David Sinclair Donscho

Napoleon's
Enfant Terrible

CAMPAIGNS & COMMANDERS

GREGORY J. W. URWIN, SERIES EDITOR

CAMPAIGNS AND COMMANDERS

GENERAL EDITOR

Gregory J. W. Urwin, *Temple University, Philadelphia, Pennsylvania*

ADVISORY BOARD

Lawrence E. Babits, *East Carolina University, Greenville*
James C. Bradford, *Texas A&M University, College Station*
Robert M. Epstein, *U.S. Army School of Advanced Military Studies, Fort Leavenworth, Kansas*
David M. Glantz, *Carlisle, Pennsylvania*
Jerome A. Greene, *Denver, Colorado*
Victor Davis Hanson, *California State University, Fresno*
Herman Hattaway, *University of Missouri, Kansas City*
John A. Houlding, *Rückersdorf, Germany*
Eugenia C. Kiesling, *U.S. Military Academy, West Point, New York*
Timothy K. Nenninger, *National Archives, Washington, D.C.*
Bruce Vandervort, *Virginia Military Institute, Lexington*

NAPOLEON'S
Enfant Terrible
General Dominique Vandamme

By John G. Gallaher

UNIVERSITY OF OKLAHOMA PRESS : NORMAN

ALSO BY JOHN G. GALLAHER

The Iron Marshal: A Biography of Louis N. Davout
   (Carbondale, Ill., 1976; London, 2000)
The Students of Paris and the Revolution of 1848
   (Carbondale, Ill., 1980)
Napoleon's Irish Legion
   (Carbondale, Ill., 1993)
General Alexandre Dumas: Soldier of the French Revolution
   (Carbondale, Ill., 1997)

Napoleon's Enfant Terrible: *General Dominique Vandamme* is Volume 15 in the Campaigns and Commanders series.

Library of Congress Cataloging-in-Publication Data

Gallaher, John G.
   Napoleon's enfant terrible : General Dominique Vandamme / by John G. Gallaher.
      p. cm. — (Campaigns and commanders ; v. 15)
   Includes bibliographical references and index.
   ISBN 978-0-8061-3875-6 (hardcover : alk. paper)   1. Vandamme, Dominique, 1770–1830.   2. Generals—France—Biography.   3. Napoleon I, Emperor of the French, 1769–1821—Relations with generals.   4. Napoleonic Wars, 1800–1815.   I. Title.
   DC146.V33G35 2008
   944.05'092—dc22
   [B]
                                                                                    2007034914

The paper in this book meets the guidelines for permanence and durability of the Committee on Production Guidelines for Book Longevity of the Council on Library Resources, Inc. ∞

Copyright © 2008 by the University of Oklahoma Press, Norman, Publishing Division of the University. All rights reserved. Manufactured in the U.S.A.

1 2 3 4 5 6 7 8 9 10

To my grandchildren,

Kathleen, Laura, Jeffrey, and Eric

Contents

	List of Illustrations	ix
	Preface	xi
1.	The Early Years	3
2.	Revolutionary General	22
3.	With the Army of the North	42
4.	Campaigns on the Rhine	71
5.	The Years of Peace	99
6.	The Austerlitz Campaign	120
7.	Siege Warfare in Silesia	155
8.	The Austrian Campaign, 1809	181
9.	Conflict with King Jérôme: The Russian Campaign	208
10.	Disaster at Kulm, 1813	227
11.	The Waterloo Campaign	256
12.	The Exile	289
	Notes	297
	Bibliography	339
	Index	347

Illustrations

FIGURES

General Dominique-Joseph-René Vandamme	2
General Vandamme, circa age thirty	147
Napoleon I	148
Jérôme Bonaparte	149
Nicolas-Jean de Dieu Soult	150
Louis N. Davout	151
The Russian Guard at the battle of Austerlitz	152
Vandamme's château at Cassel	153
Monument to General Vandamme	154

MAPS

Campaigns of 1792–96 in Belgium and 1799 in Holland	25
Campaigns of the Rhine and Danube	57
The Austerlitz and Wagram campaigns of 1805 and 1809	123
The battle of Austerlitz	134
The Silesia campaign of 1806–1807 and the campaign of 1813	159
The Ligny/Waterloo campaign	258

PREFACE

Dominique Vandamme rose from humble origins in the small town of Cassel in Northern France, without family influence, sponsors, or money, to become a general of division and commander in the Napoleonic army and the count of Unsebourg at the court of Emperor Napoleon. With limited formal education and a strong but troublesome personality, this son of provincial petits bourgeois made his way through the turbulent minefield of the military and political unrest of the revolutionary years. Denounced by both the right and the left at one time or another, Vandamme managed to keep his head—literally—while others around him lost theirs—no small accomplishment for a general in the revolutionary army of the 1790s.

Napoleon recognized Vandamme's excellent military abilities as well as the imperfections of his personality. Vandamme was rough, proud, and ambitious, as were many of the marshals and generals of the Napoleonic era. On campaign he was a superb division and corps commander; as administrator he prepared his troops well for battle; but he was frequently at odds with those under whom Napoleon asked him to serve, and with the emperor himself. He quarreled and refused to obey marshals and kings whom he considered less capable than himself. Thus, he was frequently a thorn in the side of the emperor, who had to sort out and smooth over the problems. Napoleon nevertheless bestowed honors, a title, and money upon Vandamme for the valuable service he rendered on numerous campaigns and battlefields over a twenty-three-year military career. But in the end, Vandamme remained profoundly disappointed that the emperor never bestowed upon him the dignity of the title marshal of the empire, which he believed with all his heart he deserved. His life and career, as seen in the letters and military orders of the day, epitomize the military profession during the French Revolution and the Napoleonic era, giving us a profound understanding of the military, political, and social workings of a most turbulent period of European history and of the personal relationship between Emperor Napoleon and one of his generals.

My interest in Dominique Vandamme began many years ago when I was writing a paper on the conflicting forces of political and military strategy in the conduct of the wars of the Napoleonic period. The topic I had chosen to illustrate the conflict was the Dresden phase of Napoleon's 1813 campaign.[1] The destruction of General Vandamme's First Corps at Kulm was only one major disaster of that campaign, but one that caught my attention. Some years later I learned that the Vandamme Papers were intact, filed in eighteen cartons at the Bibliothèque Municipale of Lille. Albert Du Casse had published a two-volume work on Vandamme and his correspondence, and I wondered if there could be any merit in a biography of the general, other than that it would be in English rather than in French. Upon visiting Lille and spending some time with the Vandamme Papers, I realized there was much that could still be done with this treasure of material. Du Casse's interest in Vandamme began while he was writing on Prince Jérôme Bonaparte and the Silesian campaign of 1806–1807, at which time Vandamme was serving directly under the prince's orders. In 1870 Du Casse published *Le Général Vandamme et sa Correspondance,* a wealth of information upon which I relied heavily as my notes indicate. The Vandamme family made the general's papers available to Du Casse (which, I might add, he marked up with pencil and pen, sometimes to the detriment of the documents). Du Casse was selective in the documents he included in his books. There was a wealth of letters, orders, "situations," and so on that he not did include, with which I could work. From Lille I went to Vincennes, where I found an enormous amount of material by, and relating to, Vandamme in the War Archives (Service Historique de l'Etat-Major de l'Armée) at the Château de Vincennes. There are more documents at the National Archives in Paris. Finally, on several occasions I visited the archives of the Department of the North in Lille. With this wealth of primary sources, I have tried to present a balanced portrait of a controversial figure.

When writing a biography, I find myself struggling to avoid two pitfalls. On one hand, there is the inclination to assume that the reader knows a good deal about the French Revolution and the Napoleonic empire and, therefore, to not include a history of the period because it would be redundant. On the other hand, the reader may know little of the Revolution and empire, and therefore I should include much detail. I have tried to walk a fine line in-between. Furthermore, biographers are frequently seduced by their subject. I have tried to avoid this pitfall.

The Vandamme Papers at the Municipal Library in Lille are found in eighteen cartons. Each carton has about three hundred documents. There are problems in working with these documents, and with those in other archives, inherent in the handwriting of the authors and the paper on which they wrote. In general the handwriting is legible, but in numerous cases it is difficult or even impossible to read. Signatures always pose a problem. Frequently, the signature is over or under the author's title, and in such cases the author can be identified. In other cases, I must simply state that it is not legible. Another problem is the paper upon which the author wrote. In some cases the ink has faded. In other cases the paper is so thin that, with writing on both sides, the ink has bleached through so as to make it difficult or impossible to read. Vandamme's own handwriting is quite good, but most of the documents with his signature were written by his aides and only signed by the general.

All translations from French and German are mine unless otherwise noted. The spellings of the names of individuals, towns, rivers, mountain ranges, and so on vary greatly in the archival documents and memoirs as well as in the secondary works of the nineteenth century. I have tried to select one spelling and stay with it. Any inconsistencies or mistakes remaining are mine alone.

I must acknowledge—and thank—the courteous and helpful staff at the Bibliothèque Municipale at Lille. They were most accommodating in providing me with documents from the Vandamme Papers, even microfilming many of them so that I could work with the papers at home. The staff at the War Archives at Vincennes were equally helpful, and I wish to extend my gratitude to them as well. I want to thank Glenn Lamar for lending me his copy of Albert Du Casse's *Opérations du Neuvième Corps de la Grande Armée en Silésie sous le commandement de S.A.I le Prince Jérôme Napoléon—1806 et 1807*, which I was unable to obtain by interlibrary loan. Max Deswarte kindly translated a brief history of the van Damme family from the original Flemish, a language I cannot read, into French, and for this I am very grateful. My thanks also go to David Markham for kindly providing several of the pictures that appear in this work. I am deeply indebted to Pippa Letsky for her careful copyediting of the manuscript and the excellent suggestions and corrections that she made. Finally, I wish to thank my wife, Maia, who not only put up with the seven years I worked on this study but also carefully read the manuscript and made excellent suggestions and numerous corrections.

Napoleon's
Enfant Terrible

General Dominique-Joseph-René Vandamme, count of Unsebourg, 1770–1830. Courtesy of the Museum of the Army, Les Invalides.

1

The Early Years

Dominique-Joseph-René Vandamme, count of Unsebourg, was the General George Patton of the Napoleonic army. A dedicated career soldier and an excellent division and corps commander, he was a thorn in the side of Emperor Napoleon and most every officer under whom he served. Like Patton, he was the man any king would want to lead troops into battle, but he was outspoken to a fault. His exalted opinion of his own military talents and his low esteem of his contemporaries resulted in numerous problems with those above him in the hierarchy. He was frequently engaged in damage control resulting from what he had all too publicly said or written. His clashes with Napoleon's youngest brother, Jérôme, the king of Westphalia, are legendary. He was resentful at being placed under the command of marshals Jean de Dieu Soult and Emmanuel Grouchy, both of whom he considered his military inferiors. Although Napoleon made good use of Vandamme's services, giving him command of army corps, a title, and money, he never bestowed upon him the dignity of marshal of the empire. This lack of a marshal's baton was the greatest single disappointment of Vandamme's life, and it helps to explain his ill temper in the years following 1804.

Vandamme began his career as a private in the army of King Louis XVI just before the French Revolution. He rose rapidly to the rank of general of brigade and served with the armies in the north and on the Rhine during the years of the Revolution. When Napoleon came to power, Vandamme was already a general of division. He commanded a division in the campaigns of Austerlitz (1805), Silesia (1806–1807), and Wagram (1809). In 1812 he commanded a corps in the opening phase of the Russian campaign, and in 1813 and 1815 he also commanded an army corps. Napoleon, it is alleged, once said: "If I had to make war with the Devil, I would send General Vandamme, he is the only one who could fight him on even terms." And on another occasion he reputedly said: "If I had two Vandammes, I would have one shot. But I have only one and I keep him for myself because I need him and I am unable to replace him."[1]

He was born "van Damme" on 5 November 1770 in the small town of Cassel, on a high hill, one of the most elevated points between Lille and Dunkirk. Surrounded by fertile farmland, the town is today, as it was over two hundred years ago, neither rich nor poor. A main street runs through it, and a central square serves as an open-air marketplace. Vandamme's father, Maurice Joseph Bruno van Damme, was the seventh child of René van Damme and Jeanne Marie Pyn, who had married on 31 May 1734. His mother was Barbara Françoise Baert, the attractive daughter of Dominique Baert and Thérèse de Coster. The child was named Dominique after his maternal grandfather, Joseph after his father's brother Joseph-François van Damme, and René after his paternal grandfather.[2]

The family was Flemish, with seventeenth-century origins in the town of Poperinghe in the Austrian Netherlands, present-day Belgium. Maurice van Damme was a licensed master surgeon who was officially authorized to deliver babies and care for the injured and wounded. Shortly after he married, he moved from Ghent to Cassel, France. By virtue of his profession and modest wealth, he established himself as petit bourgeois and, eventually, as one of the town notables, with some influence in the community. Dominique had a younger brother, Louis François Corneille, born in 1772 and a sister, Valentine Barbara Isabelle, born in 1774. He spoke Flemish at home and with his peers at play. Indeed, the Flemish spelling "van Damme" was used until the French Revolution when it became "Vandamme." The boy learned French at school and became fluent in both languages. His fluency in Flemish would serve him well in later years when commanding troops from Flanders and campaigning in the Austrian Netherlands (Belgium) and Holland.

Young van Damme had a difficult youth. His father was "a man of authority, abrupt, cutting in his remarks, lively, and violent." It is said that Dominique inherited a "regrettable" character from his father. When he was the tender age of five, his mother died, leaving his father with three very young children. In desperate need of a wife and a mother for the children, Maurice married Catherine Termyn, who was nineteen years his senior. Catherine was the widow of Eloi Bruneau, and she brought with her to the van Damme household her fifteen-year-old daughter, Albertine, from her first marriage. The death of his mother, his father's severe character and remarriage, and the arrival of Albertine all seem to have affected the character and emotional development of young Dominique. There is no evidence that his stepmother treated him poorly, but he is described as being rebellious to authority and difficult to discipline. Nevertheless, as an adult he remained loyal to his family in both words and deeds.[3]

Maurice van Damme made every effort to have his son Dominique well educated. He was enrolled at the Collège des Récollets in Cassel, where he received a basic education in reading, writing, and mathematics. Religion was incorporated in every aspect of the curriculum. Dominique made his first communion on 2 May 1784 and was confirmed the following year. Yet there is little evidence that this religious education affected the life of the future general. Van Damme's desire to follow a military career led to his enrollment in the military school of Marshal de Biron on 2 March 1786, but the free-spirited youth took little advantage of the opportunities available at the school. Lacking self-discipline, he found life at the military school unbearable. After two years of the severe limitations placed upon all students, he quit school on 11 June 1788.[4]

Dominique wanted to be a soldier ever since his childhood and was determined to enter the army. It is alleged that his family was concerned that the headstrong seventeen-year-old, who showed little indication he would submit to military discipline, would become a problem and an embarrassment to the family if he entered a regiment in Flanders. Therefore, through family influence, on 27 July 1788, he enlisted in the Fourth Auxiliary Battalion of the Colonies, that is, the Martinique colonial regiment. Because of the two years he had spent at the military school of Marshal de Biron, he was named corporal on 14 September of the same year. As preparations for the election of members to the Estates General were being finalized, on 2 February 1789 he boarded the *Uranie* at Lorient and sailed for Martinique.[5]

Little is known of the fourteen months that van Damme spent on Martinique. He was promoted to sergeant on 17 March 1789, and it seems on the basis of several letters dated from the period that he was a good soldier who performed his duties with energy and enthusiasm.[6] However, he soon became bored with garrison duty on Martinique, and although he had adapted to military life, his lack of self-discipline led him to seek a simple solution to his unsatisfactory situation. He decided to return to France, without the approval of his superiors, and was reported as a deserter on 29 April 1790. When his arrival in France became known, van Damme was stripped of his rank and discharged from the army, but fortunately for the young man, France—along with the army—was in a state of profound confusion.

The Revolution had begun with the revolt of the nobility against taxation and had moved into its bourgeois phase. The government's economic crisis led Louis XVI to propose new taxes in 1787, which would have fallen in part on the nobility. The Parliament of Paris, controlled by the aristocracy, refused to register the new tax laws in 1788. In the hope of solving the government's financial problems, the king then called into session the Estates General, an elected body that had not met for 175 years. This led to the historic events of the summer of 1789: the creation of a National Assembly, the July uprising that led to the fall of the Bastille, limitations placed on the king's powers, the beginning of the end of feudal privileges, and the Declaration of the Rights of Man and Citizen. The army was in an advanced state of confusion. Many officers of the king's army refused to take an oath of allegiance to the newly created National Assembly and left the service. Others, disapproving of the actions of the Revolution in general, also resigned their commissions. Although the army remained loyal to the king, many of the junior officers and most of the rank and file supported the moderate reforms of the first year of the Revolution.

Dominique van Damme would be included in this latter group who supported the reforms. There was no aristocratic blood in his veins and no reason for him to wish to see a continuation of the privileges of the ancien régime. In point of fact, restrictions on the king's powers and the reduction of the power and influence of the nobility—along with the promises of liberty, equality, and fraternity—made of him an enthusiastic supporter of the Revolution. Indeed, one might well imagine that in those days young van Damme would have supported any challenge to established authority. He joined the Society of the Friends of the Constitution in his hometown of Cassel and was active in a lesser role in the political affairs of the town. Although he had been a rebellious child, now twenty-one years of age he was living in harmony with his father in the family home and had an amiable relationship with his stepmother and Albertine. He was very attached to his sister, Valentine, and his brother, Louis.

But van Damme's first love remained the military, and on 7 June 1791 he again enlisted as a private in the Twenty-fourth Regiment of the Line (formerly Brie-Infanterie). He had matured in the two and a half years since leaving school and now stood one meter seventy-four centimeters. A handsome young man with chestnut hair and gray eyes, he was ready for a serious career in the army. His regiment was stationed at Lille, where General Anne-François Labourdonnaye (Bourdonnaye or La Bourdonnaye) had recently assumed command of the troops in and about the city. Labourdonnaye was on friendly terms with the van Damme family and had on occasion come to know Dominique personally.[7] It was through the influence of General Labourdonnaye that van Damme became the captain of a company of chasseurs.

By the end of summer 1792, the Revolution was moving to the extreme left. In fall 1791 the National Assembly had completed its work of writing a constitution for the nation. It provided for a constitutional monarchy with one elected body, the Legislative Assembly. The new constitution gave the king the power to veto legislation passed by the Legislative Assembly. It also put into writing the reforms imposed upon the Catholic Church, which virtually created a French "Gallican" church that included the confiscation of the church's lands and the election of the clergy. However, the experiment in constitutional monarchy lasted less than one year. Neither the king nor the aristocracy considered the new regime anything more than temporary, until such time as they could regain full control of the state. When France went to war with Austria and Prussia in April 1792, the war was supported by both the king and the majority of the Legislative Assembly. But the monarchy was doomed. Its days were numbered, ever since June 1791, when Louis XVI fled Paris, was stopped at Varennes, and brought back to the capital a virtual prisoner. On 10 August 1792 a Parisian mob invaded the palace of the Tuileries, the king was deposed, the Legislative Assembly dissolved itself and called for new elections. Six weeks later, on 21 September, the newly elected constituent assembly, the Convention, met and proclaimed France a republic.

The condition of the French army had begun to deteriorate in the summer of 1789. It is estimated that six thousand officers, by the end of 1791, preferred to abandon their flag and country rather than serve in a revolutionary army.[8] This mass exodus opened up the ranks of the officer corps (which under the ancien régime had been a nearly exclusive aristocratic club) to men of ability. Furthermore, the controlling majority of the National Assembly, and after them the vast majority of the Legislative Assembly, had been elected from the ranks of the bourgeoisie. These assembly members viewed the army as the "king's army" and did not trust it to protect the gains that had been made by the Revolution. As early as the summer of 1789, national guard units had been formed throughout France that were accountable to the locally elected governments, not the king. Then in 1791 there was created a "bourgeois" army that would owe its loyalty, not to the king but to the people—or perhaps more correctly, to the National Assembly elected by the people. These new military units took the form of volunteer battalions that were raised in the recently created *départements*, newly established political units that replaced the old provinces. The revolutionaries were trying to put in practice Jean-Jacques Rousseau's theory that "Every citizen should be a soldier by duty, none by trade." It was in the ranks of these volunteer battalions that many of the future generals and marshals of the Napoleonic empire began their rise to fame.[9]

In this troubled and unsettled army, Private Dominique Vandamme (he had changed the spelling of his name by this time) was given his first opportunity to display the talents that would eventually lead him to the highest rank in the army, that of general of division.[10] On 24 August 1792, he was given authorization to form a free company composed of men he recruited from his native town of Cassel and the surrounding district. The company would be made up of one hundred men, and he became its captain. He would name the lieutenant and second lieutenant, while the sergeant major, four sergeants, and eight corporals would be chosen by the rank and file. The company would establish its depot at Cassel.[11] Vandamme spent the month of September recruiting and organizing the company that was first called the Chasseurs du Mont-de-Cassel and then the Free Company of Vandamme. His ability to enlist one hundred volunteers in the region where he was known speaks well of the esteem in which he was held by his contemporaries. This also provided him with his first command and the opportunity to display his talent and to learn the problems and pitfalls of command at the lower echelon. He understood the rank and file of the army, having already served as a private, corporal, and sergeant.

For three months Captain Vandamme and his company remained at Cassel, where the men learned the basics of military life, stood guard duty, and acted as a local security force. Then on 1 December 1792, the company was ordered to join the Army of the North. By the end of 1792, the company formed a part of the garrison at Antwerp. The company, with a strength of 105 men, had yet to be engaged in combat.[12]

It was not that there had been no fighting. France had gone to war in April 1792, and the fighting had gone poorly for the French army throughout the summer. There were many skirmishes but few battles. The regular army battalions fought well, but the new volunteer battalions were unreliable. They mistrusted their predominately aristocratic leaders, were not steady under fire, and saw treason and treachery everywhere. When Charles William, duke of Brunswick, led a Prussian army over the Rhine and marched on Paris, it seemed that nothing would stop him. The fear that the army could not protect Paris from the Prussian invasion was a major contributing cause to the downfall of the monarchy in August. But on 20 September generals François-Etienne Kellermann and Charles-François Dumouriez stopped Brunswick's advance at the battle of Valmy. The Prussians were escorted back to the Rhine, and Dumouriez invaded the Austrian Netherlands in mid-October. At the battle of Jemappes on 6 November, an Austrian army of about fourteen thousand men was defeated by a French army of some thirty thousand. The significance of Valmy was that Paris was saved, and the significance of Jemappes was that the volunteer battalions fought for the first time, and they did well, beside regular army units. The French occupied all of Belgium. In the fall of 1792, General Anne-François Labourdonnaye commanded the left wing of Dumouriez's Army of North.[13] His task was to prevent the Austrians from invading northern France while Dumouriez and Kellermann stopped the Prussian invasion from the east. Fortunately for Labourdonnaye, whose troops were mainly untried volunteer battalions, the Austrians made no attempt to move south. Following the battle of Jemappes, Labourdonnaye occupied Antwerp, and Captain Vandamme was a part of his command.

General Dumouriez, having conquered Belgium by winning one single battle in which he had an overwhelming superiority of numbers, was ordered to invade Holland. When it became known in London that citizen Louis Capet (Louis XVI) had been executed on 21 January 1793 following his December trial, the French ambassador to England was asked to leave. This was quickly followed by the Convention's declaration of war on England and Holland (1 February). To bolster his invading army, Dumouriez called in troops from his right and left wings. To this end, Vandamme's company was ordered to join Dumouriez's force in mid-February. On 16 February Dumouriez's Army of the North, a mere twenty thousand men strong, crossed the Dutch frontier and quickly captured Breda and Klundert. The French general then gathered boats to be used in crossing the Rhine. It was Dumouriez's intention to cross the river and march on Amsterdam by way of Rotterdam, The Hague, and Leyden. Events on his right rear flank brought his campaign to an abrupt end, however. The prince of Coburg, commanding an Austrian army of nearly forty thousand men on the west bank of the Rhine, took the offensive. The French forces before him fled to the west in confusion and were rallied only behind Louvain. Dumouriez left his army in southern Holland and went south to take command of the army facing Coburg. Rather than taking up a defensive position, Dumouriez attacked the Austrians (unsuccessfully) at Neerwinden. Following his defeat, and realizing that his position was hazardous, Dumouriez negotiated with Coburg the evacuation of southern Holland and all of Belgium. Thus, the now designated Army of Holland with Captain Vandamme retired south, back across the French border and took up a position near Lille, from whence it had begun the campaign.[14]

The September 1792 elections had created a constituent assembly that came to be dominated by the political left. Members of the assembly were sent, usually two or three together, to all the various armies of France. These so-called Representatives of the People had full authority over the army and the civilian governments, with the power to remove a commanding general and send him to Paris to answer charges brought against him. It became all too common for generals removed by these "representatives" to be imprisoned or even executed. A general who lost a battle might well also lose his head. Following his defeat and the evacuation of Belgium, Dumouriez was frustrated and angry over interference in military affairs on the part of the government in Paris and the Representatives of the People. He attempted to march on Paris to overthrow the government, but the army did not support him. Having crossed the Rubicon and failed, the only course open to him was to desert the army and take refuge in the enemy camp. By the end of summer 1793 the Jacobins, the radical left of the French political spectrum, were in control of the government—and, through the Representatives on mission, the army. Promotions within the army were made on the basis of the officers' political views and their enthusiastic support of the revolutionary government in Paris. Pure military talent and ability were secondary. The government first had to be sure that a general would take orders from Paris and not try to overthrow the government, and only then hope he could also lead an army and be victorious in battle. Indeed, there was a general attitude among the civilian leaders in the capital that almost anyone could lead the "free" citizen-soldiers of France to victory over the "enslaved" soldiers of the European monarchies. Thus it was that promotions came quickly to young patriotic officers, while the army was purged of the greater part of the old and experienced aristocratic officers.

There was little action on the northern front through the spring and summer of 1793. Vandamme's company was assigned garrison duty first at Cassel and then at Oost-Capel, where it rested from the brief campaign into Holland and assisted in supplying the garrisons of the major fortified cities along the northern frontier and the coast.

Then, in August, Captain Vandamme was authorized to form a battalion by bringing together five free companies. These companies bore the names Equality, Saulty, The Observatory, The Pyrenees, and Vandamme.[15] The new battalion was given the name Mont-de-Cassel. Dominique Vandamme was given its command, and on 5 September he was promoted to the rank of lieutenant colonel. This promotion had more to do with Vandamme's enthusiasm for the gains of the Revolution and his support of the revolutionary government in Paris than it did with his military abilities. He was an outspoken, well-known dedicated republican with no ties or connections to the ancien régime. The revolutionary government in Paris could depend upon his loyalty. Although he had been on one campaign in the north and had taken part in several minor engagements (at Klundert, Meerdick, and Willenstadt), he had not taken part in any major battle, but in the republican army of 1793 Vandamme had the qualifications for promotion.[16]

On the same day that Vandamme was promoted to lieutenant colonel and given command of a newly formed battalion, he was placed at the head of a corps of forty-four hundred men and ordered to join General of Division Jean-Nicolas Houchard, the commander of the Army of the North. An Anglo-Hanoverian army commanded by the duke of York had occupied a small portion of northern France and was besieging the seaport of Dunkirk. General Houchard had orders to raise the siege and drive the enemy back into Belgium. The general had just received news that his predecessor, General Adam-Philippe Custine de Sarreck had been executed in Paris on 28 August 1793, and this seems to have stimulated Houchard to take the offensive without delay. His Army of the North was not concentrated, but the general had some forty-five thousand troops directly under his command in the district of Cassel and Lille. His immediate goal was to raise the siege of Dunkirk. To this end, and with the close supervision of the Representatives of the People with the Army of the North, he divided his army into several columns and ordered them to begin operations on 6 September. This brief campaign would end in the battle of Hondschoote.

Vandamme, with no opportunity to inspect, evaluate, or otherwise become acquainted with his new command, formed one of the middle columns. He drove the enemy out of the villages of Westoutre and Reningelts the night of 6–7 September 1793. The column on his left marched from Steenvoorde to attack Poperinghe; but the column on his right, supposed to advance from Bailleul to attack the enemy at Ypres, did not advance. This exposed Vandamme to attack by the Ypres garrison (about five thousand strong) on his right flank and rear. Fortunately the enemy remained within the protection of the city's defenses. Having spent the night at Provan, Vandamme's column was again on the move at 5:00 A.M. on 7 September. After a short march to Rexpoede, he halted to allow stragglers to catch up with the main body and to regroup his command. At Rexpoede Vandamme captured twenty-three wagons of the enemy's baggage and a large number of prisoners. By 4:00 P.M. his column was again marching north in the direction of Hondschoote, where an Anglo-Hanoverian force of fifteen thousand men had taken up a strong defensive position. Vandamme's advance was halted, and darkness prevented the enemy from doing serious damage to his corps. He retired to the small village of Killem, where he regrouped and rested his weary men.[17]

On 8 September, Houchard marched on Hondschoote with three of his columns, which collectively numbered some twenty-two thousand men. Waiting for him was General Walmoden with between fourteen and fifteen thousand men.[18] Walmoden was functioning as a covering force to enable the duke of York to withdraw his besieging army from Dunkirk. Walmoden's position in front of Hondschoote was anchored on the left by a stream and on the right by hedges. Houchard, therefore, decided upon a frontal attack. General Jean-Baptiste Jourdan, the future Napoleonic marshal, commanded the center, which included Vandamme's four thousand men. The superior French force drove the Hanoverians from their position back through the town and forced Walmoden in disorder to abandon the field. Vandamme distinguished himself and played a major role in the victory. But the French troops fell into great disorder in the town of Hondschoote so there was no immediate serious pursuit of the enemy. Because he was familiar with the region, the following day Vandamme was given command of three cavalry regiments to pursue and harass the retreating enemy. He captured part of Walmoden's baggage train and about one hundred of his men. York and Walmoden managed to escape with the bulk of the Anglo-Hanoverian force, however. Despite the urgings of the Representatives, Houchard refused to launch an energetic pursuit. His army was in a state of confusion, whereas York's force, which had not been engaged, was in good condition on his left flank. Thus Vandamme's battalion was given several days of well-deserved rest, and he was put in command of the region. His general headquarters were established at Hondschoote, and his troops were garrisoned in that town and the villages in the vicinity.

This was the first time that the young and inexperienced Vandamme had the opportunity to display his ability to command under enemy fire. He led his men with great courage and skill and made no mistakes. His handling of his column during the brief campaign and on the day of the battle did not go unnoticed by General Houchard or the Representatives of the People. It would be only a matter of weeks before he would be rewarded with promotion to the rank of general of brigade. However, in the meantime, his new command brought him into a most unpleasant affair. On 11 September he received the following order from General Houchard, who was himself taking orders from Paris and the all powerful Representatives of the Convention who were with his army: "It is ordered that Commandant Vandamme will burn as soon as possible the villages of Rousbruge and Poperinghe, the château of Watoue and the forest of Saint-Six." The order was by "the general in chief of the armies of the North and of the Ardennes," signed by Houchard, dated "11 September 93, in the Year 2 of the Republic."[19]

The Rousbruge-Poperinghe region had been denounced as unsympathetic to the new Republic, and its punishment was to be total destruction. Vandamme was in no position to refuse to carry out this direct order, nor did he dare even question such harsh action. Other men had been removed from command and even executed for much less. If generals were being guillotined in Paris for losing a battle or not carrying out orders, a simple new lieutenant colonel could receive the same treatment. Refusal or even hesitation would surely have been a major setback to his career, if not its end. At best, Vandamme could reason that he was not ordered to harm the person of any of the inhabitants of the towns. Whatever his feelings on this affair, the orders were carried out to the letter.[20]

It was at Hondschoote that Vandamme encountered for the first time, but by no means the last, the problem of maintaining order and discipline in his command while his troops were not actively on campaign. When he was informed that his men were mistreating the local population, he issued stern warnings to his officers to restore order and punish looters and marauders. He acknowledged that the troops had to requisition food and other military necessities from the civilian population, as the army's supply system was woefully inadequate, but his orders were that it was to be done in an orderly and proper manner.[21] It is indeed good military practice not to antagonize or make enemies of the local inhabitants of the district where one's troops are in cantonment. But one might also speculate that Vandamme, being himself Flemish, might have had sympathetic feelings toward the local population. These early campaigns provided the young officer with a school where he learned from the successes and failures of others, while honing his own skills at handling units at the battalion level.

The victory at Hondschoote and the withdrawal of the duke of York from Dunkirk enabled Houchard to shift his attention east where the fighting had not gone well. But Houchard's days were numbered. He was making enemies in the north who were quick to denounce him when he suffered setbacks near Menin. On 20 September a decree was issued for his arrest. Three days later he was taken into custody. Imprisoned at the Abbaye in Paris on the 27 September, he was tried before the revolutionary tribunal and executed on 15 November 1793. Upon the recommendation of Lazare Carnot, the Representative of the People with the Army of the North and a member of the all-powerful Committee of Public Safety, Jean-Baptiste Jourdan was named to replace Houchard. Vandamme and his small corps were still near Hondschoote when, on 8 October, he was promoted to the rank of general of brigade.[22]

Vandamme's promotion to the second-highest grade in the army is a typical example of the astonishingly rapid rise of young officers in the turbulent years of the Revolution. He was not yet twenty-three years of age. His service record was somewhat less than average. He had fought in only one major battle. It is true that the service he had rendered was quite good, but it was not necessarily outstanding. What was clearly in his favor was that he was known to be a true republican at heart, and he rendered total support for the government in Paris. The orders he received from his superiors, both military and civilian, he carried out to the letter, and this was the priority of the power structure in Paris. It should be added that along with the honorable rank of general went the responsibilities of command; and the greater likelihood that any failure, being one's own fault or not, could lead to denunciation, trial before the revolutionary tribunal, and execution. Young and ambitious Vandamme was not only willing, but enthusiastic, to accept the good and the bad that went along with promotion. He possessed the self-confidence and the belief that his cause was just, and he was prepared to do whatever was necessary to protect France from her enemies and gain glory for himself.

On 8 October, the same day that Vandamme was named general of brigade, he was given command of Dunkirk and the entrenched camp outside its walls. Replacing General Joseph Souham, he was directly under the orders of General Jean-Baptiste Davaine. He had under his command eleven battalions of infantry and one of cavalry (or chasseurs). General of Brigade Louis-Lazare Hoche, who was senior in time of rank to Vandamme, commanded one of the two brigades into which his command was divided. The high-spirited and energetic Vandamme was filled with enthusiasm and eager for a new campaign that he was confident would bring victories and glory. His experience in the battle of Hondschoote had perhaps given him an excessive self-confidence and an exaggerated impression of the invincibility of the French army, together with contempt for the weakness of the Allied army. It seems he believed that the "republicans" of the army of France would always triumph over the "slaves" of imperial Europe.[23] Thus one can imagine his joy when in mid-October he received orders to prepare to march on Furnes. On 21 October he wrote General Davaine that all his preparations were completed: "I am waiting only to know the hour to depart."[24] He envisaged a campaign not merely to Furnes, only a few miles into Belgium, but one that would take him to Nieuwpoort and Ostend.

What Vandamme did not know was that Davaine's operations on the extreme left flank of the Army of the North were designed only to distract the enemy while the major operations took place to the east. Davaine was to divide his command into three columns and advance on Menin, Ypres, and Nieuwpoort. Vandamme was assigned to undertake the movement on Nieuwpoort. It seemed that it would make little difference if he actually reached Nieuwpoort, much less captured the town. What was important was that he tied down the Allied troops before him so they could not be moved east in support of the Allied army commanded by the prince of Coburg. However, Davaine believed he did not have the troop strength to move against all three enemy positions at the same time, and he remained inactive at Cassel while Jourdan and Carnot were defeating the enemy at Wattignies.

On 21 October, Vandamme moved north in two columns. General Hoche, with one brigade, marched on Furnes while the second brigade, commanded by General Jean-Florimond Gougelot, advanced north to Nieuwpoort. Vandamme marched with Hoche's brigade and was successful in taking Furnes on 22 October. He was so filled with self-confidence that he wrote General Davaine that evening: "If the enemy camp at Dixmude does not attack me in force tomorrow, I will march on Nieuwpoort and the next day on to Ostend." In a letter to the Committee of Public Safety, written on the day he captured Furnes, Vandamme wrote: "One hundred slaves [enemy soldiers] have bitten the dust and we have taken sixty prisoners of war. In that number we found three émigrés; their trials will take place."[25] The Convention had decreed that all French émigrés taken prisoner, who were actively taking part in the war against France, should be tried for treason and, if found guilty, executed. It is reminiscent of the old expression "first we will have a trial and then we will hang them." There is no question but that Vandamme carried out the letter of the law in this matter, and that the émigrés were tried and executed. The execution of émigrés would be among the charges brought against him during the Bourbon restoration in 1815.

Leaving a small garrison at Furnes, Vandamme moved north to Nieuwpoort in anticipation of similar success. On 23 October he wrote Davaine that he had begun the attack on the fortified city. But the garrison commander ordered that the dikes be opened so as to flood much of the surrounding land. Still, with great confidence Vandamme proceeded to besiege the seaport. General Gougelot's brigade took position on the right (north) to prevent the enemy from escaping north to Ostend, and Hoche deployed his brigade on the left (south). Vandamme then called upon the town to surrender or he would destroy it by fire with his artillery. The town, being held by a garrison of four thousand men, refused to open its gates. Vandamme began the bombardment. On 24 October, with the water rising in the fields about the town, he had to move his batteries to high ground, which meant placing them on the roads that had been built up to make them usable in the event of flooding.[26] On the 25th he was informed that General Hoche had been promoted to general of division and ordered to the Army of the Moselle. He requested that the removal of Hoche from his command be reconsidered, praising that general and declaring he was a major asset to the efforts of capturing Nieuwpoort. But Hoche departed that same day. On 26 October Vandamme informed Davaine he had replaced Hoche with Adjutant General Brugant and requested that this officer be promoted to the rank of general of brigade. Brugant took over command of Hoche's brigade on the left of the siege.[27] Vandamme had captured the small fort of Viervoet on the 25th, but when the English naval squadron (some thirty vessels, according to Vandamme) opened fire on the fort, together with heavy fire from the town, he was forced to evacuate it on 26 October, and the enemy quickly reoccupied the important facility. Even so, Vandamme was still in high spirits. In his letter to Davaine he remained confident he would take the town and was ready to march on Ostend. The next day, 27 October, he described his position in glowing words: "General [Davaine], my trenches are completed, shells and bullets are raining down on Nieuwpoort, at this moment it is on fire and soon it must capitulate. The English squadron has sailed for England leaving only six ships for observation.... Tomorrow I hope to announce to you the capture of Nieuwpoort. I have decided that, if it does not capitulate, I will attack tomorrow."[28]

Despite his threats of terrible consequences if the town did not surrender, however, the commander of the garrison refused to capitulate. On 29 October Vandamme's hope for glory was shattered. General Davaine first informed him that the enemy was attacking General Souham in force, and that he was retreating. This in turn was forcing him to withdraw his forward units to the south, which was exposing Vandamme's right flank and rear to the enemy. Thus, Davaine wrote: "As for you, my dear general, I advise you to take every measure possible to prevent your position from being turned. Immediately warn General Gougelot to retreat on Hondschoote, and at the same time, you fall back on Furnes, and if you deem it necessary all the way back to your original position ... we are only left with the consolation that we have done our duty."[29]

guillotine for the words he uttered or wrote just as surely as for his actions. Vandamme, both young and undisciplined, was inclined to express himself freely and to criticize openly and often in a rash manner. Thus it was that his good friend Ernouf wrote him, cautioning him "it is necessary to be very circumspect."[36] During the Revolution and the empire, Vandamme frequently would be his own worst enemy. He would resent taking orders from anyone, except Napoleon, and would complain to the emperor about every commander under whom he served.

2

REVOLUTIONARY GENERAL

The winter of 1793–94 saw the Reign of Terror move toward its climax. The Girondin faction (it was not a party in the modern sense of the term) had fallen from power in June 1793. Many of its leaders were tried and sent to the guillotine the following November. The Jacobins (named for the Jacobin monastery in Paris where they held their meetings), although not a majority in the National Convention, came to dominate the government. They controlled the Committee of Public Safety, created by the Convention in the spring of 1793. Almost from the beginning of the Revolution they formed the extreme left of the political spectrum. The dominant members of the Committee, all Jacobins, were the lawyer from Arras Maximillien-François Robespierre, the young would-be playwright and actor Louis-Antoine Saint Just, and the crippled Georges-Auguste Couthon. Lazare Carnot was also a member of the Committee, but he was a professional soldier and never a serious Jacobin.

In the early years of the Revolution the political left was united in its opposition to the power and privileges of the king and aristocracy. As Louis XVI and the aristocracy were gradually removed from the political scene, the Jacobins emerged as the dominant faction in France. Republicans all, they succeeded in creating a republic in September 1792. Once they were in power, however, and no longer had the rivalry with monarchists and constitutional monarchists to hold them together, the Jacobins began to divide over just what the new French revolutionary government should look like. First the moderate Girondin faction split off and was eliminated. Then in the spring of 1794, personalities clashed and the Jacobins began to devour their own. The Hébertists, those who supported the radical leftist Jacques-René Hébert, were sent to the guillotine, followed by Georges-Jacques Danton and his supporters.

The creation of the Republic, the execution of the king in January 1793, the anticlericalism of the Jacobins, the foreign war with its requisitions, draft of young men, and heavy taxation, all combined to make the government in Paris unpopular in many parts of the country. In the west, the Vendée, there was open warfare against Paris. The south of France also rebelled. Toulon welcomed the English rather than submit to the republican regime. Lyon had to be besieged and taken by force. Only in the north and the east, where the republican armies were fighting, did the people not rebel, but not necessarily because they were any happier with the war or the government than their fellow citizens in other regions.

By the end of 1793, the French army's poor condition reflected that of the government and the rest of France. In a letter to Hébert, at that time still a powerful member of the Convention, General Jourdan wrote: "I am in a rage, I too! . . . The army lacks everything and, a thousand bombs, the bastards who have their feet warm want to make the infantry march without shoes, the cavalry without forage, and the artillery without horses."[1] While the government was trying, with mixed results, to address the material needs of the army, it also had to deal with the army's never-ending need of men. France had been at war for more than a year and a half. The volunteer battalions of 1791–92 were becoming reliable veteran units. Discipline had improved, the men had become accustomed to acting under enemy fire, and although far from the veterans Napoleon would lead in 1805–1807, they were not the unreliable masses of the summer and fall of 1792. The number of volunteers was declining by the end of 1792, so early in 1793 the Convention passed several decrees that created the first true modern draft, which provided for raising three hundred thousand men. The Laws of 24 February, as they came to be known, declared that the nation was in danger. If the necessary number of men could not be raised by volunteers, and no one believed it could, then a compulsory levy would complete the number. "All French citizens between the ages of eighteen and forty inclusive, not married, or widowers without children, are on call until the quota of three hundred thousand men has been filled." The levy was spread throughout the country in proportion to the population, and although not popular in most départements, it did raise the men needed to continue the war.[2]

The Laws of 24 February were only a short-term solution. As the war continued, so did the army's manpower needs. On 23 August 1793 the Convention passed the *levée en masse*, which once again declared the nation in danger, and therefore all men between the ages of eighteen and twenty-five (except married men and widowers with children) were eligible for conscription. By the end of summer 1793, France had a universal draft that enabled the government to increase the size of the army and to replace its losses.[3]

The First Coalition—as the Allied powers (primarily England, Austria, Prussia, and Spain) were known from 1792 to 1797—was held together by a common hatred of the French Republic and the general ideas of the Revolution, and by the hope of territorial gains of lesser German states or French soil. There was no great love of the Bourbon dynasty in London, Berlin, or Vienna, but if successful the Coalition would have little choice but to restore the Bourbons in the person of Louis XVI's son, Louis, or his younger brother, the count of Provence. The European powers did not really have their hearts in the war. Had Prussia, Austria, and England thrown the full weight of their combined military strength against France in 1793, they would surely have taken Paris, abolished the revolutionary government, and restored the monarchy. But Prussia and Austria were rivals in both Germany and Poland. In the east, the once geographically large but militarily weak kingdom of Poland had lost territory to Russia, Prussia, and Austria in earlier wars. To ensure they would get their share of what was left of Poland, Austria and Prussia keep major portions of their armies in the east. They were fighting the French with only part of their military strength. England, on the other hand, did not have a large army and was reluctant to commit troops to fighting on the continent. England's greatest contribution to the war effort was money and the navy. The English gave substantial financial aid to both Austria and Prussia, in

Campaigns of 1792–96 in Belgium and 1799 in Holland

order to support their troops in the field against France, but then became concerned that the Prussians and the Austrians would use the money to crush Poland, not France.

There was little fighting along the northern front during the early months of 1794. Fortunately for the new recruits and the army, Jourdan was allowed to put the Army of the North into winter quarters where the new men had time for basic training before coming under enemy fire. Vandamme's brigade continued as part of General Ferrand's division and remained in the vicinity of Hazebrouck, facing north. During the winter months Vandamme made good use of spies operating in Ostend, Bruges, and Ghent who provided him with information on enemy troop movements and the strength of enemy garrisons at Ypres, Rennegels, Poperinghe, and so on, which he then passed on up the chain of command.[4] There were also minor skirmishes. On the morning of 1 February 1794, the enemy attacked the village of Boeschèpe, just south of the French border. They plundered houses and the church and started fires. The French then came on in strength to recapture the village and take a handful of prisoners.[5] As the campaigning season approached, Vandamme moved his headquarters forward to Steenvoorde.

There was little combat with France's enemies, but Vandamme—a republican, and in 1791 a minor figure in the Constitution Club, the forerunner of the local Jacobin Club, in Cassel—managed to clash with the local Jacobins on the home front. He had not been politically active since reentering the army. At the end of February 1794, the Jacobin Club of Cassel denounced him—not for his politics, he was still a staunch republican, but for his actions. He was accused of insulting and threatening an "innocent and true republican sansculotte" on the road from Cassel to Bailleul.[6] The incident seems to have occurred more or less as described in the denunciation, which was accompanied by the testimony of three witnesses. The sansculotte insulted Vandamme, and the general then verbally chastised the man. Given his abrasive personality, the arrogant new general would not have allowed an insult to go unanswered.

The denunciation was made to General Jean-Victor Moreau, Vandamme's new division commander, who gave it little attention. Moreau had earlier served under Vandamme and the two men were good friends. But the episode clearly indicates that Vandamme's popularity in his hometown had waned. He had to fulfill the needs of his men who were quartered in the region, by requisitioning grain, cattle, and other food as well as horses and wagons. Sometimes payment was made with inflated paper money (the assignat), but most often the peasant or merchant was given a letter of credit with the promise of payment in the future. Needless to say, the promissory notes were of questionable value, and even under the best of circumstances, such practices were unpopular with the local population. Northern France had been bled white over the past eighteen months, as armies marched back and forth destroying or taking whatever they needed, or wanted. It was indeed fortunate for Vandamme, in this case, that he was on good terms with his superiors, for such a denunciation, had it reached Paris, could have led to the end of his military career—or even to the scaffold. However, all was not negative with respect to Vandamme. On 12 March 1794 the mayor and members of the municipal council of the town of Hazebrouck, where the general had his headquarters, declared that the relations between Vandamme and the city were "good and harmonious."[7] The affair along the road to Bailleul was a minor episode that passed with little notice outside the immediate region. Vandamme was to have a potentially much more serious problem in the early spring of 1794.

English agents contacted him by letter on two occasions (no dates are given). Both letters put forward basically the same proposition. The general was asked to defect to the enemy with his entire brigade and with the French plans for the coming campaign. In return he would be treated not as a prisoner of war but "as the benefactor of French Flanders," given complete freedom to do as he pleased. He would be provided with a personal guard for his protection. He would receive the sum of 240,000 French livres in addition to payment for all the pieces of artillery and all the baggage he might bring with him. His English contact would be Lord Twedel (Twedee in the second letter) at number 1650, rue de Beurre, Ypres.[8] These indeed would have been attractive offers for someone perhaps disenchanted with the Revolution, the Republic, or the direction France was taking, or for a general perhaps in fear of the guillotine. But the enemy misjudged Vandamme. A true believer in the republic and revolutionary ideals, a true republican and supporter of the government in Paris, he did not fear remaining in France. Indeed, he looked forward to the day when he might himself command the Army of the North and save France from its enemies.

Vandamme's indignation knew no limits. That the enemy would even imagine he might sell his country for pieces of silver infuriated him. He sent the letters to Moreau, who sent them to General Jean-Charles Pichegru, the new commander of the Army of the North, who in turn passed them on to the Representatives of the People. Through this chain of command, the matter reached the Committee of Public Safety in Paris. Vandamme pledged undying loyalty, and with supporting testimony from Moreau and Pichegru, the general survived. He even received congratulations from the Committee of Public Safety, signed by Carnot.[9] In these treacherous months of the Terror, Vandamme was treading through a minefield. Generals were losing their commands, their freedom, even their lives, for little or no reason.

Yet Vandamme continued to provide his enemies with material to bring him down. On 4 January 1794, he wrote his friend General Moreau: "What a confounded breed are these Commissioners of War [the Representatives of the People]! It is necessary to guillotine three-fourths [of the population] in order that the other fourth will do its duty. I no longer dare to present myself before the battalions. The soldiers, with good reason, will demand of me bread that can be eaten. The bread they have been given for the past fifteen days is poisoned, it is entirely molded. The bread distributed yesterday was dreadful, if the soldiers were to eat it they would be poisoned."[10] Such a letter, had it fallen into the wrong hands, would surely have cost Vandamme his head, despite his friends in high places. He supported the Revolution and the Republic, but he was becoming dissatisfied with the extreme actions of the Jacobins in power and what he perceived as the lack of support given the armies at the front.

The spring campaign season began in mid-April. Both armies had rested and resupplied their troops as best they could. The Allies began by sending strong reconnaissance patrols south to probe the French lines. On 12 April 1794, Vandamme fought a minor engagement when the enemy overran some of his forward posts. He regained the lost ground with little difficulty, as the enemy was only feeling out his position. He reported to General Moreau that French losses were light, but that the enemy lost a "great number and had more than twenty wounded."[11] It was standard practice to minimize one's own losses and inflate the losses of the enemy. Serious fighting began the following week.

The prince of Coburg opened the campaign on 17 April, surprising the French in the Landrecies sector. General Antoine Balland—in the absence of Pichegru, who was at Lille—rallied the French divisions and stabilized the line. Pichegru, for his part, decided to launch his left wing across the frontier to attack Menin and Courtrai. While General Pierre-Antoine Michaud covered the extreme left by moving on Furnes, General Souham occupied Courtrai. Moreau, led by Vandamme's brigade, moved on Menin.[12] Vandamme had been camped near Caestre, west of Menin. He commanded five battalions of light infantry, eleven battalions of infantry of the line, 130 cavalry, and two pieces of artillery.[13] Leaving Caestre on 28 April, he marched to Menin by way of Wervik. With support from Souham, Moreau encircled Menin and called upon the city to surrender. But the Allied commander refused, hoping to hold out for a number of days until aid could come and lift the siege. General Clairfayt with several Allied divisions did march to the aid of Menin, but he was turned back with heavy losses. Moreau launched three attacks against the city without success. The garrison, realizing that help was not on the way, decided to break out of the encirclement to the north. It was Vandamme's brigade that stood in the way.

The Allied force in Menin was not prepared for the siege that began on 28 April 1794. Vandamme received artillery support the morning of the 29th, and by mid-afternoon the town was on fire. The commander was prepared to surrender. However, the garrison included about four hundred French émigrés who made up the Légion de La Châtre. If the garrison surrendered, they would be executed as traitors. The legionnaires demanded the right to spearhead a breakout, so on 30 April, the French attacked the French. In darkness, the Légion de La Châtre surprised Vandamme's outposts; with fixed bayonets and without firing a shot, they cut their way through the Mont-de-Cassel battalion. By the time Vandamme's brigade was under arms, the émigrés had cut a corridor through the French encirclement enabling the garrison to escape to the north. It was the Mont-de-Cassel chasseurs who suffered the brunt of the fighting. The overconfident, still relatively inexperienced Vandamme was learning the hard way how to conduct siege warfare. His failure to maintain the blockage of the city did not enhance his reputation. One hundred men were left behind in Menin to man guns during the sortie. They surrendered the city the next day.[14] The withdrawal of the enemy army left the French in control of the Menin-Courtrai region. Several battalions of Vandamme's brigade occupied Menin while the remaining troops camped along the Lys River. By mid-May his headquarters were at Courtrai. On 13 May he drove the enemy back from that city in order to secure his position and to prepare for the next phase of the campaign.[15]

In mid-May the Allies were ready to launch their own major offensive. The plan drawn up by the Austrian general Karl F. Mack called for all the Allied armies in the northern sector to converge on Menin and Courtrai. The two cities would be surrounded; the divisions of Moreau and Souham would be cut off from the rest of Pichegru's army and forced to surrender. General Clairfayt advanced south from Thielt on 16 May and next day reached the Lys River at Wervik, six miles upstream (west and south) from Menin. He arrived at the river late in the day, so he delayed crossing the Lys until the next morning. On 17 May Vandamme marched south through Menin from Courtrai and took up a position at Bousbeck, just a few miles downstream (north) from Wervik.[16] To the east the enemy advanced in five columns. By the night of 18 May, four enemy columns had occupied much of the territory between Lille and Menin, with the fifth column south of Lille at Pont-à-Marcq. In this advance the northern Allied column met stiff resistance; it was stopped and forced back. This left the right flank of the Allied position exposed and caused the three center columns to halt their advance.

In the absence of the commanding general (Pichegru was with his troops on the right flank), General Souham had taken command of the three divisions in the Lille-Menin-Courtrai sector of the front. His strategy to meet the Allied onset was simple and wise. Moreau, with only Vandamme's brigade, would hold the line along the Lys River. Unfortunately, Moreau did not have his entire division with him. His second brigade, commanded by General Nicolas-Joseph Desenfans, was south of Ypres watching that section of the line and took no part in the fighting. Souham would march his own division southwest from Courtrai while General Jacques-Philippe Bonnaud's division would march north from Lille. The two would join forces and, with forty thousand men, would fall upon the center of the advanced Allied army. The French plan was successful. The Allies had spread their forces too thin and were forced to retreat to the east on 19 May. Not only were they unable to surround Souham and Moreau, they suffered a serious defeat with heavy casualties.

The battle went well for the French, but Vandamme had a difficult time on the Lys. Moreau commanded some ten thousand men, but Vandamme had only a portion of these troops with him at Bousbeck.[17] Clairfayt crossed the Lys with twenty thousand men in the early hours of 18 May and sent a strong force against Vandamme at Bousbeck. The fighting was heavy, and the village of Bousbeck changed hands several times. The outnumbered French in the late afternoon became tired and discouraged and began to give ground in a state of disorder, but when General Malbrancq arrived with two fresh battalions, Vandamme rallied his troops and drove the enemy back to Bousbeck. When darkness put an end to the fighting Clairfayt still occupied the village, with Vandamme in position to the east and the south. Both sides spent the night preparing to renew the fight in the morning. In the early hours of 19 May, however, Clairfayt learned that the main Allied army had been stopped and had begun to retire to the east. The grand Allied plan had failed. Clairfayt realized he was in an exposed position south of the Lys, vulnerable to attack by superior numbers with his back to the river, so in the hours just before dawn he began to retreat. On the morning of 19 May, Vandamme ordered an advance on Bousbeck. To his surprise he was informed that the village had been evacuated. The bulk of the enemy army had already crossed the Lys and was retiring to the north from which it had come.[18] Vandamme's brigade had suffered heavy casualties, and General Malbrancq's brigade had been marching and fighting for two days. Neither brigade was in condition to pursue an army twice their combined size that had not been defeated and was retiring in good order. The enemy withdrew virtually unmolested.

The casualty figures for the fighting on 17–19 May are conflicting and somewhat confusing. Allied losses ranged from three thousand to sixty-five hundred men killed, wounded, and taken prisoner, while there are no good figures for the French. The Allied losses are most likely closer to four thousand men than sixty-five hundred, and

French losses would have been about the same or a little less.[19] Vandamme put his losses at four hundred men, which seems rather low considering the fighting on 18 May.[20] Vandamme had handled his brigade skillfully in the face of overwhelming odds. He was rapidly becoming a seasoned brigade commander.

Pichegru returned to Courtrai shortly after the fighting ended and was determined to take advantage of the French victory. He ordered Moreau to post Vandamme's brigade in a defensive position along the south bank of the Lys between Menin and Courtrai to watch Clairfayt at Thielt. With his remaining divisions, Pichegru attacked the Allied forces on the Escaut River just north of Tournai. When the French met strong resistance and suffered heavy casualties, Pichegru withdrew and decided to capture Ypres to the northwest of Lille. Moreau's division was assigned the task of laying siege to the city. On 1 June Vandamme was ordered to march on Ypres and take up a position on the north side of the city with his headquarters at Zillebeke, while the division's other brigade was south of the city. Pichegru gave Vandamme command of all the besieging troops. Ypres was completely surrounded during the first week of June.[21]

The garrison attempted three times to break out to the north, but Vandamme's brigade had learned a lesson at Menin and each time drove the enemy back into the city. The general ordered trenches to be opened on 5 June, in preparation to take the city by assault, and despite a shortage of tools and workers, the difficult task went on using soldiers. General Michaud's division was assigned the task of keeping Clairfayt at bay, but when the Austrians decided to relieve Ypres, Michaud was driven back by superior numbers and suffered substantial losses. Pichegru warned Vandamme he could be in trouble and told him not to get caught between the enemy armies and the garrison of seven thousand men.[22]

The city garrison tried to break out of the encirclement, but again Vandamme drove it back, though he still seemed in a precarious position on the north side of Ypres. Fortunately, Pichegru with his other division came to the aid of Michaud and drove Clairfayt back north. On 14 June, Moreau informed Vandamme of Clairfayt's defeat; and Vandamme passed it on to the enemy.[23] When the Ypres garrison realized there was no hope of relief, it agreed to surrender on 18 June. Vandamme and his brigade had the honor of accepting the surrender; they watched in silence as the Allied army came out and gave up their arms. In addition to Allied soldiers, the French also captured large quantities of food and military equipment. Vandamme had been actively engaged in the seventeen-day siege, but there had been little fighting and few casualties. The city was not taken by assault.[24] The prisoners were divided into two groups. Three thousand Hessians were sent south to be held temporarily at Cassel. Four thousand Austrians were sent to Lille. General Moreau ordered Vandamme to provide an escort of one battalion plus four companies and gave very precise instructions as to their conduct. "This escort," Moreau wrote on 18 June, "will refrain from any insults they might want to heap upon the prisoners of war."[25] The escort was then ordered to return immediately to Ypres.

By the last weeks of June 1794, it had become clear to the civilian government in Paris that the Army of the North was too large and too spread out along the northern frontier to be commanded by one man. Means of communication along a two-hundred-mile front were inadequate to maintain control or react in a timely manner to enemy movements. The reorganization that took place created three independent commands: the armies of the North, the Moselle, and the Sambre-Meuse. Pichegru remained in command of the North, and Jourdan commanded the Sambre-Meuse. Moreau's Second Division, with the brigades of Vandamme and General François-Guillaume Laurent, remained with the Army of the North. The plan approved by Paris called for an advance to the north by Jourdan to attack and capture Charleroi, while Pichegru on the left flank (the west) also moved north. Fortunately for the French, the Allied high command did not take advantage of this divided command to attack and destroy first one of the French armies and then the other.

Jourdan moved out according to plan and on 26 June 1794 won a stunning victory over Coburg at Fleurus, some ten miles northeast of Charleroi. The Austrians decided to withdraw to the east along their supply and communication lines. At the same time, Pichegru advanced with little opposition. Upon learning of the French victory at Fleurus, the Allied forces (English, Dutch, and Austrian troops) facing the Army of the North decided to withdraw into Holland, while leaving garrisons in key cities in Belgium. The military planners in Paris decided that, before the armies continued their advances into southern Holland, the fortified cities in their rear must be taken.

Thus, it was assigned to Moreau's division to lay siege to and capture the enemy-held positions on the extreme left flank. His two brigades turned and marched to the west. Vandamme had informed Moreau on 23 June that his brigade was in excellent condition, in perfect order, and that when passing through cities such as Thielt not a single soldier had left his unit.[26] They occupied Bruges on 29 June and Ostend the next day, both cities evacuated by the English. On July 1 they reached Nieuwpoort, defended by more than two thousand men including four hundred émigrés, most of whom had fought their way through Vandamme's lines at the siege of Menin. Vandamme's task was to besiege the city while Laurent's brigade was to observe the enemy. Vandamme received an additional three thousand men from General Michaud's division and was ordered to occupy the key towns around Nieuwpoort and those between Nieuwpoort and Ostend.[27]

On the morning of 3 July, two small ships with émigrés and civilians managed to sail out of Nieuwpoort harbor, along a short waterway, and reach the high sea, because the artillery along the waterway was not yet in place. Vandamme quickly saw to the placement of the guns west of the city so as to prevent any further escapes. The first two ships made their way safely to the island of Walcheren, on the north bank of the West Scheldt River, occupied by the English. Then other émigrés followed their example in three small ships. These émigrés could well reason it was worth the attempt to escape from the besieged city. If they stayed behind and fell into the hands of the republican army, they would surely be shot. At 6:00 P.M. on 3 July, the ships left the harbor and made for the open sea. However, Vandamme's guns were now in position and opened fire on the slow-moving vessels. All three were set on fire or sunk. Vandamme's men took 160 émigrés as prisoners; an unknown number were rounded up along the coast. It is not known how many were killed by gunfire or drowned when the ships went down. A small number made their way back to Nieuwpoort. Vandamme wrote that his soldiers recovered considerable gold and silver from the sunken ships. The fate of the émigrés was a foregone conclusion; they were all executed. Vandamme is very specific in his letter to Moreau with respect to those unfortunate souls: "I had one émigré shot in front of each corps [of his brigade], the rest were beaten to death by our soldiers. One saw only red uniforms and bodies along the ocean shores."[28]

Vandamme made no excuses for ordering the execution of the émigrés. In his account of the siege written sometime later, he wrote: "We collected 160 émigrés, who in accordance with the laws of the Republic, were shot on the same day."²⁹ It is true that Vandamme hated those "royalists" who took up arms against their country, but there is no indication that he had any émigré executed until the Convention ordered the army to do so. Under the watchful eyes of the Representatives of the People, he was following orders from Moreau, who in turn was following orders from Paris.

On the night of 6 July, the French batteries began to shell Nieuwpoort. They were answered by heavy enemy fire. The garrison held out for two weeks until, with no hope of relief, the city on fire from French artillery, and provisions running low, the Allied commander, General Diepenbroeck, asked for terms of surrender on 18 July. In addition to the two thousand prisoners taken, Vandamme also captured about one hundred pieces of artillery and a great quantity of military supplies.³⁰ During the negotiations for the surrender of Nieuwpoort, Vandamme demanded that the émigrés, who formed a part of the garrison, be turned over to the French. General Diepenbroeck answered that he had no émigrés under his command. The general did not say there were no émigrés in the garrison, nor that there were none in the city, but simply that there were none under his command. Thus he could not turn any over to the French. Indeed those émigrés still in the city tried to hide in the ranks of the predominately German-speaking troops making up the garrison, or in the town and surrounding farms where they posed as peasants. The French troops were so incensed, however, that these émigrés had taken up arms against their country that they carefully sorted out some 160 émigrés who were promptly executed by firing squads. On 21 July Moreau wrote to the Representative Lacombe, who was with the Army of the North: "About 150 were shot yesterday, every precaution was taken so that none escaped."³¹

The capture of Nieuwpoort provided no rest for Vandamme. On 20 July Moreau marched his division along the coast to the island of Cadsand and besieged Fort Ecluse. Laurent's brigade laid siege to the fort, while Vandamme's brigade occupied Breskens and Cadsand. The defenders flooded vast areas about the fort, making it almost impossible to open trenches, the usual preparation for an all-out assault.

The garrison did not surrender until 28 August. Eighteen hundred prisoners of war were sent to France. There is no mention of émigrés among the prisoners.[32]

Moreau's division was engaged in the sieges along the coast for two months, which proved devastating to the men, not so much because of enemy fire or activities but because of sickness. The Lowlands of western Flanders with its marshes, swamps, and canals provided ideal conditions for malaria. The men came down with the "fever" and had to take to their beds. Moreau and Vandamme followed the standard procedures for the care of the men. The troops were issued vinegar and great quantities of "petite bière" (a light, weak beer), but these had no effect on the malady. In 1803–1805 the troops of Marshal Louis N. Davout's corps, which occupied the same low country, would suffer the same fever, as did the men of the Irish Legion who served on the island of Walcheren in 1809.[33] Only 120 Frenchmen were killed or wounded during military operations in July—August, but seven thousand men from the brigades of Vandamme, Laurent, and Daendels were hospitalized during the same period.[34] On 9 August Vandamme wrote to Moreau that, in the past eight days, one thousand men of his brigade had come down with it. He requested that he might quarter his men in towns and villages further inland where there was less fever.[35] The only remedies that seemed successful in reducing fever were eating large quantities of "Jesuit Bark" (containing quinine) and changing the "air," that is, leaving the low country. There is no indication that in 1794 "Jesuit Bark" was used to treat the fever, as it would be used in 1809. It was not until Vandamme's brigade departed from the unhealthy environment that the fever abated.

The capture of Ecluse completed the French occupation of western Belgium to the Scheldt River. At one point Vandamme, who was at Breskens at the mouth of the Scheldt opposite Flushing, was planning to cross the river, which is several miles wide at that point. However, the weather was bad and he had too few boats, so the amphibious operation never took place.[36] Moreau withdrew his division to the east, after destroying the defenses of the principal fortified towns, with the exception of several key places where he left small garrisons. The brigades of Vandamme and Laurent were allowed a needed and deserved rest. Away from the fever-ridden Lowlands, the men gradually regained their health and returned to their units. In mid-September

Moreau's division was ordered east to the Meuse River, which it reached on 4 October.

On 11 October, General Pichegru was compelled temporarily to give up his command of the Army of the North because of poor health. Moreau was named acting commander of the army during Pichegru's two months' absence. Although Vandamme was the senior general of brigade (promoted on 12 September 1793), General Laurent (promoted on 19 March 1794) was given command of Moreau's division. Laurent was forty-six and had been a noncommissioned officer in the king's army before Vandamme was born. He had spent twenty-three years in the ranks before receiving a commission in 1790.

The explanation would seem that Vandamme was ill with the fever and not able to take command on 11 October. In a letter to Moreau dated 19 October at Hezongen, Vandamme wrote: "Since my arrival here, my health has improved; I have begun to regain my strength." By 28 October Vandamme was apparently healthy once again, for Laurent wrote to him on that day: "General Moreau has charged me to give you command of the division; consequently, my comrade, you will give me orders." Two days later, Vandamme acknowledged his new appointment: "I have taken command of the division in accordance with the letter that you wrote General Laurent, in which you told him to give it to me so he can heal his sore leg." The command of a division generally called for an officer with the rank of general of division.[37]

During most of the month of October 1794, Moreau's division, first under his command and then under General Laurent, was besieging the Dutch stronghold of Vento on the Meuse River. The city surrendered to Laurent on 26 October, just days before Vandamme assumed command. The two divisions of the Army of the North, those of Souham and Vandamme, were ordered to move north to the Waal River to attack Nijmegen. Vandamme was assigned to besiege the city while Souham faced east on the south bank of the Rhine. General Compère, whose brigade was attached to Vandamme's Second Division, was deployed on three sides of the city, on the left (south) bank of the river. A second brigade reinforced Compère, while Vandamme took the rest of his division up the Rhine to meet the Austrians at Buderich. The Austrian general Werneck had decided to cross the river upstream from Nijmegen and give battle on the left bank.

On 10 November Vandamme attacked the Austrians at Buderich and drove them back across their makeshift bridge with heavy losses. The enemy suddenly evacuated Nijmegen, and the French were in control of the entire left bank of the Rhine in the north.[38]

With the fall of Nijmegen and the victory at Buderich, Vandamme could rest the division. His brigades went into what they thought would be winter quarters in the region around Nijmegen, and Vandamme reported to Moreau that all was quiet in his theater of operations. For the next six weeks the Army of the North rested, regrouped, and was resupplied. There were minor skirmishes along the Rhine and Waal with fighting over islands but no serious action.[39] For example, on 10–11 December Vandamme successfully attacked the island of Bethuve, captured the enemy's artillery, and drove the garrison to the right bank of the river. He then withdrew to the safety of the left bank.[40] By late November the fight had gone out of the Allied commanders. The duke of York withdrew his English and Hessians troops to Arnheim, while the Austrians prepared to make a weak defense along the Rhine. On 2 December, York left the army and returned to England, leaving General Walmoden to command a demoralized force. The weather was turning cold, and neither army was prepared for a winter campaign, but in mid-December, Pichegru, his health restored, returned to reassume command of his army. Moreau, instead of returning to take personal command of the Second Division, remained at army headquarters with Pichegru and left Vandamme, a general of brigade, at the head of the division. Vandamme spent much of the month of December in Cleves.

The weather had turned bitter cold so that the rivers and canals began to freeze. The severe cold would make it extremely difficult, if not impossible, for the Dutch to open their dikes and flood critical sections of the country to stop an invading army. With urging from Paris, Pichegru decided that Holland was his for the taking. General Jourdan would prevent the Austrians on the Rhine from interfering on his right flank or rear. The Allies were showing no interest in a winter campaign. Indeed the English army had begun a slow retreat to the east that would end on the docks of Bremen and Lehe, from which they eventually embarked for England on 14 April 1795. The Dutch, left on their own with their rivers, canals, and moats frozen solid, put up little resistance.

In the second week of January 1795, the French began to advance. Vandamme occupied Arnheim on 22 January and captured large quantities of supplies after the Dutch evacuated the city. The following day he was at Ubrecht, but still there was little fighting as the enemy continued to retire. Amsterdam was occupied without a fight on 25 January, and a small band of French infantry and cavalry actually captured a Dutch squadron of fourteen ships stuck in the ice off Helder.[41] The Dutch campaign was extraordinary. "What Louis XIV was unable to do at the height of his power, the Republic executed in less than a month." On 24 January, Moreau wrote to Vandamme: "We are absolute masters of Holland except for the provinces of Groningen, Over-Yssel and Frise, which are occupied by the English; and thus I think that it would be important to chase them out." He then ordered Vandamme to finish the conquest of Holland, and the Second Division pressed onto the heels of the enemy. On 7 February, Vandamme wrote Moreau that he would be before Loo and Deventer the next day and hoped that General Etienne-Jacques Macdonald was marching on Hardewick.[42]

The English and the Austrians were now in full retreat to the east into Germany, leaving the Dutch at the mercy of the advancing French armies. While Macdonald and Pichegru occupied western Holland, Vandamme pursued the English to the German border. In their hasty retreat the English left behind their sick and wounded in the care of a captain, a second lieutenant, and medical personnel. The English also left money to pay for the expenses of this care. In a letter to "The commander of the French troops" (that is, Vandamme), a Major Charles (last name not legible) asked that the English be allowed to care for, and pay for, their own sick and wounded. Vandamme respected this wish; and the English received humane treatment and the best medical care that could be provided under the difficult circumstances. As the English army was preparing to depart the continent, the commanding general wrote Vandamme to acknowledge that he had allowed the sick to be well cared for by English personnel and sent an additional 250 louis to pay additional expenses. Although Vandamme showed neither mercy nor hesitation in the execution of the French émigrés who fell into his hands, he treated his non-French prisoners of war as humanely as the circumstances would allow.[43]

The winter campaign was hard on the French army. It did not meet serious resistance in its occupation of Holland, but the weather was bitterly cold, and food and supplies of every kind were scarce. Prussian troops moved in to fill the vacancy left by the departing English, to a limited extent. By the winter of 1795, Prussia had lost all interest in a war with France. All that concerned Berlin was the final partition of Poland. There seemed no end in sight for the war with France. Besides, although the Prussian court still hated the French Republic, in July 1794 the radical left had been driven from power in Paris. The First Coalition was gradually unraveling. England was not happy that Prussia and Austria were spending their English pounds to gain territory in Poland rather than waging war against France. The Prussians thought the English were not contributing enough troops to the fighting on the continent. The Prussians and Austrians were competing with each other and with the Russians for Polish land rather then concentrating on the war with France. As the English were withdrawing from the continent, Prussia was negotiating with the French to quit the war. The French side was exhausted. Three years of war on its borders, civil war within its borders, and quarreling between political factions in Paris, all had reduced France to a nation struggling to survive. It is not surprising that there was little fighting in the spring of 1795.

Vandamme continued to command Moreau's division to the satisfaction of both Moreau and Pichegru. With little fighting and much housekeeping to be done, Moreau was content to leave the details of feeding and clothing the troops to someone else. Indeed, Vandamme's correspondence in April—May is filled with requests, even demands, for food to feed the army.[44] In a long letter to Moreau, dated 8 April 1795, he spelled out in some detail the terrible shortages of the division. In a desperate tone he declared: "The division I command lacks everything, someone must come promptly to its aid, and not with promises, but with real subsistence . . . you have for a long time promised subsistence, and nothing has arrived except promises, which do not fill our supply houses. At present, you promise that you will come and visit, I do not know when this promise will be fulfilled, still, I will be patient."[45] This letter shows not only Vandamme's frustration but also his abrupt and abrasive manner. Generals of division were not accustomed to being addressed in this insulting tone by their subordinates. But Moreau and Vandamme were close friends and understood one another quite well, and because there was truth in what Vandamme said, Moreau did not take offense. In the future the blunt Vandamme would continue to speak his mind freely and openly, and in harsh terms, and most of his future superiors would not be as understanding as his old comrade Moreau.

On 14 April 1795 Moreau informed Vandamme that Prussia and France had signed a peace treaty that would go into effect the night of 16–17 April, and that he should at once stop work on the fortifications of the Prussian villages he occupied. The northern sector of the front was at last quiet, the weather was like springtime, and Vandamme, who had been commanding a division for six months, was looking forward to being promoted to the rank of general of division. But this was not to be, as troubled days were ahead. Vandamme was taken by surprise when he received a letter from Moreau dated 27 April 1795: "I forward to you, general, an order from the Committee of Public Safety that calls you to Paris. They want you to give an account of yourself. In confirmation of this order, you will tell me the day you are going to leave for Paris. You will give provisional command of the division to General Compère, and you will give provisional command of his brigade to General Lacour."[46]

Vandamme had been denounced to the Committee of Public Safety as being a "terrorist." The Jacobin Reign of Terror had ended with the Thermidorian Reaction in summer 1794, and the moderate republicans had taken control of the government in Paris. No longer were generals sent to the guillotine accused of being an "enemy of the people," or for poor judgment, or "political incorrectness." Nevertheless, generals such as Vandamme who had been promoted to high rank and given favorable treatment by the Jacobins were likely to be removed from command by the Thermidorians, on the basis of little or weak evidence. Vandamme's life was not in danger, nor was it likely that he would be imprisoned without strong evidence of wrongdoing, but his military career might well suffer a severe setback.

3

WITH THE ARMY OF THE NORTH

Early in May 1795, Vandamme arrived in Paris to defend himself against two principal accusations: that he was a terrorist, and that he had delivered up the city of Furnes to pillage. If he was found guilty of these charges, he would be disgraced and sent to prison. But there was little evidence to establish that Vandamme was a Jacobin terrorist. He showed that the Jacobins of Cassel had denounced him to Moreau as being an enemy of the people, that is, an enemy of the Jacobins, which could be interpreted in 1795 as not being a terrorist. Generals Moreau and Pichegru, both of them in good standing in Paris at the time, wrote enthusiastic letters in his support, declaring that his military record and his loyalty to the government were above reproach. Vandamme had been a zealous supporter of the establishment of the Republic and the convention that governed France and carried on the war, but as the Jacobins gained control of the new government and the Reign of Terror moved toward its climax, he had become disenchanted with the men in Paris and their treatment of the army.

With respect to the pillage of Furnes, there was no evidence to show the general had profited one franc, although the pillaging was undeniable. There was no evidence that Vandamme had either allowed the pillaging or, knowing of it at the time, turned his eyes the other way. In fact, he produced correspondence in which he had condemned such acts of vandalism. The result was that the Committee of Public Safety took no action against the general, and in mid-June he returned to the Army of the North.[1] But the affair did not end there. Upon his arrival at army headquarters, he learned he would resume command of a brigade, not the division he had commanded the past winter and spring. A brief letter from General Pichegru ordered Vandamme to Malines, where he was to take command of three demi-brigades being sent to the Army of the Sambre and Meuse.[2] It was clear that, although powers in Paris may not believe him guilty of wrongdoing, there was doubt in their minds about this soldier. Moreau was most unhappy to lose Vandamme and expressed his disappointment to the general in tender terms.[3] Vandamme was disappointed to learn he would be leaving Moreau and Pichegru. He was on the best of terms with both men, who had supported him in his time of need. Furthermore, by virtue of his having commanded a division for six months, Vandamme had anticipated, clearly hoping, that he would soon be promoted to the rank of general of division. The fact that his new appointment was to command a brigade (for which his rank, general of brigade, was appropriate) meant he could see the writing on the wall: there would be no promotion in the near future. If this was disappointing to the general, there was worse yet to come.

On 30 June 1795 Moreau informed Vandamme that his name was not on the new list of officers employed with the Army of the North.[4] The Commission of Organization of the War Ministry had reorganized the armies and removed a number of generals from active duty, many of whom had been promoted by Jacobin Representatives of the People during the Terror. It is true that Vandamme had been promoted to the rank of general of brigade on the basis of his being a good republican and loyal to the government. It had not been based on years of experience and proven ability. That he was also a capable officer would become apparent as the years passed, but he was now removed from all command without explanation and ordered to leave the army immediately and return to his home at Cassel. Vandamme was devastated. On 1 July he poured out his disappointment, expressing his frustration in most vivid terms to Moreau: "At last," he wrote, "left with no alternatives, reduced to nothingness by the government, I will go to live with my parents, and eat whatever is left over."[5] Angry and bitter, he left the army and returned to Cassel. This episode marked the beginning of Vandamme's deep dislike of the Thermidorians, who now formed the government of the Directory, following the fall of the Jacobins in the summer of 1794.

The next few months found Citizen Dominique Vandamme miserable and depressed. The army had become his life, and war was what made that life worthwhile. He could not bear to be relegated to a dull, boring, provincial small town. Almost immediately upon his arrival at Cassel he began to work toward his reassignment to active duty. He requested and received letters of support from Moreau and Pichegru. He sought the assistance of the Representative of the People Isoré with whom he had worked closely while serving in the Army of the North.[6] By the end of August, Vandamme was prepared to take desperate measures to end his dreary exile. He seriously considered going to the West Indies to seek military employment and sought Pichegru's aid and advice. His former commander did not think the West Indies a good idea. He also advised him not to move to Paris, which Vandamme was also considering.[7] So he remained at Cassel.

In late September his efforts and patience (or perhaps impatience) were rewarded, and he was reinstated with his previous rank of general of brigade and ordered to the Army of the West.[8] It was most likely the intercession of Isoré that made the difference. Isoré wrote his good friend the Representative Merlin on Vandamme's behalf and informed Vandamme on 28 September that he would soon be given a command.[9] The following day Vandamme received a letter from the Committee of Public Safety dated 29 September 1795: "The Committee of Public Safety orders that General of Brigade Vandamme will be reinstated on active duty and that he will go without delay to the Army of the West to be employed in his rank with that army or with the Army of the Coast of Brest at the discretion of the general in chief of the Army of the West. The commission of organization and of movement of the land armies is charged with executing this order."[10] The order was accompanied by a letter from citizen Louis-Antoine Pille, commissioner of the movements of the land armies, instructing him to report to General Lazare Hoche (commander of the Army of the West), who would confer with General Jean Charles Pérignon (commander of the Army of the Coast of Brest) as to the best use that could be made of a newly arrived general of brigade.[11]

The armies in western France were fighting a civil war. The west was strongly Catholic, opposing Jacobin attempts to de-Christianize France, and also royalist, disapproving of the removal and execution of the king. Early in 1793 rebellion had broken out in the département de la Vendée and spread to numerous départements in the west. Fighting on the frontiers for its very existence, the government in Paris could do no more than maintain one or two understrength "armies" in the west, not strong enough to put down the insurrection. So the fighting continued, with the insurgents receiving aid from England and using guerrilla warfare tactics with some success. To be sent to fight in the Vendée was tantamount to being sent into exile. The area was a dumping ground for officers to prove their loyalty until such time as they might be sent to an army fighting the foreign enemy. It is not surprising that Vandamme, though happy to be put back on the active list, was disappointed at being ordered to the Vendée.

General Hoche, who had served under Vandamme in the Army of the North, must have been pleased to receive a general with his excellent military reputation. But before the new general had settled into his appointment as commander of the arrondissement of Ancenis, he received new orders. Jean-Baptiste Aubert-Dubayet, the minister of war, informed Vandamme on 22 November that he was to report at once to the Army of the Rhine and Moselle.[12]

By the middle of December, a very happy Vandamme was once again under Pichegru as a part of the Eleventh Division commanded by General Laurent Gouvion Saint-Cyr. He took command of General Jean-Baptiste Rivet's brigade and enthusiastically prepared to take part in the last phase of the 1795 campaign, which came to an abrupt end, however, when an armistice was signed, effective 10 January 1796. The French and Austrian armies were both in poor condition and neither wished to undertake a winter campaign. The fighting had favored the Austrians during the fall of 1795. They had driven the French back from Mayence, recaptured Mannheim, and were in firm control of the left bank of the central Rhine. On the other hand, the French still faced them in strength; and the Austrian commander, General Clairfayt, saw little possibility of further significant gain. The territory on the left bank of the Rhine had been devastated by two years of war and could no longer provide an army with either food or fodder. Clairfayt needed to be resupplied and reinforced. The

French armies were lacking everything and desperately needed rest, supplies, and to be paid.

Both armies welcomed the armistice. The only opposition came from the new government in Paris. The Constituent Assembly, elected in September 1792 to write a constitution for the new republic, had finally completed its work. It dissolved itself, and a new government, the Directory, came into existence in October 1795. The government was weakened by the remnants of the Jacobin left and the increased strength of the royalist right. When the government was informed of the armistice at the end of December 1795, at first it took the position that the generals did not have the authority to conclude a secession of hostilities, only the government in Paris could do so. But it did not feel secure enough in its position to go against the wishes of the popular generals at the front. Thus, reluctantly, the Directory gave its approval.

The armistice called for both sides to recognize the status quo even if their armies pulled back from the line that existed on 10 January. Thus the French withdrew into winter quarters in regions that had not been totally depleted of resources. Pichegru withdrew his Army of the Rhine and Moselle a number of days' march west of the armistice line. Saint-Cyr's two brigades commanded by generals Claude-Jacques Lecourbe and Vandamme took up quarters at Deux-Ponts and Sarrebruck, respectively. Although conditions on the Saar River were better than those on the Rhine, Vandamme's new command was in pitiful condition. The army's pay was months behind; even when troops were paid, it was in revolutionary paper money that was worth only a fraction of its face value. Morale was low, and the government did not provide adequate supplies, which would have greatly improved the situation. Marauding and pillaging became the norm, and officers either joined in or ignored the misconduct. Fortunately, the armistice lasted several months, and the armies were gradually resupplied. It was during this lull in warfare that General Moreau replaced General Pichegru in command of the Army of the Rhine and Moselle.

In the late fall and early winter of 1795, Pichegru had requested on several occasions that he be relieved of his command, so he might recuperate from more than three years of campaigning. The general was tired and needed a rest, but there was more to the story than that.

Pichegru had entered into negotiations with the enemy. By the fall of 1795, he had become disenchanted with the government in Paris. The armies he was commanding in the north had been shamefully neglected, and there did not seem any indication that conditions would improve in the future. His pay, in devaluated revolutionary paper money, was woefully inadequate to maintain the lifestyle he wished for. Furthermore, he had never been enthusiastic or fully supportive of the establishment of a republic in France. He probably was a moderate constitutional monarchist at heart. He certainly had come to disapprove of the Constituent Assembly's handling of the war and the excesses of the Reign of Terror, and now he did not see much improvement under the new Thermidorian Directory.

In August 1795, possibly earlier, Pichegru had made contact with enemy agents.[13] He was encouraged in this undertaking by the overall lack of support for the government in Paris following the overthrow of Robespierre and the Jacobins, and the establishment of the Directory did nothing to change his mind. He was further encouraged by the Club de Clichy, even though its members had criticized him for putting down the riots of Germinal in Paris (1 April 1795).[14] His reversals on the Rhine in the fall of 1795 served to increase his interest in overthrowing the government.

The Allied proposals to Pichegru were tempting, although their plan of action was questionable. The prince of Condé, commanding the army of French émigrés, made him a most astonishing offer for when the monarchy would be restored: "he was to be named marshal [of France], governor of Alsace, to have the *cordon rouge* of [the order of] Saint-Louis, the château and park of Chambord, twelve guns taken from the Austrians, a million [livres] in cash, an income of two hundred thousand livres [a year] . . . and [a mansion] in Paris, while the district of Arbois, from whence he came, was to bear his name and be exempt from taxes for fifteen years."[15] In return for this utopia, Pichegru would lead his army, together with Condé's French and Clairfayt's Austrian armies, in a march on Paris where the Republic would be abolished and the monarchy restored with Louis XVIII on the throne.[16] There was some question as to the concessions to the Revolution upon which Pichegru insisted, but there does not seem to have been any final or definite agreement on either just what it was that Pichegru would receive, what concessions the king would make, or when and how the Republic would be dissolved. Pichegru was careful never to commit himself totally. Thus while he contemplated, or might even have been planning, treason, there was not at the time (1795) any hard evidence, despite numerous accusations, that he actually engaged in overt acts of treason.[17]

The Directory became aware in February 1796 that Pichegru was in communication with the prince of Condé but the directors did not know the details or feel they had enough solid evidence or support to remove so popular a general.[18] Thus, when Pichegru decided it was unlikely his army would follow him to Paris to overthrow the government, he concluded there was nothing more he could accomplish by waging war against Austria or Paris. With the armistice in place and his army in winter quarters, he again offered his resignation (5 March), and this time, on 25 March, the government accepted.[19] Moreau was named to replace him, and the weary general returned to Paris.

Vandamme had not been with the army during the difficult failed campaign of fall 1795 but joined just in time to go into winter quarters following the armistice. He was not in a position to observe firsthand Pichegru's mistakes or to evaluate the actions and attitudes of the commander. Saint-Cyr, in command of a division under Pichegru, would later claim not only that the general was in communication with the enemy but that his conduct in the fall of 1795 was treasonous.[20] Some have alleged that Moreau knew of Pichegru's contacts with the enemy, but that he was not involved or did not know the details or the extent to which his friend was involved.[21]

Vandamme, on the other hand, had no knowledge of any wrongdoing on the part of Pichegru. When allegations of treason were leveled against his former commander, Vandamme came to his support. He first believed, as did the army, that Pichegru had been removed from command against his wishes. This was a man who had defended and supported him when he had been denounced, and Vandamme considered him a true friend. He wrote to the Directory a long letter defending Pichegru, praising his many accomplishments while conducting the campaigns in the north and praising his dedication to the Republic and the government. At one point in his letter, the naïve Vandamme declared that Pichegru was the "enemy of all intrigues, he scorns courtiers and flatterers." He went on: "I esteem and respect [Pichegru], if the government knew him well, I am persuaded that it would render him justice, . . . he is at this moment in Paris; but not for intrigue nor to flatter, of which he is incapable. A straightforward republican who has never wavered, a trained soldier, brave and obedient, these are the marks of his character." Then when Vandamme became aware of the Directory's offer to send Pichegru to Sweden as the French ambassador, he wrote to the general and asked that he be allowed to accompany him to Stockholm. Fortunately, Pichegru declined the offer, and Vandamme remained with the Army of the Rhine and Moselle.[22]

Vandamme's complete, enthusiastic, and open support of Pichegru did not advance his position in the Army of the Rhine and Moselle. It certainly further tarnished his relations with the government in Paris. It very probably contributed to his having to wait three more years before being promoted to general of division. Vandamme was not the most popular general in the army, but he was fiercely loyal to his friends. His support of Pichegru was also undoubtedly the basis for yet another denunciation. The charges or accusations made remain vague, but in April 1796 the Directory wrote to Commissioner Rivaud, with the Army of the Rhine and Moselle: "The Directory has received your two letters of 6 and 8 *ventòse*. It has given orders for General Vandamme's conduct to be examined with severity."[23] And this was followed by new accusations against Vandamme. On 5 May 1796, Carnot wrote to Moreau:

> The Directory has received many grave complaints of the severity of the character of General of Brigade [Vandamme], and of the actions he has taken when he experienced the slightest annoyance. . . . The Directory recognizes the patriotism and the bravery of this officer, and it is only with regret that it sees itself forced to inform you of the reproaches his conduct has merited for a long time, but the government has overlooked these faults because of the service he has rendered to the Republic. But as it appears that his presence at Saarbruck, where he has also exercised very arbitrary acts, causes fear and terror, . . . the Directory charges you, general, to

employ him immediately in a different division of the army.... If he has new complaints against him, the Directory will have no other choice but to take other measures and to dismiss him.[24]

This time the charges were more serious, and Moreau had to comply with the direct order. He moved Vandamme to command a brigade in the Seventh Division under the command of General of Division Philibert-Guillaume Duhesme.

Vandamme had two serious problems at this time. One was his personality and character; the other was the lack of material support from the government. He was abrupt, abrasive, and unsympathetic to the misery of the civilian population. A soldier virtually all his brief adult life, he understood the giving of orders and the taking of orders (though the latter was not one of his strong points), but he could not deal with local authorities in an amiable or, from their point of view, even a civil manner. He thought only of the army's needs, and that these needs overrode any discomfort or misery on the part of the local population. Since the government did not supply his troops with even the basic necessities of life, Vandamme extracted them from the district in which his brigade was quartered. If the local authority was slow or reluctant in providing the needs of the army, Vandamme was neither slow nor reluctant in acquiring what he believed necessary for the maintenance of his command. This is not to excuse his often brutal manner with the civilian population. Other commanders faced the same problems and handled them in a more diplomatic way. Civilians in the eighteenth century were always the ones who suffered the most from any war waged on their soil. They seldom, if ever, believed they benefited from wars. In any event, one should not be surprised that the civilian authorities in 1796, as they had before and would continue to do throughout Vandamme's military career, were complaining to the government in Paris of his actions. The problems of supply were corrected from time to time, particularly under the empire; but Vandamme's personality changed very little over the years.

The condition of the Army of the Rhine and Moselle improved little during winter 1796. On 2 March Vandamme wrote a long discouraging letter from Saarbruck to the Representative Woussen decrying the poor condition of his brigade and the army in general. The cavalry, he declared, was very feeble, if it existed at all. The regiments were less than half strength. "Our army is disgusted because it is so poorly paid. But even if every soldier was given one more 'sol' a day, it would not be enough. As for the officers, the generals, what are they to do? . . . They depend on the soldiers. They can not prevent the pillaging and the stealing because they are reduced to living with their troops. So the officers, disgusted by this misery, by this debasement, have no authority and no courage; the soldiers despise them and have no respect for them."[25]

When Moreau took command of the Army of the Rhine and Moselle in mid-April, he immediately informed the government that he needed at least sixteen thousand horses; he had virtually no horses or harnessing for the cavalry or artillery. He declared that the infantry lacked shoes, and that the army, in general, was discouraged. The troops were living by forced requisitions and pillaging of the countryside where they were billeted, which had led to a breakdown in discipline and a general deterioration of the army. Nevertheless, Moreau tried to show a positive attitude by declaring that everyone with the army was hopeful.[26] And indeed, he did command a force of some eighty thousand men, with the vast majority combat veterans. Most of the incompetent officers of the early years of the war had been removed. With adequate supplies, discipline could be restored and the army prepared to enter once again upon campaign. Back in Paris, Carnot, who had survived the Thermidorian Reaction, was still the dominant figure in military matters (ministers of war would come and go, but the Organizer of Victory remained in control).

Early in 1796, General Napoleon Bonaparte was given command of the Army of Italy. He had been employed in the topographical department in Paris, where he had taken part in planning a campaign for that army, so he arrived at army headquarters with a plan in his pocket that he had been influential in putting together. The Directory considered the Army of Italy something of a "do-nothing" army. No-one expected it to accomplish much more than keeping the Austrians out of southern France. Bonaparte would have a relatively free hand to conduct a campaign, without Carnot or the government taking much notice. So long as the news was not negative, all was well in the south.

This was not the situation on the Rhine. From the beginning of the war in 1792, the different governments had all considered the war on the northern and eastern fronts to be the principal threat. Allied armies in Belgium and on the Rhine were less than two hundred miles from Paris, and the major concentration of forces for both the French and the Allies were in the north and the east. With the victories in Belgium and Holland, the enemy on the Rhine consumed the military strategists in Paris. The French forces were divided into two separate armies: the Sambre and Meuse, commanded by Jourdan, and the Rhine and Moselle, commanded by Moreau. The two generals were independent of each other, but both were, for all intents and purposes, lieutenants taking orders from Carnot. The plan drawn up for the summer of 1796 called for both armies to cross the Rhine.[27] Jourdan would advance against General Wartensleben and drive the Austrians east through Frankfort, Würzburg, and Bamberg back into Bohemia. At the same time Moreau would cross the river at Strasbourg and move through the Black Forest into Würtemberg and reach the Danube and Bavaria. Jourdan would then join Moreau on the Danube, and they would extend their right flank south through the Tyrol to link up with General Bonaparte's Army of Italy.[28] The plan was ambitious and gave little credit to Archduke Charles who would command the Austrian armies in Germany.

On 20 May 1796, the Austrians denounced the armistice, with hostilities to resume in ten days. General Jean-Baptiste Kléber, on Jourdan's left wing, actually began the campaign by advancing up the east bank of the Rhine from Düsseldorf on the night of 29–30 May. The campaign started well for the French, thanks in part to Bonaparte's successes in Italy. As the Austrians were preparing to renew the struggle on the Rhine, the supreme military authority in Vienna, the Aulic Council, ordered General Würmser from Germany to Italy with twenty-five thousand men in order to confront Bonaparte, who had forced Sardinia out of the war, defeated the Austrians at Lodi on 10 May, and taken Milan three days later. Although Würmser did not leave Germany until mid-June, the Austrians had decided not to take the offensive but rather to pull back in a defensive mode behind the Rhine.

The resumption of hostilities found Vandamme commanding one of the two brigades in Duhesme's division, which made up the left wing of Moreau's Army of the Rhine and Moselle. He was before Landau facing north as the Austrians still held the entire eastern Palatinate. When Würmser was ordered to Italy, Archduke Charles was given command of the Austrian armies on the Rhine. With his troop strength reduced by twenty-five thousand men, Charles withdrew his division from the Palatinate and took up a defensive position on the east bank of the river, giving Moreau the opportunity to begin crossing the river near Strasbourg on 24 June. The crossing actually took place at Kebl and Gambsheim. General Louis-Charles Desaix with three divisions crossed the river and turned north to form Moreau's left and receive the Austrian force, sent to drive the French back to the left bank. General Pierre-Marie Férino crossed the river with three divisions, turned southeast, and marched up the Kinzig River to Hoffenberg. When General Saint-Cyr crossed the Rhine with his two divisions, he followed Férino to Hoffenberg, where he became the center of the army. Férino took up a position on the left bank of the Kinzig at Lahn, to become the right wing.[29]

General Duhesme, with the brigades of Vandamme and General Alexandre-Camille Taponnier, had crossed the Rhine and moved up the Kinzig River. He then crossed the mountains and, on 2 July, reached Oberkirch on the Murg River. Led by Laroche's division, Saint-Cyr marched on Freudenstadt. On 5 July, Desaix gave battle with the Austrians, commanded by General Latour, at Rastatt on the lower Murg. Latour, whom the archduke had sent south with a corps to drive the French back over the Rhine, was stopped at the Murg; and when he learned that Saint-Cyr was preparing to march down the right bank of the Murg with fourteen thousand men, he drew off and retired toward Pforzheim. Further north, Jourdan had reached Frankfort on the Main River and was pursuing the Austrian right to the east.

General Wartensleben was left in command of the Austrian right when Archduke Charles went south to assume personal command of the army facing Moreau. Wartensleben had no intention of engaging in battle with Jourdan, as the Army of the Sambre and Meuse was larger than his own, so Jourdan took Würzburg, Bamberg, and Nürnberg with little or no opposition. There were continuous skirmishes, but his army was still in reasonably good condition a week or so later when it reached Amberg, just west of the border of Bohemia and some thirty miles north of Regensberg on the Danube. At the same time,

Moreau was marching east, in pursuit of the retreating Archduke Charles. Charles's plan was to prevent the two French armies from uniting, while taking part of his force before Moreau and moving it north to join Wartensleben and destroy Jourdan. He would then turn south and fall upon Moreau's left flank and, with Latour's division, destroy the remaining French army.[30] In order to execute this plan, the archduke had to retreat to the east toward the Danube River, until the time was right to divide his force. As a result Moreau, like Jourdan to the north, met only token resistance marching through Würtemberg.

There were occasional engagements, not always favorable to the French. On 9 August a strong detachment of Austrian Hussardes crossed over the Danube River at Guntzbourg and caught a part of Vandamme's brigade by surprise. After creating havoc and inflicting serious casualties, they withdrew back across the river unmolested. This was an embarrassment for Vandamme but should not have been a surprise to Moreau. His army had been underfed, underpaid, and poorly supplied for a month. Now it was in a prosperous land unspoiled by previous campaigns, where both officers and men engaged in looting and pillaging.[31] Discipline continued lax, the enemy did not appear eager to fight, and commanders had become careless, not taking proper precautions each night to guard against any surprise attack. Vandamme learned his lesson the hard way and, in the future, saw to the security of his bivouacs. Discipline remained lax, however, and the army remained vulnerable.

The archduke decided to check the French advance when Moreau pressed too closely on his heels. He took up a position at Neresheim, north of the Danube and southwest of Nordlingen. The strengths of both armies were about equal on the battlefield, forty-three thousand Austrians and forty-four thousand French.[32] Both armies were scattered in southern Germany, and both commanders had only a portion of their total strength on the battlefield east of Neresheim on 11 August 1796. The archduke's intention was simply to slow down the French advance so he could break off contact. He would leave a covering force, march north to join Wartensleben, and together they would destroy Jourdan's army somewhere between the Danube and Nürnberg or Amberg. Moreau was bent on pushing the enemy over the Danube through Augsburg to Munich. He did not believe Charles wanted a major battle. Therefore, when Saint-Cyr, with only one of his divisions, came upon the Austrians, he took up a defensive position as General Moreau advised. The battle opened on the morning of 11 August, with Saint-Cyr in a weak position waiting for Desaix to come up from his left rear. Fortunately for the French, the archduke was more concerned with marching off to meet Jourdan than he was with destroying Moreau's army. He thought the French were in greater numbers than they actually were at this point of the battle. Desaix arrived with part of his corps as the battle continued throughout the day. When darkness brought an end to the fighting, the archduke decided he had accomplished his goal. He withdrew to the south, crossing the Rhine at Dillingen. Moreau claimed victory and then followed the enemy over the Rhine.[33]

While Saint-Cyr and Desaix were occupied with Archduke Charles before Neresheim, General Duhesme with Vandamme's brigade fought his own battle at Heidenheim, some fifteen miles to the southwest. Duhesme formed Saint-Cyr's right, but by 10 August they had been separated for several days. On 8 August Duhesme had received orders from General Reynier, Moreau's chief of staff, to spread his division out to the north and south of Heidenheim; however, he received no further correspondence from Moreau for four days. On 11 August Vandamme was in position before Heidenheim, with Laroche's brigade to the south and west making contact with the right flank of the army commanded by General Férino. Moreau's artillery and supply wagons were at Heidenheim, which had temporarily become the army's principal depot. Thus, when Vandamme was attacked on the morning of 11 August, Duhesme, who was with him, felt obliged to defend the town. Although the Austrian infantry was only moderately superior in numbers, the enemy had overwhelming superiority in cavalry. Duhesme called in his right wing, but Laroche was too far away to be of assistance. Vandamme held his own against the Austrian infantry, but when his modest cavalry was driven from the field he could not remain in place. Cut off from his main line of retreat to the northeast by the Austrian cavalry, he retreated to the northwest. The Austrians did not intend to follow the defeated French, there was no serious pursuit, and the fighting died away by dark. Duhesme moved north on 12 August until he reached the high road from Stuttgart and made contact with Moreau.[34] It was perhaps fortunate for Vandamme that General Duhesme was with his brigade on 11 August, because the criticism for the defeat at Heidenheim fell upon his shoulders, not those of the brigade commander.

As a part of the Thermidorian Reaction, the Representatives of the People were recalled from the various armies on campaign, which gave the generals a freer hand and the government in Paris less direct control. The Directory then replaced the representatives with so-called government commissioners. Barthélemy-C. Joubert had been sent to the Army of the North and Charles-Alexis Alexandre to the Army of the Sambre and Meuse. Nicolas Haussmann had been sent to the Army of the Rhine and Moselle, and Cristofora-Antonio Salicete and Pierre Anselme Garrau to Bonaparte in Italy. These new commissioners did not have the extraordinary power of their predecessors sent to the armies by the Committee of Public Safety, but they did have the right of surveillance and of reporting directly to the five executive directors. They were to keep the government informed of what the "real" situation was, in contrast to the rosy or dismal conditions often reported by the generals.[35]

Haussmann, known to be stern but just, was with the Army of the Rhine and Moselle at the time of the battles of Heidenheim and Neresheim. He was not with Duhesme at Heidenheim, but nevertheless, three days after the battles, he wrote a letter to the directors that was very critical of Duhesme and not at all flattering of Vandamme. He began by pointing out that, on the day of the battle, Duhesme had no idea of the whereabouts of either the army commander or his general staff; and that he was operating without any knowledge of what the rest of the army was doing. Haussmann goes on to say:

> From the report that he [Duhesme] sent me, it appears that General Duhesme had lost his head. He was persuaded that General Férino [on his right flank] had been completely beaten and had retreated to Freiburg; thus, he believed that he had to look to his own safety. He retreated well ahead of his Division [that is, Vandamme's brigade] and did not know where it was.... None of his officers had a map, and many of them did not even know the name of the town where they were. He believed that the enemy was on his heels.
>
> I think that it would be judged suitable that you citizen Directors not confer a division to be commanded by a general

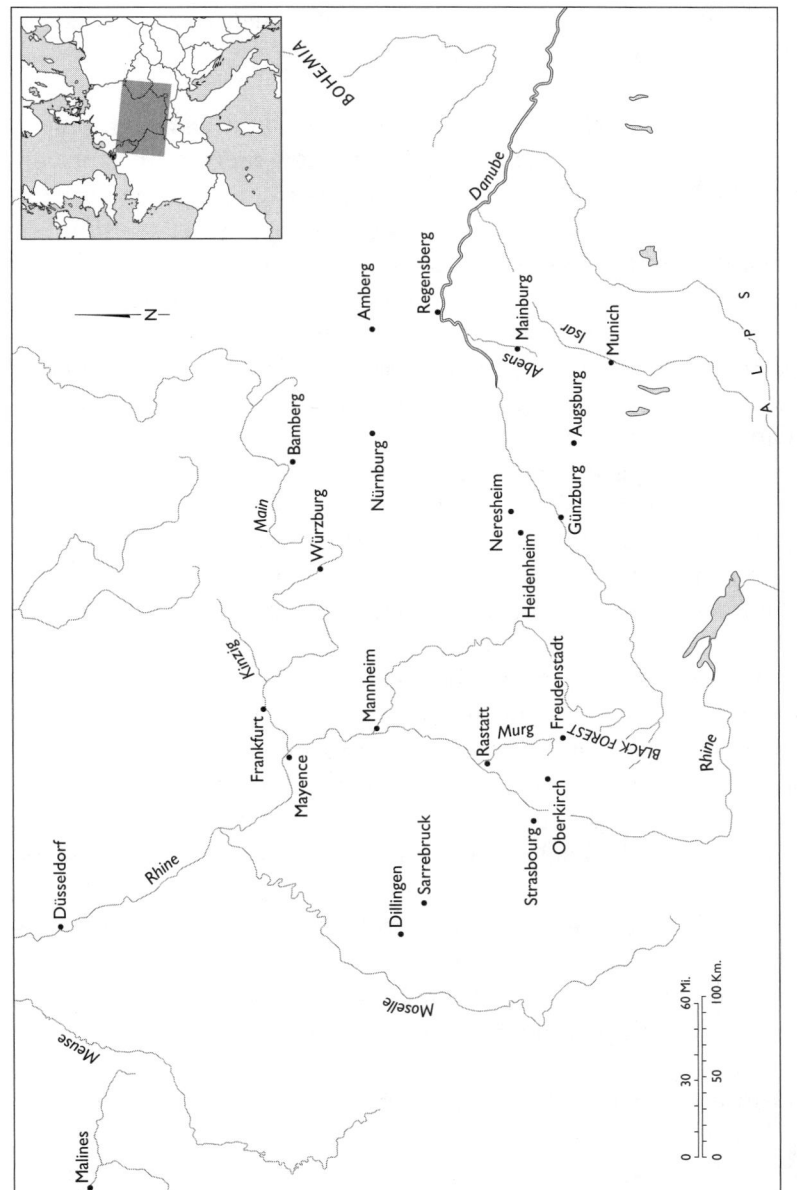

Campaigns of the Rhine and Danube

with so little dignity and who was known throughout the army as a greedy man who thinks only of making a personal profit from the victories of the army.[36]

Haussmann's remarks were harsh, but his evaluation of the general was not far off the mark. It must be said that General Duhesme conducted the battle on 11 August with some skill, extracting his command from virtual disaster and taking it to safety. That there was great confusion following the battle is true, and there was indeed room for criticism. Fortunately, the defeat had no real effect on the campaign, as the Austrians withdrew the next day.

In the same letter of 14 August the commissioner next addressed himself to General Vandamme: "His [Duhesme's] general of brigade, Vandamme, was already known to the Army of the North from previous reports, and it seems he has not broken the habits formed with that army. It is certain he has collected nearly one million [francs] of equipment that the Austrians had left behind by recommending to his Hussardes to save the equipment." Then the honest Haussmann gave Vandamme his due: "At least Vandamme has the reputation of being very brave and skillful in combat."[37] Nevertheless, he would have both Duhesme and Vandamme sent before a military consul to answer for their conduct in the conquered countries. But, he lamented, the inhabitants of those districts did not dare to come forward and testify against the generals. They were restrained by fear, Haussmann wrote, and would only talk through intermediaries. He concludes by pointing out that there had already been a number of pillagers brought before military courts, but seldom was "justice" administered. When he was unable to influence change in the Army of the Rhine and Moselle, he sought help from Paris. The Directory then ordered Moreau to search the wagons of the generals and commissioner of war and bring before military courts those officers who were found to have stolen goods. Once again there is no indication this order produced any evidence that Vandamme had in any way enriched himself by taking from the occupied territory. The armies in Germany were advancing triumphantly and the government was satisfied, the commanding generals were satisfied, it was Commissioner Haussmann who was not satisfied.[38] There was certainly disorder and pillaging, which resulted from the lack of regular supplies to the armies and the fact that the soldiers' pay was months in arrears. Haussmann indeed paints a dark, but most likely true, picture of the conditions in the Army of the Rhine and Moselle as it marched through southern Germany.

As to Vandamme, there is no documentation that any action was taken against him as a result of the commissioner's accusations. In fact, when Duhesme took sick shortly after the battle of Heidenheim, Moreau gave Vandamme temporary command of the Seventh Division. The commander in chief remembered that Vandamme had skillfully commanded a division for six months with the Army of the North in 1794–95. He had full confidence that, although still a general of brigade, his friend would account well for himself and his division.

For the next few weeks the campaign of 1796 continued to favor the French. Archduke Charles had accomplished his goal of breaking off contact with Moreau and had crossed back to the right bank of the Danube. He left thirty thousand men under General Latour to slow Moreau and to try to hold him before Munich along the Isar River. Charles, with twenty-five thousand men, marched north to join Wartensleben so as to attack Jourdan. Moreau assured Jourdan he would support him if the archduke attempted to crush him, but in fact he did not. Moreau crossed to the right (south) bank of the Danube and pursued Latour.[39]

Even when he knew that Charles was heading north, Moreau continued to press Latour toward Munich. It is true that he had orders from Carnot to advance into Bavaria, but Paris was not aware of the situation on the ground in Germany, and Carnot did not know Jourdan was about to be attacked by two Austrian armies. On 1 September the Austrians turned and attacked the isolated corps of Desaix, south of the Danube, but this general drove them off. By 7 September, Moreau was on the Abens River, and Saint-Cyr had defeated an Austrian corps at Mainburg, but Jourdan was in serious trouble. When Jourdan learned the archduke was advancing on his right, he began to pull together his scattered forces and withdraw to the west. Wartensleben and Charles joined forces near Amberg, where Jourdan fought a limited engagement to secure his westward retreat. The Army of the Sambre and Meuse was now outnumbered, and Jourdan had no desire to fight a major battle under unfavorable conditions.

On the other hand the archduke, while wanting to destroy Jourdan's army, was not willing to gamble too much. Moreau was now behind him on his left and posing a serious threat. Thus, while Moreau did very little in Bavaria, Charles followed Jourdan back to the Rhine, down the river, and escorted the Army of the Sambre and Meuse to the left bank from which it had begun the campaign.

Back in Bavaria, the Army of the Rhine and Moselle could do little without Jourdan's support. The Austrian army before it was inferior in numbers but had a superior Austrian army to its left rear; the archduke could at any time turn south and march onto the rear of Moreau's army. At first Paris ordered Moreau to hold his position in Bavaria, but by 20 September it had become clear that the Army of the Sambre and Meuse would not maintain a position on the Main River east of Frankfort, or even east of the Rhine, as Carnot had hoped.

So Moreau was given permission to retire through the Black Forest, to remove his army from the threat of encirclement. During the retreat Vandamme continued to command the Seventh Division, through the month of September and into October, and he frequently commanded the rear guard. The only battle took place on 2 October at Biberach. Latour attacked Moreau hoping to gain a great victory over the French. Vandamme played a major role in the French victory. He was part of Saint-Cyr's corps that turned the Austrian right flank; and as the battle came to a close, it was his demi-brigades (the Seventeenth and the One-hundredth) that pursued the enemy as far as Appendorf. Latour, having sustained heavy losses, then allowed Moreau to continue his retreat with only the usual harassment. The army's principal discomforts were now caused by the lack of supporting services and pay. On 21 October, Moreau wrote to the Directory describing a minor engagement with one of Latour's corps: "Despite the state of misery and fatigue of the troops, who lacked shoes and uniforms, . . . they pushed back all attacks with great courage." Moreau also addressed other problems that occurred during the campaign. Six days later he wrote that there was disorder, even chaos, among the men from time to time, but he and his officers did their best to reduce or eliminate such problems. He added, however: "It is a misfortune that will remain impossible to prevent as long as there is no regular distribution [of food and supplies]."[40]

Indeed disorder and chaos were a constant problem with the republican armies. In Italy, General Bonaparte had the same kind of troubles when he began his campaign in spring 1796. On 22 April he issued an order that condemned looting on the part of officers and civilian commissaries. He gave division commanders the authority to arrest and remove officers who allowed pillage, and to have officers and men shot who were caught in the act of pillaging. On 26 April he wrote to the directors: "There is less looting than there was. The first thirst of a famishing army is being satisfied. There are excuses for the guilty men; they have arrived in the Promised Land, which they have seen for three years from the summit of the Alps, and they want to enjoy it. A few have been shot, more put to hard labor behind the lines." On 9 May Bonaparte again wrote to Paris: "Discipline is improving every day, though we still have to shoot a good many men, for there are some intractable characters incapable of self-restraint."[41]

The problems with looting and pillaging in the armies in Germany differed little from those in Italy. Much of the blame rested with the government's inefficiency, or its inability to provide for the needs of the men. Shortages of food, clothing, and military supplies were the norm. This forced the army to "live off the land," a euphemism for disorder and pillage. Once back behind the Rhine, order was restored, and the overall condition of the army improved slowly, but food rations continued inadequate, the troops were still not paid on time, and new clothing was very slow in arriving.[42]

The retreat to the Rhine continued in an orderly manner because the archduke had followed Jourdan down the Rhine, rather than moving up the Rhine to stand between Moreau and the safety of France. Then when Charles did send a corps up the right bank of the river to cooperate with Latour, he sent only fifteen thousand men. Moreau was able, with some difficulty, to move his army to the right bank by 26 October. The campaign virtually came to an inglorious end, with the French in control of the left bank of the Rhine and Austrians in control of the right bank, except for two bridgeheads at Kehl and Huningue. The French maintained a foothold on the right bank of the Rhine at Düsseldorf. The only change that had taken place between the winter of 1795–96 and the winter of 1796–97 was that there was no Austrian army on the west bank of the Rhine, and the French had two footholds over the river in addition to that at Düsseldorf.[43]

Late in October 1796 Moreau offered the archduke a truce, which Charles wished to accept, but which the Aulic Council rejected. Charles was ordered to capture the French bridgeheads at Kehl and

Huningue. In compliance with his orders, Charles brought twenty-nine thousand men before Kehl with the intent of driving the French back across the river. Desaix was in command at Strasbourg and Kehl. A part of Saint-Cyr's corps had reinforced him. Thus it was that Vandamme, once again commanding only his brigade, came under the orders of Desaix and was a part of the defense of Kehl. General Férino's corps was left to defend the French position at Huningue, which also came under Austrian attack. Desaix had three brigades to defend the bridgehead at Kehl. Vandamme joined general of brigade Louis N. Davout. The bridgehead defenses at Kehl were in poor condition in late October; Desaix's principal, and overwhelming, task was to repair them so they might withstand a full-scale siege. Vandamme did not remain long at Kehl, however. Some time in late October or early November he requested a leave of absence, to return to Cassel for reasons of health. No immediate action was taken on his request.

Commissioner Haussmann had again denounced him to Paris—along with, it seems, most of the generals of the Army of the Rhine and Moselle. Late in October, while Vandamme was at Kehl, Moreau received a letter from the minister of war denouncing three of his generals by name and implying that there were others whose behavior should be examined. "You are informed, General, by the Executive Directory," the letter stated, "of the denouncement of many general officers of the army that you command; and, in particular, generals Antoine-Guillaume Delmas, Antoine Laroche-Dubouscat, and Vandamme." The minister enumerated charges against Delmas: that he claimed he had lost everything on the campaign, yet had many horses and seven wagons; that at the town of Lichtenau alone he had demanded twelve hundred louis that were paid to him at Carlsruhe; that he took the best carriage and twenty horses from the prince at Carlsruhe; and that he received another twelve hundred louis at Donauwörth. General Laroche was accused of extracting two hundred louis from the town of "P . . ." and the same amount at "G . . ."; while at Calw he took ten thousand florins; and then the troops he commanded pillaged the town. The minister demanded that Moreau examine these charges and take appropriate action if they were true. Such specific charges were directed against Delmas and Laroche, it is interesting there were no particular charges against Vandamme; he seems to have been included in "many general officers." There is no evidence of an investigation of Vandamme, or that any report or action was taken against him as a result of this denunciation. Even the commanding general of the army was not immune from criticism. Commissioner Haussmann, who it is presumed had initiated the denunciations against the generals, complained also of Moreau. He felt the general did not show him proper respect and did not have confidence in him. On 18 October he requested, "to be replaced by someone who would be more agreeable to the general in chief." One may well assume that the abrupt Vandamme also showed little respect toward the pretentious commissioner and that this contributed to his denunciation.[44]

In early November Vandamme was still pressing his superiors for permission to leave the army to recuperate his health. He was not alone in his desire to rest after the exhausting campaign. Saint-Cyr had been allowed to turn over his command and take a leave for health reasons. Vandamme wrote several letters to Moreau and Desaix, and the latter agreed to his leave and to send the request to Moreau whose approval was required.[45] Vandamme assumed that his friend Moreau would not object to his leave as long as Desaix was in agreement. He left Kehl and went to army headquarters at Strasbourg. There he was informed by one of his aides-de-camp that Moreau had not approved his leave, and the commanding general was angry with him for leaving his post without permission. The disappointed Vandamme sat down and penned a letter to Moreau that was both curt and apologetic: "General," he wrote, "my aide-de-camp . . . tells me you have refused to give me the leave you promised to me. I have good reason, because my health has failed totally. . . . I am not able to perform any service, and I remain in my room. If I left Kehl too soon yesterday, it was because I believed I would receive the leave you promised to me." He went on to say that he would not have requested a leave if it had not been absolutely necessary and added: "I believed that I had done my part, and that now I deserve to rest. No one can accuse me of loving my pleasures more than my duty." Realizing he had left his post at Kehl without permission, Vandamme concluded this letter: "My aide-de-camp has informed me of your anger, and it has made me very unhappy," and he asked to be forgiven, adding, "Now my fate is in your hands; do to me whatever harm I deserve."[46]

Moreau was displeased with Vandamme and wanted to keep him with the army while the two bridgeheads were under siege, but nevertheless he granted the leave, and the general left the army for Cassel. This affair probably marks the beginning of the decline in friendship between the two comrades in arms. Vandamme returned to his parents' house, where he spent the next several months resting. He was only twenty-six years old, but the campaign in Germany had been hard on him as well as on the entire army.

Back on the Rhine, the war continued. Moreau launched a major sortie from Kehl on 22 November that caught the Austrians by surprise. It was successful in destroying some of the enemy's preparations for an assault but did little more than prolong the siege. By the beginning of the new year, Moreau and the Directory had come to the realization that the two bridgeheads on the east bank of the Rhine could not hold out much longer without sacrificing both garrisons. Therefore, negotiations were opened with the Austrians, who were not anxious to sustain the casualties necessary in taking the bridgeheads by assault. The French were allowed to march out with full honors—from Kehl on 10 January and from Huningue on 5 February 1797. With the cessation of hostilities, Moreau withdrew his army from the Rhine and put it into winter quarters.

The end of the campaign of 1796 gave the armies of the Rhine and Moselle time to undergo major reorganization. Troops were sent to Italy to bolster the victorious General Bonaparte. In the Army of the Sambre and Meuse, Jourdan was replaced by General Pierre Beurnonville, who was in turn replaced on 24 January by General Louis-Lazare Hoche, who had temporarily pacified the Vendée. The armies of the Rhine and Moselle was also regrouped. General Georges-Joseph Dufour was given command of the right wing, Desaix the center at Strasbourg, and Saint-Cyr the left wing.

During this period of reorganization, Vandamme, back at Cassel, was keeping a watchful eye on events. He went to Paris for brief visits to let it be known he was still in the picture and to hear the latest rumors. And indeed, Paris was the central rumor mill of France. When Vandamme heard that General Hoche was going to be given supreme command over both the armies on the Rhine, he decided to remain at home for reasons of his health and not to return to the Army of the Rhine and Moselle. Apparently, it was his friend General Macdonald who passed to him the rumor that Hoche would be named supreme commander of the two armies on the Rhine (in fact, he was given only command of the Army of the Sambre and Meuse). Vandamme knew Hoche from their days together in 1793. Then general of brigade, Hoche had served under Vandamme at the siege of Nieuwpoort. However, during the siege, Hoche had been promoted to general of division and sent to the Army of the Moselle, while Vandamme remained with the Army of the North as general of brigade, which he was still in 1797. Hoche had become somewhat of a hero for his successes in the Vendée; and despite the miserable failure of the expedition he led to Bantry Bay on the southwest coast of Ireland in December 1796, he was held in high regard by the government in Paris. Fortunately for Vandamme, it was only a rumor that Hoche was to be supreme commander of both armies.[47]

By April 1797 it was apparent that the armies on the Rhine would soon take the offensive, and Vandamme wanted to be sure he would have an active command. Moreau recognized the general's ability in command of a brigade or division, and even though he had been angered by Vandamme's behavior the previous November, he allowed him to resume command of his old brigade in Duhesme's division, in the army's center under the command of General Desaix.[48] When Vandamme arrived at Strasbourg, Desaix was preparing to cross the Rhine as soon as the armistice was renounced. Vandamme was given the rather dubious honor of being the lead brigade to cross the river at Diersheim. The armistice was denounced on 12 April, and hostilities resumed four days later. Hoche moved his Army of the Sambre and Meuse over the Rhine and attacked the Austrian right wing.

General Latour had been given command of the Austrian army on the Rhine when Vienna sent Archduke Charles to Italy for the purpose of stopping General Bonaparte. The war in Italy had been going very well for the French ever since Bonaparte took command in the spring of 1796. Having forced Sardinia out of the war, Bonaparte marched into the Po River valley and in a series of victories drove the Austrian army from Northern Italy. The surrender of Mantua in January 1797 and the arrival of reinforcements from the armies of the Rhine enabled Bonaparte to march on Vienna by the end of winter. The overall plan, thought Bonaparte, was for the two armies on the Rhine to cross the river and march on to the Danube while he advanced on Vienna out of Italy. However, both Hoche and Moreau were slow in opening the campaign of 1797. By the middle of April, when Bonaparte was at the Leoben Pass in Austria, Hoche and Moreau had not even begun to advance.

Desaix had scheduled the crossing of the Rhine to take place under cover of darkness the night of 19–20 April, but the boats arrived without their oars. The boats had been collected up a small stream so the enemy could not see them and thus know where the crossing would take place, but the level of the Rhine had dropped, and the stream was too narrow and shallow to use the oars. The boats had to be dragged down the stream and over sand bars to the point of debarkation, and the oars were left behind.[49] By the time the oars caught up with the boats, it was 6:00 A.M., and the shore-to-shore operation then had to take place in daylight, in plain sight of the enemy on the east bank. There were enough boats to transport only a portion of Vandamme's brigade over the river at any one time. Nevertheless, Moreau and Desaix decided to go forward with the operation. Vandamme crossed with the first troops, and Duhesme quickly joined him. His "assault troops" suffered casualties even before they set foot on the right bank. Vandamme and Duhesme formed the first wave of troops into units and held the beachhead until more troops joined them. The foothold was expanded and supported by Davout's brigade, which was next to cross the river. Fortunately for the French, the Austrians could not bring up large numbers of reinforcements before Davout's brigade was in place, and the two brigades were strong enough to withstand the Austrian counterattack. During the afternoon of the first day (20 April), a pontoon bridge was erected. Saint-Cyr began to bring his corps over the river. Davout then took Diersheim and pushed south. Vandamme drove up the Kinzig River through Hoffenberg to Gengenbach. The fighting on 20–21 April was fierce and the casualties heavy. General Duhesme was wounded and had to retire from battle, but the crossing was a success. The French were well established on the right bank when news arrived that, on 18 April at Leoben, General Bonaparte had concluded an armistice with the Austrians, which included the armies of the Rhine.[50]

Bonaparte included the armies of the Rhine in the armistice because the latest news he had from Paris stated that those armies had not crossed the river and begun a new campaign. He did not know Hoche had renounced the armistice relating to the Rhine theater on 12 April and would move against the enemy within the week. Hoche and Moreau could have rejected Bonaparte's inclusion of their armies; but, in fact, both were willing to end the bloodshed (Hoche with enthusiasm and Moreau with reluctance). For Moreau the campaign had just begun, and it was going well. He was across the Rhine with superior forces to those of the Austrians; and he had every reason to believe that with the support of Hoche on his left flank he would repeat the previous year's march on the Danube. Without the approval of Saint-Cyr, Desaix, and other generals in his command, Moreau accepted the armistice, and hostilities came to an end on 22 April, after a campaign of only three days.

Vandamme and his brigade had borne some of the fiercest fighting and had covered themselves with glory. The general wrote Moreau giving high praise to the engineers and his aides-de-camp, as well as to his officers and men. He asked that the commander of the army remember them and reward them in accordance to what they deserved.[51] But the fighting had not been flawless. On the first day, when Vandamme's brigade was in position on the right bank, the Sixteenth Demi-brigade had panicked and fled to the rear. It was rallied on the banks of the river (there was no way across the river at that time) and went back into action, but the results could have been disastrous. Vandamme wrote Colonel Pinot, the commander of the demi-brigade, and ordered him to seek out the men responsible and bring them before a military court. "Find the culprits," he wrote on 27 April. "They exist. They must be tried; the cowards must be punished, the weak officers must be hunted out, only the brave and firm deserve to be rewarded."[52]

As brief as the campaign was, there was time enough for Vandamme to end up in trouble. An anonymous writer denounced him for having personally benefited from a "contribution" of thirty-six thousand livres demanded of the towns of Hoffenberg and Renchen. Both these towns had been occupied by Vandamme's brigade, and he continued to hold them after the armistice. It was common practice for French generals to demand "contributions" from towns or cities they occupied, with the money to be used to support the army or sent back to the government in Paris. On 24 April Bonaparte announced he would levy a contribution on the towns of northern Italy equal to one-half the pay of his army.[53]

The denunciation of Vandamme was made to Paris. Moreau received a letter from the minister of war instructing him to look into the allegation, and Moreau, without looking into the charge, seems to have accepted it as fact. He wrote Vandamme and demanded to know what had become of the thirty-six thousand livres. Vandamme replied in the following manner:

> General, I received this instant your letter in which you announce that you are giving the order to impose a contribution on the districts we occupy. You tell me you have been informed that I have already given the order to commissar Petit-Didier to raise about thirty-six thousand livres from the towns of Hoffenburg and Renchen; and you demand that I inform you which cash box I have put the money into. I have no knowledge of any contribution levied on the towns of Offenburg and Renchen; but I see clearly now that those who have sworn to destroy me are taking every opportunity. Be that as it may, I am accused; but having nothing to reproach myself of, I fear neither the jealous nor the malicious.[54]

Vandamme followed this several weeks later by a letter to General Reynier, Moreau's chief of staff and close confidant. After a cordial introduction, an irate Vandamme got quickly to the heart of the letter:

> I am neither an intriguer, nor am I ambitious, nor deceitful, nor mischievous; nevertheless, General Moreau treats me as if I am all of these at the same time. I do not know why he ignores who I really am. . . . perhaps my frankness is a part of my problem. Be that as it may, I will conserve the character that has always satisfied me. The fools and malicious who judge me believe they have made a fool of me. But they will be proved wrong; for I have my ways. As for them, I will know how to avoid their injustice and their maliciousness. Must I remain silent to the commander in chief after I performed my duty in crossing the Rhine? What account has he sent to the government, which can judge me only in accordance with his report? Bonaparte and Hoche rewarded their men down to the drummer boy, it seems to be less here, and I can not notice it with indifference.

Vandamme went on to declare that he had a right to expect to be promoted, as well as his aides-de-camp, but he felt they were being abused because he did not brag about his accomplishments. He also complained about the tone of the letters that Moreau was writing him after their years of serving together in the Army of the North and now in the Army of the Rhine and Moselle. Finally he wrote: "Weary of all these intrigues, I will wait several more days, and if I do not receive the satisfaction I have a right to expect, I will leave the army. I will prove, in time, that the zeal I have professed was dictated only by my love of the service here, as with the Army of the North, and not by ambition or intrigue. I see only that I have been dealt with unjustly."[55]

The friendship between Vandamme and Moreau dating back to their days with the Army of the North in 1793 was at an end. Moreau was weary of hearing accusations against his subordinate. Until this last denunciation there were few specific charges, but the claims of Vandamme's taking money for himself and complaints of his severity in dealing with civilian populations in territories he occupied had become too much for Moreau. He may have felt he needed Vandamme at the head of a brigade or division on campaign and in combat; but in time of peace, as in the summer of 1797, Vandamme was a liability. Moreau was tired of explaining and justifying him to the government in Paris. As for Vandamme, he was angry. He admitted he might have prematurely levied a contribution on the two towns he occupied, but he claimed he was not the one who collected the money, and he did not know how much was collected nor where it went. In fact, there is no evidence that he benefited from the contribution. He did not live extravagantly, nor did his family back in Cassel. Vandamme was unhappiest, however, because he felt his services to the army and the Republic were not appreciated. He saw those about him being promoted; Bonaparte in Italy was promoting his officers at a rapid rate. Vandamme had been a general of brigade for four years. He had commanded divisions in combat under Moreau in 1794–95 and again in 1796, yet he remained a general of brigade. He felt he surely should have been promoted to general of division after his service in the campaign of 1796. It appears that Vandamme's lack of promotion was linked directly to the numerous denunciations over the years, his brutal outspokenness, and his less than charming personality.

The denunciations of Vandamme have all dramatized the negative aspects of his character. But there was another side to the man. He could be compassionate when dealing with the civilian population in territories he passed through or occupied. The abbot of Schwarzach (Baden) wrote Vandamme on 30 May 1797, referring to the French occupation of Schwarzach district: "I could not be more grateful, because after the petition I had the honor to send you requesting that you reduce the number of troops occupying the village that is dependent upon my monastery, you gave the order that fulfilled the desire of the poor unfortunate residents. Faithfully interpreting their sentiments, I assure you they have already blessed you and will never forget the beneficial hand that relieved them. As for me, I am, with all the respect that you deserve."[56] Vandamme had occupied the city of Gengenbach after the April crossing of the Rhine. In mid-July Abbot Bernard of Gengenbach wrote expressing his gratitude for the general's benevolence. He concluded: "Accept the offer of my gratitude that I have the honor and the pleasure to give you. Add to that, if you will, my goodwill; and also my affection, esteem, and devotion, which I will continue until my death."[57]

4

CAMPAIGNS ON THE RHINE

In the summer of 1797, while Vandamme was sulking and contemplating once again leaving the service, political events in Paris reached a boiling point.[1] Elections had been held in April for the Chamber of Five Hundred, which gave the political right a majority. This majority in the chamber threatened to purge the Executive Directory and put the government in the hands of the anti-republicans. Paul-François Barras, with the support of two of the other four directors and the political left, carried off the coup d'état of 18 Fructidor, year V (4 September 1797). The arch-republican General Pierre-François Augereau, on loan from General Bonaparte in Italy, commanded the troops that dominated the streets of Paris. Carnot, François Barthélemy, and fifty-three leading deputies were purged. This coup put an end to the constitutional government established in 1795 and paved the way for the Brumaire coup d'état that would bring Napoleon Bonaparte to power in November 1799.

The Fructidor coup had little effect on the armies of the Rhine and Italy, but it had an effect on Vandamme. In order to gain support for the coup among the left and the center, the leaders made public General Pichegru's correspondence with the exiled royalists, thus proving his treason. This was a shock to Vandamme, who had defended his friend against such charges. Confronted with irrefutable evidence of Pichegru's treason, Vandamme ended all communication with him. Having admired and emulated Pichegru as a role model, he was devastated to know this brave soldier was a traitor.

Vandamme remained with the army on the Rhine until the end of July when he received leave to return to Cassel for "health reasons," the only way for a soldier to take a leave of absence. The continent was at peace. There seemed little chance that the English would attempt to engage the French army in the near future. During the next five months, Vandamme was in Paris on several occasions, though he was not involved in the political intrigue that flourished at that time. He also traveled in southern Germany. In the last week of November, and not by accident, he was at Rastatt, in Baden. The formal peace treaty ending the war between France and Austria had been signed at Campo Formio on 17 October 1797, but the final territorial settlement was concluded at Rastatt in November. General Bonaparte, on his way from Italy back to Paris, stopped at Rastatt for several days to put the finishing touches on the settlement. This is where Vandamme first met the future French emperor. He was already impressed with Bonaparte's accomplishments in Italy, and as one historian has suggested, he was ready to replace his fallen idol, Pichegru, with a new hero, Bonaparte.[2]

From Rastatt, General Bonaparte continued to Paris, where he arrived on 5 December in civilian clothes on the public stagecoach. The hero of Italy did not wish to appear in any way a threat to the men in power. He would simply be citizen Bonaparte, at the service of the French Republic. Nevertheless, he was the toast of Paris, which made some members of the Executive Directory and the assemblies uncomfortable. To occupy the general and remove him from the capital, they gave him command of the Army of England, newly created on 26 October 1797.

In the fall of 1797 there had been a major reorganization of the armies of France. The two armies on the Rhine—the Sambre and Meuse and the Rhine and Moselle—became the Army of Mayence; and the Army of Switzerland (Helvétie) was created, as well as the Army of England. The officers and men for this Army of England, which at its height numbered close to a hundred thousand men, came primarily from the armies on the Rhine with some contingents from Italy.[3] Vandamme remained officially a part of the Army of Mayence although he was not present with the army in the fall of 1797. Early in January 1798 he received orders to report to the Army of England. On a number of occasions he had called upon Bonaparte in Paris and was undoubtedly pleased to serve under his new hero. He wasted no time in assuming his new command.[4] But General Bonaparte was too shrewd to be put out to pasture on the English Channel, in command of an army that was not going anywhere. He realized that without naval supremacy in the Channel there was no possibility of a successful invasion of England; and the French navy, in 1798, could not guarantee control of the water between England and France. The general, therefore, returned to Paris and resigned command of the army.

An invasion of England was not the only project being put forward in the spring of 1798. When Bonaparte left the Army of England, Vandamme realized he would not go on campaign in the near future. Rumor was that General Augereau, the military commander of the Tenth Territorial Division at Toulouse, was about to form an army of Portugal. Hoping that there would be more action with Augereau, Vandamme wrote the general asking to join him should he form a new army. It was only a rumor, however, and Augereau wrote him saying as much, but agreeing to ask for Vandamme if such an expedition should take place.[5] So Vandamme remained with the Army of England through the spring and summer of 1798. With his headquarters at Cherbourg, he commanded four demi-brigades spread along the coast of Normandy from Cherbourg to Dieppe.

During his tenure with the Army of England, Vandamme was involved in several minor affairs. The most serious was the attempted expedition to Saint-Morcouf, a small island only a few miles off the coast of Normandy that was occupied by the English and a menace to coastal traffic between Le Havre and Cherbourg. The amphibious operation took place on 7 May. Vandamme was with the first wave of boats. But the affair was a fiasco. Enemy guns and musket fire prevented the French from landing; and Vandamme, whose boat suffered several casualties, returned to La Hougue, the port from which the operation had been launched.[6] He was also involved in rooting out insurgents in the departments of Manche and Calvados, over which he had military authority. Although General Hoche had "pacified" the west, French émigré insurgents, with encouragement from England, were once again active in the summer of 1798. The general was ordered to search out the bands that were active in his military district and to treat them as the enemy. He was instructed to form secret mobile columns and to move against the émigrés both swiftly and decisively.[7]

It seems that during early summer 1798 Vandamme suggested France should give aid to the Irish. General Michaud's aide-de-camp Captain Pierre-Joseph Farine wrote Vandamme, beginning: "The Directory feels the same as you do, citizen general, that it is time to send help to the United Irishmen." Farine then briefed Vandamme on the preparations for the expedition to Ireland and informed him he was to send two battalions of his command to Brest to take part in the operation.[8]

Vandamme was not happy with the Army of England after General Bonaparte's departure. The future emperor had not invited him to go to Egypt, probably because he did not really know him and he had more generals of brigade than he needed. So in September 1798 Vandamme returned to the Rhine.[9] He was given command of a brigade in the division commanded by General Filles-Joseph Sainte-Suzanne that was a part of the Army of Mayence. In the overall reorganization of the armies, General Lefebvre was named temporary commander of the Army of Mayence, then Jourdan was given permanent command of the army, and Sainte-Suzanne was transferred to the Army of Italy on 14 October. Vandamme, still a general of brigade, was given command of Sainte-Suzanne's division. With his headquarters at Strasbourg, he commanded the forts of Kehl and Auenheim on the Rhine. During the fall of 1798 his energy was directed to improving the fortifications of the two bridgeheads on the east bank of the river.[10] In less than four months after receiving command of a division, the happy Vandamme was at last promoted on 5 February 1799 to general of division. "I am informing the general in chief [Jourdan] of your promotion," the minister of war wrote Vandamme, "so that he can assign you a position in keeping with your new rank."[11] He had waited (one cannot say with patience) for nearly six years to attain this highest rank in the French army. At twenty-eight years of age, he felt that this recognition of his service and devotion to the Republic had gone too long unappreciated. Nevertheless, the promotion was just in time for the spring campaign of 1799.

General Bonaparte had sailed to Egypt in late spring 1798. Although he was successful in establishing his control over the lower

Nile, the French fleet was then destroyed at Aboukir Bay in August 1798. Bonaparte and his army of thirty-five thousand men were stranded, isolated, in Egypt. With England again providing the money, Austria was willing and eager to renew the war with France. Having never been happy with the losses sustained by the dictated peace of Campo Formio, Austria wanted to regain its dominance of Italy and southern Germany. Bonaparte had antagonized the Russian tsar Paul I when he occupied Malta in June 1798 on his way to Egypt, putting an end to the order of the Knights of Malta (Order of the Knights Hospitaler of Saint John of Jerusalem) of which Tsar Paul I was the honorary head. On 29 December 1798, for this and lesser reasons, Russia joined with Austria and England to form the Second Coalition. In a rather short period of time the Ottoman empire, the kingdom of Naples, Portugal, and some of the lesser German states also declared war on France. The rallying point of these nations was their dislike of the French-dictated Treaty of Campo Formio (17 October 1797) that ended the First Coalition. By the end of winter 1798–99 everything was in place to open the campaign against France. The burden of the fighting would fall upon the Austrian army, with some support from the Russians.[12]

The armies of France were again reorganized, in preparation for the coming campaigns on the Danube and in Switzerland in spring 1799. They consisted of about 170,000 men of which only some 128,000 were available for combat.[13] The Army of Mayence, commanded by Jourdan, would take the name Army of the Danube when it reached that river. General Masséna was given command of the Army of Switzerland (Helvétie); Bernadotte the Army of Observation (on the middle Rhine); Barthélemy-Louis Schérer the Army of Italy; and Macdonald the Army of Naples.[14] The French armies were poorly prepared for the renewal of hostilities, and even less so to undertake the offensive operations ordered by the Directory. "After two years of peace," wrote General Antoine-Henri Jomini in 1822, "the army was considerably reduced: the cavalry was feeble and generally poorly mounted; the artillery and the food trains lacked horses; a large number of brave officers had been retired for economic reasons; . . . the Army of Observation still existed only on paper. . . . To sum up, they [the government] had made insufficient preparations, in the interior and the exterior of the country, to fight a war on so wide a front."[15]

The Austrian army, on the other hand, had made good use of the two years of peace and had increased to 240,000 men, who were well trained and adequately supplied and supported. It was divided into three parts: an army in northern Italy, one in the Tyrol, and the main army under the command of Archduke Charles in Bavaria.[16] There was also a Russian army commanded by a very capable general, Aleksandra V. Suvorov-Rymmikski, on its way from Russia to join the Austrians in northern Italy.

The overall French plan, dictated from the war ministry in Paris, called for Jourdan to advance to the Danube, fight a decisive battle with the Austrians, and then march down the Danube to Vienna. At the same time Masséna would move through Switzerland into the Tyrol, and the Army of Italy would push the Austrians before it to the east. The plan was unrealistic. The Directory was thinking in terms of 1797. General Bonaparte and his Army of Italy were now in Egypt; they had won the war south of the Alps two years ago. The situation was not the same. This time the Austrians were better prepared, and the French lacked a commander the caliber of Bonaparte. Nevertheless, the opening days of the campaign seemed to go well for the French.

The Army of Mayence, forty-five thousand men, broke camp the last week of February and began crossing the Rhine at Strasbourg.[17] At the same time, General Férino, forming the right wing of the army, crossed at Basel (Bâle). When Lefebvre was granted a leave of absence for health reasons, Jourdan gave Vandamme temporary command of his advance guard. Jourdan's chief of staff, General Jean-Augustin Ernouf, wrote Vandamme on 18 February 1799: "As a result of your promotion, the commanding general has named you to command the advance guard until the return of General Lefebvre, at which time you will command the *avant-garde légère*."[18] Vandamme had two brigades at his disposal, those of generals Jean-François Leval and Nicolas-Jean de Dieu Soult (future marshal of the empire). On the morning of 1 March, Vandamme led the army across the Rhine and advanced up the Kinzig River valley through Offenburg to Biberach.[19] There was no enemy resistance because the Austrian army had wintered in Bavaria. Neither army had occupied Baden and Würtemberg. When Vandamme reached Villingen on 4 March, he received a letter from Jourdan informing him that Lefebvre had returned to the army to take command of his division and did not wish to have a general of division under his command. Vandamme was ordered to headquarters, but Jourdan added a conciliatory note: "I will not leave you long without action. I will form an infantry division attached to the reserve as soon as it arrives. I will add cavalry and artillery and give you command."[20] Upon reaching the Danube valley, Jourdan adopted the name Army of the Danube in accordance with his instructions.

When Archduke Charles learned that the French had crossed the Rhine in force and were moving toward the Danube, he crossed the Lech River on 3 March 1799 and advanced west. Jourdan believed that the archduke, while marching the main body of the Austrian army south of the Danube, was sending a strong detachment north of the river toward Stuttgart.[21] He, therefore, created a flanking corps at Tübingen and gave Vandamme command. This corps was made up of two infantry regiments commanded by generals of brigade Louis-Fursy Compère and Henri-Antoine Jardon, and three squadrons of cavalry.[22] Vandamme was ordered to advance to the northeast and report on enemy movements north of the Danube. "I have received reports," Jourdan wrote Vandamme on 18 March, "that the enemy has a project to throw a corps of troops against my left." Later in the day he wrote: "It is my intention, general, that you find out as soon as possible the movements of the enemy in the direction of Stuttgart, with intent to turn the flank of the Army of the Danube and to block its retreat."[23] This removed Vandamme from the main body of the army; Compère's brigade reached Esslingen, only a few miles east of Stuttgart.[24] On the night of 19 March, Compère informed Vandamme there were no Austrian troops at Stuttgart or at Esslingen.[25]

The French and Austrian armies approached one another at a leisurely pace. The archduke, with perhaps eighty thousand men, had a numerical superiority over Jourdan by almost two to one.[26] Jourdan did not concentrate the forces directly under his command. Férino's division (six battalions of infantry and ten squadrons of cavalry) was to the south near the Lake of Constance, while Vandamme was marching too far to the north. On 17 March, when Jourdan learned that war had been declared, Charles was in a good position to crush the French army and throw it back across the Rhine in shambles.[27]

Vandamme was very critical of Jourdan's decision to send him with half a division on a wild goose chase to the north, when the fighting was south of the Danube. In a letter to General Compère, he compared his mission to Don Quixote tilting at windmills and suggested that Jourdan be recalled by the Directory.[28] While he was off to the north, the two armies made firm contact on 20 March. The archduke did send a flanking corps of sixty-six hundred men to Ulm but recalled it in preparation for a major battle. When Jourdan realized the fighting would be south of the Danube, he recalled Vandamme.[29] But it was too late for him to march south across the Danube River to take part in the battle fought on the Ostrach River on 21 March. Lefebvre, whose division bore the brunt of the fighting on the first day, was wounded and had to quit the battle. Greatly outnumbered, Jourdan was forced to retreat west of the Ostrach to a position at Stockach. Vandamme reached the Danube and was placed under the orders of Saint-Cyr, who commanded the left flank of the army.[30] General Férino had also been called in from the right, so that Jourdan had his entire force directly under his command by 23 March.

The battle of Stockach (the French first called it Liptingen) took place on 25 March. Jourdan's plan was to attack the Austrian army, twice the size of his own force, on both flanks and in the center, thereby forcing it to retreat.[31] In the early hours the plan was going well. On the left Saint-Cyr waited until Vandamme had maneuvered to the right rear of the Austrian position at Liptingen. Once Vandamme was in position, Saint-Cyr attacked and with heavy fighting drove the enemy from the town taking from two to four thousand prisoners. The archduke moved troops from his left to meet the threat posed by Saint-Cyr. Having achieved an initial success, Saint-Cyr, his advance halted, waited for the attack on the Austrian center. This was delivered by General Soult's division, but it could not make headway. On the right flank, Férino's and Souham's divisions had moved forward, but meeting resistance they simply held their positions.

Vandamme was successful in reaching the enemy's right rear with a regiment of light infantry, three or four pieces of artillery, and six squadrons of cavalry. With the element of surprise, he made headway at first, but the archduke turned and fell upon him with overwhelming force, driving him back to the north. He withdrew in good order to join Saint-Cyr and to take with him about a thousand or twelve hundred prisoners.[32] When Soult's attack in the center was driven back and Saint-Cyr could not move forward, Jourdan ordered a general retreat.

Victory was on the side of the greater numbers; indeed, Jourdan's generals from the beginning had little hope for victory.[33]

Darkness on the night of the battle found Vandamme at Krumbach. But Saint-Cyr, believing he would be attacked and overwhelmed in the morning, withdrew to the north, across the Danube just west of Sigmaringen at Laix. While he withdrew to the west, Vandamme remained at Sigmaringen to slow down an Austrian corps coming up the river from Ulm. On 26 March Saint-Cyr moved northwest to Winterlingen and the next day to Rottweil, while Vandamme formed the extreme north flank and reached Balingen.[34] At the same time Jourdan, with the rest of the army, retreated into the passes of the Black Forest. The French had lost the battle but they avoided a disaster. The archduke, given his superior numbers, would have done better to crush Jourdan on the upper Danube—not allow him to retire with his army intact to the safety of the Black Forest and eventually to cross the Rhine. The French losses in several days of fighting were 3,654 (630 of Vandamme's command); Austrian losses were 5,921, of whom 2,953 were prisoners of war.[35] With the army safe in the Black Forest, Vandamme's division guarded the valley of the Kinzig River, which leads to the Rhine at Strasbourg.[36] The Austrians moved forward and made contact with the French in the various valleys leading through the forest, but they made no serious attempt to drive on to the Rhine until early in April.

On 2 April 1799, General Jourdan became ill. The following morning he turned command of the Army of Danube over to his chief of staff, General Ernouf, and retired to Strasbourg. Jourdan would not return to the Army of the Danube. He offered his resignation on the grounds of poor health; and the Directory, seeing that his campaign had been a total failure, accepted. Ernouf may have been an adequate chief of staff, but he was incompetent as army commander. When, on the same day that Jourdan left the army, an enemy column pressed the French outposts and captured the town of Triberg, Ernouf panicked and ordered a general withdrawal.[37] Vandamme pulled back— to Offenburg by 5 April, and then to Kehl. At this point he was given command of Souham's division to which he added his own flanking command. On 6 April the army began crossing the Rhine. Vandamme first took up a position south of Strasbourg at New Breisach. On 10

April he received orders to march south to Ottmarshein, which he reached on the 11th, and Basel on the 12th.[38]

The Directory, having accepted Jourdan's resignation, recalled Ernouf to Paris and appointed General Masséna to command the Army of the Danube and to keep command of his own Army of Switzerland. On 14 April Masséna ordered Vandamme to go east from Basel toward Zurich. He arrived on 17 April and established his headquarters at Andelfingen.[39] On 20 April, Masséna ordered Vandamme to Schaffhausen where he was to keep watch on the Rhine.[40] Masséna reorganized his army at the end of April and gave Vandamme command of the First Division of the central corps under his direct command, but as Masséna prepared to begin a new campaign in mid-May, Vandamme was once again denounced. And this time he was forced to leave the army.

In a letter dated 7 May 1799, General Louis-Marie Milet de Mureau, the minister of war, informed Masséna that Vandamme had been accused of levying a contribution for his own profit. He added: "He will be brought before a counsel of war to be judged in accordance with the law. You will issue the necessary orders to carry this out." Five days later, on 12 May, Milet de Mureau again wrote Masséna, with more specific details of allegations against Vandamme, charging the general with extorting money and supplies from the town of Vieux-Brisach under the threat of pillage and fire. "I invite you, citizen general," the minister concluded, "to order the verification of this fact, and to send me the information you find. It is the intention of the Directory and of myself to punish with severity the author of this sort of brigandage."[41] On 18 June Masséna wrote to Chef de Bataillon Coquengeiot, who had been named judge advocate for Vandamme's trial, naming three generals of division to sit in judgment: Jean-François Ménard, Henri-François Delaborde, and Claude-Juste Legrand.[42]

At the conclusion of the campaign of 1799, a number of letters were written from the department of the Upper Rhine and from Germany to Jourdan and members of the government in Paris complaining of the French army's conduct during and after the campaign. The letters fell into two categories: those from the principality of Würtemberg and those from the French department of the Upper Rhine. These charges are summarized as follows:

1. A letter addressed to citizen Trouvé, minister of the French Republic, from Count Zeppelin, minister of foreign affairs for the duke of Würtemberg, Stuttgart, 26 March 1799.
2. A translation of an official report by the Grand "Bailli" of Tübingen dated 23 March 1799.
3. Extract from a letter by citizen Roerjot to citizen Merlin, [ex-]director, Rastatt, 17 April 1799.
4. Letter from citizen Greffier (court recorder or clerk of the court) of the criminal tribunal of Upper Rhine to the Executive Directory, dated at Colmar, 22 April 1799.
5. Letter from Léopold Krauth, Greffier of the town of Vieux-Brisach, addressed to a legislator, 23 April 1799.
6. Extract of a letter from General Jourdan to the Executive Directory, dated 25 April 1799.
7. Letter of citizen Trouvé, minister of the Republic to the duke of Würtemberg, addressed to the [French] minister of foreign affairs, dated Paris, 2 May 1799.
8. Details of the private contributions that General Vandamme levied on Swabia.[43]

In a letter to "citoyen Trouvé" (citizen Trouvé), minister plenipotentiary of the French Republic, Count Zeppelin, minister of foreign affairs of the duke of Würtemberg, complained of the bad treatment of the towns of Würtemberg despite the treaty of peace between his country and France. Considering that there was a peace treaty between the two countries, Zeppelin protested "the oppressions and vexations committed in the district of Tübingen by the troops of the [French] Republic and its commanding officer during the time they spent in the duchy."[44] He included a translation from German of a report, dated 23 April 1799, from the grand Bailli of Tübingen.[45] It was this report from the Bailli of Tübingen to the duke of Würtemberg that was the basis of Zeppelin's protest.

In this report the Bailli of Tübingen laid out the grievances against the French army and its officers. The village of Kilchberg was ordered, within twenty-four hours, to provide the French with five hundred sacks of oats, fifty head of cattle, and six hundred quarts of brandy or one hundred louis if the order could not be fulfilled. The city was threatened with pillaging if the demands were not satisfied. At the same time Vandamme's aide-de-camp, Tourneur, was said to have arrived in the village of Nammerhof and demanded to receive from the Abbey of Schwirchtal the sum of fifty louis in gold. He had to settle for seven louis and some lesser coin, as that was all the money the abbot had at that time. General Compère demanded twelve horses from the village of Reutlingen. Similar demands were made upon the towns of Horb, Rottenburg, and Urach. All these demands were made on or about 20 March, at the height of the campaign, by officers and men under General Vandamme's command during the march of his flanking corps toward Stuttgart. The Bailli of Tübingen estimated that the cost to the prince of Würtemberg was ten thousand florins. The Bailli of Tübingen concluded his report with a note: "That the corps of General Vandamme, lodged and maintained in places all over [Würtemberg], did not have need of all the food supplies it requisitioned; [and] . . . that the consequences would be most costly if the demands were not met completely."[46]

There was another denunciation from Germany. Writing from Rastatt, citizen Roberjot, the French plenipotentiary at the talks in the city of Rastatt, declared to the ex-director Merlin that the discontentment in Swabia was great. After denouncing both the French and the Austrians, he declared that the war was a "War of Brigands" and then presented a "Résumé of the particular contributions levied by General Vandamme . . . on 19 and 20 March." The list contains fourteen towns with demands ranging from 25 louis (Wachendorf and Balingen) to 220 louis (Rottenburg) for a total of 1,289 louis. Roberjot concludes: "It is for this miserable amount, and for the other unjust extractions, the French name is right now abhorred in Germany."[47] There is no doubt but that the French armies, inadequately supplied by the government and frequently outmarching their poorly organized supply trains, had to live off the land. In this case it almost seems that it was the manner in which Vandamme and his men carried out the requisitions that gave offense, rather than what was actually taken from Würtemberg.

The denunciations from the French department of the Upper Rhine were similar to those from Würtemberg, but much more serious. In these letters Vandamme was accused of taking money for his own personal gain, as well as acting in a harsh and obnoxious manner, between the time that the division recrossed the Rhine, about 6 April, and when it marched south to Basel on 10 April. Conditions for the inhabitants and the surrounding district of Vieux-Brisach were indeed pitiable after six years of war. A letter from Leopold Krauth, greffier and secretary of the town of Vieux-Brisach, to citizen Metzer, deputy from the department of the Upper Rhine to the legislative Chamber of Five Hundred, pointed out the misery of the region and condemned General Vandamme. "Citizen administrators," he wrote, "the poor commune of Vieux-Brisach charged with [the care of] a French army, on the point of being exposed to a food shortage, incapable of acquiring its own bread, unable to cultivate its fields, and already suffering from having been almost entirely burned to the ground in 1793, dares to ask, citizen administrators, to have regard for its misery, and to dispense with the payments imposed upon it." The letter went on to explain that the motivation for this request was "the contribution of fifty louis in cash that it was forced, with torches in hand and under the threat of pillage, to realize within five minutes' time to the French General Vandamme and his officers."[48] Finally, from one M. Quellain, the clerk (greffier) of the criminal tribunal of the department of the Upper Rhine, came another damning denunciation. Dated 22 April 1799 at Colmar, Quellain's letter stated:

> General Vandamme, at the time of his leaving Vieux-Brisach with his division to go to the Army of Switzerland, extracted from the inhabitants of that unhappy town a contribution to his profit, of twelve hundred francs, along with other items; ... He dared to insist, and to avoid the greatest pain they [the townspeople] were obliged to take from the purses of the domestics of both sexes, to satisfy the barbaric demand.... I was not myself present at the time, but many persons of good standing from Vieux-Brisach, who are here present as I write requesting help because of their misery, affirm to the truth of this event.[49]

Finally, on 13 May 1799, the minister of war received a letter from the "Administrators" of the department of the Upper Rhine in which they described the plight of Vieux-Brisach and accusations against Vandamme. With respect to the specific charge they wrote:

"A column commanded by General Vandamme came [to Vieux-Brisach] and, instead of setting a good example for his subordinates, he summoned the inhabitants and with torches in hand and with great menaces he demanded in five minutes the sum of fifty Louis," with the threat that he would burn the rest of the town to the ground if he did not receive what he asked.[50] The accusations were serious enough that the directors and the minister of war could not ignore them. But there was a problem with bringing a general of division before a council of war. France was still at war, and the outcome of that war was still very much in doubt. Vandamme had already been ordered to stand trial for the charges against him, and the process had begun. But on 12 July the Executive Directory issued new orders in the "Vandamme Affair."

> Considering that the generals necessary for the formation of a council of war, before which General Vandamme was to be brought, can not leave their division to act as judges, and
> Considering that it is useless to wait for a time favorable to form said council of war . . .
> Article 1
> General of Division Vandamme will come at once to Paris to provide the minister of war with his defense. . . .
> Article 2
> The minister of war will provide [to Vandamme] the pieces relative to this affair, and Vandamme will make his report to the Executive Directory.[51]

The generals of division required to sit in judgment of Vandamme were leading armies against the Second Coalition and could not leave their commands to spend weeks, perhaps months, in Strasbourg listening to allegations and testimony against Vandamme. Furthermore, following the prosecution, Vandamme would have the right to present his defense in the form of numerous witnesses.

Vandamme was given copies of all the documents relating to the charges against him, and he went to Paris to defend himself. He prepared an eighteen-page document in which he first expressed his outrage at the charges, then detailed his service to France and his loyalty to the Republic, and finally addressed the charges of wrongdoing brought against him. This defense, or "Justification" as he entitled it, was published on 23 July 1799 at Strasbourg.[52] Before addressing himself to his defense, Vandamme complained in harsh terms, "It has been refused me to be judged by my peers. My innocence will not, therefore, be proclaimed in the presence of numerous witnesses to my conduct!"[53] Vandamme then briefly summarized the accusing documents and dealt with each one in its turn. First he took up the accusations from Germany.

He began by pointing out that Count Zeppelin, the duke of Würtemberg's foreign minister, "did not mention him [Vandamme] by name, but held him responsible for the actions of his officers and men." Furthermore, he had denounced the "oppressions and vexations committed in the *grand-bailliage* of Tübingen by the troops of the Republic and commanding officers." To this Vandamme replied: "I had done everything to maintain discipline in the division I commanded, and to prevent all vexations in the countries that were allied to France as well as those that were not."[54] As evidence of his good intentions, he quoted two letters from his register of correspondence for the period that his troops were in Würtemberg. Both letters were addressed from Vandamme to General Compère, who commanded the brigade that occupied the towns in question. The first letter was dated 26 ventôse, an VII (16 March 1799): "You will order, my dear comrade, that your troops essentially spare the possessions of the duke of Würtemberg and of the prince of Fürstenberg, and you will not allow any disorder in that country because we may remain here for some time and will be exposed to a lack of food. I am counting on you to maintain good order." On 18 March he again wrote Compère: "You will spare, as much as possible, the duchy of Würtemberg, and you will requisition only food or effects that are indispensably necessary; and you will take care that the delivery is in good order."[55] He concludes that, in fact, he had done everything within his power to maintain order and to respect Würtemberg and its inhabitants.

With respect to the charge made by the grand Bailli of Tübingen that General Vandamme's aide-de-camp Tourneur had demanded fifty louis from the Abbey of Schwirchtal, Vandamme declared he had never had an aide-de-camp by the name of Tourneur, and that this could be verified by the ministry of war. Vandamme makes light of the charge that his visit to Hechingen cost the prince ten thousand florins. He stayed only two days, actually thirty-six hours, at the expense of the prince and estimated that it could not have cost him one-fifth of the amount Zeppelin quoted.[56] To counter the charge that he had caused the French name to be abhorred in Germany, Vandamme quoted a letter written by the baron of Heer, on behalf of the prince of Hechingen (a relative of the king of Prussia), whose territory the general personally occupied:

> To General Vandamme, Hechingen, 22 March 1799
>
> The prince [of Hechingen], pleased by the honor you gave to him by your letter, has charged me to extend his thanks, and nothing would be more dear to his heart than to know you were satisfied with him personally and with the reception that you received. . . . Receive on my part, my general, the most distinguished homage with which I have the honor to be, etc.

Vandamme goes on to point out that there was no need for the prince of Hechingen to write him a friendly letter because the French army was in the process of being driven out of Germany. "The prince of Hechingen," Vandamme declared, "was at liberty to express his opinion on the evils I did to him and his estates."[57] He then makes a special point with respect the city of Tübingen: "No requisition for food or other necessities for the subsistence of the [French] troops was made on the city of Tübingen by my orders. That city is the home of the celebrated university that contains distinguished scholars. I wanted the sanctuary of science to be respected."[58]

The accusation by the French plenipotentiary Roberjot—that "for the miserable sum" of 1,289 louis, Vandamme had made "the French name abhorred in Germany"—was more serious. Vandamme, in his "Justification," declared that the only proof Roberjot provided was from an article by a German journalist published in the German newspaper *Mercury* of Swabia. He then pointed out that whereas the journalist accused him of extracting 75 louis from the prince of Hechingen and 450 louis from the city of Tübingen, the 75 louis was not mentioned by Zeppelin and the 450 louis was not mentioned by the Grand Bailli of Tübingen. Surely they would have known of such an extraction and would have gladly included them in their reports.

Vandamme concluded that one could not take seriously the denunciation of a French general by a German journalist who made up charges to degrade him.[59]

In concluding his defense of the charges relating to Germany, Vandamme quoted a letter written by General Jourdan to the directors dated 25 April. "General Vandamme has in effect been accused of having levied particular contributions; but those who denounced him to me did not provide me with any proof. Consequently, I was not able to pursue the matter." Vandamme added: "My justification is found entirely in this letter from the general in chief. . . . Because it affirms that those who denounced me to him were unable to provide him with proof to support the accusations."[60] He also pointed out that because Swabia (of which Würtemberg and the other small principalities were a part) was now under the control of the enemy, it was not possible to secure testimony either for or against him. He was convinced he could have secured numerous testimonies in Swabia to prove his innocence.[61] It should be noted that at no time in his defense did Vandamme declare he had not levied contributions on the southern German towns. It was standard French practice during the revolutionary wars for the armies to supplement their needs, particularly for food, by forcing the local inhabitants to feed and shelter the troops. What he denied was that he took from the German towns for his own personal profit, that his demands were excessive and unreasonable, and that they made the French name abhorred in Germany. On the other hand, given Vandamme's personality and his general dislike for Germans (all of whom he considered enemies of France), he probably was not always kind and gentle in acquiring the provisions necessary to sustain his army in the course of a difficult campaign.

The denunciations of Vandamme from the department of the Upper Rhine in the Alsace were potentially more serious. Vieux-Brisach, though ethnically German, was a part of the French Republic. Léon Nicolas Quellain, the clerk of the criminal tribunal for the department of the Upper Rhine, denounced Vandamme for having taken twelve hundred francs for himself from the inhabitants of Vieux-Brisach, who were already in a miserable state. Quellain was not at Vieux-Brisach when the alleged extortion took place but, rather, reported the affair on the testimony of others.[62] Only the first eight pages—not the entire document—were written on 27 May. The last three pages, consisting of five sections, have dates other than 27 May. But on 6 June, when Chef de Bataillon Coquengeiot, who had been appointed judge advocate of the court that was to try Vandamme, interviewed Quellain, he declared that he was not in a position to name any person from Vieux-Brisach who could verify his accusations against Vandamme. He asked for, and received, time to reexamine his memory and that of his friends so he could put forward a list of witnesses. On 12 June he provided the judge advocate with three names: Weiss, an innkeeper at Vieux-Brisach; Desept, a municipal magistrate of Vieux-Brisach; and Léopold Krauth, a clerk of the same town. In order to avoid traveling from Vieux-Brisach to Strasbourg to testify in person, Weiss and Desept put their testimony in writing. Both men declared "that they were absolutely ignorant of anything reproaching General Vandamme." Then on 22 June the two men confirmed the content of their letters before the magistrate of the town of Vieux-Brisach. The document was then certified by the French commanding officer of the town and forwarded to the judge advocate at Strasbourg.[63] Vandamme concludes that these two citizens of Vieux-Brisach would surely have known if there had been the repugnant extortion of money from their town, and the fact that they swore they knew nothing of such an affair was proof it never happened. On the other hand, one might speculate that Weiss and Desept could have been fearful of testifying against a French general of division who might at any time in the future be back in their town at the head of five or six thousand soldiers.

Léopold Krauth, named as a witness by Quellain to verify his testimony, had written a denunciation of Vandamme. But when the judge advocate went to Vieux-Brisach to secure his sworn testimony, Krauth declared: "it has never been my intention to denounce anyone, that consequently, I am not a part of this case, and am unable to indicate any person who could testify [against Vandamme]. My only intention was to return to France and to obtain work . . . not to accuse anyone." Under further questioning, Krauth declared that, if he had intended to denounce someone, he would have addressed his letter to the Executive Directory, not to his friend citizen Metzer, who was a deputy from the department of the Upper Rhine to the Chamber of Five Hundred.[64]

The combination of Vandamme's "Justification," the judge advocate Coquengeiot's *procès verbal* that discredited Quellain and contained Krauth's denial of everything, and the inability to verify accusations from Germany, led the Directory to issue the following orders, above the signature of Emmanuel Joseph Sieyès:

> Nineteen August [1799], the members of the government, enlightened on the truth of the facts contained in the accusation directed against Vandamme declare the following order:
> Art. 1. The order of 8 Floréal last [26 April 1799] by which General Vandamme was ordered before a council of war, is repealed.
> Art. 2. General Vandamme will be employed with an active army.
> Art. 3. The minister of war is charged with the execution of this order, which will not be printed.
> President of the Executive Directory, Sieyès.[65]

Vandamme had certainly made demands on the civilian population whether in France or in Germany during his campaigns. And it is certainly true that he was not always gentle and caring in securing the needs of his troops. But there is no real evidence that he personally profited, or that his demands were in excess of the needs of the army. It might be added that, when he could not provide for his men, they provided for themselves, which led to pillaging and a breakdown in discipline. Neither of the latter would have been in the best interest of the army or the civilian population.

The outcome of this "Vandamme Affair" would seem to have favored the general. There was no court martial, and the evidence, as forwarded to the Directory, was deemed inadequate to warrant any punishment; but Vandamme may well have benefited also from the uncertain political conditions in Paris. In the spring of 1799 the Directory, which owed its position in power to the support of the army in the Fructidor coup d'état, was once again navigating through troubled waters. The royalist right and the Jacobin left were both gaining strength, while the Vendée was again on the rise, and the country overall was not pleased with new demands for the army at a time when the war was not going well. The directors and their supporters needed the backing of the army, and disciplining one of its more talented and popular generals was not a course they wished to follow.[66]

On 18 August the new minister of war, General Jean-Baptiste-Jules Bernadotte, signed the letter of service ordering Vandamme back to the Army of the Rhine.[67] However, while Vandamme was very pleased with the outcome of the investigation, he was displeased with the last phrase of Sieyès's order that cancelled his court-martial, and that "this order will not be printed." Vandamme had left Paris for the north of France pleading poor health. Upon receiving Bernadotte's letter, he acknowledged his appointment to the Army of the Rhine and the order to go there at once. But the blunt Vandamme could not hide his anger, and he wrote the minister of war:

> I cannot conceal from you how much I am hurt that I did not receive in your letter the satisfaction you promised me in Paris....
>
> But, my general, why did they [the directors] suspend me from my functions with such enthusiasm and unmerited disgrace? And why today will they not proclaim my innocence publicly? So must the crime alone receive that which is due to innocence? I will go to the army as a common soldier—if necessary—but as a general of division, I can not go there until I receive from the Directory or from you public acknowledgment of the injustice that the Directory has exercised against me by removing me from the brave and excellent division of which I had its confidence and esteem, at the same moment it was going into bloody combat....
>
> I appeal to you, General; I ask you to plead my case before the Directory, and know that there is no one more devoted to the nation and its law.[68]

The day before Vandamme wrote this letter to Bernadotte (1 September) and several days before the minister received it, the minister of war had sent the general new orders, with a letter informing him that the English and the Russians had landed in Holland. Thus, before Vandamme made any preparations to join the Army of the Rhine, he was ordered to Holland to serve in the Army of Batavia under the command of General Guillaume-Marie Brune.[69] Vandamme received his new orders at Cassel and at once wrote, this time with enthusiasm, to the minister of war: "I have received tonight your orders and your letter of service for me to go to Batavia to serve under the orders of General in Chief Brune. I will leave at once, and despite my illness, I will be at general headquarters within hours. The sight of the English and the Russians will totally cure me. The two lines written in your hand at the bottom of my orders have made me partly forget the injustice I have suffered."[70] Vandamme concluded by asking that Bernadotte excuse the letter he had written the day before.

On 4 September 1799 Vandamme reached Brune's headquarters at Alkmaar and was warmly received by the future marshal of the empire, who gave him command of the First Division of the Franco-Batavian Army.[71] The two generals were acquainted but had not served together in the past. Both were outspoken republicans with good military records. Vandamme was pleased to be fighting the British under Brune, superior in time of rank to himself; Brune was happy to have an experienced French general reputed to be an excellent field commander. On 27 August an English army of some ten thousand men had landed north of Amsterdam, on the ocean side of the point of the Helder. The landing was carried out under the watchful eyes of Vice-Admiral Andrew Mitchell and General Sir Ralph Abercrombie, with the very capable General Sir John Moore in command of the first brigade to reach the shore.[72] But Abercrombie did not march immediately on Amsterdam, rather he decided to wait for the rest of the English force, and this second English expeditionary force did not land until 13 September. It included Frederick duke of York.[73] A Russian force also landed under the command of General Hermann. York was supposed to be the supreme commander, but Hermann cooperated, more or less, only as he saw fit. The only opposition to the English landing had been the Dutch division commanded by General Dumonceau, which made little effort to hamper the ship-to-shore operations. Thus the enemy established a defensive line across the peninsula and waited for reinforcements.[74]

Realizing the danger of the situation, Brune ordered the bulk of his command to move north. The French commander had about eighteen thousand French troops divided into three divisions. The First Division, soon to be commanded by Vandamme on 5 September, was seven thousand men strong and headquartered at Alkmaar, north of Amsterdam and south of the enemy landing. The Second Division was posted along the southern Dutch coast in the event of an English landing that would threaten The Hague and Rotterdam. The Third Division was scattered throughout central and eastern Holland to maintain French domination. The Batavian Directory put its two Dutch divisions under the orders of General Brune. These divisions were commanded by the Dutch generals Dumonceau and Daendels. When Brune had collected three divisions (one French and two Dutch) opposite the English position, he decided to attack and drive the enemy back into the sea, before it could be reinforced by English and Russian troops on the high sea. Vandamme's French division, the largest of the three, was on the left flank; General Dumonceau's Dutch were in the center; and General Daendels, with the other Dutch division, was on the right flank. The French advanced in good order and drove in the English outpost to reach the main enemy line of defense. Daendels's Dutch were advancing on the right when news arrived that Dumonceau's division in the center had panicked and fled to the rear. Daendels immediately fell back to his original position. This left Vandamme's leading brigade in an untenable position with its right flank exposed. When the enemy sent a strong column south along the coast, it was clear the battle had been lost, and Vandamme was ordered to fall back to his original defensive position. The English defenses were strong, and it is unlikely that Brune could have dislodged them, even if the Dutch had stood firm in the center. Nevertheless, the general laid all blame for the failure on Dumonceau's troops. In his official report of the fighting, Brune wrote: "In general, the two Dutch divisions did not show any indication of firmness. I have demanded a full report, and I will court-martial a number of their officers." Brune wrote two letters to Bernadotte, a personal friend, on 10 September, the night of the battle. One was his official report of the fighting that had just taken place, the other was a personal letter. In the first he pleaded with the minister of war to send him more French troops: "It is of the greatest urgency that you rush the arrival of the half-brigades you have destined to this army." This was followed by a personal letter in which he again pressed for reinforcements: "Send me more troops, my dear Bernadotte, or I do not know if I can hold with so many treasonous cowards and brigands surrounding us."[75]

Just four days after the battle, on 14 September, Vandamme suffered a serious fall from his horse and dislocated his left shoulder. Although it was very painful, he did not give up his command but rather continued his normal activities. English reinforcements landed on 13 September with the duke of York, who assumed command of the Allied army. The struggle was escalating, and the intrepid Vandamme was determined, despite his injury, to command his division in the coming battle. He did not have to wait long, for early on 19 September General Rostollant wrote him: "I believe that the enemy will attack in force tomorrow."[76]

The Allies launched an offensive on 19 September. The duke of York, after studying Brune's position and realizing the Allies had a substantial numerical superiority, decided to attack before the enemy could bring up reinforcements. York had thirty-five thousand English and Russians, whereas Brune, after receiving an additional several thousand French troops, could put into the field no more than twenty-one thousand men. Vandamme's First Division continued to held the left wing and a part of the center, with Dumonceau on his right forming the center, and Daendels on the right flank. Thus Brune's defensive line ran from Vandamme's left on the North Sea through Schoorl (or Schorel), then north of Hoorn to the Zuider Sea. York sent a strong Russian force, commanded by General Hermann, south against Vandamme through Schoorl to capture Bergen and Alkmaar; and an English column on his left, commanded by Abercrombie, attacked along the Zuider Sea to capture Hoorn and turn west to take the enemy in the rear. The Allied center would also advance against Dumonceau's Dutch.

The battle began well for the Allied army. While Abercrombie pushed Daendels south, Hermann attacked Schoorl. Vandamme's forward brigade, commanded by Adjutant General Claude Rostollant, felt the brunt of the Russian attack. He was able to slow—but not stop—the determined advance of Hermann's Russians, who drove the French back to Bergen. The Russians occupied Bergen, but at that moment Vandamme arrived with two brigades. He halted the enemy's advance and took back the town. Hermann's command by this time was in a state of confusion, and as Vandamme began to drive it back north, General Hermann and a number of Russians were taken prisoner. The day after the battle, General Hermann wrote a close friend at Russian headquarters: "You will count me, my dear Gernerchausen, numbered among the dead, and I do not know by what miracle I escaped death. They have taken good care of me at [French] general headquarters. They have also taken equally good care of our wounded and our prisoners with the utmost of humanity and generosity. They have given all the help necessary to our officers who are prisoners."[77]

Abercrombie, who started late, took Hoorn, but by the time he turned west, Vandamme had already won the battle on the other flank.[78] Abercrombie retraced his steps to the Allied defensive line, where he had begun the battle. In the center of the line, where the Dutch generally held their own against light English pressure, General Dumonceau was wounded and replaced by General Bonhomme. York moved English troops from the center to cover the Russian's disorganized retreat. When darkness brought an end to the fighting, both armies were back to their original positions. Brune proclaimed a great victory, and there was much rejoicing in the French camp.[79]

After the battle Brune reported to the Batavian Directory: "The English and Russians committed the greatest excesses in the villages they occupied during the fighting. The poor Dutch peasants were massacred and burned in their homes with women and children. Many villages are still on fire." On the day following the battle, Brune had high praise for Vandamme: "Your talents, the valor and courage that you displayed yesterday in commanding the French troops at the battle of Bergen, in which you played a major part, . . . all tell me that we owe this brilliant victory to your efforts. I do not know how better to reward you than to offer you one hundred Russian and English muskets."[80] Vandamme accepted the gift and then requested permission from Brune to send the muskets to the National Guard of Cassel, which was commanded at that time by his father. Brune agreed and the arms were transported to Cassel.[81] Brune also recognized the efforts of two of Vandamme's lieutenants. General of Brigade Louis-Jean Gouvion, who commanded one of Vandamme's hard-fighting brigades, was promoted on the field of battle to general of division. Then in a reorganization of his French troops Brune, having received additional reinforcements, created a second division and gave it to Gouvion, placed under Vandamme who continued to command all of Brune's troops in the peninsula. *Chef de brigade* René-François Aubrée was also promoted on the field of battle, receiving the rank of general of brigade.[82] On 28 September, shortly after the battle of Bergen, General Sir John Moore, realizing the campaign was going to fail, wrote in his diary: "The natural strength of this country is such that without a general rising of the people in our favor it is vain to hope to conquer it. [The English] Government would have done well to withdraw the army after the destruction of the Dutch fleet, making that the object of the expedition."[83]

A new Russian division landed in Holland on 25 September. This encouraged the duke of York to launch another attack on the Franco-Batavian line. The Anglo-Russian army was supplied entirely from England, and the supply system did not always function smoothly or in a timely fashion. At the same time Brune received additional troops, albeit not in great numbers, from France and the Rhine. York realized time was not on his side and that with the Russian reinforcements he had to strike as soon as possible. As early as 26 September, Brune knew from his spies that the enemy was preparing to attack all along his front, and Vandamme's forward brigades were placed on continual alert. By 30 September, General Gouvion was advising Vandamme to relieve his weary front line troops with fresh men.[84] On 1 October, news reached Brune's headquarters of Masséna's victory over a Russian army at the battle of Zurich on 25 September.[85] The same day Brune also received three thousand additional troops, with which he formed another French division whose command he gave to General Jean Boudet.

The anticipated attack came on 2 October. York sent two strong columns against Vandamme on the west side of the peninsula, General Abercrombie led an English force along the coast, and General Essen commanded the Russian division on Abercrombie's left. The French were driven out of their forward positions but held their main line of defense. Brune's center and right gave ground but did not break. By nightfall the French line was still intact, but Abercrombie had pushed south along the dunes and was threatening Alkmaar and French communications with Haarlem, still held by Vandamme. Brune ordered an overall withdrawal to a well-chosen defensive line at Beverwyck. The new French position was stronger and shorter, protected by large flooded fields. Masséna's victory had reduced the danger on the Swiss-German front and enabled the Directory to send more troops to Holland, and Brune received an additional three to four thousand French troops on 5 October.

York attacked again on 6 October. As four days earlier, Abercrombie was on the right, Essen in the center, and General Dundas on the left. The battle of Kastrikum (Castricum) raged throughout the day, in rain and fog. When darkness brought an end to the fighting, the Allied army held the French outpost; but the French had not been dislodged from their principal line of defense. Both sides claimed victory. It was in fact a draw, which was all the French really needed.[86]

Both York and Essen had suffered enough of this miserable campaign. The Russians were disheartened by the news of the defeat of General Suvorov at Zurich. They blamed the Austrians for not supporting the Russian army in that Swiss campaign, and now Essen complained that the English had not supported him in the battle of Kastrikum. York was ready to embark with his army and leave Holland behind. In a dispatch to London dated 9 October, he explained why he was asking Brune for an armistice. The English and Russian forces had suffered heavy casualties during the six weeks they had been on the continent. The Russian commander, General Hermann, had been taken prisoner; General Moore and Lord Chatham, brother of William Pitt, had been wounded. The French seemed stronger with each passing day, while his own army was growing smaller with each battle. Finally, the Dutch had shown no indication they were ready to rise up against the French and support the Anglo-Russian "Liberation Army," which added to the Allied discouragement. Following a council of war on the morning of 7 October, the Allied commanders decided to request an armistice. In this dispatch to London, York explained that the France-Batavian army was receiving reinforcements in alarming numbers. The terrain on which he had to fight was miserable: dikes, canals, flooded fields, and lakes. Winter weather had already arrived, and rain had turned the fields and roads into mud, making it extremely difficult to move artillery and supply wagons. Then he wrote: "Having maturely weighed the circumstances in which the army was thus placed, and having felt it my duty, on a point of so much importance, to consult with General Sir Ralph Abercrombie and the lieutenant-generals of this army, I could not but consider (and their opinion is unanimous on the subject) that it would be for the benefit of the general cause to withdraw the troops from their advanced position in order to await His Majesty's further instructions."[87]

York withdrew to the fortified Zype line, from which he had begun his offensive on 2 October, and the operation was completed on 8 October. It was carried out in such haste, however, that the Allied army left behind some four hundred women and children, which was reported in the English Parliament by one of its members on 9 February 1800: "The retreat [back to the Zype line] was carried out so quickly that it left behind four hundred women and children. The French, whom we represent today as cruel and treacherous, clothed the children and returned them with the women to our headquarters."[88]

The duke of York, with the approval of his government, opened negotiations with Brune for the evacuation of the Anglo-Russian army.[89] The French commander began as if negotiating from a position of strength. He demanded the return of the Dutch fleet, which had surrendered without a fight in the early days of campaign, and the return of fifteen thousand prisoners of war, the equivalent of the number of Allied troops he said would be lost if evacuated under French fire.[90] He demanded hostages, to assure that the armistice would be fully carried out.[91] There were other demands, such as the withdrawal of the Anglo-Russian army from their defensive line on the Zype, and that York leave intact the fort at Helder and not destroy the region (mainly by flooding) as they withdrew. London refused to return a single ship and offered to return only five thousand French and Dutch prisoners; York would not leave his defensive position but did agree to leave the territory he held as it was in mid-October. York also refused to provide hostages.[92]

Brune and the Directory, facing political difficulties in Paris, were as eager as York to end the campaign, however, so they reduced their demands to a minimum and the convention was signed.[93] Brune sent General Boudet to Paris with the convention that ended the fighting. On 30 October, Boudet wrote Vandamme saying: "I am engaged every day at the home of a different director. They are all very pleased to listen to me talk of the army, and they greatly desire to learn that the enemy has embarked." The enemy had actually not been defeated; and it is questionable whether Brune, even if reinforced, could have driven York into the sea. In a letter to the minister of war dated 14 October, Brune advised the negotiated evacuation of the Anglo-Russian army, which was being offered rather than a military solution. If, with further reinforcements, he were to attack the enemy's strong defensive position, it would cost the flower of his army, for as he put it, "In such an attack it is the bravest who perish." He then added: "In these circumstances, I believe it is preferable to conserve the army and assure success for the Republic rather than seek the glory of a brilliant [battle], which is always in doubt and not necessary, and which could result in the greatest disaster."[94] Furthermore, although the Dutch had not risen in support of the enemy, any sudden turn in the fortunes of war could lead to an insurrection in Holland that would be disastrous for the French. Finally, the duke of York informed Brune that, if there was not to be a cease-fire, he would break open the dikes and flood the lowlands south of his position so as to prevent any French advance during the embarkment of his army. He would also destroy the ports and forts as he left and block the roads of Texel so as to render them unusable. All of this he was quite capable of doing. Thus it was that a convention was signed on 18 October 1799, and by 19 November York and his army had left the continent.[95]

The signing of the convention marked the end of combat in Holland even though it was another month before the last of the Anglo-Russian army had departed. Vandamme, with the conclusion of the campaign, requested leave to return to Cassel. The chief medical officer of the army, after examining the general, wrote a recommendation that he be given medical leave:

> We, the undersigned, the chief medical officers of the army, certify that citizen Vandamme, general of division employed with the French army in Holland, has been suffering for the last twenty days from a dislocated left arm, and although the injury is less painful now, and even though General Vandamme continues his military duties, . . . considerable pain prevents him from using that arm. Moreover, he has had a fever for the last ten days, and in general his health in those days has deteriorated. We think that General Vandamme, to recover the use of his left arm and to reestablish his health, should retire for some time to his home to rest and recuperate.
>
> Consequently, we certify that the above named citizen should be given a convalescent leave of three months.[96]

Brune granted Vandamme leave to regain his health and assured him he would still be carried on the roster of the army in Holland. The general in chief then bestowed upon Vandamme the honor of taking the convention that ended the campaign to the Directory of the Batavian Republic in Amsterdam.[97] After passing through the capital, Vandamme retired to Cassel where he rested and recovered the full use of his arm.

5

THE YEARS OF PEACE

In the spring and summer of 1799, the Directory was once again facing a political crisis in Paris and a military crisis in Italy and Germany. Jourdan's campaign into southern Germany had been a complete failure, and the Army of the Danube was back in France defending the Rhine. The Austrians and Russians had driven the French Army of Italy out of the peninsula and the Po River valley. Although Masséna was in northern Switzerland with a formidable army, the war with the Second Coalition was not going well. After seven years of almost continual fighting, the French were weary of war, and the people blamed the Directory, even though it was only partially at fault, for the renewal of hostilities at the end of 1798. The Directory had lost popularity and whatever credibility it had enjoyed in 1795. The Thermidorians were quarreling among themselves. Especially after the Fructidor coup d'état (4 September 1797), the Directory, having lost legitimacy, ruled by virtue of the army.

In the month of Prairial year VII (June–July 1799), the political left, both Jacobin and republican, gained a working majority in the legislative assemblies. The Directory was again reorganized (read "purged") and now included the Jacobin Jean-François Moulin. With the nation declared in danger, Jourdan's *levée en masse* was enacted into law. It called for the conscription of two hundred thousand men for the army. This was followed by the Law of Hostages (12 July 1799), which was primarily aimed at émigrés and royalists in the west where violence and full-fledged insurrection had already broken out earlier in the summer of 1799. The law provided for forced loans and for taking into custody relatives of émigrés and suspect nobles who could be held responsible for terrorist acts and disturbances committed by their extended families.[1] These two provisions antagonized the masses and their import landed heavily upon the bourgeoisie. Then the tide began to turn in favor of the political right. Masséna's victory in late September and Brune's victory in early October meant the nation was no longer in danger: "Defeat [had] produced extreme measures, and victory made them unnecessary."[2]

Yet another reorganization of the Directory seemed in order. The monarchists on the right had been sufficiently alarmed by the gains made by the Jacobin left as to temporarily neutralize their strong anti-Directory feelings and activities. One aspect of political life in the fall of 1799 that everyone agreed upon was that, to bring about a new coup d'état, the army must be involved, and this involvement required a popular general with ties to the Revolution.[3] Quite by chance General Napoleon Bonaparte arrived back in Paris from Egypt at this crucial time, on 16 October. Other generals had been "consulted" discreetly with the view of providing the military arm for different factions wishing to gain control of the government: Bernadotte, Jourdan, General Barthélemy-Catherine Joubert, perhaps even Augereau and Moreau. Once Bonaparte appeared in Paris, however, he became the obvious choice. He had returned to France to save the nation from its enemies (although Masséna and Brune had already done so). The general arrived in the capital in civilian dress and did not in any way assume a threatening manner. He spent his time at the Institute, of which he was a member, and spoke in glowing terms of the Republic and the nation. At the same time, he renewed friendships and made the acquaintance of the right people. He was strategically placed when the time came to replace the Directory with the Consulate.

The principal personalities behind the Brumaire coup d'état were three ex-clergymen: the former canon of Chartres, Emmanuel-Joseph Sieyès; the former bishop of Autun, Charles-Maurice Talleyrand; and the former cleric, Joseph Fouché. Sieyès was a director, Fouché the minister of police, and Talleyrand the ex-minister of foreign affairs.

All three were well-placed, with good connections, and a comprehensive knowledge of the intricate political intrigues, plots, and ambitions that made Paris both dangerous and the city of opportunity. Bonaparte, on the other hand, was an unknown factor in the equation. He spoke as a true republican; his past suggested nothing different. He was not considered politically ambitious. He was not a monarchist, although of lesser noble origins, nor a Jacobin; both Sieyès and Talleyrand believed they could manipulate the general to their own advantage. They underestimated Bonaparte's intentions and his ability to function, not merely on the battlefield but in the political world of intrigue, which made it relatively easy for him to emerge, not as the pawn of the "professional" politicians, but as the sole head of the government.

The political crisis came to a head on 18 Brumaire of the year VIII (9 November 1799). The Chamber of Elders was informed that the Jacobins were plotting to overthrow the government and voted to move their meeting place out of the city of Paris, and thus out of reach of the Jacobins. The elders then named General Bonaparte to command the troops of Paris to protect the government. Bonaparte went to the Chamber of Five Hundred, where his younger brother Lucien presided as president, but even with Lucien's support, Bonaparte was shouted down and had to withdraw from the hall. Lucien then declared the session adjourned. The members refused to leave. With some difficulty, the legislative guard was persuaded to enter the hall and expel the deputies. Later, the elders and a rump of the Chamber of Five Hundred approved the creation of a provisional consulate with three consuls: Sieyès, Roger Ducos, and General Bonaparte. The original idea was that the three consuls would be equal; but the Constitution of the Year VIII, under the guiding hand of Bonaparte, established an executive dominated by a First Consul with two lesser consuls who had little power. Needless to say, it was Napoleon Bonaparte who emerged as First Consul.[4]

General Vandamme was still at Cassel recuperating from his fall when the news of the Brumaire coup d'état reached him. Although a true republican at heart, he had parted with the Jacobins and in the summer of 1794 had been pleased with their downfall. Now he welcomed the news of the overthrow of the Directory and the installation of the Consulate. He viewed the Directory as a corruption of the

Republic and saw it as having not promoted him for years, removed him from command on the eve of a major campaign, and ordered him to be court-martialed on false charges of misconduct. He had sought out General Bonaparte in Paris during the winter of 1797–98 to make his acquaintance. He could not, at the time of the coup, be considered a "friend" of Bonaparte, but the two men did know one another both personally and by reputation. Vandamme admired Bonaparte for his Italian campaign of 1796–97 and believed he would be good for France. In the fall of 1799 Vandamme considered Bonaparte a republican general, not a political figure in authority. He could not have foreseen the empire that was developing. The Consulate would simply give a new form or structure to the Republic. So Vandamme could be described as a pro-Bonaparte republican at the time of the Brumaire coup.

The 1799–1800 winter was relatively quiet on the Rhine and in Switzerland. General Moreau was once again in command of the Army of the Rhine. He had met General Bonaparte in Paris in October 1799, and he actively cooperated in the overthrow of the government in November.[5] The new First Consul rewarded him with the Army of the Rhine. On 8 January 1800, Moreau wrote Vandamme in the most flattering terms, inviting him to come and again serve in the army under his command.[6] Vandamme was still on the books of Brune's army in Holland, but there was not likely to be any fighting in the Low Country in the near future, whereas there would surely be action on the Rhine and in southern Germany come spring. They had experienced difficulties in their relationship, but Vandamme recognized in Moreau a capable and skillful commander whom he respected, and Moreau saw in Vandamme a skilled hard-fighting officer to head a division or to command a flank; for all their flaws, the redeeming qualities were far greater. Vandamme at this time still considered Brune a friend and was appreciative of the warm reception he received when he returned to active duty in the fall of 1799 after his disgrace of the summer. But the future was in Germany, not Holland. So on 26 January 1800, the new minister of war, General Alexander Berthier, who had been Bonaparte's chief of staff in Italy and Egypt, signed the service letter ordering Vandamme to the Army of Rhine. The following day, Berthier wrote Vandamme there was no hurry; Moreau did not yet have a command for him because the Army of the

Rhine was being reorganized. Within days the First Consul wrote his minister of war: "You will give orders . . . to General of Division Vandamme to join the Army of the Rhine without delay." However, with more general officers than needed for the army, it was not until the end of March that Vandamme reached army headquarters at Basel.[7]

Moreau gave Vandamme command of the Second Division, part of his right wing under the command of General Claude-Jacques Lecourbe. At 13,958 men it was the largest of Lecurbe's four divisions and was made up of three brigades under the orders of generals Gabriel-Jean Molitor, Jardon, and Laval.[8] Once again in command of the major French army, Moreau wanted to formulate the campaign for 1800, which, if successful, would cast him in the role of principal military commander of France. Needless to say, this was not what First Consul Bonaparte had in mind. Thus when Moreau submitted his plan for the coming campaign, Bonaparte rejected it out of hand.[9] Moreau wished to have the decisive action in southern Germany, but Bonaparte again had his eyes on northern Italy. Instead of Moreau leading the Army of the Rhine to victory and glory in Germany, he, Bonaparte, would lead the Army of Reserve to victory and glory in Italy.

It seems that the Aulic Council, which made and controlled Austrian grand strategy, did not understand the strategic positions of the two opposing armies in west central Europe. Austria's military might was divided into two armies, one in southern Germany and the other in northern Italy, separated by Switzerland and the Alps. The French occupied Switzerland, so communication between the two general headquarters had to run from the Rhine east through the Tyrol into the Po River valley and then west to Sardinia. Close coordination between General Paul Kray in Germany and General Michael Friedrich Melas in Italy was impossible; the armies could not come to each other's aid in any timely manner. In spring 1800 the French forces were also divided into two armies: Moreau's Army of the Rhine, in Switzerland and north along the Rhine, and Masséna's Army of Ligurie in northwest Italy. At the same time, a third army was being created at Dijon in east central France, referred to as the Army of Reserve and officially commanded by General Berthier, because law did not allow the First Consul to command troops.

The Austrian grand plan called for General Kray to remain inactive as long as possible; if attacked he was to fall back into a strong defensive position near Ulm or in western Bavaria. The principal Austrian campaign would take place in Italy and southern France. General Malas was to attack Masséna and drive him back across the Var River and on to Toulon. This plan was strongly influenced by the English, who were providing large sums of money for Austria to conduct the war because they wished to regain control of France's great naval base at Toulon.[10]

The First Consul also conceived a plan for the coming campaign that made northern Italy the principal theater of operation and relegated Germany to a secondary front, as a diversion to prevent the Austrians from sending reinforcements to Italy. Whereas the Aulic Council, to its later regret, managed to carry out its plans, Bonaparte had the very popular and obstinate General Moreau to deal with. The First Consul did not feel secure enough in his control of the government and the army to risk alienating Moreau. General Jean-Joseph Dessolle, Moreau's chief of staff, convinced Bonaparte it would be better, if he intended to leave Moreau in command of the Army of the Rhine, to allow him to follow his own plan of action, in which he had confidence, rather than a different plan in which he had no confidence—even if the second plan was superior.[11] So Moreau was permitted to launch a major offensive into southern Germany.

At the same time Masséna was to hold Melas in the vicinity of Genoa while Bonaparte, with the Army of Reserve, would cross the Alps via the Saint Bernard Pass and move into the Po Valley. This move would place the Army of Reserve in the rear of the Austrian army, across its line of communication, forcing Melas to give battle—and presumably on French terms.[12] General Melas caught the French off guard when he opened the campaign in Italy early in April with an attack on Masséna's Army of Ligurie. Masséna was driven back to Genoa; the First Consul urged Moreau to begin hostilities on the Rhine, and he quickened preparations for the Army of Reserve to cross the Alps.[13] Moreau's army of one hundred thousand men was organized into four corps. General Lecourbe was on the right with some twenty-five thousand men, including Vandamme's division, poised along the Rhine from Schaffhausen to the west tip of the Lake of Constance. General Saint-Cyr commanded the central corps of twenty-five thousand men, concentrated north and south of Brisach. Between Saint-Cyr and Lecourbe, Moreau commanded the reserve corps of thirty thousand men near Basel. General Sainte-Suzanne commanded twenty-thousand men in the left wing at Strasbourg.[14]

On 25 April, Moreau ordered three of his corps across the Rhine. Sainte-Suzanne moved onto the Kinzig River by way of Kehl to give the impression he would advance through the Black Forest toward the Danube. Saint-Cyr crossed the river at Vieux-Brisach and marched on Freiburg threatening to cross the mountains to the upper Danube. Moreau crossed the Rhine at Basel and marched east on Sackingen. Lecourbe remained on the left bank of the river but prepared to cross upstream at Schaffhausen. On 27 April both Sainte-Suzanne and Saint-Cyr abruptly changed direction and moved right. Sainte-Suzanne recrossed the Rhine at Kehl and marched south to Brisach, crossed the Rhine for the third time in a few days and took Saint-Cyr's place at Freiburg. Saint-Cyr marched his corps south around the mountains of the Black Forest and to join Moreau marching up the right bank of the Rhine toward Schaffhausen. On 1 May Lecourbe put his corps in motion to cross the Rhine just east of Schaffhausen.

Vandamme, being the most experienced at crossing the Rhine, was ordered to lead Lecourbe's corps over the river. General Molitor, with two battalions, made the initial crossing in boats. A bridge was quickly put in place, and Vandamme led the rest of his division into Germany. On the same day, Vandamme moved to the northeast and captured the village of Stein and the fort of Hohentwiel. General François Goullu's brigade made a second crossing at Paradies. By nightfall General Jean-Thomas Lorge's division had occupied Schaffhausen and linked up with Moreau. Thus by the end of 1 May, Moreau had his entire army over the Rhine with some seventy-five thousand men concentrated near Schaffhausen and ready to move on to the Danube.[15] By the time General Kray realized the fighting would not be in the hills of the Black Forest, Moreau was threatening his line of retreat down the Danube to Ulm. The Austrian commander ordered a concentration of his army on the upper Danube near Engen to protect his principal depot at Stokach. In doing so he abandoned the Rhine and the Black Forest but hoped to hold a line from Stokach to Engen. The prince of Lorraine-Vaudemont protected Stokach with twelve thousand men.

On 3 May, while Lecourbe's corps marched east to Stokach, Moreau took the Reserve up the road to Engen, and Saint-Cyr moved north to assist Sainte-Suzanne coming through the southern Black Forest. Vandamme formed the extreme right, moving east between Stokach and the Lake of Constance. General Leval marched just south of Stokach, and Vandamme at the head of Molitor's brigade swung north, to approach the city from the southeast. Two of Lecourbe's other divisions (generals Etienne-Marie Nansouty and Joseph Montrichard) approached from the west, Vandamme moved onto the rear of the Austrian left wing, and the Austrian position at Stokach became critical. In the following battle, the prince of Lorraine-Vaudemont was caught on his left between two French divisions, one in front and the other behind. With superior numbers, Lecourbe overwhelmed the enemy, and the city was taken, along with vast stores of food and supplies and four thousand prisoners of war.[16]

On the same day Vandamme was fighting at Stokach, 3 May, Moreau stumbled into battle at Engen. Kray had taken up a strong defensive position, intending to link up with the prince of Lorraine-Vaudemont at Stokach, but after heavy fighting, Kray was forced to withdraw under cover of darkness. With his army still in good order and his numbers equal or superior to the French, Kray gave battle at Moesskirch just east of Engen. On 5 May the two armies clashed again, and Moreau was victorious. Both commanders called in their flanking corps. Lecourbe formed the French right, and Vandamme's division captured the town of Moesskirch, playing an important role in the victory. The French had captured two major Austrian supply depots. Kray withdrew without vigorous pursuit, and in an attempt to prevent a third depot from falling into French hands, Kray decided to defend the town of Biberach on the River Riss south of the junction with the Danube. Although the Austrians took up a strong position, they no longer had confidence in their ability to withstand the steady, confident French columns that marched against them. This time it was Saint-Cyr's corps that bore the brunt of the heavy fighting.

General Kray, unable to defeat the French army in the field, withdrew to the fortified camp at Ulm on the Danube. Vandamme formed the right wing of the army as Moreau followed cautiously. He had pushed the Austrian army back to the Iller River, but now he was obligated to send a part of his army back into Switzerland in order to support the Army of Reserve that was preparing to cross the Saint Bernard Pass. Bonaparte had ordered that Lecourbe's corps, including

Vandamme, be sent to bolster his army going into Italy. Moreau had no intention of sending twenty-five thousand men, with several of his best senior officers, in accordance with an earlier agreement. Instead, he sent General Jean-Thomas Lorge with some sixteen thousand men drawn from the poorer units of all four of his corps. General Lecourbe did not wish to leave Moreau to serve under Bonaparte. It is alleged that, because he remained with the Army of the Rhine, the First Consul took personal offence and Lecourbe never held an important command in a Napoleonic army.[17]

His army had been reduced in numbers, but Moreau decided upon bold action. Encouraged by his recent successes, he would not cross the Danube and attack Kray's strong position; rather, he would cross the Iller River and march on Augsburg. Leaving the corps of Sainte-Suzanne on the left (north) bank of the Danube and Saint-Cyr on the right bank to watch the Austrian army at Ulm, Moreau started east with the other two corps (Lecourbe and the Reserve). He believed that if he threatened Augsburg and Munich, Kray would abandon his stronghold at Ulm and go to the defense of the capital of Bavaria and the gateway to Vienna. However, when Kray sent a strong corps out of Ulm and attacked Sainte-Suzanne on 16 May, Moreau quickly changed his plans. Sainte-Suzanne avoided disaster, and Moreau with the Reserve marched quickly back to the Iller to restore stability.

The German theater of the war then settled into a stalemate. The two armies were about equal in numbers. Moreau was unable to drive the Austrians from the entrenched camp at Ulm, and Kray did not dare venture forth to attack the assembled French army. Both commanders awaited the outcome of events in Italy. The campaign had come to an end in southern Germany. When Vandamme received news he was ordered to Belgium, he welcomed it and made preparations to leave the Army of the Rhine for the last time. On 22 May, General Lecourbe wrote Vandamme: "I have just received, my dear general, a dispatch from General Moreau that grieves me, because it orders you to Belgium as a result of orders from the government."[18]

It seems that, when Vandamme was in Paris before being sent to the Army of Rhine, the minister of war had promised him the supreme command of the troops in the Low Country. But as there was little chance that the English would attempt another expedition to Belgium or Holland so soon after the failure of the previous fall, and especially since the Russians had no interest in assisting, Vandamme was sent to the Rhine with the assurance that when he was no longer needed there he would be given the promised command.[19] Turning over temporary command of his division to General Molitor, Vandamme traveled north to assume military command of nine departments. In the letter Vandamme wrote to Molitor transferring command of the division, he added the following: "Before crossing the Rhine (1 May) I refused to leave [the Army of the Rhine]; but now I am able to go to my new post because I am assured that the English are menacing the coast. While you will continue to fight the Austrians, I face the possibility of defeating the English."[20] Vandamme was pleased with his new command, which he had requested. He returned home to marry his father's cousin, the pretty, charming Sophie t'Kint. Her father was a prominent *propriétaire* in the city of Ghent.

While Vandamme was living at his headquarters in Lille, Bonaparte, at the head of the Army of Reserve, defeated the Austrian army on 14 June at the battle of Marengo. This led to a cease-fire in Italy while Bonaparte wrote to Emperor Francis proposing peace along the lines of the Treaty of Campo Formio of 1797. When news reached Vienna that Moreau had occupied Munich and imposed an armistice on Kray at Parsdorf on 15 July, Emperor Francis realized his military position was extremely weak, if not desperate, and that Austria would do well to settle this conflict on the terms of Campo Formio and bide its time until conditions were more favorable to regain the losses sustained in 1796–97.

The war did not end in the summer of 1800; there was only a cessation of hostilities in both Italy and Germany. When Austria received a new very large sum of money from England for the promise that Vienna would not withdraw from the Second Coalition before January 1801, the Austrian negotiators were obliged to stall the peace talks as long as possible. During the summer and fall of 1800, France was obliged to maintain her two armies on a war footing, prepared to resume the struggle at any time if the peace talks failed to end the state of war. Following the victory at Marengo, the First Consul and Berthier turned the Army of Reserve over to the generals and returned to Paris. By the end of summer, General Macdonald commanded one of two army groups in Italy. Knowing that his good friend Vandamme no longer commanded a division in the Army of the

Rhine, he requested the minister of war to send Vandamme to Italy to serve in his Second Army of Reserve or, as it was sometimes referred to, the Army of Grisons.[21]

Vandamme's new orders were dated 8 September 1800, and the general once again bid farewell to family and friends and traveled south. He had never been in Italy. All of his service had been in the north or on the Rhine, in southern Germany and Switzerland. In northeast Italy Macdonald gave him command of the advance guard. As there was no real contact with the enemy, there was little to do except maintain a high level of preparation for the possibility of a breakdown in talks and the resumption of hostilities.

Bonaparte at last lost patience with the Austrians' delaying tactics and ordered hostilities to resume on 22 November 1800. Moreau in Germany and Brune and Macdonald in Italy engaged the enemy. This time the deciding victory fell to Moreau. On 3 December, he defeated the Austrian army under the command of Archduke John and General Kray at Hohenlinden. Before Macdonald or Brune had engaged in a single battle in Italy, the campaign was virtually ended by Moreau in Germany. Again an armistice ended the fighting. Negotiations that had been broken off were resumed at Leoben. This time the talks led to the Treaty of Luneville (8 February 1801) and the official end of the Second Coalition. England remained at war with France. It was more than a year before France was at peace with all of Europe.

By early 1801 it was apparent that the war in Italy had indeed ended. Vandamme requested permission from Macdonald to leave his command for several weeks and to travel in Italy to familiarize himself with the people and the country. This permission granted, he spent the time as an "official" tourist, returning to his division in mid-February.[22] Vandamme remained another two months in Italy; but as the war had ended on the continent, he requested and received three months' sick leave to return to Cassel. Such sick leave was usually—and in this case almost certainly was—an excuse to leave one's command. Vandamme went directly to Paris, where he arrived on 23 April to make the rounds of important people, in order to again secure command of the Sixteenth Territorial (Military) Division. He was at this time able to renew personal contact with the First Consul and the minister of war General Berthier, the two most important men in all of France for a soldier seeking favor. Vandamme's efforts were rewarded on 24 September 1801, when the command at Lille became vacant. His Sixteenth Territorial Division included the departments of the North, the Pas-de-Calais, and the Lys. As France was still at war with England, he was responsible for the protection of the coastline just twenty-one miles from Dover.

Without an ally to provide a major land army, the English were not likely to attempt a serious landing on the continent. In fact both England and France were weary of war. France was clearly the dominant power on the continent, there was little England could do to change that in 1801. On the other hand, England controlled the seas, and France could not challenge that domination. The two antagonists negotiated the Peace of Amiens, which was signed on 25 March 1802. For the first time in ten years, France was at peace with all of Europe. Bonaparte's popularity was increasing with each accomplishment. He had ended the civil war in the Vendée, defeated the Second Coalition, and ended the war with England. On 15 July 1801 he signed the Concordat with Pope Pius VII, which ended the conflict between church and state that had begun in the early years of the Revolution. The army could look forward to enjoying the fruits of its hard-won accomplishments. Vandamme, as most of the other generals, had been waging war for ten long years, suffering the hardships of campaign after campaign. Tens of thousands had been killed on the battlefields of Europe, tens of thousands more had died of their wounds or disease. Those who survived were more than ready to enjoy the good life they felt they richly deserved.

The year 1802 and the first half of 1803 were relatively uneventful in the life of Dominique Vandamme. While living in Lille, he carried out his functions as military governor of the Sixteenth Territorial Division. He lived with his wife in comfortable quarters in Lille, with family and friends about thirty miles to the west, at Cassel. For the first time in his career, Vandamme enjoyed the rewards of office without the responsibilities and hardships of command in the face of a dangerous enemy. His attachment to the First Consul grew stronger, while he continued to harbor his egalitarian republican convictions. He thought of Bonaparte as General Bonaparte and addressed him "Mon général."[23] His admiration was for the military commander rather than the head of state, although he saw no fault in First Consul's being the head of the French Republic. On 2 August 1802 Bonaparte was proclaimed First Consul for life, as the result of a plebiscite held in May. The overwhelming vote of approval for this act was a reflection of his popularity with the French people.

By May 1803, however, the English government had come to the conclusion that the Treaty of Amiens was a French treaty and no longer in the best interests of England.[24] Bonaparte did not wish to renew the war with England at that time, but he did little to avoid renewed hostilities and indeed acted in a manner, while within the bounds of international law of the day, that was clearly viewed by England as hostile. As one historian put it: "The conflict between Bonaparte and England was in reality a clash between two imperalisms." Bonaparte would not open western Europe to English merchants; "the English capitalists learned that the economic struggle would continue, and they became disgusted with a peace that profited them nothing."[25]

This time the war was going to last eleven years, and the conclusion would be much different from that of the revolutionary wars. The new struggle—or rather, the renewal of the old struggle—found both France and England in favorable positions, but neither was ready for war. France dominated western Europe from Rome to the Baltic Sea and from the Atlantic to the borders of the Austrian empire. Spain was drawing ever closer to a French alliance. It was unthinkable that England would venture to put a land army on the continent. England continued to dominate the seas, however, and Bonaparte had no desire for his navy to venture forth to challenge the English fleet. However, Bonaparte was seriously contemplating a plan to transport an army across the English Channel to invade the island kingdom. To this end he spent six weeks familiarizing himself with northwest France and Belgium. He had never campaigned in the north and had only seen the English Channel at the time of his visit to Boulogne in 1798.

Bonaparte left Saint Cloud on 24 June 1803, bound for Calais by way of Amiens, Abbeville, and Boulogne. He proceeded to Dunkirk and arrived in Lille for supper on the evening of 6 July.[26] Vandamme was in his glory. The First Consul was his personal guest, and he could show his command in the best light. Upon his arrival Bonaparte reviewed the garrison at Lille. The following day he met with the departmental and city officials and inspected the great citadel on the west side of the city. He spent 8 July inspecting the city and its immediate surroundings and departed on the morning of 9 July for the Belgium coast. Everything went well. Vandamme was pleased to receive a letter from Berthier concerning the visit: "The First Consul," wrote the minister of war, "citizen general, after reviewing your division was very satisfied with the spirit he saw among the troops and the condition in which he found all parties in your care. You have fulfilled the expectations he had of you based on your previous service. You will receive a pair of pistols that I am sending in his name. Keep them as a token of honor."[27] General Bonaparte had developed the practice of giving honorary gifts, appropriately inscribed, during his first Italian campaign. There was some question as to whether he had the authority to do so without authorization from the directors; nevertheless, he gave swords or pistols in 1797 and again in Egypt in 1798 to generals whose service he judged worthy.[28]

Following his inspection tour of the north, the First Consul decided to create an army for the purpose of invading England. Boulogne would be the principal headquarters for this new army, with corps at intervals along the coast from Normandy to Holland. General Soult was given command of the corps, with headquarters first at Saint-Omer and then at Boulogne. On 30 August, Berthier wrote Vandamme: "You have been named to command a division of the corps at Saint-Omer that is commanded by General Soult. You will not leave command of the Sixteenth [Territorial] Division until Soult gives you the order to join the army he commands. Upon leaving the Sixteenth Division, you will turn over command to General Maurice-Etienne Gérard." One week later Soult (in Paris at the time) "requested" that Vandamme go at once to Saint-Omer.[29]

Anxious to assume his new command, Vandamme turned over his duties at Lille to Gérard and became a part of the Grande Armée. He was going to serve under a general who had served under him in the past, and this would not have been Vandamme's choice, yet he was pleased to command a line division once again, in what would surely be a part of the coming campaign. He believed himself a better commander than Soult, and the two would clash in the future.

In early September 1803 there was no army along the English Channel and the North Sea. The First Consul, through the minister of war, had begun to send troops and recruits in the summer of 1803 to the various depots along the coast for the purpose of creating an Army of England. Bonaparte then organized the troops into five army corps, plus numerous other smaller detachments. With the renewal of hostilities, General Adolphe-Edouard Mortier was ordered into the English-owned duchy of Hanover, and his command became the First Corps. General Auguste-Frédéric Marmont established the headquarters of the Second Corps in Holland. Davout's Third Corps had its headquarters at Bruges, further south. Soult's divisions became the Fourth Corps at Boulogne (Saint-Omer). General Ney was designated the Sixth Corps, with his headquarters at Montreuil. Other army corps would come into existence before the campaign of 1805 was launched into central Europe.

Shortly after his arrival at Saint-Omer, Vandamme was ordered to move his division to the coast at Outreau, just south of Boulogne, and this is where he passed the next two years, organizing, equipping, training, and caring for the men under his command. The division had a large number of new recruits, unaccustomed to military life, who had to learn the most basic aspects of soldiering. The new men arrived in relatively small numbers over a period of months, so there was continuous basic training. By early 1804 the division was near full strength, and the training moved to a more advanced stage. Field maneuvers were frequent; the troops had to learn how to change formation from column to line and back again on broken and difficult terrain. They were preparing to cross the English Channel and invade the British Isles, so the army had to learn amphibious operations. They practiced embarking on and disembarking from the ships and boats both large and small that would be used in crossing the Channel. In the summer of 1804 the men were even given swimming instruction. The health of the men was an important concern. They were fed well and quartered in warm dry barracks. Hospitals were available for the sick, and many were issued wooden shoes or sabots.[30]

It was also at this time that Bonaparte reorganized the army. The demi-brigade was renamed a regiment. The number of battalions in a regiment varied between two and four, but the goal (not always met) was to have three combat and one training. Each regiment was commanded by a colonel. The composition of the division remained essentially the same, with three or four regiments, but it could be larger. The formal formation of the army corps was new. In 1796 both in Italy and in Germany, two, three, or even four divisions had been grouped together to form a wing of the army and placed under a lieutenant general who was responsible to the army commander. But now this organization became formalized, and the corps were given numbers. After May 1804, all the army corps were commanded by a marshal of the empire. Each corps was designed to be a self-contained little army that could engage the enemy in serious combat and hold its position until help arrived. Each corps was made up of several divisions and had its own cavalry, artillery, engineers, and supply system. It could operate independently of the rest of the army in a limited capacity. There was no fixed size for the corps, but it was common to have between fifteen and thirty thousand men. In 1812 Davout's First Corps numbered some seventy-five thousand men when it crossed the Niemen River into Russia.

Napoleon Bonaparte's popularity continued to rise even after the renewal of hostilities between England and France. After all, it was the English who had renewed hostilities (at sea) without declaring war, and French propaganda laid total blame on them. By the spring of 1804 the First Consul was preparing to have himself created emperor. However, he dared not make such a move without the assurance of the full support of the army. The Army of England was only three or five days' march from Paris and must be solidly behind such a coup. The generals commanding that army had been strong supporters of the Republic, almost to the man; and now they were being asked to put their republican ideals aside and back the establishment of a monarchy. Many had already thrown in their lot with Bonaparte and were ready to welcome an empire with enthusiasm. Others were skeptical, but willing to back the man who had earned their respect and admiration on the battlefields of Italy and Egypt. A small number were opposed to the renewal of a monarchy and clung to their republican ideals; but because of Bonaparte's popularity with the rank and file of the army and the masses of the French people, they were silent or extremely careful in their objection. Vandamme, as was the case of many other "republican" generals of 1793, had been wooed and flattered by the First Consul. Bonaparte had given him a lot: command of a division in 1800, of the Sixteenth Territorial Division in 1801, of a division in Soult's Fourth Corps, along with a pair of honorary pistols and the Legion of Honor.

Vandamme had become a republican at a time when the Bourbon monarchy represented oppression, inequality, corruption, and a lack of opportunity for the common man. The Republic promised young men such as Vandamme unlimited opportunity, the end of corruption in government and the oppression of the masses, and equality. But by 1804 he had few good memories of the years 1792–99. The Jacobin Reign of Terror had almost cost him his head; the Directory had humiliated him and removed him from command. Jacobin equality for "patriots" had been a questionable form of equality. The corruption of the government of the Directory seemed little different from the corruption of the old monarchy. Vandamme was no longer the twenty-two-year-old who had received with joy the overthrow of the monarchy. At thirty-four he still held to many of the fundamental ideals of the Revolution, but he had come to believe that Bonaparte would be the best custodian of these ideals. Twelve years in the army had accustomed him to taking and giving orders. There was no equality in the military, and the First Consul had been providing equality before the law. Furthermore, by 1804 Vandamme could consider himself among the elite of the French army, who could expect even more and greater favors from an emperor who valued, and would reward, his services. A future with the emperor Napoleon could bring military glory, financial well-being, and nobility. Vandamme had been a republican in the early 1790s; in 1804 he fully supported the restoration of a monarchy that he believed was enlightened and open to men of ability such as he perceived himself.

In April 1804 the corps commanders of the Army of England were polled by Bonaparte supporters as to the support that could be expected of them in the event of the creation of an empire.[31] On 12 April, after expressing his devotion to the First Consul in the most exaggerated terms, General Soult (a former devout republican) wrote: "The army wishes to tell you it desires, it demands, that you are proclaimed emperor of the French [Gaule] and that heredity is established in your family. As Frenchmen we all feel that our country needs this double guarantee, and as soldiers we would like to be the first to give the example of this patriotism." The First Consul received similar letters from the other corps commanders.[32]

Reassured of the support of the army, First Consul Bonaparte had himself proclaimed emperor of the French on 18 May 1804. The heredity of the new (fourth) French dynasty was confirmed by a plebiscite that resulted in an official approval of 3,572,329 yes votes to 2,579 nos. This figure is frequently used as an indication of the new emperor's popularity. The Republic had lasted twelve years. It was remembered by most of the French for the bloodshed and suffering of the years of the Terror, its anticlericalism, and the corruption of the Directory. There were still devout republicans, to be sure, but Bonaparte had already turned the Republic into an authoritarian regime in which he was emperor in all but name. Good government, equality before the law, good economic times, and advancement in the civil service and the military based to a large extent on merit, all seemed preferable to the vast majority of Frenchmen than the poor economic conditions, corrupt governments, and "equality" for "patriots" that had existed under the Republic. Napoleon represented the preservation of the best of the Republic and hopes for a brighter future.

The trappings of monarchy were once again put in place, but this new aristocracy was to be one based on ability and merit (the Bonaparte family being the exceptions), not based on heredity, at least in the beginning. The new empire would have to have a court, and Napoleon began by giving titles to members of his family and then to soldiers and statesmen. To tie the army to the new empire, he created the title marshal of the empire. Fourteen active and four honorary marshals were named on 19 May 1804.[33] The list of new marshals is interesting both for the names it includes and those it passes over. Davout, for example, was the youngest, and he had never commanded a division in combat.[34] Vandamme, on the other hand, had a much more impressive career commanding a division in the Army of the Danube during the campaign of 1799, in Holland under Brune in 1799, and in Switzerland and Germany during the campaign of 1800. Yet he was passed over. It is true that he had never served directly under the command of General Bonaparte, but this was true of others who received the marshal's baton. It is more likely that Vandamme was not on the list because of his reputation for being too outspoken, too abrasive, and frequently accused of wrongdoing. There can be no doubt but that Vandamme, like many other generals of division, was disappointed and felt he was more deserving than some of those who received the cherished baton.[35]

Soult announced the creation of the French empire to the Fourth Corps on 21 May. "Napoleon Bonaparte has accepted the empire," said his order of the day, "to which the will of the people and the army have called him. Today begins for us a new era and happiness for France that is assured forever." In fact, "forever" lasted less than ten years. On the same day the officers and men swore an oath of allegiance: "We swear obedience to the constitution of the empire and fidelity to the emperor."[36] Perhaps to ensure that the new monarchy would be well received, Soult ordered an extraordinary distribution of eau-de-vie for the troops. Two days after the oath, an order of the day announced that "General Soult has been named marshal of the empire."[37]

Bonaparte had already recognized that, despite the lip service of egalitarianism carrying over from the revolutionary years, total equality of man was a contradiction of natural law. Because there would always be inequality, he had established the Legion of Honor in 1802, and in doing so, he hoped to blunt the inequality of wealth that was taking the place of the old regime's inequality by birth. This five-pointed cross (or star) on a red ribbon would be given to men (only) on the basis of service or achievement. It was given not only to soldiers but also to civilians who were thought to merit it.[38] The first crosses were given to wounded veterans at Les Invalides, but the emperor soon wisely bestowed the honors upon many soldiers and civilians in order to bind them to the new empire. Napoleon is reported to have commented in more practical terms that "It is with baubles that men are led."[39] Vandamme was among the early recipients of the cross, when it was given to almost all soldiers who had already been given honorary swords or pistols.[40] Then on 15 June 1804 the grand chancellor of the Legion of Honor informed General Vandamme that he was named grand officer in the Legion. This honor carried with it a stipend of five thousand francs a year.[41] On 16 August the new emperor distributed a number of crosses of the legion in a grand review at Boulogne that found Vandamme at the head of a division.

The empire having been proclaimed, a coronation was in order. The date was set on 2 December 1804, and the place was the Cathedral of Notre Dame in Paris. Traditionally, the kings of France had been crowned in the Cathedral of Reims. Napoleon wanted a clean break from the hereditary monarchs of the ancien régime. His title, Emperor of the French, and the location of the coronation were calculated to separate him from the past. Lacking the legitimacy of the Capetian, Valois, or Bourbon dynasties, Napoleon, who greatly desired to have his dynasty accepted as legitimate, persuaded Pope Pius

VII to come from Rome and give the official approval of the Catholic Church. The pope would carry little or no weight in England, Prussia, or Russia, but his presence would be significant in Catholic Austria, Italy, and Spain. It would also impress the French clergy and the great majority of the French people. The pope did not crown the new emperor, but he did give his blessing.[42] While all of France was invited to celebrate the grand occasion, only the most privileged were invited to partake in the elaborate pageantry in the cathedral. Vandamme, although not a marshal, was among the principal generals of the new empire. He was given a prestigious place in the church, and his family was among the several thousand invited inside to witness the ceremony. Vandamme was informed that, if he intended to arrive at Notre Dame in his own carriage, he would have to do so before 8:00 A.M., several hours before the ceremony began. The pageantry on 2 December was magnificent, judging from Jacques-Louis David's enormous painting in the Louvre, despite the fact that David made full use of his imagination and made many changes from reality to suit the wishes of the emperor.

The emperor's brothers, having been made princes, had to be employed in some useful manner. Napoleon would not tolerate four capable men receiving large amounts of money to support them in a royal style and doing nothing. As the emperor had no children, Joseph, his older brother, was designated his successor. But Joseph had no military experience, and Napoleon sought to remedy that deficiency. The submissive prince accepted the rank of colonel and command of the Fourth Regiment (infantry) in Vandamme's Second Division at Outreau. Joseph took up his new command in the summer of 1804, and he and Vandamme became good friends. Their friendship outlasted the empire, and they both resided in the United States for some time after Waterloo. In the spring of 1805, Vandamme felt sufficiently close to Joseph to ask him to use his influence with his imperial brother on a matter very important to the general. On 6 March Vandamme wrote:

> My prince, you have not ceased, since the moment I had the honor of meeting Your Imperial Highness, to treat me with the greatest kindness. Every day I congratulate myself on having been close to His Majesty and having benefited from your

powerful protection; and I will make every effort to be worthy of that honor.

Dare I ask Your Highness to solicit the emperor to grant me, before his departure for Paris, the lands I requested from him? The season is very favorable for the work that needs doing. I have yet another reason for the urgency of my request to settle this matter; as there are many others asking for the same decision.[43]

Despite his letter to Joseph, Vandamme did not receive the land he wanted before the 1805 campaign.

The training and preparations for the invasion of the British Isles continued through the second half of 1804 and the first half of 1805. In addition to its normal routine, Vandamme's Second Division was called upon to increase its surveillance along the coast just south of Boulogne. Reports were reaching corps headquarters in the late winter and spring of 1805 that the English were planning to land spies on the coast of France. Vandamme was ordered to arrest all foreigners who might land on the coast for which he was responsible, as well as all suspicious Frenchmen. He was to double the sentries along the beaches, and officers were to check guards several times a night.[44] Despite the increased vigilance, or perhaps because of it, there was no indication of any spy activity in the region.

By the summer of 1805 the army was as ready to cross the Channel as could reasonably be expected. Only the final essential requirement remained: control of the water between England and France. It seems Napoleon believed that if the French navy could control the Channel for three to five days, he could transport his army from France and Belgium to England. However, as the summer progressed, clouds of war gathered in eastern Europe. The failure of the French fleet and the formation of the Third Coalition brought about major changes in Napoleon's plans.

6

THE AUSTERLITZ CAMPAIGN

In the summer of 1805, while Napoleon was facing west waiting for Admiral Pierre-Charles de Villeneuve to secure control of the English Channel, an alliance was being formed behind him in the east. First Russia and then Austria would join with the British in the war against France. The Romanovs and the Hapsburgs were offended by the creation of a new "illegitimate" royal dynasty. They had no particular love of the deposed Bourbons; but when the man they considered a Corsican adventurer made himself emperor, they saw it as an insult to the established aristocrats of Europe. Tsar Alexander I had become increasingly displeased with the new French regime's domination of Germany and its perceived aggressive Near Eastern policy. It was widely known that Napoleon wished to regain control of the Ionian Islands in the Aegean, and that he had ambitions in the eastern Mediterranean. The tsar had his own ambitions in the Mediterranean, hoping to regain control of the island of Malta. His father, Tsar Paul, had been the honorary grand marshal of the Knights of Malta when General Bonaparte captured the island on his way to Egypt in the summer of 1798, and the tsar wished to restore island control to the Knights of Malta with himself the grand master of the order. The English had taken Malta from the French, however, and the island had become an important naval base for the Royal Navy to control the central Mediterranean. Alexander hoped that his cooperation in a war against France would lead to Russian control of the island.

Austria also had reasons to renew the war with France. Hapsburg pride had received serious blows in both 1797 and 1801. The Austrians believed that the loss of two wars followed by two humiliating treaties could be avenged in one glorious campaign with the support of the Russian army and British gold. Napoleon's German and Italian policies were distasteful, as was his control of Switzerland. His mass and the singing of the *Te Deum* in the presence of Charlemagne's relics at Aix-La-Chapelle in September 1804 were clearly a slap in the face to the Hapsburgs, who carried the family title of Holy Roman Emperor and who considered themselves the heirs of the Carolingian empire. Finally, the creation of the kingdom of Italy and Napoleon's coronation as its king in the city of Milan in May 1805 could be taken only as a direct insult to the traditional dominant role of the Austrians south of the Alps. The defeat of Napoleon would drive French influence out of central Europe and enable Austria to annex territory and regain controlling interests in both Germany and Italy. The result of all these various impulses was the formation of the Third Coalition in the summer of 1805.[1]

Prussia alone of the great powers remained neutral. Spain, somewhat reluctantly, sided with France. By late August 1805, it was clear to Napoleon that Admiral Villeneuve's French fleet had abandoned their efforts to control the English Channel. It was also clear that Austria and Russia had decided on war. Following its second defeat at the hands of the French, Austria had introduced military reforms, which were, however, slow in having any real effect on the army. The war party still convinced the Austrian emperor, however, that with economic support from England and military support from Russia victory over "General Bonaparte" would restore Austrian honor, regain lost territories and influence, and restore Europe to its prerevolutionary state. To this end, the Aulic Council drew up a plan, which assumed that northern Italy would be the principal theater of operations and Germany the secondary (because the defining campaigns of 1796–97 and 1800 had taken place in Italy). That the principal French army was currently in northwest Europe facing the British Isles, not in Italy or even southern France, did not seem to enter into the decision-making. Thus it was that the main Austrian army of ninety thousand men commanded by its most capable general, Archduke Charles, was assembled in the south, facing Italy. It would advance on Mantua, drive the enemy up the Po Valley, capture Milan, and advance west into southern France. At the same time Archduke Ferdinand, with General Karl Freiherr Mack to guide him, would move into Bavaria with seventy-two thousand men and, with the support of the Russian army, take control of southern Germany in preparation to cross the Rhine and attack the heart of the French empire. Ferdinand and Mack were not intended to act alone. Tsar Alexander had promised one hundred thousand troops for the German theater of operations. This would bring the Allied strength up to almost two hundred thousand men. One last Austrian army of twenty thousand men, commanded by Archduke John, would be in the Tyrol to maintain communications between Italy and Germany.

Napoleon, always at his best when changing plans to meet changing conditions, analyzed the new circumstances and quickly adapted to a campaign in central Europe. There had been rumors of a new alliance forming against him throughout the summer of 1805. The location of the Army of England, renamed the Grande Armée, persuaded the emperor that central Europe (Germany and Austria) and not Italy would be the principal theater of operations.[2] In Italy the very capable Marshal Masséna, with fifty thousand men, would hold Archduke Charles in place so he could not send reinforcements to the north. The Grande Armée would march into central Germany and swing south to defeat Ferdinand and Mack before the Russians could arrive. Timing was most important. The Austrian army in southern Germany must be destroyed before the Russians reached Bavaria. Once that Austrian army was defeated, Napoleon would move east to meet the Russians.

The army commanded by Napoleon in fall 1805 was the finest war machine Europe had seen in centuries. It had been in training for two years along the coast. Its officer corps was young, energetic, and capable, with years of experience during the revolutionary wars. Fully half the rank and file had combat experience and was both well equipped and bored with life in the barracks. A new campaign held out hopes of glory, decorations, promotion, and excitement, with only one drawback—the possibility of being wounded or killed. By the end of August 1805, there were seven army corps, Marshal Augereau's Seventh Corps

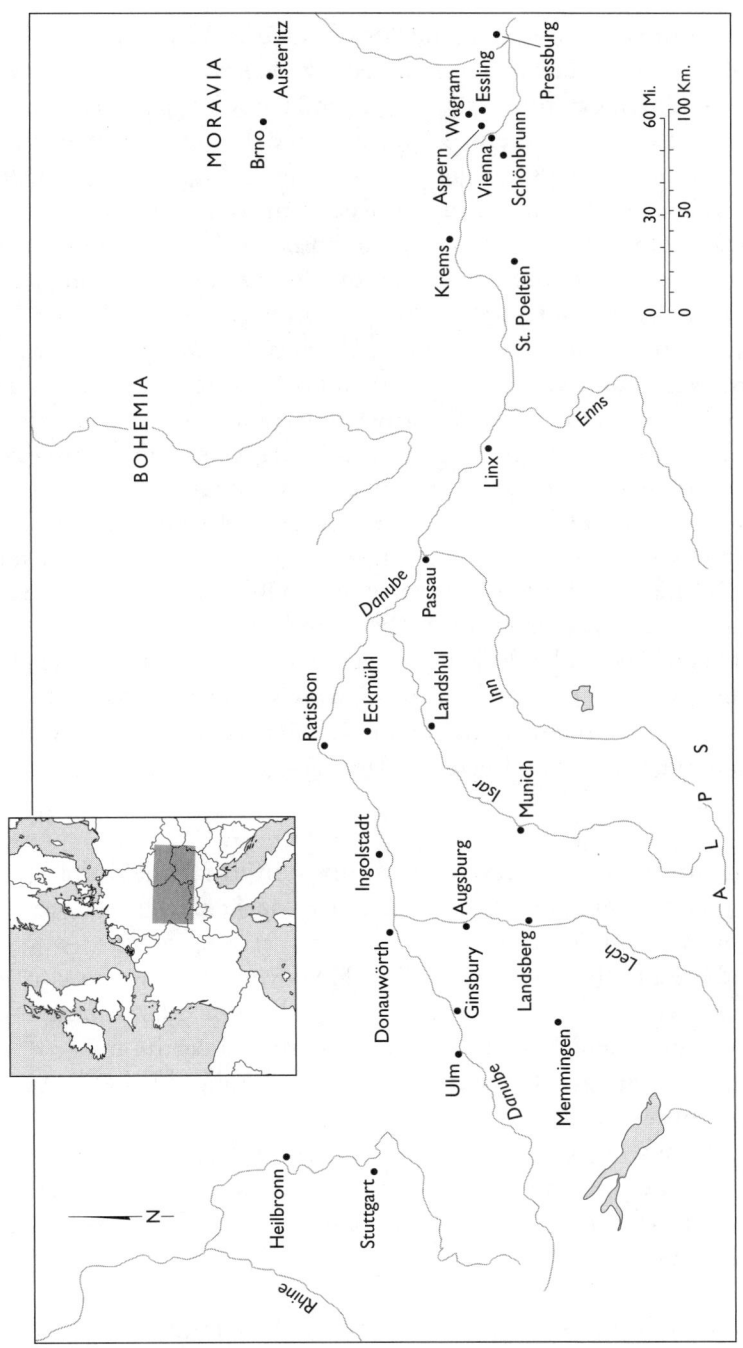

The Austerlitz and Wagram campaigns of 1805 and 1809

on the southwest coast being the latest formed. The French army had the advantage of being commanded by one man. Not only was Napoleon the finest military strategist and tactician of his day, he was also the head of government. The general and the emperor were of one mind. All the marshals and generals were subordinate to the emperor and could be brought in line or removed from command with a stroke of his pen. This unity of purpose and command was an important element in the victories of the French army during the Napoleonic years.

Marshal Soult's Fourth Corps was the largest in the Grande Armée. It consisted of forty thousand men in four divisions.[3] The divisions were commanded by generals Louis-Vincent Saint-Hilaire, Claude-Juste Legrand, Louis-Gabriel Suchet, and Vandamme. Colonel Poitevit headed the engineers. General Pierre Margaron commanded a brigade of light cavalry. General Victor-Antoine Andréossy (later replaced by General Charles Saligny) was chief of staff.[4] Vandamme's Second Division included three brigades. They were commanded by generals Charles Saligny (the Twenty-fourth Regiment of the Line and a regiment of *tirailleurs*) until he became Soult's chief of staff at the end of September; Claude-François Ferey (Fourth and Twenty-eighth regiments of the Line); and Jacques-Lazare Candras (Forty-sixth and Fifty-seventh regiments of the Line).[5] On 1 August, Marshal Berthier reviewed the division and gave Vandamme a good report, but not without criticism:

> The unexpected review [of your division] that I held today, my dear general, had as its purpose to inspect all the men you would be able to muster; . . . I counted all the men present, and I found the total to be 5,046. However, your division on paper is more than 9,000 men. I realize that one must subtract those men detached and those on guard and patrol; but perhaps you will also find a great number, who should have been present, were absent.
>
> I know, by our active surveillance, that your division is one of the finest in the army, but you must feel as I do that there is perhaps a little negligence on the part of your subordinate officers.[6]

Happy with the marshal's positive remarks, Vandamme certainly was not pleased with the criticism, but with a campaign about to begin, he did not want to ruffle the feathers of the emperor's right-hand man, who could remove him from his command with the stroke of a pen. The division was in excellent condition and up to near full strength on 1 September when it broke camp on the English Channel and entered upon campaign.

Marching orders for the Grande Armée went out from Paris on 25 August.[7] Bernadotte's First Corps moved south from Hanover while the corps commanded by Marmont (Second), Davout (Third), Soult (Fourth), Lannes (Fifth), and Ney (Sixth) marched toward the Rhine between Strasbourg and the River Main. Augereau's recently formed Seventh Corps moved into northeastern France from its staging position on the coast south of the Loire River.[8] Vandamme left his encampment on 1 September and was at Sedan on the 8th. He was joined by Soult at Verdun and reached the Rhine in the vicinity of Spire early in the last week of September. On 19 September, Vandamme reported to Soult that his division had marched in good order from Boulogne, that the food had been adequate, but that there was a shortage of brandy. He also admitted to having had a few men shot "for lack of discipline."[9] When Saligny was promoted to general of division and became Soult's chief of staff, General Joseph-François Schiner replaced him (25 September) as brigade commander in the Second Division.

On 25 September the Grande Armée was ordered across the Rhine into Germany.[10] It was the 27th when Vandamme's division crossed the river at Spire.[11] That night Vandamme invited the top officers of his division to dine with him. When the meal was completed, he requested coffee from the master of the house, who replied in a vulgar manner that he had no coffee for Frenchmen. "General Vandamme would not suffer such impertinence and, striking the man, demanded that the coffee be brought. The coffee arrived immediately."[12] The division marched through Bruchsal and Waghausel to Heilbronn, where it crossed the Necker River and pushed on to Hall, to arrive on 3 October.[13] That day, Vandamme was then ordered to Rosenberg and the following day on to Zabingen with his cavalry probing toward Nordlingen.[14] At Ellwangen the Fourth Corps made contact with a minor Austrian flanking detachment under the command of the count of Walmoden. As Vandamme's Second Division was leading the Fourth Corps through Germany, it was his advanced brigade (commanded by Candras) that first engaged the enemy and then followed as Walmoden retired south across the Danube. On 6 October, Vandamme reached the river at Donauwörth by way of Nordlingen.[15] By the end of the first week in October, Napoleon had six army corps on or across the Danube. Bernadotte (First Corps) was at Ingolstadt, Davout (Third Corps) followed by Marmont (Second Corps) at Neuburg, Soult (Vandamme's division) at Rain just east of Donauwörth, Lannes (Fifth Corps) at Münster, and Ney (Sixth Corps) moving on Gunzburg. Bessières, with the Guard, was following Soult. Murat's cavalry and Lannes's corps had crossed the Rhine at Strasbourg and feinted an advance into the Black Forest while the rest of the army moved into central Germany undetected.

The Austrians were led to believe that the principal French advance was coming directly through the forest from Strasbourg, as it frequently had before, and they responded accordingly. General Mack concentrated his forces near Ulm and sent strong advance units forward (west) to make contact with the enemy. It was only as the French army poured across the Danube taking Augsburg that he realized the difficulty of his position. Soult's orders were to cross the river at Donauwörth, but when Vandamme arrived he found the Austrians had burned the bridge.[16] Fortunately, he was able to find a bridge intact at Neuburg, a few miles down the river (east), and the Fourth Corps crossed in a timely manner. On 9 October, Vandamme reported that he had reached his destination, but his men were exhausted and in great need of food.[17]

At the same time Davout and Bernadotte moved southeast toward Munich. Soult marched south to Augsburg on the left bank of the Lech River, and on 8 October he crossed the Lech to the right (east) bank where he met light resistance. Pushing the Austrian cavalry patrols aside, Soult advanced south and reached Aicha the next day. Crossing back to the left bank of the Lech, he arrived in Augsburg. Soult was then ordered south to Landsberg, where Vandamme was given two days' rest after the forced marches from the Danube.[18] From Landsberg, on 13 October, Vandamme led the Fourth Corps west to Memmingen.[19] He remained before the town to accept its surrender and to make its four-thousand-man garrison prisoners of war.[20] Soult's First (Saint-Hilaire) and Third (Legrand) divisions crossed the Iller River and moved on to Ochsenhausen on 14 October. With Memmingen secured, Vandamme left a battalion to garrison the town and to escort prisoners of war and then joined the other divisions of the Fourth Corps as they advanced north toward Ulm.[21]

While Soult was blocking Mack to the south, Ney, Lannes, and Marmont crossed the Danube and swung west to move on Ulm. On 12 October, the pleasant early fall weather enjoyed by the French army during its six-week march from the English Channel finally came to an end. The temperature dropped to near freezing. Rain often mixed with snow turned the roads to mud. The corps had outmarched their supply trains, and the troops had exhausted the food they carried with them. The cold, the rain, the mud, the endless marching, all had taken a toll on the army's morale, but the soldiers continued to march nevertheless.

Against the advice of Ferdinand and the senior Austrian generals, Mack decided to hold a strong defensive position at Ulm until the Russians arrived. According to the Allied plan, General Mikhail Kutusov with thirty-five thousand Russians was to arrive in Bavaria by 20 October, followed by forty thousand men under General Friedrich Wilhelm Buxhöwden, and an additional twenty thousand troops commanded by General Levin Bennigsen. If Mack could hold out at Ulm for a week or ten days, help could arrive. In this scenario there were two factors that led to disaster, however. First, Russia was still keeping time on the old Julian calendar, which was eleven days behind the Gregorian calendar used by Austria and the rest of Europe.[22] It would seem that neither the Aulic Council nor Mack took this into consideration. Second, the Russians had fallen behind even on their own timetable, which meant that Kutusov would not arrive in time to save Mack from disaster.

On 12 October, Napoleon ordered Soult to reach Memmingen that night and to be on the banks of the Iller River the next day.[23] By 14 October, Napoleon had completely blocked any possible Austrian retreat to the east or south. His entire army was between Mack at Ulm and Kutusov nearly two hundred miles to the east. Vandamme, with the greater part of Soult's corps, was south of Ulm. To prevent the Austrians from escaping into the Tyrol, the Fourth Corps crossed to the west bank (left) of the Iller River, reached Ochsenhausen on 14 October, and marched northwest to cut the Ulm—Biberach road.[24] As the Austrian situation became hopeless, Archduke Ferdinand fled to the northeast with a strong cavalry escort. Pursued by Murat, he eventually reached the safety of Bohemia but not before losing the greater part of his troops. General Franz Jellacic also escaped. He took his division to the southwest through Biberach before Soult could close off that avenue of retreat, but Augereau, with his Seventh Corps on the way to join the main army, virtually destroyed Jellacic's division before it could reach safety.

Mack had hoped to hold out at Ulm until the Russians arrived to threaten Napoleon from the east. Ulm was well fortified, and the Austrians had ample military stores. But when he learned that Kutusov was still at some distance, and that the rest of the Russian army was even further to the east, he negotiated an armistice on 17 October with the stipulation that he would surrender on the 25 October if no help arrived. Napoleon accepted these terms, knowing the Russians could not possibly arrive in time. In the end, the disheartened Mack did not wait but surrendered on 20 October. Ney, Lanne, and Murat had been engaged in some serious fighting before 17 October, but overall the combat was sparse and French casualties light, with one notable exception—General Honoré Theodore Gazan's near disaster at the battles of Durnstein and Loiben on 11–12 October.

This first phase of the campaign was an enormous success for Napoleon. He eliminated an entire Austrian army in Germany. At Ulm alone he had taken twenty-five thousand prisoners of war, with all their equipment. In his eighth bulletin of the campaign Napoleon wrote, with only a little exaggeration: "From the heights of Ulm this day the 20th the emperor watched from 2:00 P.M. in the afternoon until 7:00 P.M. in the evening as the Austrian army passed before him. Thirty thousand men, of whom two thousand were cavalry, sixty pieces of cannon, and forty flags fell into the hands of the victors. . . . There were seven lieutenant generals, eight generals, and the commander in chief Mack. . . . One may estimate the total number of prisoners of war since the opening of the campaign at sixty thousand. . . . Never has a victory been more complete and cost so little."[25]

Despite his impressive victory in Germany, Napoleon's situation in central Europe was still not secure. The archdukes Charles in Italy and John in the Tyrol still commanded a hundred thousand men on his right flank. Another hundred thousand Russians, plus the Austrians of Mack's army who had escaped the encirclement at Ulm, were still before him. Furthermore, Prussia was moving toward joining the Allies and was thus posing a major threat with the possibility of ninety thousand men on his left flank. The emperor decided to push on toward Vienna, hoping to force a decisive battle with the Russians before Prussia entered the war or Charles and John could reach the Danube. To this end the Grande Armée was ordered east to Munich and on toward Austria proper. The Isar River was crossed on 25 October, and the French were quickly on the Inn River.

After a few days' rest south of Ulm while the terms of the surrender were ironed out, the Fourth Corps was back on the road. Retracing it steps through Memmingen to Landsberg, which Vandamme reached on 23 October, Soult's divisions were over the Inn River by 29 October. General Kutusov had marched out of Radziwilow, on the Austria-Galicia border, with the first portion of the Russian army (originally some forty-six thousand men strong) and had reached the Inn River by the third week of October. The long hard marching had taken a heavy toll on the troops. By 26 October he could collect only about twenty-seven thousand men because of stragglers, and a division of his army had been detached and sent east. An Austrian force of about eighteen thousand men commanded by General Max Merveldt joined Kutusov, increasing his strength to some forty-five thousand troops. However, having learned of the total destruction of the rest of Mack's army and that the French were advancing through Bavaria, Kutusov began a general withdrawal to the east.

Vandamme, with the Fourth Corps, marched east through Munich to the Inn River, then down the right bank of the Inn, and east along the right (south) bank of the Danube.[26] Murat and Lanne reached the Austrian capital on 13 November, and Vandamme arrived in Vienna the next day, where the Fourth Corps received a two-day rest. The Grande Armée had been marching hard for six weeks and was showing typical signs of the strain. Supplies could not keep up with the troops, and fatigue (more than the enemy) was taking a great toll on the rank and file. The victory at Ulm raised morale temporarily and gave the men a will to go on; but the rain, mud, and cold along with the increased shortage of food after crossing the Inn led to a breakdown in morale and discipline. Vandamme did his best to confront these problems by severely punishing those guilty of pillaging and rape, but good order would not be restored until the campaign ended after the battle of Austerlitz. In the days before reaching Vienna,

Vandamme incurred Soult's anger because he openly criticized the supply system, which was not providing adequate food for his troops. On 20 November Soult sharply reprimanded Vandamme:

> Over a period of days a number of officers of good reputation have informed me that you have been insinuating publicly that food for the army has been sold. I was very surprised to learn you had said such a thing, for I thought you knew that the administration has made every possible effort to give the troops their proper allocations; and that, if sometimes food was lacking, then it could be attributed only to shortages that we often experience.
>
> I also believe that an insinuation of this nature was unworthy of your character and that you could not help yourself. . . .
>
> When you need to make known any problems relating to your troops, with reference to abuses or to offenses, as those previously mentioned with problems in the supply service that you have unveiled, which involve my duty and authority, you are bound by honor and duty, monsieur general, to give me an account, so that I am able to remedy the problem, stop the disorder, and strengthen the lines of discipline.
>
> Your forgetfulness in this matter of your duties has obliged me to write you this letter, but I do so with regret.[27]

The outspoken Vandamme all too often lashed out in frustration against any and all whom he considered negligent. As the corps commander, Marshal Soult was ultimately responsible, and indeed the marshal took the general's remarks personally. There was no love between the two men, but they had to work together in the face of the enemy. Vandamme's denunciation of the army's support services, in which there was the usual corruption, may have been exaggerated, but the lack of a regular food supply for the troops was not. The men were forced to pillage the countryside as they moved east.[28] Large supplies of food and war matériel were captured at Ulm, Munich, and other depots hastily abandoned by the Austrians, but this resulted in brief periods of plenty followed by days of little as the army marched down the Danube through country already ravaged twice by the Russians, once when advancing west and again when retreating east. On 25 November, Vandamme wrote Soult that, while his men were in reasonably good condition, some were too sick to march and others had no shoes.[29]

Napoleon became aware of the problems when he caught up with his forward units and reviewed a part of Soult's corps at Lintz. One account describes how, after the brief review: "There, in front of the ranks, he inquired in a loud voice as to the regularity of the distributions [of food]; whether the marshal [Soult] thought the question was put merely as a matter of form, or he wanted Napoleon to be satisfied, . . . he answered that the soldiers wanted for nothing. Whereupon immediately twenty voices were raised rudely from the ranks to contradict him." The following day the emperor met General Pierre Macon, who commanded the imperial quarters. Napoleon asked him if he had any news, and the general, who had witnessed the pillage of the countryside and the disorder of the marching columns answered: "Faith, Sire, I can tell you that you are followed by a crowd of plunderers who will dishonor your army and yourself if you do not promptly put things on a proper footing."[30] Napoleon could do little to remedy the problem, however, except stop the advance on Vienna to allow the supply wagons, bogged down on rain-soaked roads, to catch up with the marching troops. As he was unwilling to do this, the army continued to plunder its way east.

Vienna was occupied without resistance because the Austrians had declared it to be an open city. Emperor Francis had already fled with the members of the court and the government. However, Vandamme had no time to enjoy one of Europe's finest cities. On 14 November the Fourth Corps camped on the outskirts of Vienna and the following day crossed the Danube and marched north. The occupation of the Austrian capital had little effect on the campaign. The armies of Kutusov and archdukes Charles and John were still a serious threat to the French army. The archdukes were retiring to the east through southern Austria. Although Masséna was following and harassing the enemy, Napoleon felt it necessary to send Marshal Marmont's Second Corps south of Vienna to protect his right flank and rear. Davout was also posted south and east of Vienna so as to be within support distance of Marmont should Charles and John attack the Second Corps. The rest of the Grande Armée crossed the Danube and moved north in pursuit of the Russian-Austrian army.

Murat's cavalry led the advance from Vienna up the left bank of the Danube. The duplicity of Murat and Lanne had led to the capture of a bridge over the river near Vienna.[31] The corps of Lanne and Soult followed the cavalry. On 15 November, Lannes's lead division (commanded by Oudinot) engaged the Russian rear guard at Hollabrünn in an indecisive battle. Vandamme reached Hollabrünn as the fighting ended. Murat was then persuaded to conclude a brief armistice with Kutusov's representative General Baron Winzgerode. When Napoleon, still at Schönbrunn Palace, was informed of it, he denounced both the armistice and his brother-in-law, who he declared had no authority to conclude such an agreement without his direct permission. The brief lull in hostilities at Hollabrünn enabled Kutusov to extract his army from a difficult position and reach Moravia where he was joined by the second Russian army commanded by Buxhöwden. The armistice denounced, the French corps quickly moved forward. Vandamme reached Znaim on 17 November and Stanitz (Steinitz) on 22 November. Kutusov had been reinforced by Buxhöwden's lead corps of fourteen thousand men on 19 November, and his Second Corps at Prossnitz two days later. The Allied army was now eighty-five thousand men strong, and Napoleon's corps were still scattered. As a result, the pursuit came to an end and preparations for a major battle began.

The newly arrived Russian troops were in reasonably good condition, but Kutusov's army was in no better shape than the French. "The forces coming from Russia," wrote one of Kutusov's officers, "were completely fresh and in splendid order. Our army, on the contrary, had been ruined by perpetual hardships, and broken down by the lack of supplies and the foul weather of late autumn. The troops' uniforms had been destroyed by the conditions in the bivouacs, and their footwear had almost ceased to exist. Even our commanders were arrayed in ill-assorted almost comic attire."[32] On 17 November Kutusov described his army to the tsar: "I dare not conceal from you, Sire, . . . [that] our troops, in spite of their zeal and their impatience to distinguish themselves, are bereft of physical strength. Exhausted by forced marches and constant bivouacs, they can scarcely drag themselves along: they often go twenty-four hours without nourishment, for lack of time to prepare their meals, constantly harried as they are by the enemy."[33]

Marshal Soult established his quarters in the château of the prince of Kaunitz at Austerlitz, and his divisions camped nearby. Vandamme remained at Stanitz from 22 to 29 November. During this time, Soult was in bed for several days with an eye infection, but by the 29th he was again on his feet and in full command.[34] The emperor established his headquarters at Brünn, where the French had found large quantities of arms and provisions.

The battle of Austerlitz was fought on 2 December 1805. For the rest of his life Napoleon considered this his greatest triumph; and whereas he gave his marshals titles of many of his other battles, he kept Austerlitz for himself. By late November his position in east-central Europe had become grave. He had major Allied armies before him and on his southern flank, and Prussia was preparing to enter the war and to march against his right flank and rear. On 25 October, Tsar Alexander had arrived in Berlin to persuade the king of Prussia, Frederick William III, to join the coalition against France. The king signed the secret Treaty of Potsdam somewhat reluctantly, pledging to declare war on France within six weeks if Napoleon did not agree to a mediated settlement. Since Austria and Russia would draw up the terms of the settlement, it was assumed that Napoleon would not agree; and Prussia would enter the war.[35]

Napoleon had to win a decisive victory over the Russians in Moravia before the situation changed to an overwhelming Allied advantage. Such a triumph would keep Prussia neutral, despite the recent treaty, and bring Emperor Francis to the peace table. The Prussians had also been bargaining with England over Hanover as the price for entering the war against France, but Napoleon's triumph at Ulm was causing second thoughts in Potsdam about which side was going to win the war. To induce the Russians to attack him, Napoleon presented a weak force before them west of Austerlitz. Alexander had joined the army, and despite the reluctance of Kutusov who advised a further retreat to the east, the tsar decided to attack and destroy the French army. The combined forces of Russia and Austria comprised some 84,000 men.[36] This was greatly superior to the 66,500 troops Napoleon had gathered between Austerlitz and Brünn in the last week of November.[37] The tsar and his general staff believed that with this numerical superiority they would be victorious, and Napoleon would have to retreat to the west. An Allied victory would greatly encourage

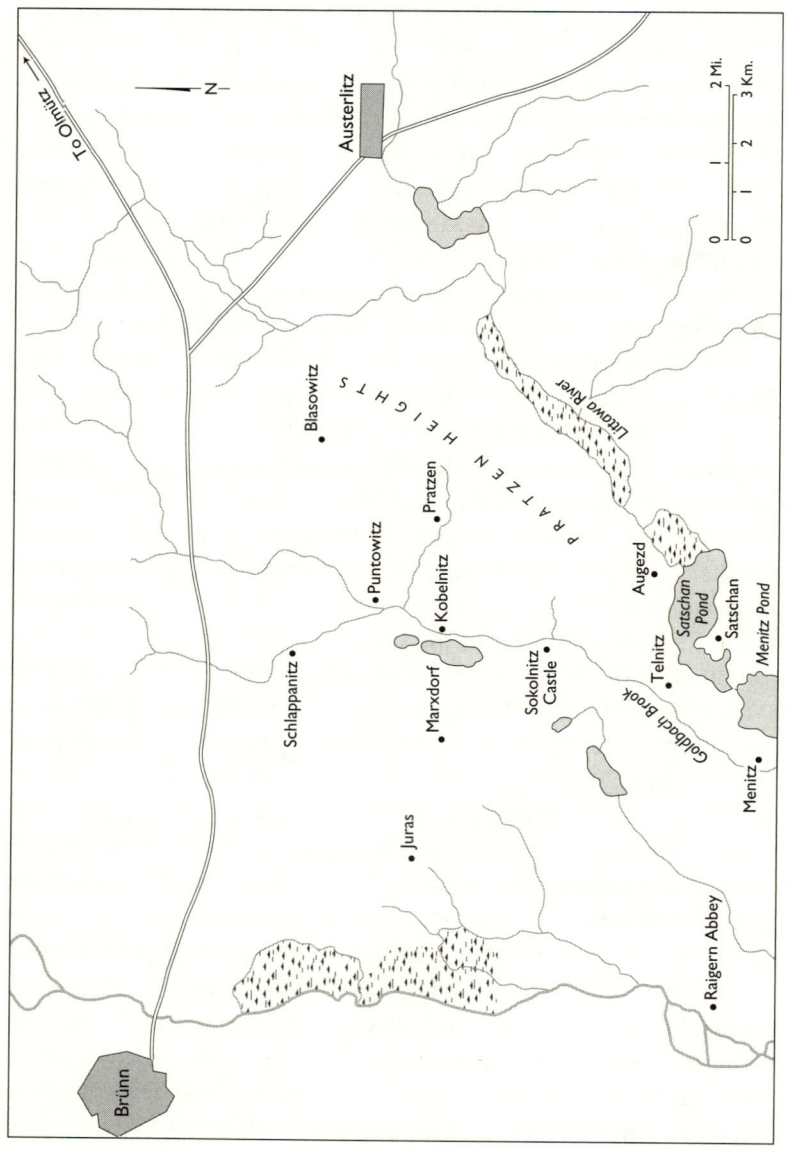

The battle of Austerlitz

MSP/WS1/0843 895717

Name: BOUSCHOR/DAVID
Date: 25JUL08
Frequent Flyer Nbr: ASXXXX694
E-ticket Nbr: 0272120819272
Flight: NW420 Coach Class

AIRLINES MVP
Conf #: N8DXYV
Request:

Gate: C16   Seat: 28-F   Board time: 11:00 AM

Depart: MINNEAPOLIS/ST PAUL 11:40 AM
Arrive: ANCHORAGE

Bag tag #NW261631

Boarding Pass

ETKT   ETKT   ETKT

the Prussians, who would then descend upon the retreating French and complete the destruction of the French army.

By 28 November the Allied army was on the march southwest from Olmütz toward Brünn. Napoleon was sure he would have his battle, and he began to plan for a clash between Austerlitz and Brünn. He deliberately presented a weak front to the Allies to encourage his enemy to attack him. Furthermore, he actually selected the battlefield. He intentionally withdrew his forces from the village of Austerlitz and the Pratzen Heights as the Russians advanced. He then placed his army corps from Santon Hill on the north (his left), south along the Goldbach Brook to the village of Telnitz by Satschan Lake. Napoleon's center would be opposite the Pratzen Heights, and here he amassed two of Soult's divisions: Saint-Hilaire and Vandamme.[38] To their left were the corps of Bernadotte and Lanne with Murat's cavalry between them. The Guard was placed behind Bernadotte so as to be in position to support either the left or the center, or to exploit a weakness in the enemy line. The right flank would be the key to the early phase of the battle. General Legrand's division of the Fourth Corps was spread thin from Kobelnitz to Telnitz. The right flank was deliberately left weak to encourage the enemy to make its principal attack at that point. Marshal Davout, at Vienna on 28 November, was at the last minute ordered to the north to bolster the right flank. If Davout did not reach the battlefield in time, Napoleon's right would be turned; and the French army would be in the gravest danger of being defeated and destroyed.

The Allied army moved into position on 30 November and 1 December. Bagration's corps took up a position astride the Brünn—Austerlitz road, facing Lanne, to form the Allied right flank. Buxhöwden occupied the Pratzen Heights (the center of the Allied position) and the terrain south to Satschan Lake. Kollowrat's corps was also placed on Pratzen Heights to back up the center. The tsar's brother, Grand Duke Constantine, commanded the Russian Imperial Guard behind the center. The plan accepted by Alexander, and somewhat reluctantly by Emperor Francis, called for a holding action on the right and in the center and an all out attack by Buxhöwden on the left. He would break through the weak French line and cut Napoleon's line of retreat south to Vienna. Then, moving north, he would drive the enemy away from its line of supplies and communications that ran south to Vienna. It was a basic and reasonable plan. It was also very obvious, and Napoleon had anticipated it even before the battle began. He would wait until the Russians were fully committed to their advance on the south flank and then attack in the center to break the enemy line.

Napoleon slept little on the night before the battle. He dictated orders and paced about the campfire in front of his hut. Sometime after midnight there was a brief skirmish on the French right near Telnitz. He sent an aide to make sure the enemy was not beginning the battle with a night attack. By 2:00 A.M. he decided to go forward and check the situation in the center of the line for himself. Satisfied all was well, he dismounted by one of the campfires. He was walking back toward his hut in the dark when he stumbled on a tree stump. Soldiers nearby wrapped up straw to make torches to light the way for the emperor. This turned into a noisy torchlight procession back to his headquarters. The word quickly spread that it was 2 December, the first anniversary of Napoleon's coronation; and the entire center of the French line erupted with torches and shouts of "Vive l'Empereur!" The incident took place in the midst of Soult's corps, and it is reported that "General Vandamme, . . . stamped up and down on the spot and shouted himself hoarse in a piercing voice, louder than his drums."[39]

On the morning of 2 December, the valley of the Goldbach Brook was covered with a heavy fog mixed with smoke from the campfires of both armies. This hid the divisions of Vandamme and Saint-Hilaire as they moved from their staging areas to their attack positions before the Pratzen Heights. At the same time, between 6:00 and 7:00 A.M., some forty-five thousand Russians and Austrians, under the command of General Buxhöwden, were moving south from the Plains of Pratzen to turn the French right flank between Telnitz and Sokolnitz. Confusion and poor visibility caused a delay in the Allied movements so that serious contact was not made with the French right until almost 8:00 A.M. This was fortunate for Napoleon, because Soult's division commanded by Legrand was spread very thin, waiting for Davout's Third Corps to arrive from Vienna. General Louis Fraint's division had left Vienna at 11:00 P.M. on 29 November and arrived at the Abbey of Raigern (five to six miles west of Telnitz) at 7:00 P.M. on 1 December. The division had covered seventy miles in forty-four hours.⁴⁰ Davout had only one of his three divisions. General Louis-Marie Caffarelli's division was attached to Lannes' Fifth Corps on the left flank; and General Charles-Etienne Gudin's division, which had been some forty plus miles east of Vienna at Pressburg, did not arrive in time for the battle. After a few hours' rest at Raigern, Friant's division moved onto the French right flank. Legrand, greatly outnumbered, fought a delaying action as best he could but in the early fighting was forced out of Telnitz. With the arrival of Friant's division, Davout, who assumed command of the right flank, was able to stabilize the line. Soult, worried about Legrand, had sent reinforcements. The fighting became fierce between the lakes and Kobelnitz, and the town of Telnitz changed hands several times. Although Buxhöwden's two lead divisions were able to cross the Goldbach, Davout held the right flank intact and stopped the enemy advance.

As the Russian divisions on the Pratzen Heights moved south and to the west in order to support the turning movement, the center of the Allied line became thinner. This was precisely what Napoleon had anticipated by showing a weak right flank. It was just a matter of timing as to when he would order Soult's two divisions up the slopes from the Goldbach onto the Pratzen Heights. The north end of the battlefield was relatively quiet in the early hours of the battle. Bagration had been ordered to hold his position while Buxhöwden turned the French right. At the same time, Lanne and Murat were also in a holding pattern astride the Brünn-Austerlitz road.

Early on 2 December, Soult, along with the other marshals, had joined the emperor to receive their last instructions. After the others had rejoined their commands, Soult was detained. Napoleon, pointing toward the Pratzen Heights, then asked the marshal: "'How much time do you require to crown that summit?' 'Ten minutes,' answered the marshal.—'Then go,' resumed the emperor, 'but you can wait another quarter of an hour, and it will be time enough then!'"⁴¹ At 8:00 A.M., as the sun rose behind the Russian line, Napoleon ordered Vandamme and Saint-Hilaire to advance and break the Allied center. Vandamme's division was assembled behind Girzikowitz and Saint-Hilaire behind Puntowitz. The troops had been given a triple ration of eau-de-vie (military brandy) to raise their spirits before going into battle from which many of them would not return.⁴²

Vandamme's objective was the high ground on the northeast side of the plateau (at Staré Vinohrady), about a mile to the east of the small village of Pratzen. At the same time, Saint-Hilaire would march to Pratzen and onto the high ground near the southeast side of the plateau (at Pratzeberg). Saint-Hilaire—less General Louis-Prix Varé's brigade, which was attached to Vandamme to serve as a link between the two divisions—reached Pratzen with only minor resistance, but he was stopped at Pratzen by the Russian divisions commanded by generals J. K. Kollowrat and Alexander Kamensky.

Kutusov was moving against the French right in five columns. Three of these had made contact with Legrand or were marching on Sokolnitz. The fourth Russian column comprised the divisions of Kollowrat and General Mikhail Andreivitch Miloradovitch. It had been thrown into some confusion and delay when the fifth column, that of Prince Johann Liechtenstein's Imperial Guard, had lost its way and marched across the front of the fourth column. When Kutusov realized there was great danger in his center on the Pratzen Heights, he redirected the Kollowrat and Miloradovitch divisions, which had been inactive on the southeast slope of the Pratzen. General Kamensky's division, a part of General A. Langeron's third Russian column, was marching on Sokolnitz. He was the rear division of that column and had not yet engaged in the fighting along the Goldbach. When he perceived the danger on the Pratzen, he turned about and marched up the slope to engage Saint-Hilaire's right flank. Vandamme, to Saint-Hilaire's left, had also encountered little resistance as he moved up the slope to the plateau. But Miloradovitch soon presented a strong front and the fighting became intense. There quickly developed a fierce struggle for control of the center of the line.[43]

Saint-Hilaire's lead battalions suffered an initial setback and lost two guns. But as the rest of the division moved into action, the line stabilized and moved forward.[44] Although Vandamme met stubborn resistance from an Austrian regiment that had occupied Staré Vinohrady, he was able to mount a sustained attack and drove the enemy from the heights. Soult's two divisions were in command of the Pratzen Heights shortly after 10:00 A.M.

The serious fighting had just begun for Vandamme. He and Saint-Hilaire broke the Allied center and found themselves between Bagration to the north and Buxhöwden to the south. Tsar Alexander was present on the battlefield east of Staré Vinohrady and witnessed Vandamme's success. He now deemed it absolutely essential to regain the Pratzen Heights in order to prevent a crushing defeat. To this end the Imperial Guard was ordered against Vandamme's division.[45] North of the Pratzen Heights the battle had begun shortly after midmorning. Both Bagration and Lannes were unhappy with their passive roles in the opening phase of the battle. As Bagration moved forward, Lannes advanced to meet him. The French left and the Allied right locked in a bitter struggle; but gradually Lanne gained the upper hand, with the support of Murat's cavalry and units of Bernadotte's First Corps, and the Allied right flank was pushed back along the Brünn—Olmütz road. On the south end of the battlefield, Davout was holding a vastly superior number of Russians and Austrians along the lower Goldbach. The determination of the French not to let the enemy pass, and the confusion and ineffective command on the part of the Allies, led to a stalemate between Kobelnitz and the lakes at Telnitz.[46]

Back in the center of the line, Napoleon was ascending the Pratzen Heights with Bernadotte's First Corps and the Guard with the intention of completing the destruction of the Allied center and crushing its left wing. But before their arrival, Vandamme's left wing (Schinner's brigade) was partially overrun on the north slope of the Staré Vinohrady by the leading regiments of the Russian Guard. When Marshal Soult noticed a concentration of enemy troops at some distance off to Vandamme's left, he ordered the general to send a battalion in that direction to investigate the enemy's intentions. Vandamme assigned the task to Major Auguste-Julien Bigarré who, in the absence of Prince Joseph Bonaparte, commanded the Fourth Regiment of Light Infantry. Bigarré took the first battalion of the regiment and—accompanied by Captain Henri-Catherine Vincent, aide-de-camp to General Claude-François Ferey—set off in the direction of the enemy force.[47] Vincent, who had ridden ahead of the battalion, returned and informed Bigarré it was the Russian Imperial Guard cavalry; and that it was moving rapidly in their direction to attack the now isolated French battalion. As the Russian guard approached, Bigarré formed his battalion into a square to receive a cavalry charge. But the Russians unmasked six pieces of light artillery and opened fire on the square. When Vandamme saw from a distance the danger in which Bigarré found himself, he ordered the Twenty-fourth Regiment of Light Infantry to his aid. Before help could arrive, however, the Russian guns took a heavy toll, and two regiments of the Guard cavalry charged. The first two attacks were beaten off, but a third Russian regiment overran the battalion, inflicting heavy causalities and capturing the eagle flag of the Fourth Regiment. The Twenty-fourth Light Infantry was also overrun; it broke and fled to the rear in disorder. In the confusion of this engagement, a noncommissioned officer of Bigarré's battalion found the eagle of the Twenty-fourth Regiment and picked it up off the battlefield. Thinking it was the standard of his own regiment, the Fourth, he thought, "no one noticed our standard was missing."[48] Napoleon's aide-de-camp, Ségur, witnessed this unhappy affair and wrote in his memoirs:

> I had scarcely returned and reassured the emperor as to what was going on in his rear, when in front of him began the attack of Alexander's horse guard. It was so impetuous that Vandamme's two battalions [of the Fourth Regiment] on the left were completely overwhelmed! One of them indeed, covered with blood, and having lost its eagle and the greater part of its arms only got up to run away at full speed. This battalion was that of the Fourth Regiment, which almost passed over us, including Napoleon himself, and our efforts to arrest it were in vain. The unfortunate fellows were utterly distracted with fear and could listen to nothing; in reply to reproaches for thus deserting the field of battle and their emperor, they shouted mechanically "Vive l'Empereur!" while they fled faster than ever.[49]

A postscript to the loss of the treasured eagle of one of Vandamme's regiments (a loss that did not enhance his reputation) provides an interesting conclusion to the affair. In 1807 Napoleon sent Colonel Marie—aide-de-camp to Joseph Bonaparte, the king of Naples—on a friendly mission to Saint Petersburg. Marie was cordially received by the tsar's brother Constantine and invited to lunch at the prince's home. After lunch, Constantine took Marie to his bedroom to show him the Fourth Regiment's eagle. The prince was using it to hold up the canopy over his bed.[50]

With Vandamme's left flank being overrun, Marshal Bessières was ordered to send the first wave of the French Imperial Guard cavalry into the melee to stabilize the line. When the last reserves of the Russian guard were committed to the struggle, Napoleon sent in the second wave of Bessière's guard and the line was stabilized. The arrival of Bernadotte's lead division, commanded by General Jean-Baptiste Drouet, was the decisive element that made victory possible for the French on the Pratzen Heights. The Russian Imperial Guard was driven from the battlefield. The remaining task was the destruction of the Allied left wing.[51]

It was about 2:00 P.M. when the battle's final phase began. The Allied center had been destroyed and the left wing was in peril. From the heights of the Pratzen plateau, Napoleon had a full view of the terrain south to Satschan and Menitz lakes and west to the lower Goldbach. The greater part of Buxhöwden's command (three Allied columns) was engaged with Davout and Legrand along the Goldbach. Saint-Hilaire was ordered down from the Pratzen to the west, so as to attack General Prebyshevsky's column from the rear as it faced Legrand north of Sokolnitz. Vandamme was wounded but remained on the battlefield in command of his corps. He advanced south and southwest from the Pratzen, with one brigade moving toward the village of Augezd, north of Satschan Lake, and the other two brigades moving toward Telnitz. To Vandamme's left was the Guard. The remnants of Miloradovitch's and Kollowrat's divisions fled east through Saratitz and Wazan.

Buxhöwden was now in a difficult position. French forces were to his front, his right, and his right rear, while the Satschan and Menitz lakes were to his left; retreat would be perilous at best. With Soult's two divisions advancing from the Pratzen, Davout went on the offensive along the Goldbach, and Legrand crossed the brook and drove south. There was a small strip of land between the two ponds that enabled some Allied troops to escape to the south and then to the east. Others managed to make their way along the north shore of Satschan Lake past Augezd and to escape to the east before Vandamme's scattered and exhausted men occupied that village in strength. Others tried to cross the frozen ponds. Seeing this, Napoleon, who was with Soult and Vandamme at the Chapel of St. Anthony on the south slope of the Pratzen, ordered twenty-five guns on the plateau to open fire on the retreating troops on the ponds. The weight of men, horses, and guns, with the French round shot from the high ground, broke the ice, which caused undetermined losses to the Russians and Austrians.[52]

Vandamme and Ségur were together on the south slope of the Pratzen Heights about 4:00 P.M. "At this moment one of his [Vandamme's] battalions came by, reduced to 150 men; and on exclamation at the sight of so small a number, he replied: 'Yes, indeed; it is impossible to make a good omelet without breaking a great many eggs!' It was, in fact, his division that had borne the brunt of the battle."[53] At about this same time, General of Brigade Paul-Charles Thiébault, who commanded one of Saint-Hilaire's brigades, alleges that as darkness approached Napoleon allowed some fifteen thousand Russians of the Allied left wing to escape. Thiébault added that this "made some people very angry. At the head of these was General Vandamme, who exclaimed on hearing of it, 'To spare them today is to have them in Paris six years hence.' Eight years hence they were there."[54]

Rain and snow began to fall as darkness brought an end to the battle. At 5:00 P.M. the cease-fire was sounded, and the exhausted French army sought campsites for the night. There was little interest in any active pursuit on the part of the men, who had been fighting the entire day. Bernadotte's First Corps did follow the enemy to the east for a few miles but without much enthusiasm. Of Vandamme's division, only General Schiner with units of the Twenty-fourth and Fifty-fifth line regiments moved south of the ponds in a limited pursuit. The bulk of Vandamme's weary troops camped as best they could on the field of battle.[55]

Austerlitz was Napoleon's greatest victory. While it is true that he had a general overall plan for fighting the battle, he had to continually fine-tune the army's operations throughout the day. This meant responding on the spot to Allied troop movements, attacks, and counterattacks. The emperor commanded a superior army, man for man, general for general. Despite the Allied superiority in numbers, the leadership failed to produce victory; the Russian and Austrian soldiers fought bravely, but the Allied battle plan was flawed, and the troops were poorly handled on the Goldbach. Buxhöwden did not break through Legrand's thin line before Davout reached the field of battle; and even after the arrival of part of the Third Corps, Buxhöwden had more than a three-to-one advantage and should have been able to drive

Davout from the field. In the center, Vandamme and Saint-Hilaire performed brilliantly on the Pratzen Plateau when they crushed Buxhöwden's wing. Napoleon was well aware of the contributions of the men and officers of the Grande Armée. In his proclamation to the troops the next day he declared: "Soldiers, I am pleased with you! On this day of Austerlitz, you have justified everything I expected of your boldness, and you have honored your eagles with an immortal glory. . . . When I have accomplished everything necessary for the happiness and prosperity of your land, I shall lead you back to France. There you will be the objects of my most tender care. My people will greet you with joy, and it will be enough for you to say, 'I was at the battle of Austerlitz,' and they will reply, 'There stands a hero.'"[56]

Nor did he forget his generals. On 8 February 1806 Napoleon displayed his appreciation in terms they most appreciated: "Wishing to recognize the services rendered at the battle of Austerlitz, by the generals named below. . . . There is assigned a pension of twenty thousand francs from the funds of the Legion of Honor to each of the generals; Vandamme, etc."[57] As special recognition of the services of General Vandamme, Napoleon awarded him the grand eagle of the Legion of Honor, the highest decoration given during the Napoleonic wars. The grand chancellor of the legion made the announcement of Vandamme's honor on 27 December 1805.

Vandamme's and Saint-Hilaire's divisions were given a day of rest. Davout's Second Division commanded by General Charles-Etienne Gudin, which had reached the battlefield the morning of 3 December, moved east in pursuit of the remains of Buxhöwden's fleeing divisions. Bernadotte's corps and some cavalry units also pursued the enemy. On 4 December, Vandamme marched east to Butschowitz to continue the campaign.[58] However, on 3 December, the emperor of Austria met with the tsar and decided the campaign was over. Alexander could think only of saving what was left of his army and taking it back to Russia. Emperor Francis, realizing his ally was deserting him, could see no alternative to asking for an armistice and concluding as favorable a peace treaty as he could in light of the circumstances. To this end, on the morning of 4 December, while Vandamme's division was on the march, the emperors Napoleon and Francis met and concluded an armistice. The details of the Treaty of Pressburg were worked out very much to the wishes of Napoleon.

Soult's Fourth Corps was ordered to Vienna in mid-December. Vandamme arrived in the Austrian capital two days before Christmas and took up garrison duty. On Christmas Day, Napoleon reviewed the division, which now numbered some 9,621 men and 337 cavalry, and expressed his satisfaction.[59] On that day Soult wrote Vandamme:

> The emperor has remarked that he is satisfied with the division you command and that His Majesty charges me to make it known to the troops making up that division. I do so with the greatest pleasure. I can only add to the honorable expressions of His Majesty, a testimony to the glorious part that your division played at the battle of Austerlitz.
>
> You will make the content of the order of the day known to the assembled companies of your division.[60]

Christmas was not so happy a day for Major Bigarré and the men of the First Battalion of the Fourth Regiment. The major records the following encounter with the emperor:

> On 25 December, the day before the signing of the peace treaty, Emperor Napoleon had Vandamme's division pass in review close to his headquarters at Schönbrunn.
>
> Arriving before the Fourth Regiment of the Line, he ordered me to form it into a square, and going into the center of the square with all his staff, he faced the center of the battalion that had lost its flag: "Soldiers," he said to the men of that battalion, "what have you done with the eagle I gave you? You swore that it would serve you as a rallying point and you would defend it with your lives; how is it that you have broken your promise?"—"Sire," I answered him, "the Fourth Regiment of the Line fulfilled its duty at the battle of Austerlitz just as it did at Arcola under the eyes of Your Majesty, and [in] all the other circumstances where it has fought for country and glory. A most unfortunate affair deprived its first battalion of the eagle that you gave it. In the melee against three regiments of cavalry of the [Russian] Imperial Guard, and against six cannons, two flag-bearers were killed, and it was only after the third flag-bearer received a dozen saber blows to

the head that the flag was taken. I swear upon my honor that no one in that battle was aware of the loss of the eagle. . . . Sire," I continued, "ask generals Vandamme and [Jacques-Lazare] Candras if the Fourth Regiment of the Line did not fight with courage at Austerlitz."[61] Your Majesty will recall that it captured a battery of enemy artillery at bayonet point on the Pratzen Plateau, captured a Russian regiment with its colonel, and here are its two flags (an adjutant-major has them in his hand) that I offer to Your Majesty in the name of the regiment of your brother [Joseph]."—"In that case," the emperor said with a smile, "I will give you another eagle." There were then a hundred cries of "Vive l'Empereur!" from the entire regiment, and this ended the scene that I am describing.[62]

The Treaty of Pressburg ending the war between France and Austria was signed on 26 December. It provided for, among other stipulations, the immediate evacuation of Vienna by French troops. Thus Vandamme resided in the Austrian capital for less than three weeks. While in Vienna, he proposed, and Soult approved, nominating 110 of his officers and men for the Legion of Honor. On 12 January 1806, the Second Division marched out of Vienna some 10,248 men strong. "The troops were superb," Soult wrote Berthier, "and there was an immense crowd to watch the last regiments, which were well dressed and marched in finest order."[63] The Treaty of Pressburg provided for the complete withdrawal of all French troops from the Austrian empire. However, there was a provision that allowed the French to occupy key positions in western Austria until the government in Vienna complied with all the terms of the treaty. Thus, Vandamme's division withdrew to Steyr on the Enns River and took up quarters in the district around the city.

Vandamme now considered the campaign to have officially ended, and he requested permission to leave the army and return on leave of absence to Cassel to spend time with his family. Napoleon granted him six weeks' leave, but with the instruction that it would not begin until his division went into permanent winter quarters at Augsburg.[64] The timing of his leave depended upon the Austrians' carrying out all the provisions of the treaty. Unfortunately, Vienna was in no hurry to comply, and Napoleon was in no hurry to withdraw his troops from

Austrian territory where they were living at the expense of the former enemy. It was not until mid-June that Vandamme was out of Austria; but he was ordered to Landshut in Bavaria, not Augsburg. Desperate to obtain leave and return to Cassel, he pleaded with Berthier, whom Napoleon had left in command of the Grande Armée:

> Monseigneur, the news of my poor health having been reported in the newspapers, my wife and her family are in a state of despair, making my position here most difficult.
>
> Now that the return of the army [to France] is certain, I beg Your Highness to permit me to take advantage of the leave that His Majesty accorded me to pass forty days in Flanders. I have another urgent need to leave the army, because I suffer daily from nervous diarrhea that has been accruing for a month. I have an indispensable need to take the waters of a spa to completely cure this dreadful suffering.[65]

With no formal system for requesting leave of absence, Vandamme, as was customary in the French army, used poor health to explain why he should be given leave. His general health was no worse or better than that of his comrades in arms. He was, somewhat reluctantly, granted two months' leave in mid-July 1806. On 16 July, General of Division Jean-François Leval was named to replace him, and within a few days Vandamme left Landshut and returned to Cassel. His farewell address, in the form of an order of the day dated 19 July, is reassuring and moving: "I can not leave you without recalling all that I have experienced during the time I have had the honor to command you.... Your valor and your wise conduct have earned the emperor's praise.... Your patience at Boulogne, your rare bravery at Austerlitz, and your wise conduct in Bavaria will always be present in my thoughts. I will always be proud to have commanded you.... War or peace, at the festivals in Paris or on new battlefields, I will be at your head."[66] Having taken leave of his command, Vandamme made his way across southern Germany and northern France to Cassel and to the warm reception of his family. It was eleven months since he had marched out of Boulogne and last seen his wife and young son.

General Vandamme, about thirty years of age.
Courtesy of the Museum of the Army, Les Invalides.

Napoleon I, emperor of the French, 1769–1821.
From the private collection of J. David Markham.

Jérôme Bonaparte, king of Westphalia, 1784–1860.
From the private collection of J. David Markham.

Nicolas-Jean de Dieu Soult, duke of Dalmatie, marshal of the empire, 1769–1851.
From the private collection of J. David Markham.

LE MARÉCHAL DAVOUST
(Prince d'Eckmühl)

Louis N. Davout, marshal of the empire,
duke of Auerstadt, prince of Eckmühl, 1770–1823.
From the private collection of J. David Markham.

The Exploit of the Mounted Regiment in the Battle of Austerlitz, 1805 (oil on canvas, 1884), by Bogdan Willewalde (1818–1903). Copyright © State Central Military Museum, Moscow, Russia. Courtesy of The Bridgeman Art Library, New York.

La Frégate, Vandamme's château at Cassel in 2004. From the author's collection.

Monument to General Vandamme in Cassel, France, in 2004.
From the author's collection.

7

SIEGE WARFARE IN SILESIA

In many respects, the campaigns of 1806–1807 continued the struggle for control of central Europe that had begun with the formation of the Third Coalition in summer 1805. There were, of course, some changes of participants. Austria was not involved in 1806–1807. Russia played no significant role in the Jena-Auerstädt campaign of 1806 but was the dominant Allied partner in 1807. The British were, as always, still at war with France but contributed only money to the conflict on the continent. Prussia was a minor player in 1805 but became the principal Allied participant in 1806 and a lesser factor in 1807. The Allied disasters at Ulm and Austerlitz convinced Austria to sign the peace of Pressburg in December 1805, which ended the war with France. The Russian tsar after Austerlitz took what was left of his army back to Russia and sent Monsieur d'Oubril to Paris to negotiate a peace treaty. But the treaty that d'Oubril brought back to St. Petersburg was unacceptable. Alexander denounced it, in an unusual turn of events, since d'Oubril had been negotiating in the tsar's name. Officially, the war between France and Russia continued, at least on paper.

Relations between France and Prussia had been reasonably normal since Prussia had withdrawn from the First Coalition in 1795. When General Bonaparte came to power in 1799, he continued the policy of maintaining the best relations possible with Prussia while aggressively spreading French influence in the German states. In June 1803, however, the First Consul occupied the British principality of Hanover, which controlled the mouth of the Elbe River. Frederick William III protested, in vain. Then in 1805, to appease the king and buy his neutrality in the approaching conflict with Austria and Russia, Napoleon promised to give Prussia the territory of Hanover in return for neutrality. But then, at the beginning of the 1805 campaign, in order to save time and distance, the emperor ordered Marshal Bernadotte to march his First Corps through Prussian territory to reach the Danube. Frederick William was not even given the courtesy of a request for permission. This infuriated the Prussian court and contributed to already strong anti-French feelings that were building in Berlin and Potsdam. Finally, as the French army marched toward Austerlitz in fall 1805, Frederick William, reluctantly, signed the Treaty of Potsdam with Alexander of Russia, which committed him to declare war on France if Napoleon would not negotiate a pro-Allied settlement. Napoleon had no proof of this anti-French agreement, but he was well informed of Prussia's intentions. Only the defeat of the Allied army at Austerlitz prevented the Prussian king from declaring war on France.

The Confederation of the Rhine, created in July 1806, was a further source of friction between France and Prussia.[1] Napoleon's total victory over Austria and Russia and his belief that Prussia would not dare engage him in war in the near future led him to form a confederation of German states under the "protection" (that is, domination) of France. Napoleon suggested Prussia might form a confederation of northern German states, but Frederick William was alarmed at French interests in southern and central Germany.

Following the battle of Austerlitz on 5 December 1805, the Prussian king, in a weak position, signed the Convention of Vienna, the Treaty of Schönbrunn (later modified in Paris in February 1806), which made Prussia a French ally. Frederick William was also assured of his possession of Hanover. But then, following the death of William Pitt in January 1806, Napoleon opened negotiations with the new British prime minister, Charles James Fox, and in a failed attempt to end the war with the island kingdom, Napoleon offered to return Hanover to King George III. When the English gleefully informed Frederick William of this duplicity, anti-French feelings ran high at the Prussian court.[2] The "war party"—centered about Queen Louise, the king's younger advisors, and the army, displeased by years of idleness—demanded war with France. The king as usual was reluctant, but with the assurance of support from Russia, he ordered a full mobilization of the army on 9 August 1806.

Napoleon wanted peace on the continent in the summer of 1806. He wrote his minister of foreign affairs, Charles-Maurice Talleyrand, on 12 September: "It is not in my interest to trouble the peace of the continent. Austria is not in a position to attempt anything. Russia and Prussia are kept apart by every kind of rivalry and dislike [that is, Poland]. . . . I do not think that they [the Russians] will again run the risk of sending one hundred thousand men into Germany." Napoleon wanted time to put his affairs in order both at home and in central Europe. A financial crisis had developed during his absence on campaign in fall and winter 1805–1806. He needed time to put the government back on a sound economic footing; affairs in Germany and Italy still needed his serious attention; and he continued to treat Prussia as a third-rate nation. He did not believe Frederick William would be foolish enough to enter into war with France in light of Napoleon's victories of 1805: "The idea that Prussia would take me single-handed is too absurd to merit discussion." Nevertheless, war did come in the fall of 1806.[3]

Vandamme spent the months of August and September 1806 with his family at Cassel. However, as war clouds gathered over Germany, he became restless. He wrote the minister of war on 27 September and requested permission to return to southern Germany and resume command of his division in Soult's corps. Berthier replied that, with hostilities about to begin, Napoleon had given General Leval permanent command of the Second Division of the Fourth Corps. Vandamme was instructed to go to Mayence, a major army depot in western Germany, to await further orders. So Vandamme sat idly on the Rhine while Marshal Davout and Napoleon destroyed the Prussian army at Auerstädt and Jena on 14 October 1806. The battles were decisive; the Prussian army was shattered. The pursuit that followed the battles has become legendary. As for Vandamme, it was not until 20 October that he was given command of General Jean-Pierre Malher's division in Marshal Ney's Sixth Corps.[4]

Ney's Sixth Corps arrived at the battle of Jena in time to assist in the rout of a portion of the Prussians and to take part in the pursuit that followed.⁵ Vandamme assumed his new command in the last week of October as the Grande Armée advanced toward the Elbe River. Napoleon was determined to reach Berlin as quickly as possible, and to this end the main body of the army bypassed the major fortified cities and drove deep into Prussia and Saxony. But this left cities like Magdeburg in his rear. To cope with this problem, the emperor was forced to assign troops to blockade such strong points. Ney was ordered to Magdeburg, and he gave Vandamme command of the siege of the city. As the completely disorganized Prussian army fled to the north, many stragglers took refuge behind the walls of Magdeburg.

The garrison plus the refugees from Jena and Auerstadt numbered some twenty-three thousand men, but the newcomers' shattered morale spread defeatism within the city walls. Neither soldiers nor civilians had any stomach for a prolonged siege they deemed useless. They all believed the city would have to surrender, as there was no Prussian army to confront the French. Vandamme began the siege on 25 October. He immediately put into place the artillery at his disposal, which included heavy guns brought in from nearby captured cities. Marshal Ney did not wish to spend time besieging the city, so it was decided to intimidate the civilian and military population into surrendering—by artillery fire. To this end, the guns opened fire on 28 October. The governor opened talks with General Vandamme the following day, but Vandamme rejected the terms put forward by the Prussians. The shelling continued, while Vandamme opened trenches and moved his guns closer to the city walls. The Prussian garrison did not show much enthusiasm in its defense. When the French artillery began to ignite fires in the city, the governor, who viewed continued resistance as simply the destruction of the city, again opened talks. This time he was ready to accept the terms laid down by Vandamme, and on 11 December the garrison marched out of the city and surrendered to the general, as his division proudly looked on.⁶

The siege and surrender of Magdeburg was not a great accomplishment militarily. The Prussians realized they had lost the war at Jena and Auerstädt on 14 October, and they surrendered the fortified city long before it was militarily necessary to do so. It is true the city would eventually have been forced to open its gates to the French, but it is also unlikely that Vandamme could have taken Magdeburg by assault given its fine fortifications and large garrison. Nevertheless,

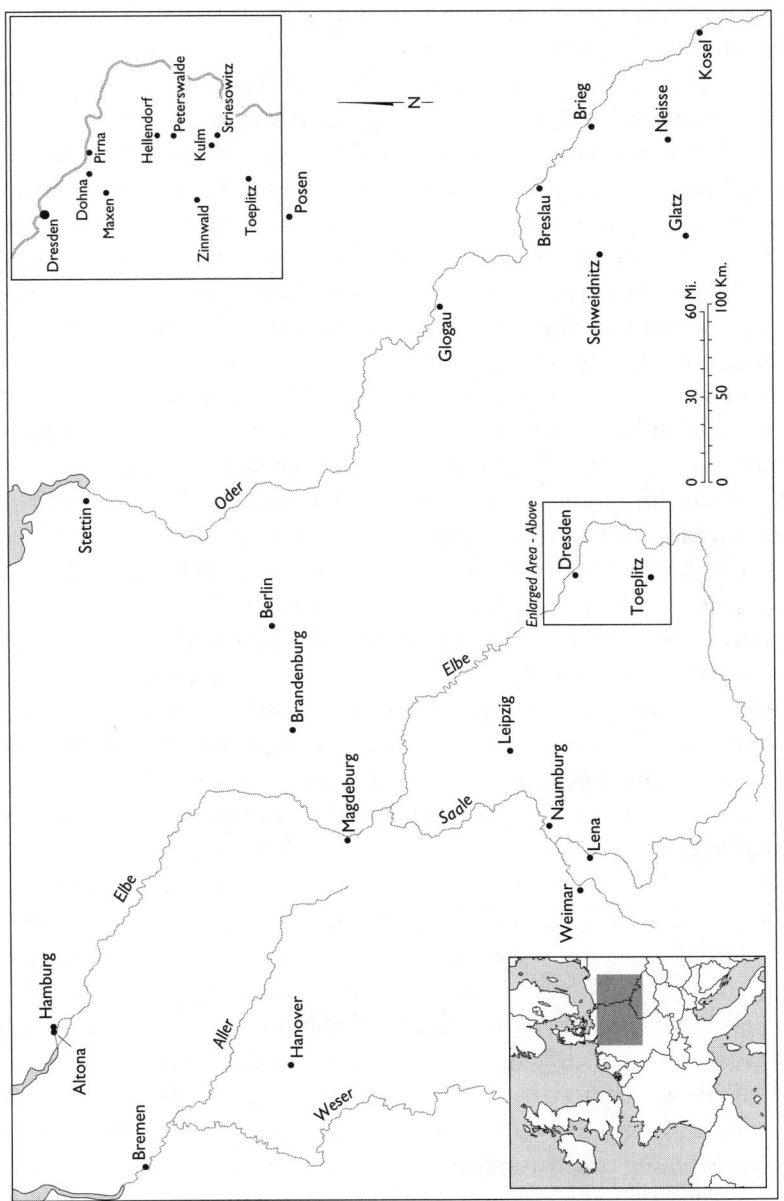

The Silesia campaign of 1806–1807 and the campaign of 1813

Napoleon praised Vandamme and Ney for capturing twenty-three thousand prisoners, more than two hundred cannon, and large quantities of food and munitions.

While Vandamme besieged Magdeburg, the Grande Armée advanced into northern Prussia, Berlin, and on to the Oder River. By the end of October, Davout's Third Corps had reached the Oder at Frankfort and Lannes's Fifth Corps was on the river at Stettin. At the same time, a corps commanded by Prince Jérôme Napoleon (Bonaparte), made up of two Bavarian divisions and one Würtemberg division, advanced through Dresden to reach the Oder at Crossen. The Prussian field army was virtually nonexistent, but isolated strong fortified positions continued to hold out. This was particularly true of the fortified towns and cities in Silesia. Napoleon wanted complete control of the middle and upper Oder. With the Russian army finally beginning to move west to the Vistula River, he did not want to leave Prussian garrisons to his right rear for concern that Russian forces would advance on his southern flank and move on to the Oder with their support. Furthermore, he hoped to draw supplies, mainly food, from Silesia, one of the most prosperous provinces in Prussia. To besiege the cities and fortified positions of the Oder Valley, the emperor sent his brother Prince Jérôme with three German divisions.[7]

Jérôme was the youngest of the five Bonaparte brothers. Born at Ajaccio in 1784, he was a rather spoiled teenager, just fifteen years old when his brother became First Consul of France and moved into the palace of the Tuileries. Napoleon first sent him to sea in the hope that he would make a career in the navy, but after his five years of reasonably good service at sea the domineering older brother decided to make a soldier of him and took him on the Prussian campaign in 1806. Jérôme was named general of division and given command of German troops. Napoleon was negotiating for his marriage with Princess Catherine of Würtemberg and planned to make Jérôme king of a German state that he would create. To this end, the emperor wished his brother to establish a military reputation. The corps Jérôme commanded was referred to as the "Allies" and was given the task of besieging the Prussian-held positions on the middle and upper Oder. Jérôme had neither the training nor the experience for the task assigned him by his brother, but Napoleon was nevertheless determined to make an army commander of the twenty-two-year-old ex-sailor. To guide and assist him—perhaps better to say, educate and train him—the emperor sent General Joseph Hédouville as his chief of staff. Hédouville was a good staff officer but not a very competent corps commander. Napoleon also sent General Vandamme, to conduct the siege warfare in actuality.[8] But the work had already begun before Vandamme arrived on the Oder.

In the first week of November 1806, the First Bavarian Division (7,484 infantry and 894 cavalry, commanded by General Bernhard Deroy) and the Würtemberg division (6,439 infantry and 1,313 cavalry, commanded by General Reinhart Seckendorf) moved up the Oder River from Crossen to begin the siege of Glogau, a fortified city that was key to Lower Silesia.[9] Commerce from Middle and Upper Silesia had to pass under its guns, which dominated the river at that point. The garrison of thirty-five hundred men, five hundred cavalry, and two hundred guns was sufficient to provide a reasonable defense.[10] It is true that the garrison was not composed of first-line troops, but the fortifications were excellent and the food supply was adequate. When French corps artillery arrived in the second week of November, Jérôme gave the order to begin firing. But the prince did not have heavy siege guns, so although he caused damage in the city, he could not force General Reinhart, who commanded Glogau, to surrender. Siege guns were requested, and on 14 November they began the journey by boat up the Oder.

By mid-November Napoleon was pressing his brother to capture Glogau, and Jérôme wished to add to his reputation by taking the city with an all-out assault. With the aid of his generals, he made plans for attack on the night of 16–17 November. On the eve of the attack, General Deroy, whose Bavarian division was selected to make the assault, informed Jérôme he could not count on his troops to carry out the operation assigned them successfully. They were not seasoned veterans like the men of the Grande Armée. They were capable of conducting a siege, he explained, and even of engaging in a defensive action, but they were not prepared to undertake an assault against a fortress as strong as Glogau when there had been no breach made in the walls. Jérôme was forced to call off the attack in disgust and to wait for the arrival of heavy siege guns. Despite Jérôme's complaint to his brother and his regret that he did not command French troops, Napoleon supported General Deroy: "His Majesty," Berthier wrote

Jérôme, "finds that observations made to you by General Deroy are correct. One does not make an assault on a city when no breach has been made. . . . His Majesty thinks that those who were advocating such an attack were very much mistaken, because one would uselessly lose a great number of men."[11]

As the Grande Armée moved east, the Russian army was moving west. Napoleon was preparing to meet the enemy and give battle. He called forward his corps and advanced toward the Vistula River. Jérôme was ordered from Glogau to Kalisch with his two Bavarian divisions, leaving only General Seckendorf's Würtemberg division to continue the siege. The prince left Glogau on 24 November and arrived with his two divisions at Kalisch on the 27th.[12] Napoleon then became concerned about operations in Silesia and instructed Chief of Staff Berthier to order General Vandamme to Silesia. At this time Vandamme was marching east with Ney's corps. He was ordered to turn command of his division over to his senior general of brigade, and to proceed with his aides-de-camp to Glogau, where he would assume command of Seckendorf's Würtemberg division and the siege of Glogau.[13]

The operations at Glogau had been more of a blockade than a siege, as Jérôme had no siege equipment and little hope of taking the city by force. On 28 November, the very evening Vandamme arrived, six boats loaded with siege equipment also arrived.[14] By 6:00 A.M. on 1 December, the guns were in position and began to shell the city with heavy mortars. The governor knew almost from the beginning of the siege that his position was hopeless unless the Russian army arrived to drive off the Allied corps. When it became clear such help would not arrive, the sixty-eight-year-old General Reinhardt informed Prince Jérôme that he knew he would have to surrender the city in the end, but that honor required him to hold out a reasonable length of time.[15] With the arrival of the siege guns, Vandamme wrote the governor: "I am informing you that if there is a long siege, I will reduce the city to ashes. Your position is hopeless, and you will be responsible for all the destruction that takes place. Thus, before I use all of the means at my disposal, I offer you the opportunity to give up the city."[16] To show the damage he was now able to inflict upon the city, Vandamme ordered the guns to begin firing. The damage they did the morning of 1 December persuaded Reinhardt that honor had been satisfied, and he opened talks with Vandamme at 9:00 A.M.

Vandamme refused the conditions that Reinhardt demanded, and the shelling was resumed after a lull of several hours of negotiations. By 9:00 P.M. the weary governor of the burning city accepted the terms laid down by Vandamme. The terms were the same as those that had been accepted by the city of Magdeburg a month earlier.[17] Vandamme had been before Glogau only three days, yet he had the honor of accepting the surrender of the city, taking 3,500 prisoners of war, 200 cannons, 400,000 units of powder, 3,000 muskets, 1,500,000 musket balls, and a considerable amount of biscuits and grain.[18] The Prussian officers were allowed to return home upon giving their word of honor they would not take up arms against France unless they were exchanged for French prisoners.[19]

While Napoleon was pleased with the surrender of Glogau, he had hoped Jérôme would have the honor of capturing the city. Needless to say, Jérôme was also rightfully disappointed; after all, he had conducted the siege for several weeks while Vandamme had been in command for only a few days. In the Thirty-eighth Bulletin of the Grande Armée, on 5 December 1806, Napoleon wrote: "Prince Jérôme, commander of the Allied Army, after strengthening the blockade of Glogau and putting the batteries about the place, took the Bavarian divisions of Wrede and Deroy to Kalisz [sic] . . . and left General Vandamme and the Würtemberg corps to continue the siege of Glogau. . . . After several hours of bombardment [on 1 December] the place surrendered and the capitulation was signed."[20] In this manner he gave credit to both Jérôme and Vandamme for the capture of Glogau.

Vandamme was immediately ordered to take the Würtemberg division up the Oder River to besiege the fortified city of Breslau.[21] He also received a flattering letter from Berthier in which the chief of staff informed him Napoleon was quite pleased with the surrender of Glogau and fully approved of the terms of the capitulation.[22] Leaving on 4 December, he marched south along the left bank of the river and arrived at Lissa, some four miles north of Breslau, on 6 December, where he established his headquarters. On 7 December he conducted a reconnaissance of the city to seek out any weak point for a future assault. He found the fortifications of the capital of Silesia well laid out and in good repair. He would also learn that the garrison was six thousand men strong and supported by ample artillery, adequate food and military supplies, and a large supportive population.[23] Vandamme's division, supported by cavalry, was inadequate to establish a creditable siege; he would have to blockade the city and wait for reinforcements and siege artillary.[24]

Despite his lack of big guns and his modest numbers, Vandamme wasted no time. On the night of 7–8 December his men began to dig trenches, and work was started on a bridge across the Oder, some two miles downstream from the city, to facilitate communications with the right bank. On 8 December, Prince Jérôme arrived to take command of the overall operation. The following day General Wrede's Second Bavarian Division arrived, commanded by General Minucci in Wrede's absence, followed a week later by General Deroy's First Bavarian Division. General Thile, the governor of Breslau, burned some of the suburbs to facilitate the defense of the city.[25] Thile was determined to hold out until a relief army could raise the siege. He had entered Breslau with Frederick the Great in December 1757, when Prussia took the city and all of Silesia from Austria; he had no intention of giving it up without a prolonged defense. On 16 December a small Prussian force made a sortie with the intention of silencing Vandamme's artillery, which was steadily increasing in numbers and size. They were driven back into the city without achieving their goal. The following day, two more heavy (twenty-four-pound) siege guns reached Breslau and were immediately put into action.[26]

By 17 December, Napoleon again believed the Russian army would stand and give battle. Jérôme desired very much to play an active role in such a battle, and he wished to join the Grande Armée.[27] Napoleon summoned him to Warsaw, telling him to leave Vandamme in command upon his departure.[28] Jérôme left Breslau on 20 December, but he took it upon himself not to follow his brother's instructions. Instead, he left his chief of staff General Hédouville at Lissa in overall control of the army, while he appointed Vandamme in command of the siege of Breslau only on the left bank of the Oder, and General Deroy in command of operations on the right bank. He did not want to give command of the Allied Army in Silesia over to Vandamme; he wanted to remain in command, with Hédouville acting on his behalf during his absence.[29]

Vandamme was insulted. He treated Deroy as if under his orders and tended to ignore Hédouville, at headquarters several miles north of the city. Jérôme's division of command might have been a serious problem if Vandamme had not assumed control. It did, quite naturally, lead to confrontation between Hédouville and Jérôme on one side and the rebellious general on the other. Fortunately, before Prince Jérôme's return to Breslau, Vandamme had secured the surrender of the city.[30] It might furthermore be noted that General Minucci, when writing to Vandamme, addressed him as Commandant du Siège de Bresslau.[31]

The intermittent shelling of Breslau on the night of 17–18 December had caused great destruction in the city and started numerous fires. At about the same time, Vandamme evacuated some of the suburbs on the right bank of the Oder to prevent spies from reporting to Thile on the activities of the besieging army.[32] By 22 December Vandamme was ready for a major assault. There would be a false attack by General Deroy on one side of the city, and the real attack by Vandamme on the other side. As a part of the preparations, generals Louis-Pierre Montbrun's cavalry and Minucci's infantry were ordered south in the direction of Ohlan and Brieg to watch for any Prussian relief army that might attack the besieging Allied troops from behind.[33] Rumors were reaching Breslau that the Prussian governor of Silesia, Prince Anholt-Pless, had raised an army of fourteen or sixteen thousand men and intended to lift the siege of Breslau. After heavy shelling on 22 December, Deroy carried out the diversion, followed by Vandamme's attack with the Würtemberg division. But the operation was not successful.[34]

Then on 24 December, Vandamme received a letter from General Montbrun informing him that Anholt-Pless had indeed assembled fourteen thousand men from the various garrisons of Upper Silesia, and it was the Prussian's intention to march on Breslau.[35] General Montbrun's cavalry was first to engage about four thousand to five thousand Prussians at Strehlen. With the arrival of portions of General Minucci's division, the enemy was driven back south to Brieg.[36] The Bavarians fought well that day; the Prussians, once they realized they could not break through to Breslau, began to give ground. The men that Prince Anholt-Pless commanded were not first-line troops. About half of his command was composed of garrison troops from the various fortified towns of the upper Oder who had never been in serious combat. The other half were citizen soldiers who had been under arms for only a month or six weeks. The Bavarians might not have been the veterans of the Grande Armée, but they were superior to the men they faced that day. The Prussians were able to defend a city from behind sturdy walls but did not hold up well in the open field.[37]

On Christmas Day 1806, sixteen heavy guns arrived at Breslau from Glogau and were immediately put into position. Vandamme then called upon the governor to surrender, but Thile refused.[38] The shelling was resumed with the addition of the newly arrived siege guns causing fires in various quarters of the city. The governor then asked to open talks for the surrender of Breslau.[39] Vandamme sent his chief of staff, Adjutant General Duveyrier, into Breslau to negotiate. During the negotiations, however, the governor received news that Prince Anholt-Pless was preparing a second attempt to raise the siege; and he abruptly ended the talks. Vandamme did not hide his anger when he wrote Berthier on 27 December. He wrote General Montbrun that he now must take the most terrible measures against Breslau, which meant heavy shelling with the newly arrived heavy siege guns.[40]

It was at this critical period of the siege of Breslau that the friction between Vandamme and Hédouville became critical. Vandamme had been ignoring the chief of staff and was giving orders to General Deroy as if he was directly under his command. On 24 December, Hédouville wrote to Vandamme:

> I assure you, dear general, that I see nothing disagreeable in your position, and that I wish, for your glory, that with the troops at your disposal on the left bank [of the Oder] you will be able to defeat the enemy's plans [to relieve Breslau] successfully. In addition, if this threat is truly creditable, I would deem it a pleasure to serve under your orders at the head of one of [General] Lefebvre brigades. I will not have any further reproach of you, and I have no fear of blame for myself, because duty and circumstances have always dictated my actions without any self-interest or pride.[41]

Hédouville did indeed find himself in a difficult and unpleasant position. Vandamme was a seasoned general of division, who, the chief of staff knew, was the most capable commander in Silesia. At the same time Hédouville was responsible to Prince Jérôme, who did not want Vandamme in command of the Allied Army. He found himself between the prince, who was in Poland, and the general, who was with the siege army, while he was some miles from the action at army headquarters. It must also be pointed out that Vandamme did not make Hédouville's life any easier. He ignored orders from headquarters and did not keep the chief of staff informed of the army operations at Breslau or of the activities of Prince Anholt-Pless further south. Vandamme surely knew it was not Hédouville but Jérôme who had created the awkward system of command. He could not take his anger out on the emperor's brother, but he could be defiant in his relationship with the hardworking capable chief of staff. It was certainly fortunate Vandamme did not know that in fact Napoleon had instructed Jérôme to leave him in command. Jérôme was kept abreast of the problems of command, and on 29 December he wrote to Vandamme and made it clear to him the chain of command:

> General, I have received your letter of the 25th [December]. I saw with pleasure the affair of Strehlen; I will include it in my report to the emperor. . . .
> I did not know when I left that my absence would be more than a few days. That is why I left my chief of staff to transmit my orders as if I was present. His Majesty had not judged it proper that generals Hédouville, Deroy and Minucci should be under your orders during my absence. You will believe me, General, that no one appreciates better than myself your talent, your zeal, and your activeness.[42]

Following his setback at Strehlen, Prince Anholt-Pless had regrouped his forces and again marched north to relieve Breslau. General Montbrun, whose cavalry and supporting infantry was keeping watch on the Prussians, informed Vandamme of Anholt-Pless's movements, and the general ordered Minucci's division south to engage the enemy. But Anholt-Pless sent only a small force of two thousand men and some cavalry to engage Montbrun and Minucci. The Prussians were easily driven back, as they had no intention of a serious battle.[43] At the same time, Anholt-Pless marched out of Brieg by secondary roads to avoid detection; and in a forced march the night of 29–30 arrived at the village of Hube where he attacked General Seckendorf's outposts at dawn. Vandamme was taken by surprise. He believed that Minucci and Montbrun would have engaged the enemy some miles to the south of Breslau. Now he found a Prussian army of about ten thousand men overrunning his pickets.

Reacting to the danger of an enemy army on one side and six thousand enemy troops in Breslau on the other, Vandamme was at his best. He ordered the siege guns to continue shelling the city, while his Würtemberg division turned its back on the siege to meet the threat from the south. With the support of field guns withdrawn from the siege, the Würtemberg battalions stood their ground. The Prussians failed to advance and soon began to give ground. Surprisingly, Thile did not attempt a sortie to aid Anholt-Pless, an action that would have put Vandamme in great danger. During the heavy fighting Vandamme sent an aide-de-camp to Minucci and Montbrun to maneuver in such a manner as to cut off the enemy's retreat. What began as an organized withdrawal on the part of the Prussians turned into a full retreat; and when Montbrun and Minucci moved to block the way, the enemy disintegrated and fled in small groups to take shelter in the fortresses and fortified towns of Upper Silesia. The Prussians suffered about five hundred men killed and eight hundred taken prisoner. They lost all their artillery and their baggage train.[44]

In his Order of the Day dated 1 January 1807, Vandamme declared: "The general of division declares his dissatisfaction with the officers who commanded the Bavarian infantry outposts on 29 and 30 December at Klettendorf, Guicchivitz, and Klein-Schottgau. Their lack of vigilance greatly compromised the security of the siege. But the valor and good conduct of those troops employed under the orders of Adjutant Commander Duveyrier repulsed the enemy attacks at Kleinburg and Kristern and saved the situation."[45] Vandamme then went on to praise the officers and men who had fought well on 30 December.

The shelling of Breslau continued for another three days. Finally, on 3 January 1807, the governor was ready to surrender the city. He had received confirmation of the destruction of Anholt-Pless's Prussian army and realized there was no hope the siege could be raised. In the negotiations of 3 January, Thile accepted the same conditions as those imposed upon Magdeburg and Glogau.[46] Vandamme had conducted the siege during its critical days and fought off two enemy attempts to relieve the city, but he received notice from Hédouville that he was forbidden to enter Breslau and that, with the Würtemberg division he should go immediately to Schweidnitz.[47] Relations between Vandamme and Prince Jérôme had deteriorated during the latter's absence. In the days after Christmas, Jérôme had learned that Vandamme sent his chief of staff, Duveyrier, to negotiate the surrender of Breslau. He was very dissatisfied with the general, who was after all still under his command. On 1 January, before the surrender of the city, he wrote Vandamme a scathing letter:

> General, I have just received your letter of 26 December. I am angry that you have made a new summation to the governor [of Breslau]. You know well that this was not my intention. I did not leave you with any doubts when I left that I was not giving up my command of the Allied army, and that I left my chief of staff to transmit my orders. . . . You had no right to send Adjutant Commander Duveyrier to treat with the governor, because it was in my name that the capitulation would be made, and it was my chief of staff who should have been in charge. M. Duveyrier is not the chief of staff of the Allied army, and the place [Breslau] should surrender to the [Allied] army, not to one division as was the case at Glogau.
>
> I hope, general, that I will not have to point this out to you again.

The prince then went on to soften the harshness of his letter by assuring Vandamme he fully appreciated his talents, ability, and actions in conducting the siege, and that he would inform the emperor of the general's accomplishment. He would also seek promotions for members of Vandamme's staff, including Duveyrier. Jérôme concluded: "The instructions of His Majesty are that you will go, without entering the city of Breslau, with the Würtemberg division and the artillery necessary to lay siege of Schweidnitz."[48]

Despite Jérôme's reassurance of his confidence in Vandamme, the general was displeased to be rebuked by the young prince. But his choices were few. He could give up his command as a means of protest, but he was not sure Napoleon would continue to employ him with the Grande Armée. The campaign had not ended, and he wanted very much to continue with a command. His other alternative was to make peace with his commanding officer. To this end Vandamme wrote to Jérôme on 5 January giving a formal detailed report of events, beginning with 23 December, as a means of justifying his actions. He concluded: "I dare to hope, Monseigneur, that you will deem to find in all of my conduct the greatest zeal for my duty and my complete devotion to you and my sovereign."[49]

Although Vandamme realized that he would have to bend to the will of Prince Jérôme, he was determined to be present when the Prussian garrison of Breslau marched out and put down its arms. To this end he wrote Hédouville on 4 January:

> I will not be able to go to Schweidnitz until the Würtemberg division has received its reinforcements and is organized in such a manner that it can present itself before that fortress without compromising the honor of the Allied Army or of myself. Furthermore, I cannot advance upon that fortress until I have sufficient artillery to undertake such an important siege. I am also not sure my health will allow me to execute His Imperial Highness's orders if I do not have a number of days' rest. I cannot hide from you that the letters I received from the prince and from you have caused me great surprise and pain.... If I have not always been satisfied with the orders or the desires of the prince, I regret it very much; but, nevertheless, I have made every effort to be victorious in the difficult situation I have found myself in. Finally, if the prince is dissatisfied with me, there are, without doubt, many other generals who would be more successful than myself, but none who would make a greater effort to merit his confidence and his approval. I hope, Monsieur Général, that His Highness's return will bring more favorable times than did his absence.[50]

While defiant in his refusal to leave Breslau, Vandamme expressed loyalty and devotion to Prince Jérôme. There is no question that he was willing take orders from his commander; one would have to question his "devotion" to the prince, however. The following day, the proud, strong-willed general put his feelings in writing to Jérôme: "I cannot conceal from Your Highness that, in the fifteen years I have been a general, I have never received from any of my commanders the reproaches you have addressed to me, after the efforts I have made under difficult conditions. . . . The order of Your Highness to march at once to Schweidnitz and forbidding me to enter the city [Breslau] I find very humiliating. I must inform you that my health has suffered greatly since your departure. . . . Finally, it appears to me from your last letter that I have lost your confidence."[51] In fact, Jérôme did not wish to lose Vandamme's services; he simply wanted the rebellious general to be submissive and obey his orders.

The capitulation was signed by both Vandamme and Hédouville, as well as Thile, and approved by Jérôme. The prince returned to Breslau by 7 January in time to preside over the Prussian garrison's formal surrender. While Vandamme was not allowed to enter the city, he did stand by the prince and watch the ceremony. Just before Jérôme arrived at Breslau, Napoleon had renamed the Allied Army the "Ninth Corps of the Grande Armée" (5 January 1807). This was an honor for both his brother and the German troops he commanded, in recognition of the capture of Glogau and Breslau, and it pleased everyone involved.[52]

The following day Vandamme marched off with the Würtemberg division to Schweidnitz, which he reached on 10 January. The city was the strongest fortified position in Silesia and alleged to be impregnable. It was situated on the Weistritz, a small stream that flowed from the mountains to the northeast into the Oder about thirty-five miles from Breslau. The old town was surrounded completely by two walls with towers and fortified gates. There were also small forts at strategic points about the town. To capture the forts, breach the walls, and take the town by assault would be a most difficult and costly operation and could not be carried out without siege guns and reinforcements. Jérôme described it in his *Mémoires*: "situated between the foot of the mountains [comté de Glatz], between Breslau and Brieg, not far from Neiss, Glatz, and Silberberg, made it [Schweidnitz] a strategic point of the greatest importance, and the effect on morale of its capture would be great."[53]

Upon his arrival, Vandamme immediately wrote the prince that he had only five thousand men "which is insufficient to blockade a garrison of fifty-five hundred enemy. . . . I need at least a full strength regiment of Bavarians and a squadron of cavalry." But Jérôme replied that the emperor had ordered him to lay siege to three fortified positions at the same time (Kosel, Brieg, and Schweidnitz), and he could not send Vandamme any additional troops. The general would have to do his best to blockade Schweidnitz until conditions changed. Vandamme's command was actually 5,295 infantry, 1,055 cavalry, and 304 artillerymen.[54] Prince Jérôme had also ordered Vandamme to call upon the commander of Schweidnitz to surrender as soon as he had invested the city. As the city had not yet been attacked, only blockaded, no one was surprised when an indignant Lieutenant Colonel Haxo, in command of the garrison, answered no. Haxo believed that Prince Anholt-Pless would come to his aid with greater success than his attempts to relieve Breslau.[55]

Vandamme established his headquarters at the small village of Wurben on 11 January; and with only one battery of light artillery, two regiments of General Montbrun's cavalry, and his Würtemberg division of infantry, he simply established a blockade of the town. Without siege equipment and without additional troops, he could not undertake a serious siege. For the next three weeks there was a standoff. Deserters from the garrison trickled out daily and were interrogated and sent to Breslau.[56] There were several sorties—neither serious nor successful—on the part of the Prussians.[57] Vandamme tried with partial success to deprive the town of water. The principal source of water for Schweidnitz came from the Weistritz through a water pipeline. Vandamme cut the pipe, but the town continued to get enough water from the stream to sustain itself. The general then tried to divert the stream around the town but again was only partially successful. Although there was a scarcity of water, the garrison was able to survive.[58] On 24 January a serious sortie took place. Five hundred infantry and ninety cavalry overran a French advanced post but were then driven back into the city.[59] The opening of trenches was delayed because the ground was frozen and the French had a shortage of trenching tools.[60] Then on 28 January, Prince Jérôme wrote Vandamme to convey information to him that he had gained from deserters and spies. Prince Anholt-Pless was said to have assembled some eight thousand men in an entrenched position near Warthe, and he was preparing to march to the relief of Schweidnitz. Vandamme was ordered to send out strong reconnaissance to verify these rumors and to take the appropriate action to meet such a threat. At the same time Jérôme moved two battalions of infantry closer to Schweidnitz to support Vandamme if attacked and ordered General Minucci, with four thousand men, to move onto Anholt-Pless's rear if he attacked Vandamme.[61] The crisis did not materialize, however. Anholt-Pless remained in his strong defensive position; and it was in Poland that the campaign took an ugly turn for the French.

When the Russian army showed no desire to make a stand against the victorious Grande Armée in December 1806, Napoleon ordered his men into winter quarters in Poland with the intention of resupplying, reorganizing, and resting his weary troops. He would reevaluate the situation in the spring. He preferred to negotiate a favorable peace with Alexander I as he was not prepared to invade Russia. Nor did he want to undertake such a difficult—if not impossible—campaign in the middle of winter. The army corps had scarcely settled down in the harsh forbidding Polish countryside when the Russians launched a major offensive in mid-January. The French were caught by surprise, as they thought the Russians were also suspending hostilities for the winter, and Marshal Ney's Sixth Corps fell back in confusion. The emperor quickly gained control of the situation, stopped the enemy advance, and moved onto the offensive. At Eylau, on 8 February 1807, the Russian army under the command of General Levin August Bennigsen turned and fought. The Russian line gave ground but did not break. Under cover of darkness, Bennigsen retreated to the east. Losses on both sides were enormous. Napoleon had no desire to continue the struggle; his army was not prepared for a winter campaign. The Russian army was now also ready for a lull in the fighting. Thus both armies went into winter quarters to prepare for the next phase of the war.

Back in Silesia, there was no lull in operations. Vandamme was ordered to take Schweidnitz by 20 February. Napoleon had told Jérôme, and the prince, through his chief of staff, informed Vandamme of the emperor's wishes. When Jérôme thought that Anholt-Pless was preparing to march on Schweidnitz, he ordered the various detached units of the Würtemberg division to rejoin Vandamme at the siege, which increased his numbers by fifteen hundred men in early February.[62] By the end of January, siege guns and equipment had begun to arrive at Schweidnitz, but not without delays. Vandamme had sent horses to Breslau to be used to bring the needed artillery and supporting material to Schweidnitz. However, with the renewal of hostilities in northern Poland, Napoleon wrote his brother on 28 January that it was urgent he send food and munitions immediately to

Warsaw for the Grande Armée.⁶³ In order to comply with this demand, Jérôme had to use the horses Vandamme had sent to carry supplies to Warsaw. Despite these problems, the artillery began to arrive the evening of 30 January and was immediately put into place before the city. The following day trenches were opened using both troops and pressed civilian workers. By 3 February all the siege artillery and munitions had arrived and were in position. At noon on the same day Vandamme began to shell the town.⁶⁴

The shelling of Schweidnitz halted at darkness but resumed the next morning. Fires broke out in the town and caused extensive damage because of the shortage of water. Desertions increased dramatically, for panic was beginning to take hold among the civilian population. Prince Jérôme arrived at the siege and took personal command of the operations. On the night of 5–6 February, 1,943 projectiles were fired into the town and at the ramparts. So violent was the shelling that the Prussian soldiers abandoned the section of the ramparts opposite the French batteries. When, on the morning of 6 February, Jérôme was informed by deserters that the town was in total disorder, he silenced the guns and sent his aide-de-camp Prince Hohenzollern to demand that the governor surrender Schweidnitz. Following brief negotiations it was agreed that, if no relief arrived by 16 February, the garrison would march out and surrender. Jérôme was willing to grant this time concession because he knew full well that no help was on its way. The conditions of the capitulation were the same as those that had been granted to Breslau.⁶⁵

Before the ink was even dry, Jérôme had departed for Breslau leaving Vandamme once again in command. The general had conducted the entire operation at Schweidnitz, Jérôme's presence for a few days was little more than ceremonial, but the prince had returned by 16 February to preside over the formal surrender.⁶⁶ It was still Napoleon's intention that his brother should be credited with the capture of all the fortified cities and towns in Silesia while commanding German troops, so as to create a military reputation for his youngest brother. He believed this would make Jérôme more acceptable to the German people of the new kingdom that the emperor intended to create in the near future for him. Thus, in the Sixtieth Bulletin of the Grande Armée dated 17 February, which announced the capitulation of Schweidnitz, Napoleon mentioned General

Lefebvre by name for a minor engagement in which he commanded, and one Colonel Backer who commanded a regiment in that affair; but the name of Vandamme, who commanded the successful siege of Schweidnitz, does not appear.[67]

The Prussian garrison that filed out and surrendered on 16 February was only thirty-two hundred men strong. It had been reduced by more than two thousand troops, of whom most had deserted during the blockade and the shelling. Large quantities of food and military supplies, including some 247 pieces of artillery, also came into the hands of the French. It has been estimated that the garrison could have held out for more than three months rather than a mere four weeks.[68] An Austrian garrison had held out for ninety-four days against the army of Frederick the Great in 1762. With the French occupation of Schweidnitz, the Würtemberg division received new orders. On the very day of the formal surrender, Vandamme received orders to march his division to Neiss. He was to go by way of Friedland and Glatz to lay siege to Neiss. At about this same time, Prince Anholt-Pless was replaced by the count of Goerzten. The count had been given a substantial amount of English money while in Vienna and was able to raise an army of ten thousand men at Glatz. The French knew he was preparing some sort of an offensive operation, but they did not know in which direction.

Napoleon had fought a bloody battle with the Russians at Eylau, and he proclaimed a great victory, although it was not a decisive affair. The Russian army had retreated in good order to the east, so the battle was in fact a draw. There was no vigorous pursuit because the French army had been badly mauled and was exhausted. As the Russians retreated to the east, Napoleon began to search desperately for troops to replace his losses. Jérôme was ordered to send at once ten thousand of his best men, about one third of the Ninth Corps, to Poland. To fulfill this quota, on 18 February, Vandamme was ordered to send four battalions (twenty-five hundred men) of his Würtemberg division as soon as possible to Breslau.[69] The loss of one-third of his army corps caused Jérôme to reorganize his forces and scale back siege operations at Kosel, which General Deroy had been conducting since mid-January, and at Neiss, but the remnants of the Würtemberg division still left Schweidnitz on 18 February to undertake yet another siege.[70]

In accordance with his orders Vandamme marched first to Glatz by way of Friedland and Waldenburg. As instructed, he called upon Glatz to surrender on 20 February; and when the governor refused, as was expected, Vandamme marched on to Neiss through Frankenstein and Munsterberg. He reached Neiss on 23 February 1807; and although he had only half the Würtemberg division (about three thousand men), he began to lay siege to a fortified town garrisoned by some five thousand men.[71] Neiss was a strongly fortified town with two walls and a deep moat filled with water. Heavy rains had swollen the Neiss River, which separated the town on the left bank from Friederichstadt, a heavily fortified position on the right bank. The river's high waters had flooded large areas on the right bank, rendering operations most difficult. Nevertheless, Vandamme set about the task of laying siege to the town. To prevent the Prussians from marching from Glatz to the relief of Neiss, Jérôme put first General Montbrunt and later Lefebvre in command of a corps of cavalry and light infantry with orders to contain the Prussians in the vicinity of Glatz. Siege equipment was on its way from Schweidnitz to Neiss. Until it arrived, Vandamme sealed the town, prepared positions for the guns, and opened trenches.[72] The situation changed drastically in early March.

Following the occupation of Schweidnitz, there was some confusion and misinterpretation in the correspondence between Napoleon and his brother. Jérôme first believed he was to concentrate on making Glogau the only stronghold in Silesia, and to scale back his efforts to capture Kosel and Neiss. The fortifications of the captured towns and cities of Silesia were to be dismantled, and only Glogau fortified and strongly manned with adequate supplies to withstand a prolonged siege. It seemed Napoleon was saying he wanted Jérôme to hold his present position in Silesia so as to send supplies from the Oder Valley to the army in Poland.[73] To this end the siege of Neiss, which Vandamme had just begun, and the siege of Kosel by General Deroy's Bavarian division were put on hold. At the same time, the siege equipment from Schweidnitz intended for Vandamme was ordered to Breslau, Jérôme's headquarters, and then on north to Glogau. Thus Jérôme ordered both Vandamme and Deroy to stop siege operations and simply blockade Neiss and Kosel.

Then Jérôme received clarification of Napoleon's intentions, which included an active siege of both towns. During most of March, however, Vandamme just sat before Neiss and did very little.⁷⁴ On 7 March 1807 Vandamme wrote Jérôme that the artillery from Schweidnitz was on its way to Glogau, along with four battalions of the Würtemberg division, and that he had posted a cavalry regiment to keep watch in the direction of Glatz in case the Prussians attempted to raise the blockade of Neiss or march on Breslau. He also mentioned that there were minor skirmishes but nothing serious.⁷⁵ Vandamme was not fully apprised of the emperor's intentions and had requested additional troops and siege equipment. "I know the position you are in," Hédouville wrote him on 11 March, "but at this time I can not send the reinforcements you have requested.... The wisest measure you can take is to hold your position.... I know you need money, a siege requires money. I will write to Berthier about this matter." It was not until late in the third week of March that Jérôme, with new instructions, asked Vandamme if, with the troops he commanded, he could renew the siege of Neiss. If the answer was yes, then he would send a small park of artillery.⁷⁶

When Vandamme answered in the affirmative, the siege began again in earnest. The troops under his command comprised 2,219 infantry, 748 cavalry, and 150 artillerymen, to a total of 3,117 men.⁷⁷ During the lull in activity in the first half of March, Vandamme had engaged in negotiations with the Prussians with respect to the exchange of prisoners; but Jérôme, reprimanded in the past by his brother for undertaking such negotiations without first obtaining permission, wrote Vandamme to end all such talks of exchange until receiving approval from Berthier. Napoleon rejected the exchange of prisoners at that time but said that, if soldiers had already been exchanged, Vandamme was to keep them.⁷⁸

It was not until 13 April that siege equipment began to arrive at Neiss. The guns' positions had already been prepared, and they were quickly ready for action. The newly arrived artillery, twenty heavy (twelve- and twenty-four-pounders) and twenty-five mortars, opened fire on the town on 16 April, causing much damage and many fires. The shelling continued intermittently during the following days and nights, but despite substantial damage to the town, there were no signs the garrison would surrender. Jérôme came to visit the siege on 20 April and approved of Vandamme's conduct with respect to the operation.⁷⁹ There were sorties from time to time, but none of a serious nature. The most intense combat took place at the end of the month. On 30 April Vandamme attacked and captured several fortified positions just outside the walls of Neiss. Jérôme wrote his brother in glowing terms: "The general officer [Vandamme], despite great difficulties and a shortage of troops at his disposal, put himself at the head of his troops and captured the works with a bayonet charge the night of 30 April. All enemy troops were killed or captured. This included three officers, one hundred prisoners of war, and five pieces of artillery." Vandamme may well have caused Jérôme problems in the course of the Silesian campaign, but the prince admired his bravery and respected his talents as a field commander. In his *Mémoires* he wrote: "Vandamme, who was neither easygoing, easily persuaded, nor disciplined, was extremely brave in the presence of danger, [but] he was not obedient."[80]

Despite minor achievements, it was not until the end of May that the governor of Neiss was ready to negotiate the surrender of the town and its garrison.[81] On 29 May a French bomb from a mortar caused a large magazine in town to explode, resulting in serious damage. Two-thirds of Neiss had already been destroyed by shells and fire, and it was now clear that the Prussian governor of Silesia could not relieve the besieged garrison. The town could have held out for weeks, but surrender was certain in the end, and continued resistance seemed pointless. The governor accepted Vandamme's offer to negotiate an end to the struggle. The capitulation was signed on 30 May, with the stipulation that the garrison would march out and surrender on 16 June if the siege was not lifted by that date. The terms were similar to those given at Breslau and Schweidnitz. The officers were allowed to keep their swords and were sent home upon their word that they would not take up arms against France until they had been exchanged. Thus, the longest siege of the Silesian campaign came to an end. On 16 June, fifty-five hundred Prussians marched out of Neiss before Prince Jérôme and General Vandamme and laid down their arms. Three hundred twenty-eight pieces of artillery with three hundred thousand pounds of powder also came into the hands of the French.[82] This time Prince Jérôme gave full credit for the capitulation to General Vandamme. The prince, having had very little to do with the operations, wrote to Napoleon: "I take this occasion to inform Your Majesty that it is impossible for anyone to have shown more zeal, ardor, and devotion to service, than did General Vandamme. I am extremely satisfied with this general officer."[83]

While Vandamme was before Neiss, the Grande Armée was relatively inactive in the north. Except for Marshal François-Joseph Lefebvre's Tenth Corps besieging Danzig (which capitulated on 27 May 1807), the rest of the army was in winter quarters.[84] Then, on 5 June, with the improvement of the weather and the road conditions, General Levin A. T. Bennigsen began the second phase of the Polish campaign. This time the French were prepared and reacted quickly and effectively. The Russian attack was repelled, and Napoleon gathered his forces to renew the struggle with an intensity that would bring the war to a successful conclusion. The decisive battle came at Friedland on 14 June 1807. The victory was complete. The shattered Russian army retreated east across the Niemen River and back into Russia. Tsar Alexander now knew that Prussia and Poland were lost. With his army unable to stop the tide flowing from the west, he decided to make peace before the victorious French army invaded the Russian motherland. Napoleon, although victorious, did not want to cross the Niemen and undertake a campaign on hostile Russian soil. What he wanted was a favorable understanding with Alexander, and the cooperation of Russia in his war with England. Thus it was that both monarchs agreed to peace talks at Tilsit.

The news of the victory at Friedland was received with great joy at Neiss, but it did not mean the end of the war, only that it was being won on the battlefield. In Upper Silesia, Count Goerzten still held Glatz and Silberberg, where General Lefebvre had failed to contain the small Prussian army. The surrender of Neiss enabled Jérôme to send Vandamme's Würtemberg division to Glatz where, with the addition of Lefebvre's troops already in the vicinity, a proper siege could be carried out.[85] Goerzten was reported to have twelve thousand men.[86] Although siege work had begun, the heavy guns had not arrived, and the strength of the garrison put any immediate assault on Glatz out of the question. While Vandamme was still conducting the siege on 13 July, news arrived that the treaties of Tilsit had been signed—first with Russia on 7 July and then with Prussia on the 9th. Thus the war with both nations had ended. Vandamme, who desired very much to return to France, was ordered to turn over command of the Würtemberg division to General Camrer and proceed immediately to corps headquarters at

Breslau.[87] The campaign concluded, he was given a two months' leave to return to Cassel and rest.

In the spring of 1807 there had occurred an unpleasant and embarrassing episode, generally referred to as the Strasbourg Affair. Vandamme's unjust reputation as a plunderer provided his enemy (and he had many) with an easy target. On 4 March 1807 he had dispatched from Neiss a wagon filled with personal belongings to Cassel. Philippe-Pierre Bertin was charged to escort the wagon. Its departure was made known to the minister of war who was informed that it contained valuable loot that Vandamme had pillaged from Silesia. Acting on this information, Berthier issued orders to the commanding general at Strasbourg to take possession of the wagon and make a detailed inventory of its contents. The eighteen boxes and chests were impounded at Strasbourg, opened, and a full description of their contents was made and forwarded to the minister.[88] At the same time Philippe Bertin was placed under arrest. However, the contents of the wagon proved to be personal items that Vandamme had purchased or had been given to him: bolts of fine cloth, table cloths and napkins, drapery material, several hunting guns, two pistols, and so on. When the minister realized that the items being sent to France were indeed Vandamme's personal belongings, such as a general of division might reasonably acquire, he ordered the boxes and chests to be sealed and sent on to Cassel. The completely innocent Bertin was set free. Vandamme was furious when he heard of the affair and wrote the minister two letters, on 28 April and 21 May, in which he barely concealed his anger. In his first letter he blamed General Legrand for denouncing him and described Legrand as "a bad officer, without service or talents."[89]

The affair was an embarrassment to Berthier. That the denunciation was taken seriously is a clear indication of Vandamme's reputation in the army, however. It also might explain why Vandamme was not allowed to enter Breslau after he had forced its capitulation. Nevertheless, the Strasbourg Affair very probably helped Vandamme's reputation more than harmed it as the accusations made against him proved totally unfounded.[90]

8

THE AUSTRIAN CAMPAIGN, 1809

During the year 1808 Emperor Napoleon was preoccupied with the affairs of the Iberian Peninsula. With the decrees of Milan (November 1806) and Berlin (November 1807) he had closed to British shipping the ports of Europe over which he had control, and he had secured the cooperation of Tsar Alexander at Tilsit in 1807. He pressured Spain into closing its ports to British ships; but Portugal, traditionally a friend of the British, was not cooperating. In 1807 Napoleon sent General Andoche Junot at the head of an army to bring that small country into line; but although Junot was able to occupy Lisbon, a British army landed north of the city, and the French were obliged to evacuate the whole country. After this failure, Napoleon put his brother Joseph on the throne of Spain in the summer of 1808. When the Spanish rebelled, a French army was sent to secure Joseph's throne. The Spanish resistance, supported by a British and Portuguese army, led Napoleon to increase the size of his forces in the Peninsula and even to go south of the Pyrenees himself late in 1808. Thus, at the beginning of 1809, with the emperor and the bulk of the Grande Armée occupied in Spain, central Europe appeared vulnerable. The French army was spread from the borders of Russia to the Straits of Gibraltar, and Austria decided to act.

Napoleon had defeated Austria three times; and the humiliated Austrians were eager to regain respect, influence in central Europe, and territory they had lost. After the disastrous campaign of 1805, the Austrian army had undertaken meaningful reforms, and Archduke Charles was given extensive—but not complete—control of the army. He was not the one who decided to go to war with France in the spring of 1809. It was the Aulic Council, the court, that decided on another war with France. Charles, although he supported a war, argued that he needed more time; the reforms were not complete and the army was not ready. However, the war party in Vienna pointed out to Emperor Francis I that it was necessary to attack France as soon as possible. The Austrian army had been reorganized and reequipped, and sufficient reforms had been introduced over the past three and a half years since Austerlitz. Furthermore, in the winter of 1808–1809, Napoleon and the bulk of the Grande Armée were busy, occupied down in Spain. Austria would have numerical superiority in central Europe and would be facing a relatively weak French army, stretched thin across the continent. A large portion of this army was made up of recent recruits who had no combat experience. It was supported by troops of the South German Confederation, who were considered less enthusiastic about war and less effective in combat than the French. The time to strike was before Napoleon could return from Spain with his army. The French would have to fight a two-front war with her best troops a thousand miles from the proposed theater of operations in Germany. It was these arguments that won out over Charles, and early in 1809 Austria decided on war.

The Austrian plan for the 1809 campaign was to fight in Italy and Germany at the same time. The Austrian army had been reorganized into nine army corps. The Army of Italy, consisting of two corps (76,000 men), was placed south of the Alps under the command of Archduke John. The remaining seven corps (209,000 men) were given to Archduke Charles north of the mountains. Charles originally planned to mass the bulk of his force north of the Danube River and strike west into central Germany, while two corps would advance into Bavaria south of the Danube. He hoped to catch the French by surprise and penetrate deep into Germany before his enemy could react. This would discourage and demoralize Napoleon's German allies; and after fighting a victorious battle against a smaller French army, he would be on the Rhine before the French emperor could react in any serious way.

Napoleon, for his part, did not want a war in central Europe in the spring of 1809. He had committed more than two hundred thousand of his best troops to Spain in order to secure the Spanish throne for his older brother, Joseph, and he wanted to finish the work south of the Pyrenees before again engaging Austria in Germany. Furthermore, his troops in Germany were questionable in the event of war with Austria. Only Marshal Davout's Third Corps was made up of first-line troops. Almost two-thirds of the French soldiers available were untried young recruits. It is true that the southern German states could provide perhaps one hundred thousand men, but there would be little enthusiasm for a war between France and Austria. Napoleon had reduced Prussia to a second-rate power after the 1806–1807 campaigns and did not think Frederick William III would risk another war with France so soon after the humiliation of Jena and Auerstädt. Tsar Alexander had become an "ally" at Tilsit and had reaffirmed his friendship in October 1808 at Erfurt, just before Napoleon went to Spain. But whereas Alexander promised to support France if attacked by Austria, he also let it be known in Vienna that he really had no intention of becoming involved in a war between France and Austria. As for Austria, Napoleon realized the country was not satisfied with the status quo in Europe; but he hoped (perhaps even believed) that it would not make war against him without the support of a major land army such as Russia or Prussia. England was still at war with France, of course, and would provide money to support the Austrian army, but the British ally could expect little in the way of military support on the continent. There might be a landing in Holland or Belgium to provide a distraction; but Napoleon had just driven the English expeditionary force out of the Iberian Peninsula in January 1809, and Austria could not expect any serious assistance from France's perpetual enemy.

Had Archduke Charles been ready to move in the first weeks of 1809, he would have caught the French unprepared and the army on a peacetime footing. But the Austrian attack did not come until the second week of April. Napoleon returned to Paris on 23 January and immediately took up the Austrian problem. He was receiving reports from Marshal Davout in Warsaw that Austria was moving troops into Bohemia in ever-increasing numbers.[1] He quickly realized he had a new war to fight in Germany. The only question was when? He could not be fully ready until late April at the earliest. He would have to create a new Grande Armée in Germany. In a broad sense, he planned to repeat the campaign of 1805, in that he would amass his army and threaten to advance down the Danube toward Vienna, while his stepson, Eugène Beauharnais, held Italy. As French and Allied forces concentrated on both sides of the Danube, the Austrians decided to change their plans. Instead of attacking into central Germany from Bohemia, they decided to shift the bulk of the army south of the Danube and attack through Bavaria. At the same time two army corps—General Heinrich Bellegard with forty-eight thousand men and General John Charles Kollowart with twenty thousand men—would advance out of Bohemia onto the upper Danube. By the beginning of April, Charles had two corps in Bohemia and four corps (those of Archduke Louis, Prince Franz Rosenbert, General Johann von Hiller, and Prince Friedrich Franz Hohenzollern) plus cavalry and artillery in Austria along the Inn River, which formed the border with Bavaria. His brother Archduke John commanded another seventy-six thousand men facing Eugène in Italy.

In early March 1809, Napoleon's forces in central Europe were scattered from southern Germany into Poland. He did not want to give the Austrians any pretext to begin the war before late April. It must be Austria who attacked him, so he could have a defensive war to rally the army and the home front to a "just" cause. Nevertheless, as quietly as possible he was preparing for a new campaign. Early in April he created the Grand Army of Germany that, when all was collected, numbered some 172,000 men. Marshal Davout commanded the Third Corps, with 62,000 men forming the core of the new army. Marshal Masséna was at the head of the Fourth Corps, some 38,000 strong. Marshal Lefebvre's Seventh Corps with 27,000 men, General Oudinot's Second Corps with 21,000 men, Vandamme's Würtemberg division (soon renamed the Eighth Corps) with 11,800 men, plus some smaller units, made up the field army Napoleon would command when hostilities began in the second week of April.[2]

Still hoping to have the element of surprise on his side, Archduke Charles launched his army across the Inn River into Bavaria on 10 April 1809. At the same time, the two Austrian corps in Bohemia marched into eastern Germany north of the Danube. Napoleon had remained in Paris for political reasons while naming Marshal Berthier commander in chief of the Army of Germany, which was not yet ready to enter upon a new campaign. The emperor was working feverishly on its organization, equipment, personnel, and supplies. His delicate position in Europe at that time, particularly in the lesser German states, made it essential that he not be seen as the one who provoked the war. It must appear to the German princes and people that it was Austria who started the war. Therefore, Napoleon remained in Paris until the Austrians began hostilities. The Army of Germany headquarters had been established in France at Strasbourg. Berthier was an excellent administrator, who as chief of staff had served Napoleon well in Italy, Egypt, Germany, and Austria in 1805, and again in Germany and Poland in 1806–1807; but he was not a competent army commander. He was accustomed to working directly under Napoleon's eyes at headquarters. He did not give orders; he transmitted orders. He did not make decisions; he passed on Napoleon's decisions. Now, in spring 1809, he found himself in Strasbourg trying to manipulate an army spread all over Germany and Poland in accordance with instructions coming from Paris. It should not be any surprise at all that the French nearly suffered a catastrophe on the Danube in April 1809.

As rumors of war in central Europe became more creditable in the late winter of 1809, Vandamme became less content with his comfortable command of the camp at Boulogne in northern France. He had received proof of the emperor's satisfaction with his conduct in the 1807 Silesian campaign, when Napoleon named him count of Unsebourg on 19 March 1808 (confirmed by patent dated 1 April 1809). It was not the marshal's baton that Vandamme desired, but it was a sign of favor on the part of the emperor. Then in mid-March he received the letter he had been looking for, from Marshal Berthier.[3] Napoleon was pleased with his handling of the Würtemberg division in the Silesian campaign, and despite Vandamme's strong desire to command French troops, he was ordered to Stuttgart to command Germans again. Vandamme turned over his command at Boulogne to his senior general of brigade and left for Paris. Departing the capital on 26 March, he arrived in Stuttgart on the morning of 31 March.[4] The following day, 1 April, the minister of foreign affairs presented Vandamme to Frederick I, king of Würtemberg. The general was given command of the Würtemberg division with exaggerated pronouncements of the king's affection, and his pleasure that Vandamme was to command his troops. But Vandamme, not pleased with his new command and feeling he should have the title of marshal of the empire, wrote Berthier: "I am taking command of troops who are under the command of a [Würtemberg] field marshal whose rank is superior to mine. I will refrain from all observations in that regard."[5] On 3 April Vandamme had an amiable dinner with the king and left the next morning, in accordance with Berthier's instructions, to proceed to Heidenheim where the Würtemberg division was stationed. On 5 April he began the inspection of his new command and found it in good condition. He reported to the major general that its strength was at 12,290 men.[6] He spent the next days inspecting and becoming acquainted with his new command.

Vandamme was still at Heidenheim when the Austrian army began the campaign. On 11 April, the following day, Marshal Lefebvre informed him that Archduke Charles had crossed the Inn River at Braunau and was marching on Munich. Vandamme was informed that his Würtemberg division was to be known as the Eighth Corps of the Army of Germany; and that he would be under the command of Marshal Augereau, supposed to be on his way to join the army. In accordance with orders from Strasbourg dated 11 April, Vandamme marched his corps southeast to Dillingen and then on toward Donauwörth where he arrived on the 13 April and secured first the bridge across the Danube and then the bridge over the Lech River at Rain.[7]

Napoleon left Paris on 13 April and arrived at Donauwörth, the new army headquarters, on the 17th. He found the army in a most dangerous position. The various orders for the concentration of the army should the Austrians attack before or after 15 April had been both delayed and misinterpreted by the major general.[8] The result was that Davout, who had begun to fall back toward Ingolstadt, was ordered back to Ratisbon just as the Austrian army advanced over the Isar River and threatened to reach the Danube upstream (west) from Ratisbon. This would have cut Davout off from the rest of the army; and with Kollowart's corps advancing on Ratisbon from the north and supported by Bellegarde's First Austrian Corps, the Third Corps was in danger of being destroyed before help could arrive.

Napoleon perceived the danger at once. He ordered Lefebvre (Seventh Corps) to intercept and slow the Austrian advance while

Davout, leaving a regiment to hold the bridge at Ratisbon, marched west along the south bank of the Danube to unite with the rest of the army.[9] At noon the next day, Oudinot (commanding the Second Corps) and Masséna (commanding the Fourth Corps) were ordered to march by way of Pfaffenhofen toward Landshut, to threaten the enemy's left flank and rear. Napoleon hoped that these two corps would draw troops away from Charles's advance on the Danube, which was threatening the Third Corps's very existence.[10]

On 18 April, Vandamme was moved forward to Ingolstadt.[11] The next day he was ordered to march to the support of Lefebvre. Marshal Augereau had still not joined the army in Germany (in fact he never did arrive), and Vandamme was placed temporarily under the orders of Lefebvre.[12] In fact Napoleon, at Vohburg on 20 April, was directing every aspect of the campaign in person, and on that day, at 6:00 A.M., he ordered Vandamme from Neustadt, where the Eighth Corps had spent the night, to Siegenburg.[13]

When Archduke Charles learned that Napoleon had reached the army and taken command of the campaign, he slowed his advance and became overly cautious. He decided to move against the isolated Third Corps at Ratisbon, but Davout fought his way past Hohenzollern's Third Corps and linked up with Lefebvre and the rest of the army. Napoleon then reorganized, taking two of Davout's divisions (Morand and Gudin) and two cavalry divisions (St. Sulpice and Nansouty) to form a new provisional corps for Marshal Jean Lannes, who had just arrived from Spain. When Davout reported that Hohenzollern was retiring to the south, Napoleon believed that the whole Austrian army had begun to retreat. On 20 April, he moved from defense to offense. He issued orders for a full pursuit. His center (Lannes, Lefebvre, and Vandamme) was ordered forward; his right (Masséna and Oudinot) was to march on Landshut to cut off the Austrian retreat over the Isar River. Davout, with about half his corps, was to hold his position east of the Saal River near Teugen. The Austrian left (Archduke Louis and General Hiller) gave way before the French offense. Hiller fell back all the way to Landshut in order to protect the road to Vienna; Louis retreated east across the Laber River.

On 21 April Napoleon believed he had won the battle and ordered the pursuit to move forward with haste. He wrote Davout at 5:00 A.M.: "Yesterday and the day before are another Jena."[14] Vandamme was ordered to march at once with Lannes and General Karl Philipp von Wrede's Bavarian division of Lefebvre's corps at Landshut.[15] But the Austrians were not in full retreat. Colonel Coutard, whom Davout had left at Ratisbon with only one regiment, was forced to surrender the town and its bridge intact when he was attacked from the north by Kollowart and from the south by Lichtenstein. This opened up a new line of retreat for Charles over the Danube into Bohemia in the event of defeat. As Napoleon believed that the Austrians were retreating, he ordered Davout to attack what he thought to be only the rear guard of General Rosenberg's Fourth Austrian Corps. The fighting was heavy, and even though the French were outnumbered, Davout held his position until darkness put an end to the struggle. The marshal informed Napoleon that he was facing the greater part of the Austrian army, and the enemy showed no signs of retreating. At last realizing that the bulk of the Austrian army was indeed not retreating but instead converging on Davout, the emperor ordered all available troops toward the town of Eckmühl.

Vandamme, who had reached Essenbach the night of 21 April, received his orders early on the 22nd to march north immediately on the road to Ratisbon. He was to be at Ergoldsbach by 9:00 A.M. and to continue by forced marches on northward.[16] Lannes was given overall command of four divisions (Morand, Gudin, Wrede, and Vandamme) with orders to reach Eckmühl by noon if at all possible.[17]

Early on 22 April the emperor himself left Landshut to reach the battlefield. Davout, Lefebvre, and Montbrun's cavalry division faced Archduke Charles in command of four corps (Lichtenstein, Hohenzollern, Rosenberg, and Kollowart) plus cavalry. Charles knew he had superior forces. He planned to turn Davout's left flank with Kollowart's Second Corps and destroy the French before help could arrive. But the turning operation was slow in developing, and Montbrun was able to hold Kollowart at bay until almost noon. Rosenberg (Fourth Corps) and Hohenzollern (Third Corps) were to attack Davout and Lefebvre in the front in order to hold them in position, but they decided to wait until Kollowart's movement onto the flank of the French Third Corps was well under way. Thus Davout and Lefebvre were relatively inactive during much of the morning. By the time the Austrians were pressing hard, and Davout was in a difficult position, Vandamme had arrived south of Eckmühl.

He began to threaten the Austrian left. He had led his corps on the march north from Essenbach and fought his way through Ergoldsbach to reach Lindach shortly after noon. He immediately attacked the town of Eckmühl and, with Gudin's division on his right, captured it and threatened to turn the Austrian left flank. In the attack on the town, Vandamme was wounded while leading his troops in person. His wound caused him much suffering but did not force him to give up his command and leave the battle.[18] As other units of the French army arrived from the south and west to join in the battle, Davout and Lefebvre went on the offensive. With his left flank being overrun, the archduke decided to retreat to the north across the Danube. Under cover of darkness, the Austrian army withdrew to Ratisbon where the bridge was still intact.

The corps of Vandamme, Lannes, Masséna, and Oudinot were exhausted from two days of marching and fighting with almost no rest. Napoleon decided they were in no condition to undertake a vigorous pursuit. Davout and Lefebvre had borne the brunt of the fight and could not be asked to press the enemy in the darkness. Therefore, Napoleon had to be content with ordering only a cavalry pursuit, which spent the night in confusing engagements with the Austrian cavalry while Charles's infantry reached Ratisbon. The Austrian army had suffered heavy casualties (thirty thousand men) and was in a state of disarray. It had been defeated, but by no means destroyed. It fought a successful rearguard operation as it filed over the Danube to safety and then on into Bohemia with the French never far behind. Napoleon did not try to follow the archduke in force. He sent Davout's Third Corp and Murat with cavalry to escort the Austrians out of Germany. At the same time he turned his back on Ratisbon and made for Vienna. There was only a feeble Austrian force, Hiller's Sixth Corps plus reserves, between himself and the Austrian capital.

On 23 April Vandamme had marched with the rest of the army on Ratisbon. His Würtembergers did not take part in the capture of the city, and the next day he was ordered back to Eckmühl.[19] The battle won and the immediate danger past, Vandamme, with the approval of Berthier, reorganized the top-level officers of his Eighth Corps—to the displeasure of several of its generals. When he took command of the division in early April, the appointment of general officers had not been his affair; the king had chosen the generals, and not always for their military abilities. Having observed these officers for almost a month, and in particular during the week of combat, Vandamme deemed it necessary to make some changes. The Würtemberg officers were not entirely pleased to be serving under a French general, who was not even a marshal of the empire; and they were inclined to exercise excessive independence. Furthermore, they felt free to communicate directly with their king and to receive orders from him. On 24 April a frustrated Vandamme gave General Neubronn command of the two brigades of infantry of the line, General Hugel command of the brigade of light infantry directly under Vandamme's orders, General Wollowart command of the cavalry, and Colonel Schnadow command of the artillery. In a letter to Neubronn he wrote:

> Immediately order the chief of staff, Kerner, and the officers under his command, and all the commissariat to come to me to receive my orders. Inform everyone, including you, general, that I am the commander in chief and that I want every person to do his duty; that I am not unjust to anyone, but that I will use whatever authority is necessary to fulfill the intentions of His Majesty the emperor and the interests of your king. . . . I have concealed the faults of individuals and of corps. I have highly proclaimed the deeds of those who have conducted themselves well and in a brave manner. No one can tread on my reputation. It has been established over many years. All the orders I have given you this morning, whether they are to your liking or not, must be carried out at once.[20]

The Würtemberg officers immediately reported Vandamme's heavy handedness to the king. Frederick, who had written amiably to the general just a few days earlier, now expressed his dissatisfaction. On May 5 he wrote Vandamme:

> I have received your letter of 24 April and I cannot conceal from you that it seemed strange, at the same moment that the emperor,[21] all the army's generals, and you yourself have given the highest praise to my army corps, and to the generals who commanded it, that you have found in its organiza-

tion reason to show your dissatisfaction and are obliged to make changes. I accept your right to control military operations, but not the internal command [of the Würtemberg division] in the manner that I make reports and transmit my orders. Nothing can be changed, and Lieutenant General Neubronn, for his part, has received my orders and is solely responsible to me.[22]

General Vandamme, with the backing from army headquarters, ignored the king and tightened his control over the generals of the Eighth Corps.

As the army moved east toward Vienna in April 1809, Vandamme marched to Muhldorf (25th), Landshut (26th), and along the left bank of the Inn River to arrive at Braunau on the 30th.[23] On 1 May Vandamme was ordered at once to Altheim. On 4 May, Napoleon wrote Berthier telling him to send the Eighth Corps on to Linz, where Vandamme was to repair the bridge over the Danube that had been destroyed by the retreating Austrians and take command of the city and province. On the same day Davout was also ordered to Linz, and Vandamme was placed under the orders of the marshal for as long as he remained in the region. The first meeting of these two strong-willed soldiers did not go well.[24]

Vandamme arrived at Linz on 5 May, put troops across the Danube, and gained control of the north approach to the bridge. Still suffering from the wound he received at Eckmühl, he took to his bed. On the morning of 6 May, Marshal Davout arrived in Linz. According to common military courtesy when a superior officer arrives at his command, Vandamme was expected to call upon the marshal in person. But he was suffering from his wound, and he sent his first aide-de-camp, Commander Vincent, in his place. The Iron Marshal was not a man with whom one could trifle. He received Vincent rudely, denounced Vandamme for his lack of respect and courtesy, and abruptly sent the aide back to his master. Vandamme knew Davout's reputation very well and had no intention of engaging in a confrontation he knew he would lose. He immediately wrote to the marshal: "Informed yesterday of the arrival of Your Excellency in this city, I was attentive to give the necessary orders due to a person of your rank. I was not prepared myself to present my homage." He then described the difficulties he had encountered in securing the left bank of the Danube and went on:

> I returned to my quarters overcome with fatigue and suffering greatly from my wound. I developed a fever and much perspiration that night and I still have these troubles today. I was not able to come to you. I sent you my first aide-de-camp to give you an account of those things that would be of interest to you and to receive your orders. I learned with surprise and great pain the manner in which this officer was received. I did not know Monsieur Marshal that you judge generals like myself with such disfavor.... I command here in the name of and by the orders of the emperor. If I had been able to get up from my bed, I would have come to see Your Highness.[25]

Vandamme then wrote to Napoleon a full account of his encounter with Davout. The emperor, who knew of Vandamme's stormy relations with his superiors in the past as well as how sharp Davout could be with anyone who crossed him, nevertheless thought it necessary in a letter to the marshal to add: "You will treat General Vandamme well and don't fight with him." In the long run, relations were not too difficult between these two brave and headstrong soldiers: Vandamme was careful not to give Davout cause for friction, and Davout treated Vandamme with the respect due to a general of division who commanded an army corps. Indeed, in his almost daily reports to the emperor, Davout spoke well of the work Vandamme was doing at Linz.[26]

On 9 May 1809 Napoleon wrote Davout that Archduke Charles was moving south from Bohemia, but that he was not sure at what point the Austrians would approach the Danube. The emperor thought he would most likely come to Vienna, but that he might send a strong force to Linz or Krems to threaten the French line of communication. When this information was passed on to Vandamme, he sent a strong reconnaissance force along the right bank of the river to try and make contact with the enemy. When Napoleon learned of this, he wrote Davout, who was at Saint-Poelten at the time but still in overall command of the Lenz–Saint-Poelten region: "My cousin, General Vandamme's movement on Krems makes no common sense.... If an enemy party presented itself, that column would be cut off. That manner of waging war is mad. You will recommend to General Vandamme that he continue with his instructions to guard Linz.... If he wishes to push [a reconnaissance] as far as Budweis, that would be acceptable."[27]

With Davout's Third Corps moving ever closer to Vienna, preparing for the army to cross the Danube to meet the archduke, Napoleon ordered the Ninth Corps (the Saxon corps) commanded by Marshal Bernadotte to go east to Linz in support of Vandamme. On the day the Ninth Corps arrived at Linz (16 April), Vandamme was ordered to send a strong formation to Steyer.[28] Before he could carry out this order, however, he received information that several Austrian columns, more than twenty thousand men under the command of General Wollowart, were converging on the Danube at Linz. Once across the river he engaged two of Wollowart's columns on the morning of 17 April. Bernadotte came to his support as a third column approached the battlefield. Vandamme's Würtembergers drove the Austrians from the battlefield, while Bernadotte's Saxons forced the third column to retreat down the Danube toward Vienna. Vandamme took fifteen hundred prisoners, including thirty officers, and six pieces of artillery. In his account of the battle to Napoleon, Marshal Bernadotte had high praise for Vandamme. "General Vandamme's conduct," he wrote the day after the fighting, "was above all the praise I could make to Your Majesty who himself knows the intrepidity and all the distinguished qualities that characterize this excellent general."[29]

Following the defeat of the Austrians on the left bank of the Danube, Vandamme made preparations to carry out his instructions to take a strong force south to Steyer. The Austrian Army of Italy, commanded by Archduke John, had been outflanked by Napoleon's march to Vienna. John was obliged to fall back toward the middle Danube at Pressburg. In doing so, he threatened the exposed right flank of the French army. Napoleon was not sure just what action John might take, so Vandamme's Eighth Corps was given the task of protecting his line of communication and supply that ran along the right bank of the Danube. Steyer became an important outpost for the French, in case the Austrian Army of Italy turned north and marched on the Danube between Linz and Krems.

On 20 May, Vandamme began his movement south from Linz, but that same morning he received new orders from Berthier. He was to move his headquarters from Linz to Enns and send only two thousand men to Steyer, while holding the rest of his corps ready to meet the enemy on whichever side of the Danube it posed a threat.[30] Bernadotte, who greatly appreciated Vandamme's military talents, was sorry to have him removed from his command. On 21 May, upon learning that the general was leaving Linz, he wrote the emperor: "It is with regret that I see myself separated from General Vandamme. The talents and energy of this general officer have supported me very well.... He is the only general officer who is capable of replacing me in case I should be killed or wounded."[31] Considering the lofty opinion Marshal Bernadotte held of himself, this was indeed a high compliment paid to Vandamme.

On 21 May, Napoleon crossed the Danube a few miles south of Vienna on a bridge hastily constructed by his engineers. The following day, before his entire army could cross to the left bank, Archduke Charles attacked his position at Essling and Aspern, and the bridge was destroyed. Davout's Third Corps sat idle on the right bank while the outnumbered French fought a desperate battle. Napoleon had to retreat to the safety of the island of Lobau. His army had suffered heavy losses that included the deaths of Marshal Lannes and General Louis-Vincent Saint-Hilaire. This battle was a serious setback for the emperor, who then had to regroup his forces. Reinforcements arrived at Vienna in the form of part of Eugène's Army of Italy. The remaining units of the army followed Archduke John to Pressburg.

On 21 May, the same day that Napoleon was crossing the Danube, Vandamme reported to Bernadotte the position of his troops and the situation in the region about Enns. To the south, in the mountains, there were numerous Austrian patrols, while chaos reigned throughout the province. He would require a substantial force to restore order and maintain control of the region. While the Würtemberg corps began the campaign with a total strength of 12,864 men, on paper, he could count only 9,947 men under arms; and they were spread along the Danube from Linz to St. Polten.[32]

Napoleon was building a stronger bridge below Vienna with piling upstream to protect it from floating objects such as had destroyed his first bridge. He intended to move the bulk of his army onto the island of Lobau, then cross the narrow strip of water that separated it from the left bank and once more engage Archduke Charles. This time he would not be outnumbered, and he would have a secure link to the river's right bank. As Napoleon gathered his army near Vienna, Vandamme was ordered closer to the city. On 24 May, Berthier instructed the general to move his headquarters to St. Polten. Davout would move his Third Corps to Vienna, and Vandamme's Würtembergers would replace it, patrolling the right bank of the Danube from Moelk to Vienna. On the same day he was ordered to move his headquarters, Vandamme sent a party of three hundred men across the Danube to attack an Austrian camp that had been established opposite Moelk. The operation was successful; Major Kechler, who led the raid, took more than eighty prisoners of war and drove the remains of several companies from the area.[33]

Then suddenly, to the surprise of Vandamme and his Würtembergers, an Austrian force of about twelve hundred men crossed the Danube between Krems and Hollenburg on 31 May, posing a serious threat in the rear of the French army. At first it was not clear whether this was simply a raiding party in strength to harass the French, or the advanced guard of a major thrust against the French lines of communication and supply. Vandamme reacted swiftly and energetically. He gathered his forces near Moelk and marched to meet the Austrians. With superior forces he had no serious problems driving them back across the river.[34]

No sooner had he restored control over the right bank of the river than he received instructions from the emperor to fortify several of the great monasteries along the Danube. On 5 June Napoleon told him to fortify and prepare the monastery at Moelk to be used as a hospital. The fortifications were to be such that five or six thousand men could hold out for a long period of time.[35] He was later ordered to do the same with the monastery at Gottweg. The establishment of such strong positions at strategic points along the Danube was undoubtedly sparked by the Austrians crossing of the river near Moelk, and the anticipation of thousands of wounded from a great battle he was planning. Indeed, following the battle of Wagram, on 16 July, Napoleon wrote Berthier: "I am authorizing the seriously wounded [from Wagram] to be sent to the abbeys of Moelk, Goettweig, and Klosterneuburg. . . . Six thousand to be sent to each one."[36]

Napoleon spent the entire month of June preparing to cross the Danube again and destroy the Austrian army camped across the river. For Vandamme it was a month of administrative headaches, disciplinary problems, minor military actions, and so on. He was not in the front line—that is, his army corps was not slated to form part of the French army that would engage the enemy. He would protect the flanks and the rear of the main army and maintain order in the hostile territory occupied by his corps, which eventually would include the city of Vienna. Thus, when eleven of his Würtemberg chasseurs were assassinated in a small town, he received the following instructions from Berthier: "It is necessary, General Vandamme, to take hostages in the village where eleven Würtemberg chasseurs were assassinated and to have an equal number of guilty persons shot. You are also authorized to levy a heavy contribution on the village for the assassination of those eleven chasseurs." On 17 June, Vandamme sent his reply to Berthier: "I am informing you that this morning a council of war of the Würtemberg corps has condemned to death one Leopold Digner, an innkeeper, and Drechsler de Neulemback convicted of having taken part in the massacre of eleven Würtemberg cavalrymen from Wilhousbourg. Furthermore, in conformity with your orders . . . I have imposed a contribution of thirty thousand florins on the village where the soldiers' assassination took place."[37]

The most serious problem Vandamme faced at this time was in controlling the behavior of the officers and men under his command. The irregular supply system led his subordinates to engage in levying unauthorized contributions on towns and villages they occupied. Such practices, condemned by Vandamme but to little avail, were reported to imperial headquarters.[38] Although there were no accusations of wrongdoing on the part of General Vandamme, he was criticized for not being able to control the Würtemberg troops under his command, officers as well as men. The officers extracted contributions from towns and villages to feed and supply their men. Although Vandamme ordered them to stop the practice, he must have sympathized with them at least somewhat because the supply system was so irregular. Napoleon complained that the towns and provinces could not meet his demands because of the illegal contributions being collected by local commanders.

In the early hours of 5 July, Napoleon sent three army corps onto the left bank of the Danube, followed by the rest of the army, and engaged the Austrians at Wagram. In the two-day battle, Archduke Charles was forced to abandon the field and withdraw to the north. The French were too exhausted to mount a serious pursuit. Much to the disappointment of Vandamme, this major Napoleonic victory was accomplished without the aid of his Würtemberg corps. He had to watch the battle from a high point on the other side of the river. But the war still had not ended. The Austrians retreated to the north with the French following close behind. When the leading French corps caught up with Charles at Znaim on 10 July, he asked for an armistice. He realized that Austria had lost the war, and that sooner or later he would have to bring it to an end. On 12 July an armistice was signed and, for the Austrians, the campaign came to an inglorious conclusion. But as it was only a brief halt in hostilities, not a peace treaty, there was the possibility that the fighting could be resumed.

On 10 July Vandamme had been placed under the orders of Prince Eugène, viceroy of Italy. He immediately went to the headquarters of the Army of Italy to receive orders from Eugène and to report the strength and location of his Eighth Corps.[39] On 14 July, Napoleon instructed Eugène to send the Eighth Corps south through Neustadt to the Semring Pass with the intention of marching south to occupy the fortified city of Gratz, some seventy-five miles south of Vienna.[40] Gratz was the key to the control of southern Austria.

When Vandamme reached Kindberg on 16 July 1809, on his march south, he came in contact with Austrian advance posts. The Austrians had received news of the battle of Wagram but had not been informed that an armistice had been signed. Vandamme agreed to a truce while the enemy sought to verify that Gratz was to be turned over to the French.[41] On 17 July he received news from Berthier that Marshal Macdonald had been ordered south to join him and to take command of Gratz. With Macdonald's corps on its way, Vandamme informed the local Austrian commander, General Giulay, that his orders were to march on Gratz and if Giulay did not give way hostilities would begin.[42] The Austrians gave way, and Vandamme continued his march toward Gratz. Reaching the city on the 21st, he named his chief of staff, Colonel Kerner, as commander and settled his troops in the surrounding towns and villages.[43] Macdonald soon arrived and assumed command of the province, and on 23 July Vandamme was ordered to move the Eighth Corps back north to Nesstadt.[44]

The region around Neustadt had already provided food and money for the French army since its arrival in the region in May. When Vandamme complained to headquarters that he could not live off the land and the supply system was totally inadequate, he was given permission to spread his troops over a wide area; but still the Württembergers acquired what they needed with a heavy hand.[45] By the end of August, the major general was receiving complaints from the local Austrian authorities: "I have been informed," he wrote Vandamme, "that in the communes near where the Würtemberg troops are quartered there is frequent misconduct. The military police who were sent to stop the disorder have been badly received by the officers. You will give orders to put an end to reprehensible conduct." Just five days after being reprimanded by Berthier, an angry Vandamme wrote his chief of staff: "I am sending you a report that I received from the commander of the military police regarding the reprehensible conduct of the Würtemberg troops. . . . I order you to take the most severe measures to put an end to these abuses." But the army system was not providing adequate supplies for the troops or the officers, and the abuses continued, although on a lesser scale. Then on 6 September 1809, Vandamme intervened on behalf of the officers in a letter to the major general: "I must inform you that the Würtemberg officers having such a feeble pay, it is impossible for them to live in an honorable way. Therefore, I ask that you supplement their income."[46]

Despite Vandamme's efforts to restore discipline in his German troops, pillage and the illegal levying of contributions continued. On 14 September Berthier wrote of Napoleon's displeasure: "Complaints by the government of Styrie have been reported to the emperor, Monsieur Général Vandamme, concerning the illegal requisitions that have been made by the Württembergers who were quartered in that province. They are certified by the original documents that accompanied the report to His Majesty." There followed three detailed accounts of illegal contributions levied on the towns of Gleisdorff and Feldbach, and the arrondissement of Herberstein. "The emperor,"

Berthier continued, "is very displeased that the Würtemberg officers are acting in this illegal manner. . . . His Majesty orders, as the consequence of these acts, that you punish the culprits and take measures to put an end to these practices. You will inform me, general, of the actions you are going to take to carry out His Majesty's intention."[47]

Despite the court-martial of several officers, Vandamme received only meager support from the Würtembergers and was never able to put a complete halt to the illegal practices.[48] The war was over. His troops wanted to go home, and they continued to treat the Austrian territory in which they were quartered as enemy territory. At the same time as Vandamme tried to maintain discipline, his relationship with the general officers serving under him was strained.

In the middle of October he clashed with Count Wollowart, the ranking Würtemberg general of the Eighth Corps who was second in command. Vandamme had criticized General of Brigade Hugel in the presence of other officers at Mautern. On 19 October General Wollowart wrote the following letter to his commanding officer:

> Monsieur General, as it appears by your letter of the 17th that you will soon leave Germany and that your relations with the Würtemberg army will end, I am taking the liberty to make the observation, M. General, that there is still a general officer to whom you owe amends.
>
> It is M. General de Hugel, whom you grievously offended at Mautern in the presence of officers of your staff . . . and who insists to obtain from you suitable reparation.
>
> As it would be cruel for me that you were to depart without correcting this matter, I am asking you, M. General, to satisfy General Hugel in a public manner.

An angry and insulted Vandamme answered Wollowart the same day:

> I have received this instant your letter dated today and have the honor to reply to you. What were you thinking of, general, when you signed that letter? What do you know of this affair? Is General Hugel ignorant of who I am? What! I grievously offended that major general at Mautern because I reproached him for his negligence, for the bad positioning of his artillery,

for the faulty disposition of his troops, the carelessness he showed by not visiting his lines that day, which enabled the enemy to cross [the river] without being opposed . . . where were General Hugel's cannons? . . . I reprimanded him in severe terms, but not improperly. I sent him orders simply to distance himself from me because he was extremely impertinent. . . . You yourself, general, have been indignant with respect to his conduct and surprised at my indulgence [toward him]. Today you are his advocate and, forgetting the duty of your rank and of mine, you address me a letter that will very much astonish His Majesty the Emperor, to whom I will send your letter. I reproach myself for only one thing; and this is that I have given him a strong reputation greater than his merits, and that I have treated him too well in every respect.

Vandamme did send General Wollowart's letter and his own reply to the major general at headquarters. With the two letters he added a third, to Berthier. This melancholy letter announced new abuses by the Würtemberg troops and decried the fact that his reputation was being destroyed by events he could not control. Contributions were being made in his name that he had not ordered and of which he had no knowledge until well after the fact. He referred to his command of the Würtemberg corps as "a long series of bitter disagreements."[49]

Vandamme remained in command of the Würtemberg corps, however, and General Wollowart was still directly under his orders. Realizing the extent to which he had antagonized his superior, Wollowart quickly penned a letter to Vandamme in an attempt to make amends, explaining that the general had mistakenly interpreted his letter in a negative manner. On 21 October, he wrote: "I am in despair because of the effect that my letter has had upon you which is very much contrary to my intention. I did not act so as to insult you, M. General, I wanted only to call upon your justice and your kindness, to beg you to repair the wrong that you have committed toward General Hugel. It is not the judgments or the reproaches that were offensive, it was the unsuitable words. The choice of other words, an honorable mention in an order of the day, would repair everything."[50] Despite this letter, which certainly was not an apology, relations between these two generals remained tense for the remaining weeks they had to work together. Finally Vandamme was ordered to give up his command of the Würtembergers and return to France.

Vandamme's discouraging letter to the major general and his heated exchanges with General Wollowart can be seen in the context of his disappointment resulting from what he perceived to be a lack of gratitude on the part of Napoleon. Following the battle of Wagram, in which Vandamme had not been given the opportunity to take part, generals Oudinot, Macdonald, and Marmont were named marshals of the empire. Vandamme believed he should also have received the coveted baton, that he was being overlooked, and that he was more deserving than these three men recently named marshal. On 16 October, just three days before receiving General Wollowart's letter, he had written the emperor of his dissatisfaction:

> I will not conceal, Sire, that for some time now I have been distressed. I have kept my sadness to myself so long as the resumption of hostilities was uncertain. But now that Your Majesty has again brought peace to France, I feel I can make known my chagrin. Sire, to remain profoundly forgotten as I am overwhelms me, while I see the entire French army receiving great benefits and favors, and right before my eyes my equals are gratified with rank, dignity [that is, the marshal's baton] and immense fortunes.
>
> What am I now to think, Sire? What will my family think and those who know me? Am I in disgrace or can I still count on the goodness of Your Majesty? Without doubt, if one looks at my conduct, one must believe that I deserve Your Majesty's goodwill rather than the bitterness of disfavor.

He went on to remind the emperor of his service in the fighting at Donauwörth, Abensberg, Ratisbon, and Eckmühl and added that the only reason he had not been at the battle of Wagram was because Napoleon deemed his services more necessary elsewhere. Vandamme concluded by requesting that he be sent home, if he was to remain in disfavor. The war was over. There was no reason for him to remain with the army in disgrace.[51] This letter is one of the clearest examples of Vandamme's frustration at seeing others named marshal of the empire while he was passed over. It was a continuing source of unhappiness for the general, for the rest of his life. As he watched men who had served under his command, junior in rank to that of general of division, men whom he considered inferior to himself in military talent—or, in some cases, perhaps his equal—receive the cherished marshal's baton, Vandamme's frustration and dissatisfaction increased.

The Treaty of Schönbrunn, officially ending the war, was signed on 14 October 1809. Despite Prince Charles-Maurice Talleyrand's urgings for a lenient peace with the Austrians, Napoleon dictated a "French" treaty, and Emperor Francis had no other choice but to sign. Napoleon was displeased with the Austrians for trying to take advantage of his deployments in Spain. After all, this was the fourth time he had fought and defeated Austria; and he was in no mood to be understanding or reasonable. The treaty called for the gradual withdrawal of the French army from occupied Austrian territory. On 15 October Vandamme moved his Würtemberg corps across the Danube to Krems, where it arrived on the 17th, in preparation for its return to Germany. Vandamme, who had been at Vienna for several weeks, left the Austrian capital on 25 October to join his command, which had moved to Linz.[52]

Three days after Vandamme's arrival in Linz on 26 October, Napoleon informed the minister of war, General Henry-Jacques Clarke, that he was ordering Vandamme to Antwerp where he would be given a command in the Army of the North. The emperor added that this was appropriate because Vandamme knew the locality.[53] Nothing could have pleased Vandamme more than being relieved of his command of the Würtemberg corps and sent to northern France. However, he quickly received a letter from Berthier ordering him to remain in command of his corps until properly relieved, which would most likely be about 20 November. All things being in order, Vandamme turned command of the Würtembergers over to his senior general, Wollowart, and on 19 November he left Lintz.[54]

The general went directly to his family at Cassel and then to Paris to receive new orders. The emperor's original intent was for Vandamme to receive a command in Holland under Marshal Oudinot, but Vandamme reminded the minister of war that he had been given a two months' leave to recover his health. Then on 27 January 1810, he was ordered to Berg-op-zoom to command a division in the Lowlands of Belgium. Again he begged out of the command on grounds that the climate in the malaria-infested regions of the lower Scheldt River aggravated his rheumatism, and that he was still on leave.[55] Finally Vandamme was given command of the camp at Boulogne. This pleased Vandamme. He would remain in France and close to Cassel. He quickly made preparations to assume his new post, but the arrival of the new commander in chief quickly became a major embarrassment for all concerned.

On 13 February 1810, the mayor of Boulogne, M. Menneville, received a letter from General Vandamme's aide-de-camp Captain Fournier informing him that the general would arrive in two or three days or so in order to assume his new command; and that M. Menneville should prepare proper living quarters for him. The mayor wrote back at once that there were no suitable lodgings available for the general, but that the house of M. de Chanlaire, where Marshals Soult and Brune had stayed, could in time be made available. The building was at present being used by the city treasurer and his staff. He also mentioned that in the upper city there might be a place that would suit the general. In the meantime, and as he did not know the general's wishes, he would make temporary arrangements for him at the Hôtel de Britannique or some other location.[56] Vandamme arrived in Boulogne on 21 February between seven and eight in the evening. He did not go to the Hôtel de Britannique but to the Hôtel de France, where he stayed until the 22nd. The mayor went to Vandamme's lodgings, but the general would not receive him.

Senator Suzanne was at that time residing at the mayor's home and had been for some six months. On the night of 22 February, he abruptly moved out. The next morning at seven o'clock, six gendarmes arrived and took over Suzanne's apartment in the house. Menneville was not consulted in any way. General Vandamme arrived at eleven the same morning and received the mayor, informing him that he would reside in the quarters evacuated by Suzanne.[57]

In a six-page letter to the minister of war, Menneville detailed the history of Vandamme's arrival in Boulogne and then complained of the manner in which the general treated him in his own house. He had been dishonored and humiliated before the leading citizens of the city and asked that his honor and his home be restored to him. Finally, he concluded by saying that General Vandamme had no respect for civilian government officials and the services they rendered; that he considered military service the only honorable way a man could serve his country. Only soldiers had the general's respect. The minister of the interior informed Napoleon of Menneville's letter and explained the facts as provided by the mayor. Vandamme was given direct orders to move out of Menneville's house, and he was relieved of his command for a brief period.[58]

Now it was Vandamme who was humiliated. And he, in turn, wrote a long letter to the minister of war, dated 21 March, explaining his side of the story:

> I have testified to Your Excellency how much it pained me to receive the order to leave the apartment that I occupied in the house of Mr. Menneville. . . . General Olivier Harty, my chief of staff, has taken command of the camp during the time prescribed by Your Excellency, and yesterday he sent you the army report.[59]
>
> I do not look to make any protest or to evade what has been so severely prescribed. I have proved my complete submissiveness, but I still must, Monseigneur, request a few moments of your time to present my case. It is not to dispute the cause of the affliction that overwhelms me, because the damage has already been done, but rather to correct the unfavorable opinion of me created in the reports, which are not entirely correct. I wish to clarify for Your Excellency the reasons these events took place.
>
> From the first time I was in command of the camp of Boulogne, I occupied the same lodgings as Colonel General Gouvion Saint-Cyr, and that was in the house [now occupied by] Mr. Menneville.[60] After I left [for a new assignment] M. the Senator Rampon occupied that apartment, and after him M. Suzanne whom I found there [when I arrived]. Quite naturally, I thought I would occupy the same quarters as I had left to my successor, and that they would serve as the general headquarters of the commander in chief. That building, the only one that represents power, is situated on the place d'Arme; and for the good of the service, it is useful that the general in chief would be lodged there.

I know that Mr. Menneville dislikes me very much, and he resented the placing of gendarmes in his house. They were put there to protect the effects of General Suzanne after his departure and to assure my entrance.... But I used no violence, Mr. Menneville was not evicted from his house. Another reason that I did not think of lodging in a different place is that I would have had to evict those who already occupied the building. And it is at this point, Monseigneur, that I must point out the error.... They [Menneville] affirmed that lodgings had been prepared for me upon my arrival. This is totally untrue. When I arrived in Boulogne I had to reside in an auberge at my own expense, as no arrangements had been made because there was not a vacant building, and this is the truth....

[Vandamme goes on to describe how Menneville allowed Senator Suzanne, and others, to live in his house for months at a time.] Why did he reserve for me the most pronounced injustice, refusing me the same accord that he extended to others? I will ask, Monseigneur, was I to be permitted to accept that insult and bend to the scandalous will of an individual who finds himself overwhelmed with the profound contempt of every person in the city?[61]

It is certain that Vandamme treated the mayor of Boulogne shabbily and showed him no respect. Menneville was absolutely correct when he wrote that the general had no respect for civil administrators. Vandamme—a soldier all of his adult life, who had survived innumerable hardships and dangers on so many battlefields and campaigns, and who had shed his blood for France—truly believed that only military service, in combat, merited his respect. The above letter to General Henry-Jacques Clarke clearly indicates his humiliation in this affair. Had Berthier still been minister of war, Vandamme might have hoped for more understanding and less punishment. But the Irishman Clarke (born in France of Irish parents) was not a combat officer. Like Menneville he was a professional administrator, albeit in the army, and he had little patience for the likes of the undisciplined Vandamme. In the end, there was really nothing the general could do but accept the situation that his inflated pride had brought upon him. Needless to say, the general did not see it in this light.

The remainder of the spring of 1810 passed uneventfully enough, but in the second week of June the tranquility at Boulogne was again disrupted. On 10 June, the general of division Jean Sarrazin deserted and went over to the English. Sarrazin was one of Vandamme's division commanders who had risen through the ranks during the revolutionary wars to the rank of general of division. He took part in the expedition to Ireland with General Jean-Joseph Humbert in 1798 and was sent to San Domingue in 1802. Back in France by the end of 1803, he commanded military districts until he was given command of a division at the camp of Boulogne in February 1809.

On the morning of 10 June, General Sarrazin, accompanied by his servant, hired a fishing boat, the *Saint-Laurent* of Camiers, to take him from the port of Petite-Garenne to Etaples. Along the way he would fish. But once in the open sea he saw a British ship patrolling on the coast and ordered the captain of the boat to take him to the enemy ship because, he said, he had orders from the commanding general to open talks with the British. When the crew refused to do as ordered, Sarrazin and his servant showed their pistols and were taken to the enemy ship. The general then gave the crew a written statement declaring that he had ordered them to take him to the British brig.[62]

General Sarrazin was second in command of the camp at Boulogne, and his defection was an embarrassment for Vandamme. When he had gathered all the facts, Vandamme wrote the minister of war on 14 June to give him the full details and to explain how the defection came as a complete surprise to himself and all the officers and men under his command. "The desertion of this general officer took the entire army by the greatest surprise," Vandamme wrote. "The generals, all the officers, even the soldiers, cannot understand what happened; and I myself was the most surprised as I had received from that general the greatest testimony of his zeal, his love of duty, and his desire to assure the good of His Majesty's service. No one displayed more support or greater devotion to the duties of his command. . . . The day before his flight, he sent to me a report on the troops that he commanded. Monseigneur, after all this, it was utterly impossible to have even the slightest suspicion of this general officer."[63]

As there was never any indication that anyone else was involved in Sarrazin's defection, it had no effect upon Vandamme's career. However, the commander did change all passwords and took measures to ensure that whatever information Sarrazin might give to the enemy would have no effect upon his command.[64] As a concluding note to this affair, General Sarrazin was tried by a military tribunal at Lille on 15 November 1810, and condemned to death; but as he had fled the country, the sentence was never carried out.[65]

The years 1810 and 1811 were peaceful years north of the Pyrenees. Britain remained at war with France, but Prussia, Austria, and Russia desired no confrontation with the seemingly invincible Grande Armée under the leadership of Emperor Napoleon. In the Iberian Peninsula, however, it was quite different. Spanish resistance continued to varying degrees in various parts of the kingdom. King Joseph controlled only those sections of the country that were occupied by French troops in strength. In Portugal the situation was less favorable. The British had returned with an expeditionary force under the command of General Arthur Wellesley, duke of Wellington. With the aid of Portuguese troops, Wellington posed a serious threat to Joseph's control of Spain. In 1810 Napoleon placed Marshal Masséna at the head of three army corps and sent him to capture Lisbon and gain control of Portugal. But the campaign of 1810–11 proved a failure; and after Masséna's withdrawal from the Torres Vedras Line protecting Lisbon, the French were on the defensive in the Peninsula. Vandamme never served in Spain, which was certainly very much to the general's satisfaction.

Despite the continued bad news from the south, life was good for Vandamme in northern France. He was close to his family and friends and, except for the affair with Menneville and the desertion of Sarrazin, life was routine. He was named president of the administration college of Hazebrouck and presided over its meetings.[66] Indeed, the period from the spring of 1810 to the spring of 1812, when he rejoined the army in central Germany, might well be called the good years in the life of Dominique Vandamme.

9

Conflict with King Jérôme
The Russian Campaign

By the summer of 1812 France had been at war for twenty years with but a brief eighteen-month "truce" following the Treaty of Amiens. The nation was weary of the continuous drain on its young men and its resources for the army. The annual military drafts to fill depleted ranks south of the Pyrenees became increasingly unpopular. The prospect of war with Russia was also unpopular, and the population was becoming restless and yearning for peace. The French people saw neither Spain, Portugal, nor Russia as a threat to themselves or their nation. Yet there was still faith, or at least hope, that the emperor would solve the international problems one way or another. True to his nature, Napoleon decided to solve them on the battlefield.

The failed campaign in Portugal in 1810–11 had been a major disappointment to Napoleon, and the situation in Spain only worsened through 1811 and the first half of 1812. More than two hundred thousand of his finest troops were on the Peninsula, and still the position of his brother Joseph on the throne of Spain was anything but secure. An Anglo-Portuguese army had followed Marshal Masséna's army out of Portugal and was driving deep into western Spain.

Europe, excluding England, had been reasonably tranquil since the defeat of Austria in 1809. Napoleon divorced Josephine in 1809 and married the Princess Maria Louise of Austria in 1810. The royal couple produced a son in 1811. In many respects these were good years for France and the French, unless one happened to be sent to Spain. The rest of Europe was not particularly pleased with French domination, but at least there was no warfare north of the Pyrenees. Prussia, humiliated in 1806 and relegated to second-class status, was reforming and reorganizing its limited army but was in no position to challenge Napoleon. Austria after Wagram wanted no confrontation with the master of the continent. The Italian states were totally dominated by France. Holland had been annexed in 1810. Denmark was an "ally," Poland a client state, and the German state was submissive to the will of the French emperor. England alone remained at war with France. However, with the English navy in total control of the seas since Lord Horatio Nelson's brilliant victory at Trafalgar in 1805, Napoleon had no hope of conquering the island nation with his army. France had defeated all the major armies on the continent, so that England had little hope forcing Napoleon to the peace table. The leopard and the shark had reached a stalemate. To be sure, Wellington was having some success in Spain, and Napoleon was trying desperately to put real teeth into his Continental System. Yet, from the fall of 1811 Napoleon's attention was more directed to the east, with the idea that once Russia was brought into line, England would follow.

At Tilsit, Emperor Alexander had made peace with Napoleon on French terms. Napoleon gave his approval for Russia to take from the Ottoman empire the principalities of Wallachia and Moldavia and for the annexation of Swedish-owned Finland. But Alexander had to abandon his ally Prussia, agree to take part in the Continental System, and recognize French domination of the European continent west of the Niemen River. This included the restoration of a Polish state, nominally under the king of Saxony but actually controlled completely by Napoleon. Alexander felt humiliated by the military defeat at Friedland, and what the Russians considered a shameful treaty at Tilsit. By the fall of 1808 the situation began to change. The Spanish quagmire had begun, and Napoleon wanted Russian support in eastern Europe while he went to Spain. Alexander was treated more as an equal than the defeated enemy he was at Tilsit. When Austria went to war with France in 1809, Russia remained neutral and even gave moral support to Austria. By 1810 Russia no longer felt restrained by the Continental System and even placed heavy tariffs on

French imports. Relations between the two empires became strained. Before the end of the year, Napoleon began early preparations for war with Russia.

In 1811, to tighten the continental blockade, Napoleon annexed the German Baltic states including the duchy of Oldenburg. Alexander's daughter, Princess Anne Pavlovna, had been refused to Napoleon as a wife in 1810 and had then married Peter Frederick, duke of Oldenburg. Although the French offered compensation in central Germany, Alexander refused the token and considered Napoleon's action a personal offense. Neither emperor wanted a war, but they both wanted peace on their own terms, that is, as they considered in the best interests of their own state. For Napoleon this was Alexander's complete compliance with the continental blockade that forbade any trade with Great Britain, and the adherence to all the terms of the Treaty of Tilsit signed by Alexander in 1807. For Alexander it meant French withdrawal from eastern Europe (Poland and Prussia), the restoration of his son-in-law to the duchy of Oldenburg, and the freedom to determine Russian trade interests and foreign policy according to the best interests of Russia, not France. The desires of the two emperors were not reconcilable, however, and war became inevitable. Despite Napoleon's rhetoric that Alexander refused to honor his commitments made at Tilsit, there is little question that he was the principal architect of the war of 1812.

This was a year of misfortune for Vandamme, and of disaster for Napoleon and France. The general remained at Boulogne in command of the camp and the Sixteenth Military Division until he received new orders, dated 24 August 1811, to proceed to Cherbourg and take command of the camp there and the Fourteenth Military Division.[1] On 21 February 1812, with the invasion of Russia just months away, Vandamme was ordered to Germany to assume command of the Westphalian corps, to be known as the Eighth Corps of the Grande Armée, being assembled in central and eastern Europe.[2] Napoleon had been pleased with Vandamme's handling of the Würtemberg divisions in Silesia in 1806–1807 and in Germany and Austria in 1809. This time Vandamme was again given the command of German troops; not the Würtemberg division, which he had left at the end of the 1809 campaign, but the troops of the kingdom of Westphalia. Vandamme would have much preferred to command French troops. He felt that his services commanding foreign divisions, often relegated to secondary duties, had deprived him of the opportunity to take part in the major battles of the campaigns of 1806–1807 and 1809 (that is, Eylau, Friedland, and Wagram), and that this was why he had been denied the coveted marshal's baton. He believed that Oudinot and Macdonald were named marshals because they had fought under the eyes of the emperor at Wagram; and that if he had commanded a corps at that battle, he too would be a marshal of the empire. Furthermore, as Jérôme was now king of Westphalia, Vandamme would once again be directly under the orders of a man for whom he had no respect. Vandamme considered Jérôme utterly incompetent of commanding troops on campaign or in battle. The relationship between the two men was strained in Silesia when last Vandamme served under Jérôme. Napoleon was fully aware of the difficulties between them, and of Vandamme's unmanageable personality. He was asking for trouble when he threw the two of them together as he did. The general feared that if he declined the command offered him, then Napoleon would leave him behind in command of a military district in France. By accepting this new command, he would perhaps have the opportunity to win his baton on a battlefield in Russia.

Vandamme left Paris on 2 March and arrived at the court of King Jérôme at Cassel, Westphalia, on 8 March.[3] After a quick revue of some of the Westphalian troops, he reported to Berthier that they were in very good condition, indeed "magnificent."[4] After exchanging pleasantries with the king, Vandamme was officially given command of the Westphalian corps. The troops were quartered in the duchy of Anhalt between the Saal and Elbe rivers. Vandamme established his headquarters in the city of Dessau. But the duchy of Anhalt was suffering greatly from the burden of quartering so great a number of Westphalian troops in so small a principality and with little relief from the king of Westphalia. On 16 March the duke of Anhalt-Pless wrote to Vandamme seeking relief:

> Since the 6th of this month [March] a considerable number of Westphalian troops have been in cantonment on my estates in such numbers that no village has been spared. Last year's harvest having been very poor, and the importation of food as well as forage being halted completely because of the

cantonment of troops everywhere, we are exposed to a general food shortage.

In this extreme situation, I do not hesitate to communicate to Your Excellency my sorrow, . . . and to implore your assistance to deliver us from this scourge that menaces us. If it pleases Your Excellency, would you remove the troops that are quartered with us as soon as possible.[5]

Vandamme had no authority to move his troops, and it was not until 23 March that he received orders to take his corps across the Elbe. Feeding the Westphalian corps had been a problem while they were in Anhalt, but not a serious one. Using bridges at Alten and Elbhause, he took his new command over the Elbe. In the last week of March and first two weeks of April, Vandamme marched from the duchy of Anhalt to Kalisch in western Poland. This took him through Saxony and Silesia where he crossed the Oder River at Glogau, a city he had forced to capitulate some five and a half years earlier.[6]

The march into Poland presented difficulties. On 9 April, Vandamme informed Jérôme that there were more than 150 officers and men in the hospital at Glogau, and he wanted either to leave the men there in the care of the civilian government or to create an army hospital for the men until they would be well enough to rejoin the army.[7] The long march also caused desertions from the ranks, and on 19 April Vandamme informed the king that he was conducting court-martials to deal with the problem. Of greater concern to the commander was the flight of the civilian population in advance of his marching columns. The inhabitants were fleeing into the forests and taking their livestock and food with them.[8] This made it difficult to acquire food from the local population as the army moved east. The army supply system was not keeping up with the marching men. On 22 April, General Adam von Ochs, commander of the Twenty-fourth Division, informed Vandamme he did not have enough food or wine for his men the following day. He wrote: "I have authorized each commander of a cantonment to take whatever measures necessary to obtain food. If these measures are irregular, Your Excellency will know that I have no other choice."[9]

The Polish population had not yet recovered from the devastation of the campaigns of 1806–1807 and 1809. French troops had been quartered in Poland, at Polish expense, since 1807; and Napoleon's demands to raise troops for the Russian campaign had placed an additional hardship on the population and the economy. The influx of several hundred thousand troops in the spring and early summer of 1812 in preparation for the invasion of Russia was a devastating burden on the Polish people and its economy. The result was that Vandamme was unable to meet the needs of his troops from local regions. Nevertheless, in an order of the day dated 21 April, he pointed out that the Polish were a strong supportive ally of France, and that the inhabitants should be treated as friends and in a just and fair manner.[10] On the eve of the campaign, Vandamme put the strength of the Eighth Corps at 17,833 men and 2681 cavalry.[11] The chief of staff was Adjutant Commandant Revest. General Jean-Victor Tharreau commanded the Twenty-third Division, and General Adam von Ochs commanded the Twenty-fourth Division.[12] The corps also included a brigade of light cavalry under the command of General Hammerstein and forty-two pieces of artillery.

Vandamme wrote Jérôme on 23 April, concerning the increasing scarcity of food and other necessities:

> Our suffering will increase as our position becomes more and more critical. The surrounding country is in a food shortage. The closer we approach the Vistula [River] the more our situation worsens. Already inhabitants are dying of hunger, while the others are living on acorns. Your Majesty will judge the anxiety in which I find myself. The prince of Neufchâtel [Berthier] assured me there would be supplies at Kalisch; Your Majesty knows there was nothing upon the arrival of the Eighth Corps. I hope that the wisdom of Your Majesty will deliver us from the scourge that menaces us.[13]

On the same day Vandamme issued an order of the day in an attempt to raise the morale of the troops and reduce the marauding and plundering of the countryside.

> Westphalians!
> We are in Poland, a country that is our ally and is particularly affectionate to the great Napoleon. They are brave people, and

their soldiers have everywhere mingled their blood with the blood of the French to defeat the enemies of the Napoleonic dynasty.... These lands offer at this time little in the way of resources. We are suffering here at this time and our pain will increase, but help will arrive. Your king knows your position.... On your part, it is necessary to have patience, sobriety, and confidence; a soldier must know how to bear suffering and to have confidence.... On my part, I am completely satisfied with you.[14]

However, the lack of a regular supply system meant that the troops had to supplement their rations as best they could on the backs of the local population. The result was that both the inhabitants and the army went hungry, and the soldiers' marauding led to a breakdown in discipline.

In the last days of April, Vandamme received orders from Jérôme to move the Eighth Corps on to the Vistula River. His right flank was to rest on the north bank of the Pilica River and his left to reach north to a point just south of Warsaw.[15] However, there was some confusion concerning his orders. On 27 April, General Marchand, Jérôme's chief of staff acting in the absence of the king, ordered Vandamme to the Vistula south of the Pilica River. Vandamme had already issued all the necessary orders, two days before receiving new instructions from the king. Thus he had to countermand his orders of 28 April and, he thought, was made to look foolish in the eyes of his command. In a letter to Jérôme dated the same day he received the king's new orders, he explained how he had received one set of orders from Marchand and a second set of quite different orders from him. "Nothing," he continued, "causes more discouragement and negligence among the troops than this uncertainty as to which orders to follow, and nothing is more frustrating and conflicting to the well-being of the troops than the continuous and useless movement. In the days that the other corps of the army are resting, a rest that is very much needed, we are marching and countermarching for no useful purpose. I beseech Your Majesty not to permit the smallest change [in orders] without serious reflection."[16]

The general went on to complain that so many units from his corps had been detached that he commanded little more than General

Ochs' division, and he asked that his troops be returned. Needless to say, King Jérôme resented being scolded by one of his subordinates. Their relationship had been strained in Silesia in 1807, but after a five-year separation most of the old animosities had subsided. Now, however, new wounds were being opened. Vandamme's lack of respect for the young king as a general, or for that matter as a monarch, was unmistakable in this letter; and it drove home to Jérôme just how difficult his corps commander had been in the past, and what he could expect in the future.

Unhappy as the general was, he carried out the king's orders, and the Eighth Corps advanced to the banks of the Vistula, camped, and scoured the region for food. The Polish villages and countryside were overwhelmed by the massive influx of soldiers in the late spring and early summer of 1812. Just able to feed themselves as a result of previous poor harvests, the Poles could not feed the additional hundreds of thousands of Napoleon's army as it prepared to invade Russia. The troops were dependent upon supplies being sent from central Europe. In the case of the Eighth Corps, those supplies were to come primarily from Westphalia. The chief supply official was a man named Dupleix, who was a relative of the king. Vandamme's troops were suffering from the lack of supplies, and Dupleix was spending his time with the king at Cassel and then Warsaw; Vandamme wrote him a sharp letter on 3 May: "I am astonished," he wrote him, "that I do not see you here [with the troops] anymore, and dare not guess what your motives are to remain constantly in the rear. It is not from there that you are able to assess the needs of the army. You give the orders, but I repeat that it is not through correspondence that it is possible to determine our needs. Where you should be is up front, in Galicie."[17] He went on to say that it was only by illegal measures—that is, requisitions on the local inhabitants—that the generals and officers were able to feed their men. This sharp criticism of Jérôme's relative and official served only to exacerbate the tension between the king and his subordinate.

Vandamme was also complaining directly to Jérôme of the lack of food and supplies reaching the troops. On 12 May one of the king's ministers, the count of Fürstenstein, wrote the general a sharp rebuke: "Monsieur le comte, the king has received your letter. His Majesty charges me to tell you that he has not given any false interpretation to your intentions or to your conduct, and that you have proof of his confidence in that he has given you command of his troops. But he observes that all his orders must be punctually executed, and that all negligence in this regard is subject to the greatest inconvenience; it is necessary that he be assured that these orders will be carried out. This has not been the case."[18]

At the same time, friction developed between Vandamme and General Marchand, the king's chief of staff. It might be recalled that Vandamme did not have a good working relationship with General Hédouville, Jérôme's chief of staff in Silesia in 1807. The problem arose from Vandamme's practice of bypassing the chief of staff and writing directly to the king, and the fact that he tended to pay little attention to orders he received from Marchand. When he failed to keep Marchand posted as to his movements and location, the frustrated chief of staff wrote on 12 May: "M. General, in the letter I wrote you on the 6th of this month, I asked you to inform me of the position of your general headquarters, so that when the king asked me where you are I would not have to say I do not know. You realize, Monsieur General, that when I write you, it is always by order of the king, and that I never add a single word or phrase to what His Majesty tells me to say to you." Vandamme continued to write directly to Jérôme, but he also informed Marchand in some detail as to his location and that of his divisions.[19]

In the latter days of May, Vandamme was greatly annoyed by a lavish review of his Westphalian troops by their king. It was not that Jérôme was to review his command, but that he was coming down from Warsaw with six festive carriages, for which Vandamme was ordered to provide relays of horses. In addition, he was to provide a mounted escort of fifty troopers and more horses in the event that some of the members of court wished to ride part of the way. With war imminent, Vandamme resented what he considered a wasteful use of the Eighth Corps horses to throw a grand party for the king and his court followers. His denunciation of the pompous display, so characteristic of the outspoken general, quickly reached Jérôme and worsened the relationship between the two men.[20]

In the last days of May Jérôme was complaining to his brother of his difficulties with Vandamme. Local authorities were also complaining of the requisitions being made by the Westphalians on the local population as they moved east. This all culminated on 1 June with a sharp rebuke from Berthier on the part of Napoleon: "Monsieur General Vandamme," he wrote, "the emperor has ordered me to inform you of his extreme displeasure with respect to the excesses committed by the troops of the contingent of His Majesty the king of Westphalia every place they passed through. The complaints are general in this regard. The emperor orders you to reestablish order in the corps under your command, to execute those who have committed such offenses against inhabitants, to send back to Westphalia the officers who permit those actions that are not authorized to all of the corps of the army."[21]

Feeling that this harsh criticism of his handling of the Eighth Corps was not justified, especially in light of the lack of regular food and supplies reaching the Westphalians, Vandamme tried to justify his action in a long letter to Berthier on 4 June. "Nothing can give me more pain," he wrote, "than the letter Your Highness wrote me on behalf of the emperor, to express His Majesty's extreme displeasure regarding the excesses committed by the Westphalian troops." He went on to declare that he thought there was a plan against the Eighth Corps, and that his troops, though young and inexperienced, had conducted themselves "with the greatest reserve." He admitted that there might have been some abuses, such as always happen with an army on the march, and blamed them on the lack of support from the rear, without mentioning anyone by name. Vandamme also blamed much of the reported abuses on the Seventh Corps, a Saxon corps, that had moved through the territories in front of the Eighth Corps. In conclusion, he assured the major general that everyone was doing their duty, that he was issuing orders to maintain the strictest discipline in the ranks, that men were being punished for abuses, and that deserters were being punished. Despite Vandamme's attempts at damage control, there can be little doubt of the negative impression forming at imperial headquarters.[22]

Jérôme did make some attempts to get food and supplies to his troops. On 26 May Vandamme wrote to Dupleix that the king had ordered his minister of interior to send two hundred head of cattle to the corps—but there is no indication they ever arrived. On 30 May Vandamme informed Dupleix that the emperor had ordered every corps should have on hand twenty days' supply of flour or biscuits, and that every soldier should have eight days' supply of biscuits in his knapsack. This was not the case with the Westphalian corps. Vandamme was particularly concerned about the shortage of food, because he believed that the campaign was to begin on 5 June, and he was forbidden to take anything from the local population. From time to time some food did arrive from the rear, but the Eighth Corps remained poorly supplied and the troops frequently went hungry.[23] This led to foraging parties, which in turn resulted in a breakdown in order and discipline as the corps began its final approach to the Russian frontier. In mid-June Vandamme was ordered east from the Warsaw region. His destination was the Niemen River at Grodno. Reaching Sierock on 17 June, he rested his men for three days; and renewing the march on the 20th, the Eighth Corps was near Rozan on 21 June when the Russian campaign began.

The Napoleonic Grande Armée was truly a European army. Only about 55 percent of the troops were French. The remaining troops were from allied countries. There were Germans, Poles, Italians, Dutch, and even some Spanish. Prussia and Austria had also contributed substantial corps on the flanks. The figure most frequently given for this army crossing the Niemen River in the last week of June is 420,000 men.[24] This army was divided into three parts. In the vicinity of Kovno on the Niemen, Napoleon had five army corps under his direct command. On his left Marshal Macdonald's Tenth Corps prepared to cross the river at Tilsit. King Jérôme was given command of three corps plus cavalry on the southern flank (the right flank). Jérôme's command consisted of three infantry corps: Prince Joseph Anthony Poniatowski's Fifth Corps, General Jean-Louis Reynier's Seventh Corps, and Vandamme's Eighth Corps. General Marie-Victor Latour-Maubourg's Fourth Cavalry Corps was also under the king's command. Well south of Jérôme was an Austrian corps commanded by Prince Schwarzenberg to keep an eye on the Third Russian army south of the Pripet Marshes.

The Russian forces opposing Napoleon numbered about 180,000 men divided into three armies. The First Army of the West was commanded by General Michael Barclay de Tolly, who was also the minister of war and thus acted as the overall commander of the Russian forces in the west. The Second Army of the West was commanded by General Peter Bagration. The Third Army of the West, which would play no role in the opening phase of the campaign, was commanded by

General A. P. Tormassov. The Russians also had a second and third line of defense with additional troops of varying quality. Describing the Russian army, Carl von Clausewitz, who served in Tsar Alexander's entourage in 1812, wrote: "The result of this reckoning appears, first, that the Russian army's proper effective strength was six hundred thousand men.... Second, that in the year 1812 not above four hundred thousand regular troops were actually forthcoming. Third, that of these four hundred thousand not more than a hundred eighty thousand could be opposed, in the first instance, to the French."[25] Barclay was positioned to oppose Napoleon, while Bagration was facing Jérôme.

Why did Napoleon give command of the right wing of the army to his young, inexperienced, and unproved brother? The question is continually asked. The emperor left no written explanation, nor did he feel it necessary to explain his decision. That Jérôme was part of the imperial family with the title of king was surely a major factor. Napoleon's other option was to give that important command to one of his marshals. But whichever one he chose (Davout would have been the logical choice), the choice would have increased the jealousy and friction among his corps commanders. Furthermore, if Jérôme were to take part in the campaign, would he (a king) have had to serve under a mere prince? Indeed, when Napoleon did place Jérôme under the command of Marshal Davout, prince of Eckmühl, the king gave up his command and went home.[26] Napoleon's stepson, Eugène, the viceroy of Italy who commanded the Fourth Corps, might have been a choice. But Napoleon had been trying to make a reputation for Jérôme as a military commander that would enhance his status as king of Westphalia and as a Bonaparte.

Finally, there is a theory that he gave Jérôme command of the right wing of the army as part of a grand strategy to encircle the Russian Second Army and destroy it before it could retreat to join Barclay's main army. According to this theory, Jérôme was set up as a weak and inefficient commander who would tempt the aggressive Bagration to attack him in Poland, while Davout drove east and swung south to encircle the Russians and, with the support of the right wing of the army, destroy the Second Russian Army of the West. Even if Bagration did not attack when hostilities began, if he simply remained in place, Davout could advance onto his rear and, if not destroy his army, at least force it to retreat south into the Pripet Marshes, where it would not be a factor in Napoleon's destruction of Barclay's First Army of the West. In this scenario, Jérôme's incompetence would work to the benefit of the overall strategy.[27]

The central army's leading corps was ordered to cross the Niemen River near Kovno on 23 June 1812, to begin the Russian campaign. On 22 June, Napoleon wrote the major general: "You will write the king of Westphalia to inform the Fifth, Seventh, and Eighth Corps [that the campaign began] only on the morning of the 26th."[28] Thus Jérôme was not to be informed of the commencement of hostilities until three days after the war had started. It is true that Napoleon continually wrote his brother of his concern that Bagration might attack into Poland between Jérôme's force and Schwarzenberg's Austrian corps further to the south. This would threaten the French right flank and rear.[29] Napoleon obviously did not want his right wing to engage the Second Russian Army of the West in the opening days of the campaign. In the "Order for the Passage of the Niemen" issued on 23 June, there is no mention of the three army corps commanded by Jérôme. The Eighth Corps was ordered simply to continue its eastward march on 23 June to Raygord.[30] Neither Vandamme nor Jérôme, or anyone else in the right wing of the army, knew what was taking place to the north until the campaign had been underway for three or four days.

As the Eighth Corps moved toward the Russian frontier, Vandamme complained that his men were not receiving the supplies that had been promised. On 21 June the general informed the king that M. Bathomauf, the ordinance officer who had been sent to him to secure supplies from the local authorities, had produced nothing. The following day he again wrote Jérôme that for several days his troops had not had any bread. Not a day passed that Vandamme did not write Jérôme, the major general, or Dupleix to complain that his troops were not being fed, and that he was not allowed to requisition food on his own authority.[31]

Vandamme continued his march to the Niemen. Passing through Lipsk on 30 June, he reached Grodno on 2 July. The condition of the Eighth Corps by this time was deplorable. Nothing he could do had improved the supply system for his men. Foraging and plundering had reduced discipline in the ranks. To try once again to convince Jérôme of the deplorable conditions of his Westphalian troops and to demand relief in the form of food and supplies, Vandamme wrote the king on

3 July: "Sire, the misery of the Eighth Corps is at its height, and if Your Majesty does not see to correct the situation afflicting all the corps, I will be forced to request permission to give up to another the command bestowed upon me by the emperor. It is impossible for me to continue any longer to witness the conditions about me. There is no order and violence is everywhere in the name of Your Majesty. They violate the land and properties; ... and no one will inform Your Majesty. I am obliged to do so because of my attachment to you. I plead with Your Majesty to intervene on our behalf ... there is no time to be lost."[32] The general had no real intention of giving up his command just as the campaign was at last beginning. He hoped that, if he threatened to quit (a tactic used by French generals during the revolutionary wars and to a lesser extent in the Napoleonic army), more serious attention would be given his requests for supplies. What was completely unexpected was the letter he received from Jérôme in reply to his 3 July threat:

> I received your letter today. In the case of what you call disorder [the irregular supply of food], I see on the contrary the regular establishment of the measure I prescribed. No one has the right of self-service.
>
> The Eighth Corps ordinance official's letters that you submitted to me as proof of disorder, I see as showing the contrary, ... that the men have had half rations of bread and the rations will be complete this night. I see nothing to indicate disorder; as a result, after your letter, and as I will not change anything with respect to the established order, *you are authorized to proceed to Warsaw where you will await orders from His Majesty the Emperor* to whom I am sending your letter in order to inform him of what is taking place.
>
> You will turn over command of the Eighth Corps to General of Division Tharreau to whom I will send orders with respect to you.[33] (Emphasis added.)

At the same time Jérôme wrote his wife, Catherine: "I have been obliged to remove Vandamme from his command of the Eighth Corps. He has done everything, pillaging, robbing, insulting.... It is unbelievable the hatred his name inspires in the country. The inhabitants have an inconceivable fear of him. I presume that the emperor will send him home or give him a command in the rear."[34]

Vandamme was stunned and horrified by Jérôme's reply to his letter. He had no intention of leaving the army. He did not believe the king had the courage, much less the authority, to relieve him of a command Napoleon had given him, although it was the king who had given him the command of the Westphalian corps. Nevertheless, Vandamme knew full well that, without his brother's backing, Jérôme could not remove him from his command. He, therefore, at once wrote to Napoleon to present his side of this affair.

> By the time this is delivered Your Majesty will have already received the report from the king of Westphalia.
>
> On the basis of my well-founded and respectful letter that I addressed to the king, and of which I am including a copy, it pleased His Majesty to relieve me of the command of the Eighth Corps and to send me to Warsaw to await the orders of Your Imperial Royal Majesty. Not having horses at this time to go to Warsaw, nor Vilna, I am forced to remain at Grodno awaiting your orders.
>
> Sire, after I have made every possible effort to merit the confidence of the king of Westphalia I feel I have some rights, but I find myself all of a sudden without a command.
>
> I implore Your Majesty not to forget my good, long service and to be persuaded that I have committed no other fault than to have served the king who again yesterday expressed his compliments.
>
> I beg Your Majesty not to leave the men very long in a state of anxiety that overwhelms me at a time when there are Russians to fight.[35]

Displeased with the bickering between troublesome Vandamme and his ineffective brother Jérôme, and with so many more important matters at hand in the early days of the new campaign, Napoleon did not bother even to answer the general's letter.

The right wing of the army was ordered to advance and engage the enemy so as to hold Bagration's Second Army of the West in place, or at least slow its retreat. This would enable Davout's First Corps to swing to the southeast from Vilna and cut off the Russian retreat, forcing Bagration to fight a battle in which he would have Jérôme on one side and Davout on the other. In this manner Napoleon hoped to destroy the First Army of the West in the opening weeks of the war. But Jérôme was too slow in advancing, and Bagration skillful in his retreat. When the Eighth Corps moved east out of Grodno toward Bielitsa, Vandamme followed without a command. By 11 July he realized that Napoleon had no intention of responding to his plea for a new command. Out of sheer desperation, he wrote a humble letter to Jérôme asking to be given back command of the Eighth Corps.

> It is to Your Majesty that I address myself with confidence to implore you to end my uncertainty. Having not yet received orders from the emperor I could not remain long at Grodno, so far from the army that will soon be fighting the Russians.
>
> I am not guilty of the reasons Your Majesty has sent me away from the army. I believe that it depends very much on you for me to take command of the Eighth Corps where I have never ceased to make every effort for the good of your service and that of the troops.
>
> Your Majesty has honored me with such kindness during the course of this campaign . . . I rest assured that Your Majesty will tell me what I hope for, having committed no action to merit your disaffection.
>
> I beseech Your Majesty to reach me at Bielitsa with your orders or your response.[36]

Having rid himself of a troublesome corps commander, Jérôme had no intention of giving back to Vandamme command of the Eighth Corps. Be that as it may, the course of events was catching up with both Vandamme and Jérôme.

Napoleon was not pleased with the conduct of his young brother in the opening weeks of the war. On 4 July he wrote Jérôme: "It is impossible to make war like this: you do not occupy yourself with it, you speak only of *babioles* and I see with pain that everything is petty in your camp. . . . You are compromising the success of the entire campaign on the right."[37] The statement that "you speak only of *babioles*" was a direct reference to his complaints against Vandamme and the fact that he had just relieved the general of his command the day before. This was followed the next day (5 July) by an even stronger condemnation of the king's handling of the army's right wing. "My cousin," he wrote Berthier, "you will write to the king of Westphalia that I have received today his dispatch of 3 July.... You will inform him that I am extremely dissatisfied that he has not placed all his light infantry under the orders of Poniatowski to the detriment of Bagration, to harass his corps and stop his retreat. That having reached Grodno on the 30th [of June], he should have attacked the enemy at once and pursued him aggressively. *You will tell him it is impossible to maneuver worse than he has*. That having ignored all rules [of war] and instructions, he is allowing Bagration to have all the time he needs to retreat" (emphasis added).[38]

The following day the emperor issued a secret order that was sent to Marshal Davout but not to the king of Westphalia: "Order, Vilna, 6 July 1812. His Majesty orders that, in the case of the union of the Fifth, Seventh, and Eighth corps of the army and the Fourth Corps of reserve cavalry with the corps commanded by the prince of Eckmühl, the overall command will go to the prince of Eckmühl as the senior general. The emperor orders that His Majesty the king of Westphalia will recognize the prince of Eckmühl as the supreme commander when the corps of the army is united."[39] Davout was instructed not to make known this order until such time as he joined with Jérôme's corps.

This was the situation on 15 July, when the king of Westphalia's secretary, Baron Sorsum, replied to Vandamme: "Monsieur Count, His Majesty received the letter you wrote him from Bielitsa on the 11th. He orders me to inform you that the emperor has approved General Tharreau to command the Eighth Corps, and as a result orders are being sent directly to him. The major general [Berthier] announces that he will send you the emperor's orders at Warsaw." Sorsum went on to inform Vandamme: "His Majesty the king ... has given his command of the different corps of the [army's] right wing to the prince d'Eckmühl."[40] Thus, Jérôme no longer commanded the Eighth Corps and (as he had left the army to return to Westphalia) no longer had any influence over who would command that corps. When Jérôme made contact with Davout on 12 July, the marshal, in a last desperate attempt to prevent Bagration from joining forces with Barclay, informed the king of Napoleon's order authorizing him to assume command of all the forces on the army's right flank. Refusing to take orders from the prince of Eckmühl, with whom he had argued when part of the marshal's corps was quartered in his kingdom, Jérôme gave up his command and went home. He wrote a very submissive letter to his brother, requesting permission to leave the army, and then did so without waiting for an answer. He wrote Berthier his true feelings: "I can see nothing else in this disposition except a complete lack of confidence on the part of the emperor, and a strong desire on the part of His Majesty to humiliate me."[41]

One can certainly to some extent sympathize with Jérôme. He was a Bonaparte, but he was not a Napoleon. His brother had put him in a position far beyond his ability and talents. It would be wrong to criticize him for ridding himself of the troublesome strong-willed Vandamme. Their relationship had degenerated to the point that they could not work together for the good of the army. That he failed as commander of the right wing of the army would reflect on the poor judgment of Napoleon who put him in a position for which he was not qualified, either by experience or by talent. The emperor must have known the task was beyond his brother's ability. Jérôme should never have been given such an important command. Any one of his three corps commanders—General Reynier, Prince Poniatowski, or Vandamme—would have been a much better choice. But Jérôme was his brother. In the end, Napoleon lost the use of a perfectly good, albeit difficult, corps commander. He also lost the king of Westphalia, but this was probably more to the benefit of the army.

Vandamme remained with the army after having been removed from his command in the hope of either being reinstated by Napoleon or being given another command. When, after two weeks, the emperor still had not answered his 3 July letter, he wrote Berthier on 18 July. He explained that he had followed the Eighth Corps because he believed it would be engaged with Russians near Mir. He acknowledged that General Tharreau had been given command of his corps, and that the king of Westphalia no longer commanded the right wing of the army. He concluded: "I can only be extremely sensitive with respect to what has happened to me, having done nothing to merit the loss of the goodwill of His Imperial and Royal Majesty. Without question, the faults of others have been attributed to me, and these lies have embittered my sovereign against me. Nevertheless, I have nothing to reproach myself with.... I have a great need to see the emperor so as not to be a victim of false reports, for I have every hope, and I attend with confidence, that His Majesty will render me justice." As with the letter Vandamme had written Napoleon, he received no answer from Berthier. Becoming desperate, he again wrote Berthier, from Bielitsa on 27 July. This time he wrote a minihistory of the events, as he saw them, that led to his present situation.[42] Again he received no reply. Napoleon had no time for—and no interest in—General Vandamme. Still the general persisted; and on 4 August, still at Bielitsa, he wrote Berthier a third time, requesting a command so as to rejoin the campaign. This time, and to end the affair once and for all, Berthier expressed the will of the emperor. On 6 August, Berthier wrote Vandamme: "Monsieur General Count Vandamme, I have put before the eyes of the emperor the letters you have written to me. Having not authorized you to quit your command, His Majesty found it necessary to replace you. He has done so. As a result, you are no longer employed in the army, and you must return to France where you will be at the disposition of the minister. I will inform the minister of war."[43]

The reasoning for sending Vandamme back to France can hardly be justified. He had left his command by orders of his commander, not of his own will, as he had threatened. Nevertheless, at this point, Bagration had escaped encirclement, and Napoleon was angry with everyone on the right flank: Vandamme, Jérôme, even Davout. On 20 July he wrote Berthier: "My cousin, write the prince of Eckmühl that I am not satisfied with his conduct toward the king of Westphalia; that I had not given him command except in case the union had taken place."[44] There was nothing left for Vandamme to do but follow orders and return to France. On 16 August he began the lonely journey west. He traveled by way of Posen, Berlin, and Wesel and arrived at Cassel on 14 September 1812.[45]

10

Disaster at Kulm, 1813

Following Vandamme's departure from the Grande Armée in August 1812, Napoleon marched deep into Russia in pursuit of the tsar's army. After General Barclay was replaced by General Kutusov, the Russians turned and gave battle at Borodino on 7 September. Both armies suffered enormous losses; but the Russians were obliged to retreat under cover of darkness, and Napoleon occupied Moscow. Despite Napoleon's overtures for peace, Tsar Alexander refused even to discuss an end of hostilities so long as even one French soldier remained on Russian soil. Unable to assure adequate supplies for his army of one hundred thousand men through the winter of 1812–13, Napoleon ordered a withdrawal to the west. He hoped to stop and winter at Smolensk, but the withdrawal became a retreat, and the retreat a disaster. The emperor left the remnants of his once mighty army in Poland and returned to Paris. There was little he could do by remaining with the army, whereas if he were back in Paris, he could consolidate his position and raise a new army to continue the war in central Europe.[1]

Napoleon never seriously considered a diplomatic solution to end the war and stabilize Europe. He had always solved problems on the battlefield, and to his advantage. He intended simply to create a new army, defeat his enemies, and once again be master of the continent.

To this end, his days were consumed with the administrative functions of government and the army.

The quagmire in Spain continued to tie down two hundred thousand men, and the war was not going well. Fighting on two fronts at the same time was an enormous burden on the resources of the empire. The creation of a new army in the spring of 1813 created a major strain, not only on France, but also on the annexed territories, the satellite kingdoms, and allied states. There was resistance to the draft throughout western Europe, and even in France. Nevertheless, Napoleon was able to add two hundred thousand troops to the remains of the Grande Armée and was ready to move onto the offensive by late April 1813. When he left the army early in December 1812, he gave command of it to his brother-in-law, King Joachim of Naples (Marshal Murat), who then left the army to attend to "urgent" affairs in his kingdom. Prince Eugène, the emperor's stepson, was given command of what was left of the army. Eugène was struggling unsuccessfully to hold the line along the Elbe River in central Germany. Fortunately, Napoleon arrived with reinforcements and assumed command in the third week of April 1813. Austria had declared its neutrality. He hoped his father-in-law, Emperor Francis I of Austria, would remain on the sidelines in the upcoming campaign. If he could win a major victory in Germany, he believed, Austria would not turn against him, and he would reestablish his reputation, which had been tarnished by the previous year's devastating campaign. Furthermore, such a victory would keep the wavering German princes in line and would demoralize the enemy.

During the hardships of the 1812 campaign, the Russian army had suffered almost as much as the French. The army was reluctant to advance into central Europe without the support of the Prussian and Austrian armies. However, with the presumed support of Prussia, and the hoped-for support of Austria, Alexander ordered his generals to continue to pursue the enemy through Poland and into Germany. General Kutusov's health was failing, and he was not an enthusiastic supporter of this decision. He believed the army needed rest, supplies, and reorganization. So he did not press the retreating French. Then the sixty-eight-year-old general died of a fever at Breslau, in the last week of April, and was replaced by General Ludwig Adolf von Wittgenstein. When the advancing Russian army liberated

Prussian territory in February 1813, King Frederick William III renounced his alliance with France and joined Russia to form a new coalition against Napoleon.

Sweden joined the Coalition also, in the spring of 1813. In 1810 the Swedes had chosen Marshal Bernadotte to become crown prince and heir to the throne. He was now known as Crown Prince Charles John of Sweden. His relationship with Napoleon had been strained since 1806.[2] In 1813 he saw Sweden's best interest to be in joining Russia in the war against his native France. Russia had taken Finland from Sweden in 1808–1809, and Sweden wanted to take Norway from Denmark as compensation for the loss. Denmark was allied to France, thus Napoleon would not give his approval. Alexander had no ties to Denmark and could care less what happened to the Norwegians. When the courts of St. James and St. Petersburg approved Swedish acquisition of Norway, Bernadotte took his adopted country into the Coalition.[3] Denmark wanted to remain neutral and just keep the territory it had and perhaps gain a little in northern Germany. However, under pressure from Napoleon, the Danes reluctantly remained an (almost passive) ally of France.

Vandamme spent the fall and winter of 1812–13 at home in Cassel without a command. He was clearly out of favor with the emperor because of his relations with Jérôme the previous summer. After Napoleon's return to Paris, Vandamme went to the capital on several occasions to repair his relationship with the emperor. As Napoleon created a new army in preparation to undertake a new campaign in the spring, he was in need of good officers. Although he may have been displeased with Vandamme's manner in treating the king of Westphalia, General Bonaparte was willing to overlook such past affairs in order to make use of the talents of a proven division commander. So, on 8 February 1813, the minister of war wrote Vandamme asking if his health would allow him to return to active duty. The general replied at once that he was physically fit and ready to serve the emperor again just as soon as he received new orders. He then reminded the minister that he had not yet been reimbursed for considerable expenses incurred returning to France after having been sacked the previous summer by Jérôme.[4]

With the new organization of the army in the spring of 1813, Napoleon created twelve army corps.[5] As part of this organization he ordered the recruitment and training of three divisions between the Weser River and the Elbe, and he sent Vandamme to organize and command this new corps. Vandamme's objective was to reinforce the sparse French troops in the lower Elbe region. As the French army retreated to the west under Eugène, Magdeburg on the middle Elbe became the army's focal point. But Eugène did not have enough troops to hold the line of the Elbe from Hamburg to Dresden. The Russians captured Dresden and crossed the Elbe in force. At the same time, a Russian and Prussian force was advancing through northern Germany. News reached Hamburg that Coalition forces were meeting little resistance in the north. The citizens became restless and threatened to revolt. General Claude Carra Saint-Cyr, commanding a modest force in Hamburg, received information that a large enemy army was approaching. He evacuated Hamburg on 14 March 1813, without a shot being fired, and retired to the southwest. Then only a small "free corps" arrived at Hamburg and occupied the city.[6] The region of the lower Elbe had been annexed to France, and Napoleon considered Hamburg a "French" city. The emperor was angry with Carra Saint-Cyr.[7] He ordered Vandamme to retake the city, the key to the lower Elbe. Vandamme was named commander of the Thirty-second Military Division, which included the three departments of the lower Elbe (Lippe, Bouche-du Weser, and the Elbe). He was also given command of the Second Division commanded by General Jean-Baptiste Dumonceau, the Fifth Division commanded by General François-Marie Dufour, and a depot training division at Wesel on the Rhine. But his two line divisions were not at full strength and required organization.[8] Although Napoleon was writing to his lieutenants of twenty-eight battalions, on 6 April, Vandamme was able to muster only eight or ten battalions on the Weser.[9]

Before Vandamme's new command was even organized, he was informed that Marshal Davout was given command of the Thirty-second Military Division and all the troops in the North. Although the general would keep command of his three divisions, he was placed directly under the marshal's orders. He had been under Davout's authority for a brief period in 1809, and their relationship had begun with an unpleasant scene. He would now have to work with the marshal in a combat situation. Vandamme had no love for Davout. General Paul-Charles Thiébault—who also served under the marshal in 1813, and who despised him—wrote in his *Mémoires* that to "merit serving under [Davout's] orders, you must have killed your own father and mother."[10] Thiébault also records a conversation with Vandamme when he was about to leave Hamburg to join the main army: "I understand you are now employed with this corps of the army and are waiting at Hamburg, he [Vandamme] said to me, and I extend to you my compliments and condolences on your unhappy service with Marshal Davout, a man whose indignation is impossible to escape. As for me, I thank God I am leaving. In fact, if the emperor had not removed me from here, I would have removed myself."[11]

One can be sure that Vandamme was not pleased with his new position. He had been general of division when Davout was still a general of brigade. But although Vandamme had little respect for most of the marshals of the empire, he could not ignore Davout's outstanding reputation, based on the marshal's victory over the Prussian army at Auerstädt in 1806 and his service at Austerlitz, Eckmühl, Wagram, Eylau, and Borodino. He had reason to respect the marshal and fear the man. Yet he had hoped for an independent command in the north where he would be given credit for retaking Hamburg and pacifying the north. Now it would be Davout who would get the credit. Although these two soldiers cared little for one another, they were able to cooperate for the common good. Davout treated Vandamme with the respect due a general of division under his command, and Vandamme dared not treat Davout with the disrespect he had shown other marshals or the king of Westphalia. The marshal recognized a capable and experienced commander whom he would have to keep on a short leash. Vandamme knew that if he stepped out of line in the least manner Davout would destroy him in both words and action. The two men understood each other, and both kept to as harmonious a relationship as possible.[12]

Davout did not go immediately to the Thirty-second Military Division, for there was some confusion and misunderstanding of the orders. As a Coalition force was marching on Magdeburg, Eugène kept Davout and his First Corps close to his concentration point at that key city. The marshal was at Salzweld in the last days of March and then at Stendal in the first week of April and remained near the middle Elbe until the third week of April. Thus Vandamme remained in command of the troops on the Weser with little interference from the marshal. His headquarters were at Bremen. He used the first three weeks of April to organize and train the new recruits sent forward from France, and to reestablish order under French authority after the region revolted in March.

He faced numerous problems for these were confusing and uncertain times. The English, it was reported, were about to land troops on the German coast. In fact some five hundred English soldiers landed at Cuxhaven.[13] There were minor revolts on both sides of the Weser, which Vandamme put down. Rebels were treated as French citizens. They were captured, tried for treason, and shot. On 12 April the Russian general Tettenborn, in command at Hamburg, wrote Vandamme: "Monsieur General, the rumors here are that you have had two magistrates of Oldenburg shot, and that you have designated the same fate for many other respectable persons. I do not believe these atrocities are true; but, if they are, I have the honor to inform you that I will take revenge and that all of the French military and employees who are currently under my control, or who will come under my control, will be put to death. . . . You should know, Monsieur General, that I will keep my word. . . . I would further point out to you that in your situation you will be responsible for all of your terrorist actions." Despite Tettenborn's threats, Vandamme continued to send rebel leaders before military courts, and those found guilty were executed. When a revolt at Boryfeld was put down, he wrote Berthier on 19 April: "Today I have given orders to capture the authors of this open rebellion, and I will administer justice."[14]

The two line divisions commanded by Vandamme would not be ready for combat until the third week in April; and even then, the raw recruits, who had never been under enemy fire, had little or no artillery and very little cavalry support.[15] The two combat-ready units under his command were General Morand's division and General Carra Saint-Cyr's corps. Morand was operating on the lower Elbe; Carra Saint-Cyr, having withdrawn from Hamburg, was between the Elbe and the West River.

It was reported to Vandamme that General Morand had been wounded and taken prisoner.[16] Vandamme blamed Carra Saint-Cyr for not supporting him, and he denounced that general in his usual damning terms. The prefect of Bouche-du-Weser had requested protection from rebellious citizens; and Carra Saint-Cyr, who had been supporting Morand just south of the Elbe, marched his entire division back to the Weser. Morand was attacked by superior Russian forces, and his two thousand men were overrun. On 8 April, Vandamme declared to Berthier that a battalion or two was all that was needed in Bouche-du-Weser to maintain order, and that Carra Saint-Cyr should not have left General Morand alone and exposed to an enemy army. "General Saint-Cyr," he wrote Berthier, "is in no condition to lead his troops into the least danger. This general is finished, worn out, useless, and without character. . . . General Carra-Saint-Cyr gives only timid and uncertain orders. . . . [He] is no longer able to serve usefully in this region. It was his lack of character, more than all other causes, that brought about the troubles and the revolt at Hamburg."[17] Despite this criticism, however, Carra Saint-Cyr continued to command a division under Vandamme's orders.

In the third week of April, Davout was ordered to take personal command of the Thirty-second Military Division, and on 22 April he was at Nienburg on the middle Weser River. From this city he assumed total command of all the troops in the north. "Now I am here," he wrote Vandamme at Bremen, "there must be no troop movements without my orders . . . because it would be too inconvenient for you to be giving orders on your own and for me to be doing the same."[18] The following day the marshal arrived at Bremen, and Vandamme found himself as a general of division who was second in command. Displeased with his new inferior position, he asked to be relieved of his command at Bremen. On the same day that Davout arrived, Vandamme wrote Berthier: "Monseigneur, the prince of Eckmühl arrived this afternoon at Bremen. I have given him an account of the political and military situation of the Thirty-second Division, and I have turned over to His Excellence all the papers relative to this command that the emperor had conferred upon me, and that it pleased His Majesty to take from me. I have a strong desire to continue to be of use to the service of His Majesty, but I doubt I can succeed here under the orders of the prince of Eckmühl. I will try by new efforts to merit the approval of my sovereign."[19] Napoleon had more important problems; no attention was paid to Vandamme's letter, and he remained with Davout.

Napoleon had left Paris in April and joined the army east of the Rhine. He ordered the main army to advance from the Weimar area toward Leipzig so as to threaten both Berlin to the north and the Coalition forces, commanded by Prince Wittgenstein, to the south. From Leipzig Napoleon planned to send a column to Berlin while he marched to Dresden. In this manner he hoped to force the Coalition army either to give battle or to retreat east of the Elbe. At the same time, Davout was to take Hamburg again and dominate the lower regions of the Elbe. To carry out his instructions, Davout gave Vandamme the task of taking Hamburg while he held the left bank of the Elbe between Hamburg and Magdeburg with his First Corps. Davout would be close enough to the main army to support it if this became necessary. Davout was aware of Vandamme's successful siege operations during the Silesian campaign of 1806–1807, and he was pleased to have such an experienced officer under his command. He could give Vandamme a free hand at Hamburg knowing that the general was competent of the task assigned him. It might be added that Davout's reputation was already well established and he did not need credit for the capture of Hamburg; Vandamme, on the other hand, was still seeking a marshal's baton, which had seemed to be just out of reach for the past nine years.

The key to taking Hamburg was in the nine thousand Danes commanded by General Wegener near Altona, the Danish city at the mouth of the Elbe adjacent to Hamburg. Denmark found itself in a difficult position in the spring of 1813. England was hostile, Russia was backing Swedish demands for Danish territory (Norway), and Coalition forces were on its southern border at Hamburg. A Napoleonic army had been destroyed in Russia, and the Danish court could not be sure the emperor would restore his control over central Europe. Denmark was trying to remain neutral until it could see which side was going to emerge victorious. The Danes, quite understandably, wanted to end up on the winning side. While the tsar would have preferred Danish support, he at least wanted its neutrality. On the other hand, Napoleon was pressing for a military alliance. To this end Vandamme was instructed to send an officer for the purpose of establishing friendly communication with Colonel Haffner, who commanded the Danish troops at Altona. The only effect of this mission, however, was to alarm the Russians. The Danes had no intention at the time of antagonizing the Coalition. In early May, Vandamme and Davout were in no position to cross the Elbe and lay siege to Hamburg. They had to settle for minor military actions and major diplomacy.

What tipped the scale in favor of the French at Copenhagen was Napoleon's victory over the Coalition army at Lutzen on 2 May. The battle of Lutzen was a major victory for Napoleon, but it was not decisive. Wittgenstein retreated under cover of darkness and withdrew east of the Elbe to fight another day. Nevertheless, Europe was impressed, and the emperor encouraged. He took a harder line with the Danes and the city of Hamburg. On 7 May, Berthier informed Davout of the actions to be taken once Hamburg was restored to French control. It was to be treated as a French city that had rebelled against the imperial government. The marshal was to arrest all members of the senate, the governing body of Hamburg during the rebellion. They were to be sent before a military court, and Davout was to have the five most influential leaders shot by a firing squad. The others were to be sent to France to a state prison. The wealth of all senators, in money and property, was to be confiscated. He was to disarm the city and execute all the officers of the Hanseatic Legion, which had been the military force defending the city, and then send all men who had served in the legion to France to be put to hard labor. Davout was to make a list of the fifteen hundred richest individuals of the Thirty-second Military Division. He was to arrest and confiscate the belongings of those who had taken the most active part in the rebellion. Then a contribution of fifty million francs was to be levied on Hamburg and Lubeck, and Davout was to take measures to have this sum apportioned and promptly paid. He was to disarm the countryside, arrest all traitors, and confiscate their property. Berthier concluded: "All of these actions are rigorous; the emperor does not leave you free to modify them in any way."[20] But Hamburg would not be punished so harshly, for Davout interceded on behalf of the population.[21] There is no indication that Vandamme knew of the orders Davout received regarding the punishment of Hamburg. These orders clearly reflected Napoleon's anger and frustration with respect to the ("German") population of the region.[22]

Vandamme's one serious offensive operation in early May was to capture several islands that were occupied by the enemy in the Elbe near Hamburg. On 7 May he personally led the attack on the island of Wilhemsburg, between Haarburg and Hamburg. Two other less important islands (Ochsenwerder and Altenweerder) were also occupied by French troops. Knowing the importance of Wilhemsburg, the enemy sent reinforcements, and lively fighting was underway when the Danish Colonel Haffner appeared to act as an intermediary. He proposed that the islands in the river should be neutral. In accord with the French policy of appeasement toward the Danes, Vandamme agreed and withdrew his troops to the left bank of the Elbe. He brought back with him one hundred fifty prisoners of war, fifteen or twenty Cossack horses, and several pieces of artillery.[23] Haffner also proposed to Vandamme that the French not take Hamburg by storm. When the general informed Davout of Haffner's mission, the marshal replied immediately: "The neutrality of the islands is not acceptable," although he approved of Vandamme's actions. As to the recapture of Hamburg, Davout instructed the general to send an officer to Altona to tell Haffner, "we do not want to take Hamburg by force, and it is up to the wise inhabitants to prevent that extreme measure; they should give up the city."[24]

Vandamme carried out his commander's instructions and reoccupied the islands in the Elbe on 11 May. He was careful to carry out Davout's orders promptly and to the letter, and then to inform the marshal he had done so. At the same time Davout was being instructed by imperial headquarters to handle the general with care. On 7 May, Berthier wrote Davout concerning Vandamme: "It is necessary to take care, prince, in managing this general, for *hommes de guerre* are becoming rare."[25] Indeed, Davout's reports to headquarters were always favorable of Vandamme. The day after Vandamme had retaken the islands in the Elbe, the marshal wrote Berthier: "It is very fortunate that this general [Vandamme] is here; it is his presence and the élan he gave the troops that produced these results."[26] Such praise from Davout, always sparing in his compliments, was not taken lightly at headquarters. Again, when Vandamme requested the promotion of his chief of staff, Adjutant Commandant Revest, to the rank of general of brigade, Davout assured Berthier "that the best harmony exists between General Vandamme and myself, that we both will think only of the good of the service, and that this motive will eliminate the minor altercations occasioned by our competing characters."[27] Napoleon also was satisfied with Vandamme's organization and training of the new recruits he commanded, and in the way he was conducting his phase of the campaign. On 7 May, Berthier expressed these sentiments: "The emperor, Monsieur General Vandamme, has instructed me to tell you that he is content with your conduct at Bremen, and that he will provide you with a good command. Until then, support the prince of Eckmühl [Davout] in every way you can."[28]

On 20–21 May, Napoleon won a second victory over the Coalition army, this time at Bautzen, north of Dresden. The enemy army retreated east into Silesia, which had several direct effects upon the situation at Hamburg. When the news of the new Russian-Prussian setback reached Copenhagen, the Danes decided that Napoleon was in the process of regaining control of central Europe, and they began to draw closer to the French. The Danish commander in Holstien, General Wegener, was instructed to cooperate with Davout and Vandamme on the lower Elbe. On the other hand, Berlin was now threatened and Hamburg was outflanked, which meant that Tettenborn, if he remained at Hamburg, would soon find himself surrounded and besieged with little hope of escape or of being relieved.

With the Danes no longer cooperating with Hamburg's defenders, Vandamme launched another amphibious operation. When it appeared that the city might be taken back by the French, Charles John of Sweden (the former Marshal Bernadotte) had ordered the two battalions of Swedes reinforcing the Hamburg garrison out of the city. This weakened the defenses but still left a respectable Russian and German force. On 28 May, Vandamme landed troops on the Island Oschen-Werder, the last obstacle to an all-out assault on the city. He took every defensive measure so as to be sure he could withdraw his troops should they be attacked by overwhelming Coalition forces. However, rather than attempt to drive the French back to the left bank of the Elbe, General Tettenborn evacuated the city the night of 29 May.[29]

Vandamme was caught by surprise. He had plans for crossing the Elbe in force to encircle Hamburg, with Danish cooperation, but he was still several days from launching the attack. With the sudden departure of the Russian troops and the Hanseatic Legion (made up of German troops), a delegation from the city opened its gates and invited the Danes to occupy Hamburg. Davout immediately ordered Vandamme to cross the river and replace the Danes in control of the city. The general was to surround Hamburg and prevent anyone from leaving. He was not to enter into negotiations with any representatives of the population, "because there is no longer any question of capitulation." The city was to be totally disarmed. French troops were to occupy all positions. The Danish troops were to withdraw as they were replaced by French troops. Finally, Vandamme was forbidden to make any kind of arrangements with any of the citizens of Hamburg.[30]

Vandamme acted promptly on his commander's orders, and when Marshal Davout arrived in Hamburg the following day he found his instructions had been carried out to the letter. However, as he reported to Berthier, he also found that "none of the principal inhabitants remained in the city. Those who had taken part in the Hanseatic Legion had departed with the Russians or disappeared; others are in Denmark. . . . The officers of the Hanseatic Legion who have been taken prisoner up to this day are almost all foreigners, Prussians." Davout was particularly pleased that not one single member of the rebellious Hamburg government fell into his hands, nor any of the officers of the Hanseatic Legion who were "French" citizens, so he was not obliged to execute anyone. Other measures of the 7 May orders to punish Hamburg were carried out, but with moderation.[31]

A week before Hamburg was reoccupied by the French, Napoleon instructed Berthier that, as soon as Hamburg was in Davout's hands, he was to "send General Vandamme with the Second and Fifth divisions and the necessary artillery in the direction of Mecklenburg and Berlin to cover the left flank of the corps that is advancing on Berlin."[32] Knowing that Vandamme would no longer be directly under his orders, Davout praised the general and gave him the credit for the successful operations at Hamburg. "I would like you, Monseigneur," he wrote to Berthier, "to tell His Majesty that these results [the reoccupation of Hamburg] are entirely due to the good disposition of General Vandamme, . . . I must add that since General Vandamme has been put under my orders, I have had only praise for his excellent spirit. The emperor knows the ambitions of General Vandamme [a marshal's baton]. He has acquired, in these circumstances, a new right to the benevolence of His Majesty."[33] Such praise from the Iron Marshal was not common. Vandamme may well have been glad no longer to be serving directly under Davout (he wanted his own command, an army corps, directly under the emperor), but the marshal recognized his ability and, despite the general's personality, would have been pleased to have retained the services of such an excellent general of division.

By 3 June, Vandamme was in western Mecklenburg with the divisions of Dufour and Dumonceau trying to make contact with the retreating Russians. There was also a Swedish corps of some twenty or twenty-five thousand men commanded by Prince Charles John in the vicinity, but Napoleon was uncertain just where it was and what the Swedish intentions were. The emperor still hoped, despite Sweden's alliance with Russia, to be able to neutralize the Swedes. To this end Vandamme was instructed not to take hostile action against Swedish troops and to send a senior officer to Charles John (once Vandamme's personal friend) with friendly letters and to inquire as to the intentions of that nation.[34] On 7 June, Vandamme sent M. de Richardot to deliver three letters to Charles John personally. But the prince would not receive Richardot, and the general did not receive an answer until 18 June. In his response, Charles John said that Swedish troops had only reclaimed Swedish Pomerania, which had been taken by the French; and that they would defend Swedish territory against all enemies. He declined to discuss any political matters because Vandamme's role was purely military. The former marshal of the empire concluded: "I remember with great satisfaction, Monsieur Count, the times we fought together, and the proof of the attachment you gave me will always remain in my memory. I renew my good feelings for you and assure you that this sentiment extends toward you and your family. . . . Your affectionate and ancient brother in arms. Charles John."[35] In fact, Richardot's mission and the prince's reply were rendered temporarily moot by the Armistice of Neumarckt (also referred to as Pleiswitz or Poischwitz) that was signed on 4 June between the belligerent powers. The terms stated that hostilities would end on 8 June, with the demarcation to be the position of the armies at midnight. It was stipulated that the end of hostilities would last until 20 July. Vandamme did not receive news of the armistice until 9 or 10 June when Davout wrote him from Hamburg.[36] With a cease-fire in place and the operations against Hamburg a complete success, Napoleon wrote Davout on 7 June: "My cousin, show my satisfaction to General Vandamme on the occupation of Hamburg."[37] Vandamme was once again in the emperor's good graces.

The Armistice of Neumarckt was nothing more than a temporary cease-fire. Neither party was interested in a compromised peace. Both Napoleon and the Coalition monarchs believed they could still win the war and impose their terms on the other. However, the two armies were in great need of rest, supplies of all kinds, and reorganization. Napoleon's army was made up of a great number of young new recruits. They had been marching and fighting for three or four months and were in urgent need of rest. Spring recruits were being readied for the army but needed time before they were organized and sent forward into central Europe. The French cavalry had been decimated in Russia and could not be replaced as easily as infantrymen because there was a serious shortage of horses, and the training of men and animals was a slow process. Napoleon also had to bring forward every type of military supply from the Rhine to the Elbe. If, in retrospect, he is criticized for accepting the armistice, at the time there seemed many good reasons for the delay.[38]

The Russians and the Prussians also had good reason to desire a temporary cease-fire. The Russian army had suffered like the French army in the 1812 campaign. The troops needed rest, reinforcements, and supplies. In the early days of June the Prussian army was not yet up to strength. Gerhard Johann Scharnhorst had introduced reforms in the army and was rapidly increasing its number, but he needed time.[39] Equally important to the Coalition was bringing Austria into the war on its side. Austria had not been satisfied with the expanding role of France since 1797. There were four humiliating defeats at the hands of Napoleon and four equally humiliating peace treaties. Despite the marriage of Napoleon and the Austrian princess Maria Louise in 1810, the Austrian court wanted to join the Coalition and reshape the map of Europe more to its liking.

The stated purpose of the armistice was to enable Austria, in the person of Prince Clemens Lothar Metternich, to negotiate peace between the belligerents. But everyone knew that Napoleon would never accept the terms proposed by Metternich—that France must withdraw behind the Rhine, the Alps, and the Pyrenees.[40] Still the charade was played out in Prague through July and early August with Armand Caulaincourt representing the emperor. The armistice was renounced on 11 August. On 12 August, Metternich informed Napoleon that Austria had joined the Coalition and was now at war with France.[41]

During the weeks of the cease-fire, Napoleon continually regrouped and reorganized his army. On 18 June he formed a new corps for Vandamme, which would be designated the First Corps of the Grande Armée. With his headquarters at Magdeburg, the general was given forty battalions of infantry formed in three divisions. He also had forty-six pieces of artillery and headquarters staff befitting an army corps for a total of twenty-four thousand men. By 2 July, Napoleon was referring to Vandamme's command as the First Corps. This, undoubtedly, was the "fine command" that had been promised to Vandamme during the siege of Hamburg.[42]

Whereas the French army had a unified command in the person of Emperor Napoleon and internal lines of communication and maneuver, the Coalition had three monarchs plus Charles John of Sweden and an equal number of generals with different interests, goals, and strategies, and difficulties with communication and cooperation. Eventually they were able to agree upon a general plan for the renewed campaign. Charles John would have overall command in the north, with General Friedrich Wilhelm von Bülow to do the actual fighting. The Prussian General Blücher would command ninety thousand men in Silesia, and the Austrian General Schwarzenberg would command the main Coalition army in Bohemia, over some one hundred thirty thousand men strong. Schwarzenberg would have a king and two emperors helping him to make the right decisions. In fact, Tsar Alexander of Russia tended to dominate even though the Army of Bohemia was a predominantly Austrian force. The Coalition leadership had, by August 1813, at last learned one important lesson: that they should not give battle to a French army when Napoleon was in command on the battlefield. Therefore, they adopted what has come to be known as the Trachenberg Plan. Although the details were never put in writing, the plan was simply that none of the three armies should give battle if Napoleon commanded the enemy army before them. The army facing Napoleon would retreat while the other two armies would advance; and if the conditions were favorable, engage the less capable marshal commanding the force before them. In this manner they would wage a war of attrition. Talent may have been on the side of Napoleon and the French, but time, numbers, and resources were on the side of the Coalition.[43]

With hostilities about to resume, Napoleon made general plans to renew the campaign. His tentative plan was to divide his forces into two parts. There would be a smaller army in the north and the main army in Saxony. Marshal Oudinot, with eighty thousand men, would march on Berlin and then to the Oder River, relieving the besieged French garrisons in the north. Davout would support him on his left with the newly created Thirteenth Corps (thirty-two thousand men, on paper). The main army, with its principal depot at Dresden, would hold in the vicinity of Silesia and then invade Bohemia to take Prague. All of this was assuming that Austria would join the Coalition and would depend upon the actions taken by the enemy. Napoleon was a master at making plans and then being able to change them in accordance with the movements of his opponent. In late July and the early August, Vandamme was to make up part of Oudinot's command and to advance on Berlin.[44] But on 11 August the emperor wrote Berthier: "My cousin, give the order to General Vandamme to leave tomorrow, the 12th; for his First Division to take up a position at Torgou and Eilenburg in a manner to be able to reach Dresden in three days' march. The Second Division will take a position at Wittenberg and Duben so as to be able to reach Dresden in four days, and his third division (the Twenty-third) will be at Dessau, Wittenberg, and Duben so as to reach Dresden in five days. . . . His general headquarters will be at Dessau until new orders." Then the following day (12 August) Napoleon informed Davout that he was calling Vandamme to Dresden.[45] In these instructions one can see that Napoleon was modifying his plans. Vandamme was being positioned to join the main army rather than Oudinot's command in the north.

By the third week of August the fighting had resumed, and the armies were on the march. Vandamme received orders to move east to the Stolpen-Bautzen region by 19–20 August so as to be in close support of Marshal Saint-Cyr in the vicinity of Dresden. He was to establish his headquarters at Bautzen and push his cavalry as far east as Hoyerswerda. In this position he could move on Zittau or Dresden as the need arose. The situation was not clear, and Napoleon did not know the exact location of the Coalition Army of Bohemia or in which direction it would move. Thus Vandamme's divisions were ordered to Rumburg, Stolpen, and Koenigstein. He was instructed to fortify the pass through the mountains between Zittau and Gabel in the event that the enemy would move north by that route. Furthermore, the First Corps would also be in position to march south into

Bohemia. He was to send reconnaissance patrols into Bohemia in search of the enemy.[46]

Then on 23 August, Napoleon wrote Vandamme that he had fought the enemy (Blücher's Army of Silesia) and driven it back east. He declared that he had in hand one hundred thousand troops to march on into Bohemia to Zittau or to Dresden. His plans were still not finalized. But Marshal Saint-Cyr had informed him that an enemy corps had occupied Peterswalde on the Elbe, east of Dresden, and he believed that the main Coalition army was not far behind.[47] With this information, the emperor ordered Vandamme to march west to close on Dresden. He was to leave a rear guard at the pass until it was relieved by units of General Poniatowski's Eighth Corps. On 24 and 25 August the First Corps moved toward Saint-Cyr, who was holding Dresden with just one army corps.[48] On 25 August Napoleon received an urgent letter from Saint-Cyr telling him that the entire Army of Bohemia, more than one hundred thousand strong, had crossed the Erzgebirge Mountains and were preparing to attack Dresden on 26 August. Napoleon still thought of a movement against the enemy's rear by way of Pirna with Vandamme's First Corps leading the way. He informed Saint-Cyr that Dresden should be able to hold out for six days while he marched on the rear of the enemy, but after receiving a report from one of his aides, sent to assess the situation at Dresden, he decided to go to the aid of Saint-Cyr.[49]

In the afternoon of 25 August, Vandamme received the emperor's new orders. He was instructed to march onto the Koenigstein Plateau and attack or occupy Pirna on the Elbe. Although Napoleon abandoned plans to march with his whole army onto the rear of the enemy in Bohemia, he still hoped for a movement through the mountains to take the Coalition army from behind. "If the information we have received," he wrote Vandamme, "gives us to believe you are able to advance to Basra and Hellendorf so that you can occupy the passes and fall on the rear of the enemy, ... I will support you with the Young Guard." On 26 August, Vandamme wrote the emperor: "I will be master of Pirna tomorrow at an early hour," but he said he did not have his heavy guns (the twelve-pounders), which had been sent on to Dresden. On the same day Napoleon informed Vandamme that the entire enemy army was before Dresden; and, thus, the force facing the First Corps was "quite small." He ordered Vandamme to march on to

Hellendorf as quickly as possible and, he added, "I hope that during the day you will find yourself in the rear of the enemy."[50] As early as 26 August it was clearly Napoleon's intention for Vandamme to operate against the rear of the enemy army. At Hellendorf the First Corps would be astride the main road (the high road) from Dresden to Prague, thus blocking the Coalition's principal line of retreat from the Saxony capital.

In accordance with his most recent orders dated 26 August, Vandamme attacked the enemy corps before him, which was commanded by Prince Eugène of Würtemberg and supported by a Russian corps commanded by General Ivan Ostermann-Tolstoy.[51] He drove the enemy up the left bank of the Elbe along the road toward Peterswalde.[52] In the late afternoon of 27 August Vandamme reported to the emperor that he had sent an advance unit on the high road from Pirna to Dresden (on the left bank of the Elbe) in search of the enemy in that direction, while he followed the main enemy force south. He also reported that he had taken prisoners and found five hundred wounded Russian soldiers in the hospital at Pirna. The weather was bad, and his troops were tired but in good spirits.[53] The First Corps was still without its heavy twelve-pound guns. Napoleon ordered the guns to be returned to the First Corps, but the artillery commander did not know where to find Vandamme.[54] Nevertheless, on 28 August, Vandamme fought his way south to Hollendorf, which he occupied before darkness brought an end to the fighting. Würtemberg, despite heavy losses, continued to retreat down the road to Peterswalde in reasonably good order.

On 26 August the Coalition Army of Bohemia, more than one hundred thousand strong, attacked Dresden where Marshal Saint-Cyr commanded only his Fourteenth Corps of about twenty thousand men. Schwarzenberg's troops pushed in Saint-Cyr's outpost and overran several of his five redoubts, as well as most of the Grosser Garden. But Napoleon arrived and took personal command of the battle as the reinforcements he brought with him began to cross the Elbe and move to the support of the hard-pressed Fourteenth Corps. Late in the day, Napoleon was able to go on the offensive and retake some of the ground that had been given up in the course of the day's fighting. French reinforcements continued to flow into Dresden during the night, and Napoleon made plans to attack the enemy on the morning of 27 August. Much to his surprise, however, the Coalition army had retreated during the night. In keeping with the Trachenberg Plan, the decision was made not to fight a pitched battle with Napoleon in command of an army approaching the strength of Schwarzenberg's force. When the emperor realized the enemy was in full retreat, he issued orders for pursuit. The Erzgebirge Mountains run east and west just south of Dresden. The Elbe flows from Pirna east to west at that point. Thus the Coalition army, in order to reach the safety of Bohemia, had to retreat through the mountains. Vandamme blocked the high road into Bohemia, which ran from Dresden to Pirna and then south through the mountains to Töeplitz. Indeed, that was a major factor in the Coalition's decision to retreat the night of 26–27 August. Schwarzenberg's corps had to move on several different poor roads through narrow defiles and overpasses. The French pursuit was equally difficult and suffered the added problem of abandoned Austrian carts, wagons, and supplies along the narrow roads.

Napoleon was not sure that the enemy was in full retreat until the morning of 28 August.[55] When he was certain of it, he issued urgent orders for a full press pursuit. Three army corps—commanded by marshals Saint-Cyr, Ney, and Murat, plus Marshal Adolphe-Edouard Mortier, who commanded two divisions of the Guard—were ordered to pursue the enemy. Saint-Cyr, on the left, was to march on Dohna and then join up with Vandamme. Together they would move onto the rear of the enemy at Töeplitz. At the same time, Mortier was ordered to occupy Pirna and to support Vandamme from the rear, if the general needed support. Berthier was ordered to inform Vandamme of the movements of Saint-Cyr and Mortier.[56] Murat, forming the French right, followed the Austrian left, which was separated from the main army and retreating to the southwest. Marshal Ney followed the enemy center almost directly south into the mountains toward Altenberg and Töeplitz.

On 28 August Vandamme believed that Saint-Cyr was marching to join him on his right flank in pursuit of the enemy, while Mortier would be in support behind him. Berthier wrote to Vandamme at 8:00 A.M. on the 28th that the emperor was on his way to Pirna to take personal control of the pursuit.[57] This was followed by new orders issued at 4:00 P.M. the same day. Vandamme was to move forward immediately to Peterswalde with his entire corps. The major general wrote:

"The emperor desires that you reunite all the forces that he has put at your disposition, and that with them you will penetrate into Bohemia and fall upon the prince of Würtemberg, if he wants to oppose you. *His Majesty thinks that you will be able to arrive upon the enemy's communications at Teschen, Aussig, and Töeplitz and be able to take his equipment, his ambulances, his baggage, and in fact everything that marches behind an army*" (emphasis added).[58]

In response to Berthier's instructions, at 8:30 P.M. that night Vandamme reported he was at Hellendorf. The enemy had put up a fight but was driven south with heavy losses. "I will attack at daybreak and march on Töeplitz with my entire corps unless I receive orders to the contrary."[59] Having received no new orders, at 8:30 A.M. on 29 August, Vandamme informed Berthier: "I attacked the enemy at dawn today. It was routed after defending Peterswalde. I will pursue the enemy. . . . Our infantry conducted itself perfectly and, I might say, covered itself with glory. . . . *I am continuing my march on Töeplitz in accordance with my orders from the emperor*" (emphasis added).[60] This is the second time Vandamme informed Berthier that he was marching on Töeplitz as ordered. Clearly, and without question, Vandamme believed his orders were to push the enemy before him and reach Töeplitz so as to capture the enemy's baggage and cut Prince Schwarzenberg's retreat southeast out of the Erzgebirge Mountains. That Napoleon was fully aware of what Vandamme was doing—and that it met with his approval—is seen in a letter the emperor wrote Murat on 29 August: "My brother, today the 29th at 6:00 A.M. General Vandamme attacked the prince of Würtemberg [actually Ostermann] near Hellendorf: . . . He is leading the advance with drums beating. They [the enemy] were all Russians. *General Vandamme marches on Töeplitz with his entire corps*" (emphasis added).[61]

On the morning of 29 August 1813, Vandamme placed two brigades under the command of Prince Reuss-Schleiz to lead the attack against the enemy. The unfortunate Reuss was struck on the left thigh by a cannon ball. Evacuated to Hollendorf, the general died within hours.[62] The French advance continued as General Ostermann, who commanded the enemy rear guard, fell back fighting. Vandamme crossed the pass of the Erzgebirge Mountains and descended into the plains of Kulm. He was then on the south side of the mountains and only six or seven miles from Töeplitz. He reported that he had taken thirteen hundred prisoners of war including thirteen officers, one of them a colonel.[63]

Napoleon had left Dresden on 28 August to go to Pirna and personally direct the pursuit into Bohemia, but before reaching that town he received news that Marshal Oudinot had been defeated by General Bülow at Gross Beeren. Oudinot was falling back onto the Elbe. This drastically changed the situation in the north, and the emperor returned at once to Dresden. Instead of being close behind Vandamme, as the general believed, Napoleon was thus at a much greater distance from the fighting. This made communication between the general and headquarters more difficult, as it took a greater length of time for Vandamme's information to reach headquarters and for new instructions to reach the battlefield.

The return to Dresden did, on the other hand, put Napoleon in closer communication with Saint-Cyr, Ney, and Murat. Because of the defeat at Gross Beeren, however, the emperor pulled Ney from the pursuit of the Austrians and sent him north to replace Oudinot. On 28 August, Saint-Cyr also had been ordered to pursue the enemy, actually the Prussian corps of General Frederick Heinrich Kleist, in the direction of Dohna. This took the marshal parallel to the Elbe on the left bank of the river. At Dohna he was just a few miles west of Pirna and moving directly toward Vandamme, with whom he had been ordered to join forces. But on the morning of 29 August, Napoleon instructed Berthier: "Give the order to Marshal Saint-Cyr to follow the enemy to Maxen and *in whatever direction it would take*" (emphasis added).[64] Maxen was to the southwest, so Saint-Cyr, still following Kleist, was moving away from Dohna, and away from Vandamme.

Vandamme reached Kulm at about 11:00 A.M. on 29 August and found that Ostermann had taken up a defensive position across the main road leading to Töeplitz. The main Coalition army of Schwarzenberg was retreating down the Dresden-Altenberg-Töeplitz road. Most of its baggage train was still near Töeplitz, and it was vital for the Coalition that Ostermann stop Vandamme's advance at Kulm, in order to keep the road open through Töeplitz and on south toward Prague. "Ostermann and his grenadiers understood what was being asked of them.... The valley of Töeplitz had become their 'Thermopylë.'"[65] Tsar Alexander and the Prussian king Frederick William were at Töeplitz on 29 August, and they ordered all available troops forward to support Ostermann. When Vandamme made first contact with the enemy, he had only the late Prince Reuss's brigade commanded by his chef d'état-major Jean Revest. The rest of his corps was spread along the road behind him. The road from Kulm to Töeplitz ran east and west parallel to the mountains, less than a mile to the north. Ostermann anchored his left on the village of Straden at the foot of the mountains and his right near the village of Karwitz. The fighting line was more than a mile between the mountains and Karwitz, with the road and the village of Priesten in the middle. The village of Kulm was less than one mile behind Vandamme.

Vandamme ordered Revest to attack the village of Straden immediately, on the enemy's left, while General Corbineau's cavalry division occupied the ground on his left. Revest was about to occupy the village when the enemy launched four squadrons of the Russian guard at the same time that enemy troops attacked the French right flank from the woods at the base of the mountain. This drove the French back, but Vandamme sent forward reinforcements as they arrived down the road from the pass and moved up his division artillery. However, he did not have his corps artillery nor adequate cavalry or sufficient troops to push the enemy back. Yet the line was stabilized, and the fighting continued. Vandamme's corps continued to move onto the plain and was ordered into the line. On the other side, Schwarzenberg's troops had begun to reach Töeplitz and were ordered at once to Kulm so as to hold the French at bay. Thus both armies continued to receive reinforcements, and the day ended in a stalemate.[66]

On the morning of 30 August, Vandamme had in hand fifty-two battalions, a division of cavalry and eighty guns, a force of perhaps thirty-two thousand men. At the same time major Coalition forces from Dresden had arrived south of the mountain, which allowed Schwarzenberg, who assumed command at Kulm, to confront the French with by noon some forty-five or fifty thousand men.[67] At 6:30 A.M. Vandamme informed Napoleon: "The enemy is determined to defend the road to Töeplitz with vigor. His forces were strengthened [overnight]. I can only hold my position and await Your Majesty's orders. I have concentrated my forces and I am prepared to execute your instructions. . . . My reserve artillery has still not joined me. I lack munitions. My company of horse artillery that followed the Twenty-third Division has not returned to the First Corps . . . we have no source of substance. The enemy has burned everything."[68]

Vandamme believed that Napoleon was at Pirna personally conducting operations. If so, he could receive new orders by noon. He also believed that Saint-Cyr was still moving onto his right flank and that Mortier was not far behind him. Therefore, his intention was to hold his position until one or both of the marshals arrived to support him. This decision was supported by General Nicolas Haxo and the other generals of division.[69]

Schwarzenberg was not quick in developing his forces on the morning of 30 August. His plan was to hold the French in the center and on his left while outflanking the enemy on his right. The fighting resumed on a moderate scale by 7:00 A.M. when Vandamme ordered an attack against the enemy left. But Austrian reinforcements were sent forward and a counterattack followed. Fighting continued without either side making headway. At 8:00 A.M. two more Austrian divisions began to arrive on the enemy's right, and Schwarzenberg ordered the turning maneuver to begin in earnest. Vandamme sent support to his left, but the progress of the Coalition forces could only be slowed, not stopped. By noon the First Corps was giving ground in the center and the left. General Philippon, with the Twenty-fourth Division and one brigade of Dumonceau, held firm on the right. The day after the battle he reported to headquarters: "I was ordered to hold my position. I held until 3:00 P.M. . . . by which time the left flank of the [French] army had been turned. At that time, Vandamme gave me orders to retreat to Pirna, which was no longer possible."[70] Despite the fact that he was outnumbered and the tide of battle was turning against him, Vandamme continued to hold his position during the early afternoon in the expectation that help was on its way. But finally all hope disappeared.

Shortly after noon, General Kleist, with the First Prussian Corps, some thirty thousand strong, began to appear in Vandamme's rear. Kleist had retreated through Dohna and Maxen to Barenstein, but finding the Altenberg–Töeplitz road so cluttered with wagons and retreating troops, he decided the only way he could save his corps was to move off to his left. He would march east to the high road and fight his way across Vandamme's rear to rejoin the main Coalition army.

The Prussian corps marched most of the night of 29–30 August. Unfortunately, Marshal Saint-Cyr did not press hard on the enemy, which let Kleist make good time moving onto Vandamme's rear. Led by Colonel von Blücher (son of the famous general), the Prussians reached Nollendorf. Learning of the battle taking place at Kulm, Kleist ordered a right turn to fall upon the rear of the already outnumbered and hard-pressed French. At the same time Kleist sent a strong column toward Peterswalde, in the event that Napoleon was sending help to the now encircled First Corps.[71]

When Vandamme and the French first heard cannon fire behind them, they believed it was either Saint-Cyr or Mortier coming to their rescue. They took heart and renewed the struggle with vigor. But they soon came to realize it was not French guns announcing their arrival but enemy fire. By 3:00 P.M. all hope was lost, and Vandamme ordered a general retreat. He sacrificed his artillery that was covering the retreat, because there was no way it could be saved. He ordered the caissons burned, the munitions destroyed, and the guns spiked. Most of the gunners were saved. "The general," he wrote in his notes, "seeing that his orders for retreat were not being carried out precisely as he had given, decided to remain behind and personally conduct the retreat. He exposed himself on many occasions and was in constant danger directing the rear guard."[72]

As Kleist's corps emerged from the defile onto the plains, it took up a position astride the main road blocking the French retreat. But the center and left of the First Corps had no choice but to use that road. Thus heavy fighting now occurred east of Kulm with the newly arrived Prussian corps. In desperation, the French cavalry, supported by infantry units and stragglers from the artillery and support trains, attacked the Prussian line and destroyed its center, which enabled the French to pour through the breach and reach safety. The Prussians had been marching all night, without food or rest, and had little interest in trying to stop the desperate French column. The men of both armies were thinking first of saving themselves. The Prussians were quite satisfied to get out of the way of the thundering cavalry and the desperate men following. Kleist himself was almost overrun and took refuge with his troops in woods flanking the road. Losses on both sides were heavy, but a substantial number of French troops (perhaps five thousand) and horses escaped to reach Prina eventually.[73] The French right flank had held its position until 3:00 P.M. By the time General Philippon received orders to retreat, it was too late to fall back onto the high road. He had Russian columns in front of him and Austrian divisions turning his left flank. The divisions of the right would have to surrender or flee into the wooded mountains on their right. Choosing the latter, most of Philippon's command was saved and eventually linked up with Saint-Cyr. The day following the battle, Philippon wrote to Berthier: "I have about ten thousand infantrymen and five hundred cavalry that have escaped."[74] The enemy, exhausted by days of marching and fighting, made no serious attempt to pursue the defeated French into the mountains. Its principal aim was to save the Army of Bohemia, and with Vandamme's defeat, this goal was achieved.

More than half of Vandamme's command escaped to fight another day. In addition to Philippon's ten or eleven thousand, Napoleon informed Berthier on 1 September that the Forty-second Division had assembled five thousand men at Pirna.[75] However, their commander in chief was not among the fortunate. Vandamme, having remained behind to direct the retreat, was taken prisoner by Russian troops. The senior Russian officer was Paul Andréiévitch Kolzakov, who held the rank of naval captain and was aide-de-camp to the grand duke Constantine Pavlovitch, Tsar Alexander's brother.[76]

Kolzakov in his *Mémoires* has left a description of Vandamme's capture on the afternoon of 30 August.[77] He made no attempt to describe the battle of Kulm but wrote: "I simply want to mention an episode to which I can testify as an eyewitness, and in which I played a role." As one of Constantine's aides, Kolzakov was, for the fourth time, carrying orders to Kleist in the defile. On his return he had to dismount his exhausted horse and was walking back through the confusion of the French retreat. Suddenly, a handful of French officers came riding toward him with Cossacks in hot pursuit. From the opposite direction more Cossacks joined Kolzakov. The French were surrounded and about to be put to the sword when, Kolzakov wrote: "I heard a loud cry 'Russian General save me!' . . . I cried out 'Halt, Cossacks, halt! Do not strike them!' I was able to stop them in time. The French were surrounded on all sides and made prisoners."[78]

> The French General [Vandamme] dismounted animated by what he was going to do. His chubby face was all red and the sweat ran in great drops down his cheeks that were covered with dust, as was all of his uniform. After catching his breath, he turned towards me; and thinking that I was a general officer—without doubt because of the naval hat—he said, while handing me his sword with a theatrical gesture, "I give to you, General, my sword that has served me during many years for the glory of my country." I refused to receive it, saying that he would have to give it personally to the Tsar [Alexander], to whom he would be conducted, and I asked him his name. I learned that it was General Vandamme himself.

Kolzakov wrote that Vandamme appeared to be drunk [*ivre*] as he was completely exhausted. He requested that he be allowed to rest a little before going on. The request was granted. The French officers who were with Vandamme dismounted, and the general shook each man's hand and said: "My brave friends, we cannot always be lucky."[79] Vandamme then told Kolzakov that two of his officers had been wounded and were back along the road. The Russian said he would see that they were cared for. Russian cavalrymen then escorted the French to Emperor Alexander, while Kolzakov rejoined Grand Duke Constantine. When informed that Vandamme had been taken prisoner, the grand duke set off at once to meet the French general. Arriving at imperial headquarters at about the same time as the French, Constantine approached Vandamme. The general, believing Constantine was the emperor, again drew his sword and with the words and gesture as before tried to present his sword. Like Kolzakov, Constantine refused and pointed out his brother. For the third time, Vandamme presented his sword and made his brief speech. This time it was accepted, and Alexander replied: "General, I am indeed sorry, but such is the way of war!" He then signaled Prince Volkonsky to return the sword to Vandamme and ordered the prisoners to be sent to the rear. "'Sire, one more word,' Vandamme said to him, 'I pray Your Majesty the grace not to turn me over to the Austrians.' The tsar smiled at the emperor of Austria and told Vandamme that his request was granted."[80] Vandamme was escorted first to Töeplitz and then on to Prague, where he was shown, somewhat discreetly, as a trophy of war. Finally he was sent to Moscow.[81]

The question of who was at fault for the defeat at Kulm was one in which everyone involved on the French side pointed to someone else. Napoleon's secretary of the cabinet, Baron Agathon Jean Fain, who was at headquarters at the time, records the following account of the emperor when he received the news of Kulm:

> Napoleon received the details of his losses coldly. What he could not understand was how Vandamme could let himself be drawn into Bohemia. "With an army that is fleeing," he [Napoleon] repeated, "it is necessary to give a bridge of gold or to oppose with a barrier of steel. Vandamme was not able to be a barrier of steel." Then turning to the major general "could you have written to him something that could have inspired that fatal thought? Berthier, go find your minutes: Fain, you do the same; verify everything that we have written." The major general soon brought his book of orders; the secretary of the cabinet produced his minutes; they reread all their letters, and they found nothing that authorized the unhappy general to quit his position at Peterswalde.[82]

After some reflection on the course of events and his present situation, Napoleon is reported to have said: "*Eh bien*, he said to the duke of Bassano [Hughes-Bernard Maret], you will come to understand that with war, it is up in the morning and down at night.... From triumph to fall it is often only one step."[83]

Napoleon put the entire blame for the disaster at Kulm upon Vandamme. On 1 September, just two days after the battle, he wrote his brother-in-law, King Joachim Murat: "The unhappy news has arrived of the First Corps.... General Vandamme, who seems to have been killed, did not leave a sentinel on the mountains, nor a reserve of any part; he rushed forward without looking to either side."[84] It was in Napoleon's and Berthier's best interests to find no direct order sending Vandamme to Töeplitz. Thus the disaster at Kulm was entirely the fault of the commanding officer. However, it clearly had been Napoleon's intention for Vandamme to move onto the rear of the retreating Coalition Army, capture its baggage train, and harass its withdrawal. It is also clear that Vandamme believed he was following orders, and that he was being supported on his right flank by Marshal Saint-Cyr and in his rear by Marshal Mortier. In retrospect, it is easy to criticize him, as Napoleon did, for not leaving a rear guard in the pass. Yet even a few battalions would not have halted Kleist's Prussian Second Corps of thirty thousand men desperately trying to avoid encirclement. Vandamme felt that Saint-Cyr and Mortier did not give him adequate support; he blamed Saint-Cyr for not pursuing Kleist with sword in hand, and Mortier for not following him in close support when he knew, or should have known, that the First Corps was moving into a dangerous position across the path of a vastly superior retreating enemy army.

While all the French commanders were attributing blame for the disaster at Kulm to someone else, it seems that the real explanation lies with the Coalition forces. Ostermann's stand behind Kulm on 29 August enabled Schwarzenberg to reach the battlefield with superior forces on the 30th. Vandamme was defeated on the battlefield. He may well have retreated and saved his corps if Kleist had not arrived on his rear. It was Kleist who turned the French defeat into a disaster. Blame, from the French point of view, and credit, from the Coalition point of view, should go to Kleist, Ostermann, and the Coalition Army.

Although Napoleon won a major victory over the Coalition Army of Bohemia at Dresden, his generals were defeated: Oudinot at Gross Beeren, Macdonald at the Katzbach, Vandamme at Kulm, and Ney at Dennewitz on 6 September. Napoleon regrouped his forces, and on 16–18 October he fought the battle of Leipzig. Outnumbered and outgunned, the emperor suffered his greatest defeat, and the French army retreated behind the Rhine into France. Napoleon fought a fine campaign in 1814 but lost the war eventually to attrition. Paris was occupied on 31 March 1814, and the French emperor abdicated his throne on 6 April. With the conclusion of the war, Louis XVIII was put on the throne of France, and all prisoners of war were sent home.

Little is known of Vandamme's captivity in Russia. He spent about four months in Moscow where he was relatively free to move about with a Russian escort. His movements were monitored and reported to St. Petersburg. On 31 January 1814, the Moscow governor wrote Tsar Alexander: "After the report I sent Your Imperial Majesty [24 September 1813], you will see that Vandamme did not frequent the premier homes of Moscow. Since his arrival, I have seen him only once, in order to gain his impression of the battle of Leipzig. I have an idea of the character of this villain of a man; but having received no particular orders with respect to him, I have treated him no different from any other general prisoner, and I have taken upon myself to have an officer of the police accompany him."[85] From Moscow Vandamme was sent to Viatka (also called Kivov), some three hundred miles to the east, where he remained until released from captivity.

The war ended with Napoleon's abdication in April 1814, and prisoners of war were allowed to return home. On 13 July Vandamme arrived at Riga, and the following day obtained passage on the *Anne Dorothea* for himself and twenty-six French officers and civilians to return to France.[86] The ship flew the Danish flag out of Copenhagen, and her captain was Johan Peterson. The arrangement was to transport the French to Dunkirk for the sum of 6,150 francs. The *Anne Dorothea* sailed from Riga on 28 July and stopped at Copenhagen for several days before sailing on to Dunkirk, arriving on 1 September 1814. As Vandamme had made the arrangements and signed the documents, he was held personally responsible for the payment of the 6,150 francs when neither the new French government nor any of the other passengers would provide any money. The so-called *Anne Dorothea* Affair dragged on for several years, but in the end it was Vandamme who paid. In December 1820 the affair was closed with an agreed-upon amount of 4,811 francs.[87] Upon his return to France, Vandamme joined his wife and son in Paris where they resided at number 17 rue Joubert until 7 October 1814, at which time he returned to Cassel.

11

THE WATERLOO CAMPAIGN

General Vandamme returned to a France that had undergone enormous changes since his departure. Following his defeat and capture at Kulm at the end of August 1813, the defeat of Marshal Oudinot at Gross Beeren, Marshal Ney at Dennewitz, and Marshal Macdonald at the Katzbach, Napoleon was forced to wage a defensive war. He still commanded a dangerous army, but the Coalition, with superior forces, began to close in on him. Prince Charles John (Marshal Bernadotte) of Sweden from the north, Blücher from the east, and Schwarzenberg from the south brought the emperor to bay at Leipzig on 16 October. In three days of fierce fighting, the battle of the Nations settled the fate of central Europe. Napoleon was defeated on the field of battle, and the crippled and demoralized Grande Armée limped back across the Rhine for one last campaign in northern France. But the die was cast; and although Napoleon waged the campaign of 1814 with great skill, there was little hope he could prevail against the superior forces now marching against him. The emperor conducted the campaign like the Napoleon of old, but the army he commanded was not the Army of Austerlitz or of Jena-Auerstädt. Nor was the Coalition army facing him the same force he had defeated so many times in the past. Russia, Austria, and Prussia were now united in their determination to destroy

Napoleonic France. Paris was occupied on 30 March, and Napoleon abdicated at Fontainebleau on 6 April 1814.

The French emperor was given the island of Elba for his "empire." Louis XVIII assumed "his" throne in the nineteenth year of his reign.[1] The royalist émigrés returned from exile to reclaim their lands, positions, and status in society. The Bourbons restored the monarchy, but they could not turn back the clock to 1789. Twenty-five years of revolution and the Napoleonic empire could not be ignored. Louis granted France a charter that established a constitutional monarchy, but one in which authority flowed from the king downward, not from the people up. Many of the changes introduced since 1789 were accepted, in particular those pertaining to the army and the church. The king recognized titles of nobility and military rank granted by Napoleon. Thus Lieutenant General Vandamme remained the count of Unsebourg. At the same time, many officers of high rank in the army were forced into retirement and replaced by royalists. The army was downsized. Its morale plummeted. France was thankful that the years of warfare—with the odious conscription that had sent so many young men to die on foreign battlefields—had ended.

With the removal of Napoleon and the restoration of the house of Bourbon, the victorious powers of Europe set about restoring the old regime to their liking. Because their "ally" Louis XVIII was back on the throne of France, they did not treat the country as an enemy. It was Napoleon, they declared, who was the enemy, and he was at Elba. France was restored to the 1792 boundaries, that is, the boundaries as they had been when the Revolution overthrew the monarchy. It was into this "new" France that Vandamme arrived on 1 September 1814.

The general went directly to Paris where his wife and son were waiting for him. He pledged his support for the king and sought the aid of the duke of Aumont, the First Gentleman of the Chamber, to gain an audience with Louis XVIII. When he received no reply, he informed the duke that he had no request of the king except to be presented, as the other general officers had been on returning from captivity. Vandamme then went to court where, together with a large crowd, he watched the king enter the throne room. He thought he would be admitted; but instead, a bailiff sent by d'Aumont told him that he could not remain at the audience and that he must leave immediately. He

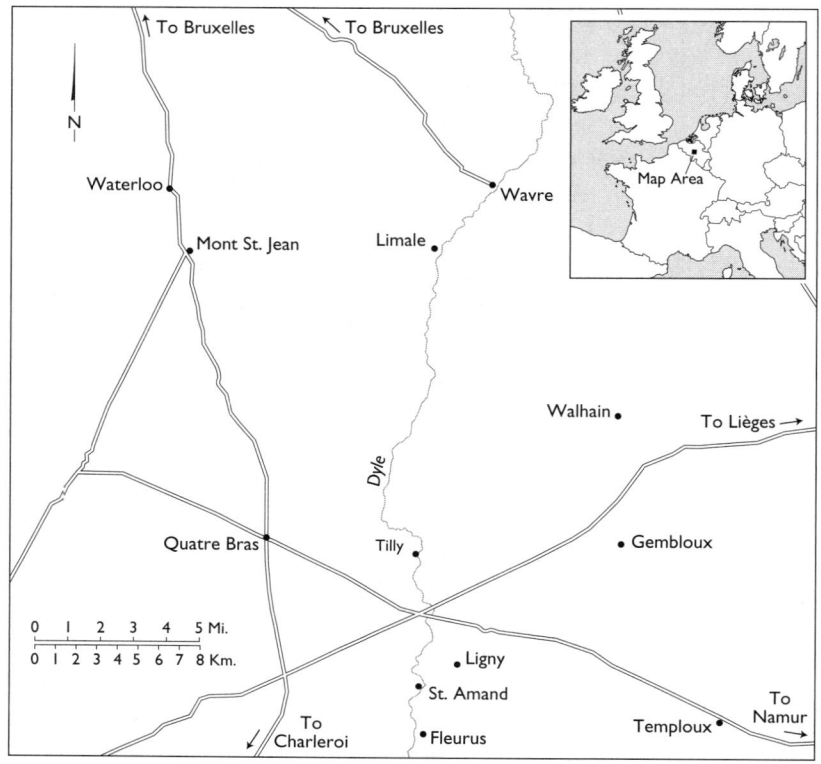

The Ligny/Waterloo campaign

later wrote that "I was consumed with humiliation," and he left at once.[2]

Vandamme was still residing at 17 rue Joubert on 10 October 1814 when, sometime between midnight and one o'clock in the morning, he was awakened and an officer of the minister of war presented him with an order to leave Paris within twenty-four hours. The order named Cassel as his new place of residence. "Torn from the arms of my family," he later wrote, "I left my wife and son in the greatest anguish," and obeying the order, he left the capital the following day. That night, 11 October, an officer of the minister of war returned to the rue Joubert to be sure that the general had departed. Vandamme wrote several letters to the minister of war asking for an explanation of why he had been ordered out of Paris, but he received no answers. He also requested that he be placed on trial so that he could defend himself in public. Again he received no reply.³

The explanation seems to be that the royalists considered him a confirmed Bonapartist, who had been a radical republican and antimonarchist during the revolutionary wars. He had been denounced to the king as having personally executed émigrés taken prisoners when his troops captured the city of Nieuport in 1793. A letter printed in a German newspaper some time in the early 1790s, reported to have been written by the general, quoted him as having said, in part: "Their [the émigrés] trial was made on the spot, my pistols and saber did their work."⁴ This appears to be the main reason that Vandamme was not accepted at court or in the army and was exiled from Paris.

Needless to say, Vandamme immediately set about to clear his name. He wrote the minister of war: "A vile slanderer has told the king that I killed émigrés with my own hands, which is false to the point of absurdity. . . . A brave soldier such as myself fights and kills but never assassinates."⁵ To accompany his letter, which also pledged loyalty to France and the king, Vandamme sent an undetermined number of letters to former commanding officers and comrades. It is not known how many of his former comrades in arms he requested letters from, nor how many replied, but four of these letters exist in the War Archives at the Château de Vincennes—from Marshal Jourdan, Marshal Macdonald, General Dejean, and General d'Erlon, all of whom served with the Army of the North in 1793.⁶ All declared that they had no knowledge of such an atrocity at the time (1793), nor had they heard any rumors of such action on the part of General Vandamme. The very respected Marshal Jourdan reflects the views of the others: "I presume, Monsieur General, that like all of the other military commanders, you carried out the law that ordered all Frenchmen taken prisoner with arms in their hands who were in the ranks of the enemies of France be sent before a military tribunal. But I declare that it never was known to me that any of these were executed by your hand. You may, general, do whatever you consider convenient with my letter."⁷

In mid-February 1814, when the Coalition armies occupied northern France, Russian Cossacks vandalized La Frégate, Vandamme's château at Cassel. On 17 February, Baron Geismar, a colonel in the Russian army who was second in command of the army commanded by the duke Regent of Saxe Weimar, ordered his aide-de-camp Major Count Pückler to take a patrol of forty or fifty Russian Cossacks to Cassel. The Baron Geismar claimed that Vandamme, when in Germany in 1813, had stolen three hundred thousand francs and two very large silver andirons from his father and uncle. The object of this mission was to recover the money and the andirons from Vandamme's château. There was no money, as the Vandamme family had fled to Paris leaving only the servants behind. The Cossacks pillaged La Frégate with the aid of one of the general's servants, M. Salome, taking what they could carry. They also sent a wagonload of wine to army headquarters. But there is no mention of the andirons.[8] The damage to the château was not serious, as the campaign was still in progress and the Cossacks were ordered out of Cassel the following day. To show their anger and disrespect, the portrait of General Vandamme was slashed by a sabor.[9]

The Vandamme family maintained a low profile and lived quietly in Cassel through the fall and winter of 1814–15. Their income was greatly reduced, as at the close of the war they had lost the holdings in Belgium and Germany that had been given to the general by Napoleon. Vandamme spent his time caring for his gardens and the park that made up his estate on the south side of Cassel. The damage at La Frégate was estimated at about twelve thousand francs, most of which was from the items carried off by the Cossacks. There was little damage to the château itself or its grounds. In any event, the Vandammes were hard-pressed for money in the winter of 1814–15. As the general had no command, he had little income. He busied himself trying to collect 6,000 francs in back pay from the summer of 1813, and 4,164 francs for the losses he suffered at Kulm when taken prisoner.[10] Life for Vandamme and his family might well have remained peaceful and uneventful had Napoleon not returned from Elba in the spring of 1815.

On 26 February, Napoleon sailed from Elba and landed at the Gulf of Juan on 1 March. He had received constant information from Paris and from Vienna where representatives of the crowned heads of Europe were redrawing the map of Europe. He had been informed that Louis XVIII was not popular with the people, and that the army, in particular, was disgruntled. His informants assured him that the great powers were divided over a number of issues, mainly with respect to the fate of Poland and many lesser German states. The territorial ambitions of Prussia and Russia were opposed by Austria and Great Britain. Talleyrand, representing the king of France, was siding with the Austrians and the British. If the Coalition of 1813–14 could not hold together, and if the army could be won over to his side, Napoleon believed, he could return to Paris and reestablish himself as French emperor. His march to Paris was a victorious triumph. At Grenoble and at Lyon, the soldiers rallied to their emperor, and on 20 March 1815 he entered Paris to the cries of "Vive l'Empereur." The king fled to Belgium under the protection of the Coalition army, and the empire was once again proclaimed.

It is true that not all Frenchmen were happy to see the emperor return. Royalist resistance had to be put down in the south and in the west. But, in general, the French people preferred Napoleon to Louis XVIII, particularly when the emperor proclaimed that he wanted peace in Europe. There is little doubt that he did indeed want peace. The army had been put on a peacetime status and was not at all ready to undertake a military campaign. The government had to be reorganized, money had to be raised, and the army had to be put on a war footing in case the powers of Europe did not accept the new regime. When the news of Napoleon's successful return to power reached Vienna, the antagonists put aside their differences and pledged unity in the common goal of once again removing him from the throne of France. Britain, Austria, Prussia, and Russia all pledged again to march major armies to the borders of France to restore Louis XVIII to his throne.

Despite his declaration for peace, Napoleon was declared an outlaw, and the Coalition forces prepared for war. Europe did not believe he could live within the boundaries established in 1814, or with Europe's boundaries as they were being drawn in Vienna. Thus Napoleon was faced with war, and all of Europe was opposed to him. From a strategic point of view he seemed to have two options: he could wait until the Coalition armies invaded France and fight a defensive campaign, or he could attack the enemy and wage an offensive campaign. The first option would give him more time to increase the size of the French army and prepare for war, but it would also give the Coalition all the time it needed to bring massive forces against France and to choose the times and the places where the campaigns would be fought. On the other hand, if he chose to attack the enemy before it was ready, that is, before the Russian and Austrian armies were in position on the Rhine and the Alps, he could win major victories over the Prussian and the Anglo-Dutch-German armies in Belgium. He could then march against the Russians and Austrians. As this seemed to hold the greater hope for ultimate victory, Napoleon set about preparing the army to invade Belgium.

The army as a whole rallied to the emperor. Many former soldiers who had been dismissed from the king's peacetime army returned and rapidly increased the army's size. Not everyone was enthused about yet another campaign, however. Some marshals and generals chose to sit out this war, and others were not acceptable. Napoleon was still angry with Murat, for he had joined the Coalition in the last days of the 1814 campaign in order to save his throne at Naples; and Ney was initially refused a command because of his negative reaction to the emperor's return. Perhaps the greatest loss was Berthier, who was weary of war and remained neutral until his untimely death on 1 June 1815. But once the king had left the country, others such as Marshal Davout and Vandamme, who had never been received at court or given a command in the royal army, were relatively free to take service with Napoleon. Later they would maintain that they had served their country when it was attacked by its enemies.[11] With the rapid expansion of the army in the spring of 1815, Napoleon was in need of good generals, and Vandamme was still one of his best. He was given a command and ordered to Dunkirk.

On 9 April, Napoleon wrote Marshal Davout, whom he had named minister of war: "My cousin, send tonight a lieutenant general or a *maréchal de camp* that is capable and firm to command at Dunkirk.... The émigrés and the enemy are concentrating all their efforts to take control of that city."[12] The same day the minister of war ordered Vandamme to Dunkirk, and he took up his new command on 11 April.[13] His very presence in the vulnerable port city seemed enough to end the attempt on the part of the émigrés and the royalists to gain control of Dunkirk for use as a base in France to oppose the new regime. The threat removed, on 20 April, Napoleon gave Vandamme command of the Third Corps of the army and of the Second Military Division, with his headquarters at Mézières, just north of Reims.[14] The months of April and May were taken up with the organization of the Third Corps and the training of new recruits. There were also rumors that the duke of Wellington was preparing to invade France by way of Vervins and Laon, which kept part of Vandamme's corps on constant alert.[15] The general was also faced with the problem of desertions from a Swiss battalion that was a part of his command.[16]

In the third week of May, the Third Corps was ordered to the region between Rocroy and Philippeville where it became a part of the right wing of the Army of the North. It was while he was at Rocroy that Vandamme learned that he had been named a peer of France. He was then ordered to Paris where he was officially installed at the Palace of Peers.[17] Then, on the eve of the campaign, Vandamme was ordered to concentrate his corps before Beaumont, just south of the Belgium (the kingdom of the Netherlands) border. On the morning of 15 June, the French, led by Vandamme's Third Corps, crossed into Belgium, and the Waterloo campaign began.

The Coalition forces in Belgium comprised two separate armies, each with their own independent commander. The duke of Wellington, with his headquarters at Brussels, commanded 96,000 Dutch-Belgiums, Germans, and English. Field Marshal Gebhard Leberecht von Blücher, with his headquarters at Namur, commanded a Prussian army of 123,000 men. In addition, there was a Russian army commanded by General Barclay marching through Germany on its way to the Rhine; and two Austrian armies, one commanded by Schwarzenberg advancing on to the Rhine at Basel, and the other in Italy preparing to invade southern France. The overall Coalition strategy was to wait until all these armies were on the French border, presumably about 1 July. Then Wellington, Blücher, and Barclay would march on Paris, while the two Austrian armies (Schwarzenberg in Germany and General Frimont in Italy) would strike into central and southern France. Until such time as all Coalition armies were in place, Wellington and Blücher had their own understanding. Wellington's army was not united but was spread out in camps from north of Lille to a point east of Quatre Bras. The Prussian army was spread out from the east flank of Wellington to Liège. Wellington and Blücher were well informed of the gathering threat in northern France. Spies and travelers kept them posted as to the movements of the French army, so they were not taken by surprise. Their original plan was to concentrate their two armies, in the event that Napoleon would take the offensive and invade Belgium. However, they could not be sure just where the main French attack would take place—against Wellington or against Blücher. Thus on 15 June the two armies had made no effort to unite.[18]

Napoleon believed that his invasion of Belgium would catch the Coalition forces by surprise. His plan was to strike at their most vulnerable point, that is, where the two armies joined between Quatre Bras and Sombreffe. His army of some 128,000 men was made up of five army corps plus cavalry and the Imperial Guard. The corps were commanded by General Jean-Baptiste Drouet, the count of Erlon, First Corps; General Honoré-Charles Reille, Second Corps; Vandamme, Third Corps; General Maurice-Etienne Gérard, Fourth Corps; and General Georges Lobau, Sixth Corps. Marshal Grouchy, whom Napoleon had just named marshal of the empire, commanded the right wing consisting of the cavalry corps of Exelmans and Pajol. General Kellermann commanded the cavalry on the left. This army would be divided into two wings and a reserve. The initial goal would be the town of Charleroi just across the border. Then the left wing (Reille, d'Erlon, and Kellermann) would advance toward Quatre Bras to engage Wellington's advanced units, while the right wing (Vandamme, Gérard, and Grouchy) would move on to Fleurus against the Prussians. The Guard and Lobau (Sixth Corps) would act as a reserve to support whichever of the two wings first met serious resistance. In this way the emperor hoped to engage the Coalition armies one at a time before they could unite.

Vandamme's Third Corps, preceded by a cavalry screen, led the army north. To facilitate the army's rapid advance, Napoleon had ordered all baggage and equipment vehicles to be sent to the rear, to follow the last marching column. Any wagon or cart, other than munitions or hospital, that was found with the advancing columns would be burned.[19] Although it was the emperor's intention for the Third Corps to be on the road by 3:00 A.M., Vandamme did not move out until almost 5:00 A.M., because the aide carrying orders to the Third Corps fell from his horse and broke his leg. Vandamme was still awaiting orders from headquarters when the Sixth Corps (Lobau), which was to follow him, arrived at his encampment. All this meant that the campaign began with an unfortunate delay that was never overcome.[20]

General Hans Joachim von Zieten commanded the First Prussian Corps at Charleroi. His brigades were not unified, as it remained uncertain as to just where the French would attack. The Prussian advanced posts were pushed back to Charleroi with the lead cavalry units reaching the city about 8:30 A.M. Zieten was able to slow the French advance, but he was forced to continue the withdrawal.[21] The Prussian First Corps was ordered to fall back fighting to Fleurus, as Blücher needed time to unite his Prussian corps. From Charleroi, Vandamme led the right wing of the army toward Fleurus, while the left wing, now commanded by Marshal Ney, advanced on Quatre Bras.

On the morning of 15 June, General Louis-Auguste Bourmont, who commanded the Fourteenth Infantry Division of Gérard's Fourth Corps, deserted to the enemy with members of his staff. Although he gave the enemy a full account of Napoleon's plan for the opening phase of the campaign, this had little effect on the course of events. Wellington and Blücher either already knew from their spies and from travelers or had assumed how the campaign would go in the early days of a French attack.

When the news that Napoleon had crossed the border reached Blücher at his headquarters at Namur, he immediately ordered the concentration of his four army corps between Ligny and Sombreffe. Zieten's First Corps was to fall back fighting. The Second Corps, commanded by General von Pirch (1), was near Namur.[22] General Johann Adolf von Thielemann's Third Corps was centered at Cindy. These three corps could converge behind Ligny in twenty-four to thirty-six hours. However, Blücher's Fourth Corps, under General Friedrich Wilhelm Bülow von Dennewitz, was at Liège, perhaps a march of a day and a half from the time it would receive orders. At Brussels, on the other hand, Wellington was slow in ordering his scattered army to concentrate, because he was not sure whether the French advance on Charleroi was the true thrust of the enemy or just a diversion that would be followed by a major attack against his forces.

One of Zieten's brigades was quickly united on the morning of 15 June and put up stubborn resistance as it fell back on Charleroi. But when Vandamme launched an attack on the town, the outnumbered Prussians were ordered to retire in the direction of Fleurus. At Charleroi there was only one bridge over the Sambre River that could be used by both cavalry and infantry, and much time was lost in the pursuit, which allowed Zieten to bring up a second brigade. The Prussians took up a strong position behind the village of Gilly and waited for the French. Napoleon came forward and personally directed the advance. Yet it was not until 6:00 P.M. that Vandamme was ordered to attack the enemy position. Formed into three columns, the Third Corps advanced while General Exelmans's cavalry moved onto the Prussian left flank. Realizing that he could not hold his position, Zieten ordered a general retreat and fell back fighting to Fleurus. At Fleurus he united his entire army corps and took up a strong position.

By the time Vandamme reached the Prussian line in strength, he believed it was too late in the day to begin a serious battle. Marshal Grouchy, whom Napoleon had named commander of the right wing of the army, wanted to launch an attack and drive the Prussians back toward Sombreffe. To do so he required the support of Vandamme's Third Corps, but Vandamme had already begun to camp his troops for the night. Declaring that his men were exhausted, he refused to advance any further without direct orders from Napoleon. He is reported to have said, "he had never received his orders from a cavalry commander [Grouchy]."[23] Napoleon had indeed given Grouchy command of the army's right wing, but he never informed Vandamme he was to take orders from the marshal. On the evening of 15 June, the general still believed his orders came directly from the major general (Soult) or the emperor. Thus the first day of the campaign ended with the French, before Fleurus, having suffered some six hundred casualties while the Prussians had lost more than twice that number.[24] As the center and the right wing moved through Charleroi and Fleurus, Marshal Ney, with the left wing of the French army, advanced in the direction of Quatre Bras. Wellington's advanced position was driven back by overwhelming numbers, but by nightfall Ney was still some three miles south of that important road junction.

On the morning of 16 June, the Prussian Second and Third Corps continued their marches to join the First and, they believed, Fourth corps between Sombreffe and Ligny. But Bülow did not perceive the urgency of the concentration and was slow in moving the Fourth Corps from near Liège. The result was that this corps did not arrive in time to take part in the battle of Ligny. Nevertheless, Blücher decided to give battle. He fought a defensive engagement on 16 June with the expectation of support from Wellington. Then on 17 June the combined armies of Bülow and Wellington would defeat Napoleon.

Blücher's decision to fight at Ligny had several interesting facets. Wellington went to Prussian headquarters in the mill of Bussy at Bryeon shortly after noon on 16 June. The two commanders pledged to support one another if either were attacked in strength. Wellington agreed he would support Blücher if Napoleon attacked him at Ligny. Major General Friedrich Carl von Müffling, who was at the meeting, quotes the duke as saying: "Very well! I will come so long as I am not attacked myself."[25] Blücher believed that, even with just three of his army corps, he had a numerical superiority over Napoleon. Finally, he wished more than anything in the world to defeat Napoleon on the battlefield and believed that this was going to be his opportunity.[26]

As the result of Vandamme's refusal to take orders from Grouchy on the evening of 15 June, Soult wrote the general at 8:00 A.M. on the 16th: "His Majesty orders that you will take orders from Marshal Grouchy as commander of the [right] wing of the army. Thus you will send to him an officer of your staff to request your orders."[27] Napoleon personally directed the operations on the 16th, however, so Grouchy did not actually give orders to Vandamme on that day. The emperor ordered the Third Corps forward on the morning of 16th in support of Grouchy's cavalry. Vandamme had reached the plains before St. Amand and Ligny by noon. As the Fourth Corps was some distance behind him, and the reserves and the Sixth Corps even further to the rear, his troops were rested while Gérard's corps moved forward. In the morning Napoleon believed either that Blücher was retreating along his line of communication back to the Rhine or that a continued show of force would lead him to do so. When he was informed later in the morning by Grouchy, whose cavalry was advancing toward Sombreffe, that strong Prussian columns were moving west to support Zieten at St. Amand and Ligny, Napoleon rushed forward to join Vandamme's leading column in order to assess the Prussian situation. At first he saw only one Prussian corps drawn up behind the villages Ligny and St. Amand. When he realized that Blücher intended to stand and fight, he moved the Third Corps into position before St. Amand. Girard's division, detached from the

Second Corps, and General Jean-Simon Domon's cavalry division were placed under Vandamme's orders. As Gérard's corps arrived, it was posted before the town of Ligny to form the French center. Grouchy was given command of the right wing of the battlefield facing east. It was made up of one of Gérard's divisions (that of General Etienne Hulot) and the cavalry corps of generals Exelmans and Pajol. When assembled, the French forces numbered 67,000 infantry and 12,000 cavalry supported by 210 guns.[28] In a strong defensive position, Blücher was able to amass 84,000 troops (including 8,000 cavalry) and 224 guns.[29] Zieten's First Corps faced Vandamme while Pirch's Second Corps moved in behind him, facing Gérard at Ligny. The Prussian Third Corps, under General Thielemann, arrived in the mid-afternoon and became Blücher's left wing, facing Grouchy.

The Guard artillery gave the signal for the battle to begin at 2:30 P.M. Vandamme sent General Lefol's division against St. Amand in three strong columns. In heavy fighting, the French drove the Prussians out of the village, but when counterattacked, they were in turn driven out. The village changed hands frequently during the course of the afternoon. General Girard was ordered into the battle to support Lefol on his right. In the fierce fighting the general was mortally wounded, and the commander of the Eighty-second Regiment, Colonel Matis, assumed command of the division. In the center of the line, Gérard was able to occupy the part of Ligny that was on the south side of the Ligny Stream but could not break through the center of the Prussian line. Grouchy, on the right flank, with only one division of infantry and his cavalry did not press hard on Thielemann's Fourth Corps. By 5:00 P.M. Napoleon believed the time had come to send in the Imperial Guard to break through the center of Prussian line. But just as he was giving the orders for the Guard to advance, an excited aide from Vandamme informed the emperor that a column of perhaps twenty thousand men was marching on his left flank rear. He did not know if the column was from Wellington or Ney. Napoleon could not take a chance and launch the Guard, his only reserve at that time (General Lobau's Sixth Corps had not yet reached the battle) into the center of the battle if an enemy column was about to attack Vandamme on his exposed flank. If Vandamme was overemotional and overconcerned, it may have been that he still remembered Kleist arriving on his rear at Kulm. The Guard was ordered to stand down, while an aide was sent to determine the intentions of the advancing column.

Sometime after noon on 16 June, when Napoleon realized he would be fighting a major battle, he wrote Ney to send a part of his command to Ligny. Then in about mid-afternoon he sent a second aide-de-camp to Ney calling for assistance. This second aide came upon d'Erlon's Second Corps and presented the general with a message addressed to Ney ordering him to Ligny. The message, written in pencil, did not survive the campaign. There is some question as to just who wrote the order, whether it was Napoleon or his aide when he unexpectedly found d'Erlon marching north toward Quatre Bras.[30] The general must have thought it came from the emperor, because he turned his column to the right and marched toward Ligny. However, as the head of his corps came within sight of the battlefield, d'Erlon received an urgent message from Marshal Ney who was heavily engaged with Wellington at Quatre Bras. Ney ordered d'Erlon, who was directly under his command, to come as quickly as possible and take the enemy on his left flank. The general, who had no direct orders from, or contact with, Napoleon, save the questionable pencil note addressed to Marshal Ney, turned his corps about and marched in the direction of Quatre Bras. Thus, at the crucial point of the battle, Napoleon learned, to his dismay, that twenty thousand men were marching away from Ligny.[31]

The arrival of a strong unidentified column to the northwest of the battlefield caused Vandamme's troops much consternation so that the fighting diminished on the left wing. At the same time, Napoleon held the Guard in place, and Gérard's men were unable to advance, which gave Blücher time to regroup his scattered and shaken troops. He had realized by this time that neither Wellington nor Bülow would arrive to support him; that the best he could hope for was to hold his position until dark (between 9:00 and 10:00 P.M.), at which time he could either withdraw or regroup to await the arrival of Bülow, perhaps even Wellington. He could then give battle on the 17th under more favorable conditions. To hold his position, the field marshal launched an attack against the French left. Vandamme's weary men were caught off guard; and the Prussians, led by Blücher himself, drove them out of St. Amand. Then Napoleon sent a division of the Young Guard to bolster his left. These fresh troops recaptured

St. Amand, restored the courage of Vandamme's men, and together they took back the ground that had just been lost.

By 7:30 P.M. Napoleon had decided he could wait no longer to launch the Guard against the enemy center. The "bearskins" moved forward in two columns on the east and the west of Ligny. At the same time Gérard's weary men drove the Prussians out of the half of the village they still held on the north side of the stream. The Guard moved up the slope beyond Ligny toward Bry. In one last desperate charge to stop the advancing French, Blücher put himself at the head of his cavalry and led the charge. The French formed squares that could not be breached. The field marshal's horse was killed under him in this action, and he lay near unconscious pinned beneath the animal as the French cavalry rode past him. When the Prussians checked the French cavalry, they rode back past the injured commander in chief. Fortunately for the seventy-two-year-old veteran of so many battles, his men rescued him, put him upon a horse, and led him from the field of battle. For Blücher and his brave Prussians the battle was lost. Although the center was shattered, the two wings were still in reasonably good order, however. Outflanked on his left, Zieten withdrew to the north through Bry, while Thielemann fell back behind Sombreffe. The battle was won by 8:30 P.M., but the fighting did not die out until after 10.00 P.M. Vandamme's exhausted men slept on the north side of the battlefield.

Napoleon, having slept very little in the previous forty-eight hours, was exhausted at 10:00 P.M. and retired to his headquarters in Fleurus without giving any orders to pursue the enemy. Marshal Grouchy, whom the emperor had named commander of the army's right wing, arrived at headquarters about 11:00 P.M. to receive his orders for the following day. He was told that Napoleon was sleeping and could not be disturbed, but he should return in the morning at 8:00 A.M. It was indeed quite unlike Napoleon not to order a vigorous pursuit after defeating an enemy army. However, a night pursuit is both difficult and dangerous, which was especially true in this case. Although the Prussian center had been broken and driven back, Zieten's First Corps and Thielemann's Third Corps had not been defeated. Zieten's corps had suffered heavy casualties but had retired from the field in reasonably good order and was still a force to be reckoned with; Thielemann's corps was still in good condition. The fighting on the Prussian left had been light, and the Third Corps had only fallen back behind Sombreffe because the collapse of the center had exposed its right flank. Thus, there was still a Prussian army capable of effective resistance. Furthermore, General Bülow's Fourth Corps, which had taken no part in the fighting on 16 June, was marching to join Blücher and could be facing the French army at any time. While in retrospect Napoleon is criticized for not pursuing the Prussians in the night, there was a reasonable explanation for why he did not give the orders. There was yet another reason for him to be cautious. He had not received news from Ney all day. He did not know if the marshal had been successful at Quatre Bras against Wellington. If Ney had been defeated and forced to retreat, Napoleon would be exposed to a flanking attack by Wellington on the morning of 17 June. He had to know the situation at Quatre Bras before he could launch a pursuit of the Prussians.

On the morning of 17 June, Grouchy returned to headquarters and met with Napoleon. The emperor then had the marshal accompany him on a review of the previous day's battlefield. At about 11:00 A.M., a courier arrived from Ney saying that Wellington's army was drawn up at Quatre Bras, that he had held his position the day before. This was the information Napoleon had been waiting to hear. He at once gave Grouchy oral orders to take command of the army's right wing and to pursue the defeated Prussians. Grouchy would have under his orders the Third and Fourth corps and the cavalry of Exelmans and Pajol. Because it was unlikely that either Vandamme or Gérard would accept the marshal's authority without written orders from headquarters, General Henri-Gatien Bertrand, in the absence of the chief of staff (Marshal Soult), wrote instructions for the two corps commanders. The "Bertrand Orders," as they came to be known, were dispatched within the hour.

The decision to give Grouchy command of the army's right wing was problematic. He was a good cavalry commander when serving directly under Napoleon's orders, but he had no experience as an independent commander of all three arms (infantry, cavalry, and artillery) operating on his own and out of immediate communication with the emperor. There was another problem also. Grouchy had been named marshal of the empire just two months before the campaign began on 15 April 1815. He had received this honor after a successful minor campaign in the south of France against a ragtag royalist force. Vandamme, who thought that if there was to be a new marshal named he should have been the one, was bitter at seeing a man he considered his inferior receive the prize he had been seeking for ten years. It was surely a mistake for Napoleon to place General Vandamme under the orders of Marshal Grouchy. Gérard also resented taking orders from a cavalry officer who had received the marshal's baton that should have been his. But although he disliked Grouchy, he was not as bitter as Vandamme. The two corps commanders had no choice, after they had received written orders in the name of the emperor.

Before Grouchy left Napoleon at noon on 17 June, he explained that the Prussians had begun their retreat shortly after the battle ended at 9:00 P.M. the night before and they had a fifteen-to-sixteen-hour head start with little interference as no pursuit had been ordered. Furthermore, neither he nor Napoleon knew in which direction the enemy had retreated.[32] Napoleon was convinced that Blücher was retreating to the east or the northeast along his lines of communication back to the Rhine. Indeed, Grouchy had sent General Pajol's cavalry in the direction of Namur (that is east) early that morning, and he had reported the capture of several pieces of Prussian artillery. Although this was only a small isolated Prussian unit, separated from the main army, it seemed to confirm Napoleon's belief that the enemy was moving away from Wellington, not to the north or the west. Furthermore, Napoleon informed Grouchy that he would march with the Guard and Lobau's Sixth Corps to Quatre Bras and, with Ney, attack Wellington.

The marshal was not happy. He went on to point out to the emperor that his new command was scattered over the plains of Ligny, that they were cooking lunch and cleaning muskets, and that it would take several hours to put the two corps on the road. What disturbed Grouchy the most was that no one knew which way the enemy had retreated. Unless Napoleon gave him specific orders as to the direction, he told the emperor, he would move to the east, which was away from the rest of the army. "I would find myself isolated," he wrote in his *Mémoires*, "separated from him [Napoleon], and out of the circle of his operations." Nevertheless, Napoleon received Grouchy's observations coolly and repeated the orders he had given. The emperor then added, Grouchy wrote later, "that it was for me to discover the route taken by Marshal Blücher."³³ Clearly Grouchy did not want command of the pursuit. Either Vandamme or Gérard would have been a better choice. It is unlikely that the appointment of either of these two men would have changed the outcome of the campaign, but in fact Napoleon could not—or rather would not—give a general of division such as Vandamme or Gérard command over a marshal of the empire.

Even before Grouchy's army began the pursuit, it was too late to prevent at least a major portion of the Prussian army from reaching the battlefield at Waterloo the following afternoon. The First and Second Prussian corps had marched directly north from Ligny in the direction of Wavre. They spent the night between Tilly and Mellery, and the morning of 17 June they were on the road early to the north. Before Grouchy's corps had begun to march, Blücher's lead battalions had crossed the Dyle River at Wavre. Thielemann's Third Corps withdrew through Gembloux on 17 June covering the retreat of the First and Second corps. He was joined by Bülow's Fourth Corps, which had marched from Liège, and together they marched on Wavre.³⁴

Upon leaving imperial headquarters at Fleurus about noon, Grouchy sent marching orders to Vandamme and Gérard. The Third Corps was ordered to take the road to Gembloux with the Fourth Corps to follow. Unknown to Grouchy, Exelmans had already made contact with Thielemann's rear guard at Gembloux but was not sure of the direction in which the Prussians were retreating. Vandamme and Gérard were slow in their preparations to begin the march to the northeast. Having received no orders by noon, they, along with their men, had come to believe that their corps were being given a day of rest. Thus, it was not until mid-afternoon that the Third Corps was on the road. The road was in terrible condition from the previous day's rain and the fact that twenty thousand Prussians (Third Corps) with their artillery and wagons had used it in the morning. It was 6:00 P.M. before Vandamme reached Gembloux where he stopped to spend the night. The Fourth Corps joined him a few hours later. Thus on the night of 17–18 June, the First and Second Prussian corps were at Wavre with the Third and Fourth corps between Wavre and Gembloux, whereas Grouchy's command had only reached Gembloux and was still not certain of just what direction Blücher was retreating. Finally, by 10:00 P.M., Exelmans had determined that the Prussian army was retreating in the direction of

Brussels by way of Wavre, and he informed Grouchy of his findings. The marshal wrote at once to Napoleon: "I occupy Gembloux and my cavalry is at Sauvenière. The enemy, about thirty thousand strong, continues to retreat. It would appear . . . [that the enemy] must have taken the road to Wavre. It may perhaps be inferred from this that one portion [of the Prussian] army is going to join Wellington; and that the center, which is Blücher's army, is retreating on Liège. . . . According to their [cavalry] report, if the mass of the Prussians is retiring on Wavre, I shall follow them in that direction, so as to prevent them from reaching Brussels and to separate them from Wellington."[35]

Thus it was not until the night of 17 June that Grouchy even knew that the Prussian army was retreating to Wavre—and, he assumed, on to defend Brussels. Armed with this information, the marshal sent written orders to Vandamme and Gérard.[36] The Third Corps was ordered to march at 6:00 A.M. up the main road from Gembloux to Wavre, and the Fourth Corps was to follow at 8:00 A.M. As it would be daylight between 3:30 and 4:00 in mid-June, it is curious that the army was not ordered to march until 6:00 A.M. In any event, Vandamme was not on the road until 8:00 A.M., with Gérard behind him. Exelmans's cavalry made contact with the Prussian rear guard south of Wavre at about 10:30 A.M. on the morning of 18 June, but the slow advance of Vandamme's corps delayed the arrival of all his divisions until early afternoon.

At Quatre Bras, Ney and Wellington had fought to a stalemate on 16 June. At about 7:30 A.M. the following morning, Wellington received news of the Prussian defeat at Ligny and learned that Blücher was retreating north to Wavre. This exposed his left flank at Quatre Bras, and at about 10:30 A.M. the duke began to withdraw. Ney, with orders only to occupy Quatre Bras, did not press the enemy. It was not until Napoleon arrived in person in the early afternoon that Ney moved forward. The French advance was slowed by a thunderstorm that turned the roads and fields into seas of mud. The French reached Wellington's position shortly before dark, and the two armies spent the night hardly a mile apart. During the night of 17–18 June, Blücher assured Wellington that he would march to support him on 18 June if the duke gave battle. It was the knowledge that the Prussian army was at Wavre and would march at dawn to join him that gave Wellington the fortitude to stand and fight on that day.

The battle of Waterloo began about 11:30 A.M. At Welhain, twenty miles east as the crow flies, Grouchy heard the artillery beginning the battle. General Gérard, with several staff officers, was with him at the time. Gérard immediately advised the marshal to march to the sound of the guns, but Grouchy at first believed they were hearing the sound of Wellington's rear guard. As the artillery on both sides increased their fire, it became clear that Napoleon and Wellington were engaged in a full-scale battle, but still Grouchy maintained that his orders were to pursue and engage the Prussian army and that he would follow his orders. Furthermore, the bad condition of the roads, the distance (more than twenty miles by road), and the fact that his own two corps were strung out on the road between Gembloux and Nil Perriaux meant that he could not reach the battlefield before dark. When Gérard asked for permission to take just his Fourth Corps and march to the battle, the marshal flatly refused. He believed that the entire Prussian army was before him at Wavre, and to divide his force would put Vandamme's Third Corps in great danger should the enemy turn and give battle.[37] Thus the march on Wavre continued.

When Exelmans met stiff resistance just south of the town, he had to wait for Vandamme's lead division to push the Prussians north of the Dyle River. In hard fighting Vandamme was able occupy that part of the "suburb" that was on the right bank of the river. However, as the two bridges over the river at the village were barricaded, the Third Corps was unable to fight its way into Wavre. Thielemann had decided at noon on 18 June that the French were not going to attack in strength that day. Leaving three battalions at Wavre, he began to take his corps on the road west to follow Blücher to Waterloo. When Vandamme appeared and launched his lead division against Wavre, the Prussian Third Corps countermarched and took up a strong defensive position on both sides of the town. Grouchy soon joined Vandamme, who had committed the bulk of his corps to the battle. The marshal ordered Exelmans, supported by a battalion of infantry, to Basse Wavre, half a mile downstream from Vandamme. But the bridge at that village also had been barricaded and was well defended. As Gérard's corps and Pajol's cavalry arrived, Grouchy ordered them to force a crossing of the Dyle at Bierges a mile upstream from Wavre. When this failed, he moved his troops further upriver to Limale. At this point Pajol and the Fourth Corps were able to force a crossing and gain a strong foothold on the left bank. At about the same time, 5:00 P.M., Grouchy received a message from Soult dated at 1:30 P.M. It informed the marshal that a Prussian force was approaching from the east, and that he should march west so as to take the enemy column on its flank or rear. By the time Grouchy received this order, however, it was clearly too late for him to arrive in time to have any effect on the outcome of the battle. Therefore, he continued the flanking operation against Wavre. The fighting continued into the night. When it ended, about 11:00 P.M., the Prussians still held the village. Vandamme had not been able to force a crossing of the river and drive the enemy back. The Third Corps had suffered heavy casualties in the fighting and camped for the night on the south bank of the Dyle. General Gérard was seriously wounded in his attack on a strong Prussian position at Bierges and had to leave the battle. His corps and Pajol's cavalry spent the night on the left bank about a mile upstream from Wavre.

While Grouchy's wing of the army marched on Wavre, Napoleon fought a pitched battle at Mont St. Jean (Waterloo). Wellington, in a good defensive position, was able to hold his ground through the early afternoon of 18 June. Early in the morning, Blücher had Bülow's Fourth Corps on the road marching west to support Wellington. The Prussian First and Second corps (commanded by Zieten and Pirch) followed the Fourth Corps. Only Thielemann, reinforced by one division, remained at Wavre to hold Grouchy on the Dyle. Bülow's advance guard arrived within sight of the battle in progress shortly before 1:30 P.M., but it was not until after 4:00 P.M. that he made contact with the French right flank. Napoleon was forced to move troops to his right in order to meet this serious threat. As the Prussian numbers increased in the late afternoon, the French became significantly outnumbered. When the Old Guard was unable to break the enemy center, the entire Coalition army began to advance. The Napoleonic army was driven from the field, and a disorderly retreat followed.

On the morning of 19 June, Grouchy still had no knowledge of the disaster at Waterloo. Indeed at midnight he had written Vandamme that he had no news of the battle Napoleon had fought that day, and it was his intention to push back Thielemann and rejoin the emperor. Vandamme was given orders with the assumption that all had gone well at Waterloo. The Fourth Corps with Pajol's cavalry, already on the left bank of the Dyle, would attack Thielemann while Vandamme held his position before Wavre. The marshal expected to drive the Third Prussian Corps to the northeast and continue his march north to join the emperor and advance together to Brussels.[38] Thielemann learned early that morning that Napoleon had been defeated; he expected that Grouchy also knew the results of the battle, and he thought that the French would begin to retreat. But when Gérard and Pajol attacked, Thielemann ordered a general retreat to the north at 10:00 A.M. The Prussians evacuated Wavre, and Vandamme crossed the river and pushed them to the north.

It was not until 10:30 A.M. on the morning of 19 June that Grouchy received news of Napoleon's defeat at Waterloo and that the French army was in full retreat to the south. Grouchy was ordered to take action to bring his corps back into France and to join the main army at Laon.[39] He ordered Exelmans to send a strong cavalry corps to Namur to secure the bridge across the Sambre River. The Fourth Corps, with the wounded and baggage, crossed the Dyle again and took the high road toward Namur. Vandamme retired through Wavre and took the road through Chaumont, Tourinnes, Grand Leez, and St. Denis and reached Temploux about 11:00 P.M., where his weary corps spent the night. Gérard's corps also spent the night near Temploux. Thielemann was slow to realize that the French had finally begun to retreat, because Exelmans's cavalry had masked the Third Corps's withdrawal. By the time the Prussians realized the enemy was in full retreat, it was too late in the evening to undertake a serious pursuit. However, Blücher, not forgetting that Grouchy was on his left flank, ordered Pirch's Second Corps to march east and cut off Grouchy's retreat. The Prussians were at Mellery the night of 19 June and ready at dawn to move on Namur.

With the knowledge of Napoleon's defeat, Grouchy gathered his senior generals about him to explain why he had maneuvered as he had on 18 June:

> My honor makes it a matter of duty to explain myself, with regard to the dispositions which I took yesterday. The instructions that I received from the Emperor left me free to maneuver in no other direction than Wavre. Therefore, I was

obliged to refuse the advice which General Gérard thought he had a right to offer me. I freely admit General Gérard's talents and brilliant valor; but doubtless you were as surprised as I was that a General Officer, ignorant of the Emperor's commands and all of the information which influences the Marshal of France under whose orders he was placed, should have presumed to dictate to the latter his line of action. The advanced hour of the day, the distance from the point where the cannonading was heard, the condition of the roads, made it impossible to arrive in time to engage in the battle which was taking place. At any rate, whatever the subsequent events may have been, the Emperor's orders, the content of which I have disclosed to you, did not permit of my acting otherwise than I have done.[40]

The night of 18–19 June, Grouchy sent his marching orders for the next morning. However, Vandamme had left his headquarters to sleep in a house, and he did not return at an early hour. Grouchy had ordered the Fourth Corps to march on Namur first, with the Third Corps to follow, acting as rear guard. In the absence of the corps commander, the division commanders of the Third Corps took it upon themselves to begin early to march on Namur, which uncovered the flank of the Fourth Corps. At dawn, Thielemann sent a Prussian cavalry corps to harass the French and slow down their retreat so that his infantry could catch up. To meet this threat Grouchy, himself at the head of General Louis Vallin's Hussars, attacked the Prussian cavalry and drove it off. Vandamme rejoined his corps in time to face a Prussian attack. Again, Grouchy arrived to support Vandamme, and together they drove off the enemy. Grouchy then ordered Vandamme to take up a defensive position before Namur to enable the Fourth Corps to cross the Sambre with the wounded and supply wagons. When the Fourth Corps had cleared the bridge, Vandamme began sending his division over the river. General Teste's division fought a rearguard action until dusk and then skillfully withdrew and burned the bridge. With the enemy unable to immediately cross the Sambre, Grouchy was out of danger and the retreat proceeded in a more orderly manner.[41]

The march from Namur to Dinant on 21 June was relatively uneventful. Teste's division was placed under Vandamme and provided the rear guard for the column. The Fourth Corps led the way with the Third Corps behind. Vandamme barricaded the bridges and narrow passages behind him. In keeping with his orders, Grouchy turned west at Dinant and marched to Philippeville.[42] Marshal Soult, the army's chief of staff, had ordered him to join the main army at Laon. However, the main army was retreating by several roads in poor order with Blücher in close pursuit. Therefore, to prevent his corps, which had not been defeated and were retiring in good order, from being swallowed up in the confusion of Soult's fleeing troops, Grouchy turned south and entered France at Rocroy on the night of 22 June. To accelerate the march, Grouchy ordered all unauthorized wagons and carts destroyed. His corps reached Mézières on 23 June and Rethel on the 24th.[43]

Unknown to Grouchy and his command, Napoleon had left Marshal Soult in command of the army and retired to Paris where he arrived on 21 June. Events in the capital had progressed rapidly in the confusion and uncertainty following news of Waterloo. News of the victory at Ligny had reached Paris on 18 June and caused much jubilation. Then the news of the defeat at Waterloo began to arrive on the night of 20–21 June. Napoleon reached the Elysée, which he had made his residence in the weeks before the campaign, exhausted in both body and mind. The emperor remained lethargic throughout the morning of 21 June while events moved quickly behind closed doors at the Chamber of Representatives. Led by Fouché, with the support of all those who hoped to endear themselves to whatever new order would emerge from the chaos overtaking France, Napoleon was pressured once again to abdicate.

The emperor realized that for him all was lost. The army, except for Grouchy's two corps and cavalry, was retreating in shambles. It may have been possible for him to defend Paris for a few weeks or to continue resistance behind the Loire River, but the war had been lost on the battlefield at Waterloo. Napoleon, therefore, abdicated on 22 June in favor of his son, the king of Rome (a step no one took seriously), and prepared to leave Paris. On 25 June he left Paris, never to return, and resided at Malmaison until 1 July when he departed for Rochefort. Although the original intention was to sail to the United States, Napoleon surrendered himself to the British who blockaded the port. With the abdication of the emperor, Marshal Davout as minister of war became the supreme military commander and began to issue orders to the field commanders.[44] On 22 June, Davout informed Soult of the emperor's abdication and indicated that, as major general of the army, Soult should inform the generals under his command.[45]

The Army of the North was then reorganized and renamed the Army of Paris. Soult left the army, Grouchy was named commander, and two corps were formed. General Reille was given command of one corps, made up of the remains of the army that had fought at Waterloo (that is, the First, Second, and Sixth corps). Vandamme was given command of the other corps, comprising the old Third and Fourth corps, and this was formed into three or four divisions. The new corps commanders were authorized to name their division commanders.[46] It might be noted that Grouchy was the only marshal of the empire left with this army. With this new organization the French army continued its retreat toward Paris.

In the capital, the Chamber of Representatives spontaneously formed an executive government commission that began acting as an executive body following Napoleon's abdication. Among its first acts was to gain the approval of the army. It was this body that reaffirmed Davout as minister of war and named him commander of the Army of Paris. Furthermore, on 23 June 1815, the executive commission, having elected Fouché its president, wrote Vandamme to express its satisfaction with the manner in which he had handled his corps.[47]

The rallying point for the army was at Soissons, and Grouchy intended to unite his forces in that city. On 24 June he ordered Vandamme to march by way of Reims to Soissons. Vandamme reached Reims on the 25th and Soissons on the 26th. The forced marches had taken a toll on his troops. There were many deserters; and because the army no longer had a functioning supply system, the troops were pillaging the towns and villages through which they passed.[48] Reille was unable to slow the Prussian advance. Thus, on 27 June, Grouchy ordered Vandamme to take his corps to Paris as quickly as possible: "The movement on Paris becomes more urgent with the passage of time; the enemy is marching down the Oise River.... There is not a minute to lose."[49] He was to march by way of Villers-Cotterêts, as was Grouchy and the remains of the other corps. From Villers-Cotterêts, Vandamme took his corps south to Meaux (28 June), while General

Reille led the rest of the army directly to the capital on the high road.[50] Vandamme arrived at Paris on 30 June, with about twenty-three or twenty-five thousand men and virtually all the equipment of the two corps. He was ordered to quarter his troops at Montrouge to defend the city on its northeast side.[51]

By 25 June it had become clear to almost everyone, including Davout, that it was useless to continue the war. It would only postpone the inevitable Coalition victory, and at a terrible cost to France in lives, property, and money. The arrival of the armies of Austria and Russia combined with Wellington and Blücher would have, without question, overwhelmed any army the French could muster. It was also becoming clear that the only reasonable solution was to welcome back Louis XVIII, and to make the transition as smooth as possible. First an attempt was made to stop the enemy advance on Paris by seeking an armistice.[52] Neither Blücher nor Wellington would have any part of such negotiations, however. Blücher was determined to enter Paris as a conqueror, as Napoleon had entered Berlin in 1806.

Next, an effort was made to submit to the king if Louis would give certain guarantees to the army. The king also refused to negotiate with Paris, since the outcome of the struggle was a foregone conclusion.[53] As Vandamme reached Paris from the east, Blücher's advanced units reached the French outposts of the city on the north. Finding the capital strongly defended on the north, the Prussian commander ordered a flanking movement around Paris on the west, by way of St. Germain and Versailles. When, on 1 July, Blücher rashly sent a cavalry brigade across the Seine with little infantry support, General Exelmans, with the bulk of the French cavalry, stopped the Prussian advance at Versailles. Then at Roquencourt, with General Hippolyte-Marie Piré's support, he destroyed the entire enemy brigade, taking some nine hundred prisoners while an equal number were killed or wounded.[54]

On 1 July, the same day, an address from the army was read to the Chamber of Representatives.[55] The address had been drawn up the night of 29–30 June in Davout's forward headquarters at Villette. It first declared the army's loyalty to the government (that is, the Chamber of Representatives) and to France, but it went on to reject the return of Louis XVIII. This document was signed first by Marshal Davout, then by General Vandamme and the other generals at Villette.[56] It would be used against Vandamme in the weeks and months to come to prove his anti-Bourbon sentiments.

Upon his arrival at Paris, Vandamme began to prepare his troops to meet the oncoming Coalition army. He became responsible for defending the northeast approach to the capital. The Chamber of Representatives, anxious to know the condition of these troops and the degree of support the government could expect from the officers and men, sent a number of deputies to inspect the army. After reviewing troops with the deputies, Vandamme took them back to his headquarters, assuring them of the loyalty of himself and his officers and men. He also wrote to the president of the Chamber of Representatives. After requesting that the government treat the army with the respect it deserved for its gallant victory at Fleurus (Ligny) and its "glorious" fighting at Wavre and Namur, he concluded: "I take this occasion, Monsieur le président, to assure the Chamber that the seven divisions of infantry, six divisions of cavalry, troops of artillery and engineers that I have had the honor to command from Wavre to Namur and Namur to the capital are animated with the greatest respect [for the government]. They have been constantly victorious. . . . I wish to present to the Chamber the assurance that all of my troops are ready to accept all the intentions of the government, and that they will act only in the interest of the *patrie*."[57]

On 3 July the president of the Chamber of Representatives acknowledged Vandamme's letter and declared: "I have the honor to address to you an extract of the *procès-verbal* of today's meeting where is found the declaration of the Chamber's profound satisfaction with your letter."[58] No mention was made of the king in either letter, as Vandamme was pledging his loyalty and that of the troops he commanded to the nation and the elected representatives of the people. However, political events in Paris were moving more rapidly even than Blücher's army.

The politicians, led by Fouché, were determined that the blame for the evacuation of Paris, when it would surely occur, would fall upon the army and not the government. To this end, the minister of war was ordered to hold a council of war to be attended by all the marshals and commanding generals in and about Paris. The council, attended by General Vandamme, met at Davout's headquarters the night of 1 July; and the marshal penned the reply the following morning. He stated that the army could hold Paris for perhaps several weeks, but that in the end the city would have to be given up to the enemy.[59] This was all the politicians needed to hear. The army prepared for battle on the night of 2–3 July. Vandamme issued orders for the disposition of his two army corps and moved his headquarters to the Petit Montrouge in preparation to fight the next day. But Fouché and company were preparing for the army's evacuation of Paris and the return of Louis XVIII. In the morning of 3 July, Davout was informed that representatives were being sent to negotiate an end of the war with the enemy. An armistice was signed on the evening of 3 July, and fighting gradually came to an end as word spread along the lines.[60] On 4 July the French army began to withdraw to the south to take up a position behind the Loire River. When the army began to pull out of the Paris region, Vandamme was instructed to keep his two corps in place until he received new orders.[61]

The morale of the officers and men of the army was at its lowest point as they moved south in the July heat. There had been serious desertions during the retreat from Belgium, but many had believed the army would fight once again before Paris. When word came that the capital would not be defended, and the army would retreat behind the Loire, discouragement reached a new depth. If the army was not going to defend the homeland, then why remain with the colors? And if the king returned, even the tricolors (red, white, and blue) would change to the Bourbon white. Desertion was rampant. The minister of war put out orders for the corps commanders to take special steps to prevent men from leaving the ranks. Vandamme received his marching orders on 4 July. He would take his two army corps (previously numbered Third and Fourth) and the Third and Sixth cavalry divisions south to Jargeur on the left bank of the Loire. He left Paris on the morning of 6 July and bivouacked at Lonjumeau. He would spend the nights at Etampes (on the 7th), Angerville (on the 8th), Artenay (on the 9th), Orleans (on the 10th) and reach Jargeur on 11 July. Provisions for the men and horses would be provided by the quartermaster corps so the troops had no excuse to pillage or leave their ranks to seek food. Vandamme was to take every measure to maintain good discipline during the six-day march.[62] Even so, thousands of men deserted on the long hot march from Paris to the Loire. On 7 July General Pierre Berthezène, commanding the Eleventh

Division of Vandamme's former Third Corps, wrote Davout: "I have eighty-one deserters from the Thirty-third [Regiment], and eighty-seven from the Eighty-sixth; in my artillery the desertion is so high that there remain only six men for each train."[63] Vandamme issued orders to his division commanders to take stern measures and to make examples of deserters.[64] But nothing could stop the exodus.

When Vandamme reached Jargeur as scheduled, he began immediately to deploy his command in accordance with Davout's instructions.[65] As there was no mention in the armistice of where the Coalition forces would be stationed, Blücher sent his corps south on the heels of the French to take up positions along the right bank of the Loire. Furthermore, neither the Russians nor the Austrians had signed the armistice that ended the fighting between Wellington and Blücher and Davout. Thus all Coalition armies were advancing into France, and it was very questionable as to whether they would stop at the Loire or continue the campaign. Vandamme formed the right wing of the army, now referred to as the Army of the Loire, and deployed his forces in anticipation of either a Prussian crossing of the river or an Austrian attack from the east.

The army was in a most difficult position. The king reached Paris on 8 July and began to reestablish his government. Fouché's provisional government dissolved itself and pledged allegiance to Louis. Davout was receiving neither orders nor instructions from Paris. The Army of the Loire was an army without a government, seeming to have only two choices—either civil war, or submission to the new regime in Paris and swearing allegiance to Louis XVIII. Civil war was out of the question with the armies of the Coalition backing the king. As early as 9 July the decision was made for the army to submit to the government in Paris and swear allegiance to the king. Davout sent a delegation to Paris to represent the army. It was composed of lieutenant generals Count de Valmy (François-Etienne Kellermann), Count Gérard, and Count Haxo, and it was to plead the army's case. The delegation was given a letter of instructions, signed first by Marshal Davout, and then by Vandamme followed by the rest of the lieutenant generals of the army and several other generals and colonels. After justifying their actions, the instructions read: "Consequently, the army is prepared to swear fidelity to the king and to the laws that govern the nation. It [the army] demands only that which honor prescribes; that no Frenchman be deprived of his rank, civil or military, and that the army will be preserved in its present state until all foreigners have left France."[66]

The army representatives informed the new minister of war, Saint-Cyr, of the army's willingness to submit to the king and the laws of his government under certain conditions. The minister replied that it would not be dignified for the king to bargain with the army until after it had given its unconditional submission. In fact, before Louis XVIII even entered Paris, he issued a proclamation from Cambrai to pave the way for the army and the people of France (Paris in particular) to accept the restoration of the monarchy. He "promised to forget and forgive 'those Frenchmen who had gone astray,' but he added, 'I must however, for the dignity of my throne, the welfare of my people and the peace of Europe, exempt from pardon those instigators and authors of that horrible plot. They will be designated for punishment by laws to be passed by the two chambers, which I propose to call into early session.'"[67] The delegation was told that there would be no further guarantees and no negotiation until the army swore allegiance to Louis. St.-Cry then added, referring to the Cambrai proclamation: "I promise you that you will be content with the king and that he will probably give you more than you demand."[68]

On 13 July, with seemingly no other reasonable choice, Davout wrote to the delegates in Paris: "You have acquired by your conduct the esteem of the entire French army. . . . If you judge that a pure and simple submission would be useful to our unhappy nation, make it; but save the honor of the army, because without that it would no longer be of any use, it would break up entirely."[69] It should be noted that on 9 July, General Edouard-Jean Milhaud, who commanded the Fourth Cavalry Corps, had written to the minister of war and offered the unconditional submission of himself and the officers and men under his command.[70] Milhaud, having voted for the death of the king's brother Louis XVI in 1792, hoped to win favor with the Bourbons. The royalists had a long memory, however, and the general was first placed on inactive duty on 9 September and then retired from the army on 18 October. Nevertheless, his actions clearly gave the impression in Paris that the army may not have been all of one mind.

On the twenty-sixth anniversary of the storming of the Bastille in Paris, Marshal Davout, with the support of the generals of the army, wrote the king: "Sire, the army, united in its intention and its affection, submits purely and simply to the government of Your Majesty, without the need of any particular reservations." Six copies of the submission were sent to various corps and division commanders in order to secure the signatures of as many high-ranking officers as possible. The troops were administered the new oath of allegiance, and the tricolor flag of the Revolution and the empire was replaced with the white flag of the house of Bourbon. The army believed the king had promised it would not be purged. A few generals and a number of officers accused Vandamme of having received two million francs to deliver the army to the king. However, there is absolutely no evidence to support such a claim. The general denied the accusations and replied: "This accusation . . . in no way changed my conduct; I continued to profess the same principles. It is certain that I never sought a career of titles from the king; my intention was not to seek employment and become a dishonest courtier. I sincerely urged the return of His Majesty because a united France was the only way to avoid the pain that was about to descend upon us."[71]

The army having become a part of the France of Louis XVIII, and France now being an ally of the Coalition, Davout ordered a general withdrawal from the positions held along the left bank of the Loire. Army headquarters moved to Bourges. Vandamme was ordered to leave one division south of Orleans between the Loire and the Cher rivers. His new headquarters were established at Vierzon, about twenty-five miles down the Cher from Bourges, with his six divisions deployed along the Cher and north and east of Bourges. At the same time the army was reorganized. The grossly understrength regiments of five hundred or seven hundred men (the result of massive desertions) were consolidated into full-strength battalions. The excess officers and noncommissioned officers were sent to Poitiers. As the result of massive desertions, Vandamme's two corps numbered only 8,139 men on 26 July.[72] The army's supply system had deteriorated since its withdrawal from Paris. The new government had no money and little inclination to support an army that was withholding its allegiance from the king. The result was major shortages of food for both men and horses.[73] As if the army did not already have enough troubles of its own, Vandamme was informed that an Austrian corps had crossed the Loire in the east and was marching into central

France. Fortunately, when the Austrians were informed that the army had indeed submitted to Louis and was now the "king's army," they withdrew back across the river and no longer posed a threat.[74] The conditions of the Army of the Loire reached their lowest point when the king issued the Ordinance of 24 July.

Despite efforts on the part of Marshal Davout and of the delegation he sent to Paris, the army had received no specific assurances that individuals would not be arrested, tried, and shot. Disregarding the proclamation of Cambrai, in which the king had promised to leave punishment in the hands of the legislature for the actions of men during the Hundred Days, the royalists demanded blood. They rightly believed that it was a "Napoleonic" army, in which many generals had been revolutionary republicans, even Jacobins, who had voted for or supported the execution of King Louis XVI. It was naïve of Davout and others to think that the brother of the guillotined king would, for the second time, pardon those who had supported his dethronement and exile. Louis had been reasonably generous with respect to the army in 1814 (although Vandamme would not have agreed). This time examples would have to be made. On 24 July the king signed an ordinance listing fifty-seven names, of which nineteen were army officers. There were actually two lists. The first listed those who were to be arrested immediately and tried for treason. The second listed those who were to be removed at once from the army and placed under police surveillance until such time as a decision was made as to their fate. The lists were drawn up by Fouché, who had been appointed minister of police as a reward for his services in restoring the monarchy. As Talleyrand sarcastically put it: "We must give [Fouché] the duke of Otrante credit for one thing, he did not forget any of his friends in drawing up the list."[75] General Dominique Vandamme's name appeared on the second list.

An angry and disheartened Davout informed Vandamme he was on the list of those who must be removed from the army and placed under surveillance. However, as the marshal had not yet received the official document, he ordered Vandamme to remain at his post until further orders.[76] Rather than preside over this purging of the army, Marshal Davout resigned his command of the Army of the Loire.[77] On 1 August, Marshal Macdonald arrived at Bourges as his replacement. During Davout's last few days in command of the army, he did everything in his power to make it possible for all the generals on the first list—that is, those in danger of being tried for treason and execution—to avoid arrest and trial.[78]

As Vandamme was not on the first list, he remained at his post for several more days. However, the minister of war, Marshal Saint-Cyr, wrote Macdonald even before he had reached his new command: "You know of the lists published 25 July [signed by the king on the 24th]. It is indispensable in these perilous circumstances to remove those generals who are on the second list. You will replace them as you see fit. . . . Those on the first list should be executed."[79] Macdonald took immediate action, and on 3 August, having been ordered to withdraw from the army, Vandamme turned over command of his corps to his senior general of division, Pierre Berthezène, and retired to a farmhouse that he rented near Limoges. This was the inglorious end of Vandamme's military career. There was no acknowledgment of gratitude from the government or the army, only the threat of imminent arrest followed by exile. All of this he could accept. What grieved him the most was that he never received the marshal's baton he had fought for so valiantly on so many fields of battle.

12

THE EXILE

Louis XVIII was once again upon his throne and the royalists were in control of France. The bitterness ran deeper among the royalists in the summer of 1815 than it had in the spring of 1814. This time there was a demand for blood to flow. On 2 August, Marshal Brune was assassinated by an angry crowd in Avignon, and his body cast into the Rhône River. The "White Terror" was particularly bloody in the south of France. In Marseilles and Toulouse, both real and perceived enemies of the monarchy were murdered. An estimated one hundred men lost their lives, and a much larger number were imprisoned. At Bordeaux and in the west of France calmer heads prevailed, and in the departments of the north and northeast occupied by Allied armies the authorities were able to control the situation.[1] But the overall mood throughout France was ugly.

Following his departure from the army, Vandamme rented a farmhouse near Limoges where his wife and son joined him. He was placed under police surveillance and not allowed to leave the house without first receiving permission from the authorities.[2] The Vandammes had hardly settled into their new quarters when the general received a letter from the prefect of the department of the Haute Vienne, in which he was ordered to leave the department within twenty-four hours. "I do not know the motive for this decision," he later wrote.³ It would seem that the reason for his removal from the Limoges area was twofold. Too many people were under surveillance for the police to handle; and although Vandamme could not leave his house, too many officers were coming to visit him.⁴ In any event, he left at once and went to Olivet. Then, however, the prefect of the department wrote the minister of war, complaining that the general was too close to the line of demarcation between the Allied and French armies. He suggested that Vandamme not be allowed to remain.⁵ Thus, Vandamme was again told to move on. This time the town of Vierzon was designated as the "official" residence for him and his family while he awaited the government's decision as to what action would be taken against him.

The Vandammes resided at Vierzon until early February 1816. None of the authorities of the regions south of the Loire wanted the responsibility or the trouble associated with the general's residing in their jurisdiction. But after he had been expelled from two towns, the minister of police wrote the minister of war: "I must observe to Your Excellence that it has been perhaps very inconvenient to keep assigning different locations for those included on the lists of the Ordnance of 24 July."⁶ As late as 25 January 1816 Vandamme was still being refused permission to return to Cassel.⁷ Then at the end of January he was exiled from France. He was allowed to retire to Belgium, which had become a part of the kingdom of the Netherlands, but was forbidden to pass through Paris.⁸ Although his wife and son were able to pass through the capital, the general had to leave the carriage and travel by foot around the west side of Paris to St. Denis and then continue on to the north.⁹ He was allowed to pass through Cassel to see his estate. During the family's absence from Cassel, their château, La Frégate, and park had been vandalized for the second time.

Whereas it had been Russian soldiers who pillaged La Frégate in 1814, this time it was the citizens of Cassel. The White Terror reached the departments of northern France in the summer of 1815, although not with the intensity or the violence to individuals that gripped the south. Madame Vandamme had fled to Paris with their son as the Allied armies moved south in the last week of June, leaving the general's widowed sister, Madame Valentine Deswarte, and his father living in the town. Early in August 1815, on the pretext of getting foliage to celebrate the return of the king, a crowd invaded the

Vandamme estate. They did much damage to the gardens and the park and invaded the wine cellar, which had already been emptied by the Russians a year and half earlier. The authorities were never able to find, or never interested in finding, who was responsible for these transgressions. Then on Sunday, 3 September, a large angry crowd went to the Vandamme estate with intent of doing great harm.[10]

The townspeople had a long-standing grievance with Vandamme, because he had built a wall around his garden and park that had blocked off a "public" passageway that crossed his land. This was a source of inconvenience for some of the inhabitants and an overall matter of principle. There were also erroneous accusations in the press that threats had been made in Vandamme's name to burn the town and to do bodily harm to citizens. The general was also accused of being vastly rich. He denied all the charges and concluded: "for twenty-two years I have been a general, and I have always had important command. All that I personally possess is at Cassel in the department of the North and is of modest value."[11]

It seems that, following the first episode at the château in 1815, Madame Deswarte, to the annoyance of the general population, had spoken loudly and frequently of the inhabitants of Cassel as being insurgents and Jacobins. Then on 1 September 1815, upon leaving his house on the Grande Place, Vandamme's father struck one M. Clement Haeuw with his walking stick because, it seems, the man had insulted him. When M. Vandamme returned home, Haeuw struck him and pulled the walking stick out of his hand. This was followed on 3 September 1815 by a crowd who went to the estate to destroy the hated wall. The mayor of Cassel requested the Chef de Bataillon Morard de Galles, who commanded a detachment of the Second Legion of the North, stationed at Cassel, to send troops to restore order. Morard sent an officer and six men. However, this number was too small to control the large crowd in a foul mood. The soldiers were disarmed, and it was only with great difficulty that the officer was able to keep his sword. Upon hearing of the violence taking place, Morard, at the head of his entire troops, rushed to the château. The crowd had already calmed down by the time the commander and his troops appeared, and the people dispersed without further incident, but the more militant vowed to return the following day. Much of the hated wall had been demolished, hedges had been uprooted or cut down, and there was general destruction. Fearing a renewal of the violence, Morard informed General Louis-Auguste Bourmont, the governor of the military division at Lille, and he sent two hundred men to keep order at Cassel. Thus, there was no disturbance on 4 September. The events of 3 September seemed to have satisfied the anger of the people.[12] However, because of this display of hostility, Vandamme did not linger in Cassel. After a quick visit to his estate, he left France.[13] He took his wife and son to Ghent in Belgium to live with her parents rather than leaving them in Cassel in the care of his father and sister who remained in the town.

Valentine's husband, Charles Deswarte, had died of complications from surgery on 21 March 1809. She had been left with four young children: Marie-Thérèse, aged eleven; Uranie, aged nine; Alcide, aged six; and Pauline, aged one. In 1815 they lived with her sixty-three-year-old father in Cassel on the Grande Place. Although she herself had a modest pension, her brother had assumed responsibility for the education of the children. Dominique and Valentine had always been very close, perhaps as the result of the early death of their mother, the untimely death of their brother, Louis, at the age of fourteen, and the entry into the home of a stepmother and her teenage daughter following the remarriage of their father.[14] But although Vandamme finally received 4,164 francs for his losses at Kulm two years earlier, he was falling ever deeper in debt.[15]

Vandamme had hoped to live with his wife and son at the home of his in-laws at Ghent until such time as he would be allowed to return to France, but that was not to be. When it became known to the Dutch authorities that General Vandamme, whose name was on the second list of the Ordinance of 24 July 1815, was residing in Ghent, he was informed that he must leave the country as quickly as possible. In vain he implored the Dutch authorities for permission to live quietly with his family. After all, there were already some thirty-eight individuals who had been proscribed by the ordinance living in the kingdom. The only concessions made, however, were that his wife (having been born in Ghent) and her son would be allowed to live with her parents; and that the general had until 15 May 1816 to find a new country that would accept him.[16] Knowing full well he would not be welcome anywhere in Europe, Vandamme decided to retreat to the United States.

Many officers of Napoleon's Grande Armée who had been forced out of the army of Louis XVIII had immigrated to America. They were scattered up and down the east coast and as far west as New Orleans.[17] The emperor's brother Joseph had settled in Pennsylvania, and the city of Philadelphia soon boasted a thriving Bonapartist community. Marshal Grouchy—under whom Vandamme had served in 1815 and who was also exiled by the restored Bourbon regime—made Philadelphia his temporary home. So in the spring of 1816 Vandamme arrived to a warm welcome. When, in 1803–1804, Napoleon had tried to make a soldier of his lawyer brother, Joseph, he had placed him with the rank of colonel under General Vandamme. Although Joseph lasted only a short time in the army, his relationship with Vandamme was an amiable one; and the two men remained friends throughout the years of the empire. It may well be because Joseph was in Philadelphia in 1816 that Vandamme decided to settle in this city. It is most likely he met with Joseph, but there is no documentary evidence to verify a social relationship.

Specific information on Vandamme during the three years he spent in the United States is scarce.[18] It would seem that it took some time for him to get established in Philadelphia. He had to live modestly, on credit and on money he brought from Europe. It was not until November 1817 that the general received letters of introduction from a Mr. Talcott, which enabled him to make business connections with Misters Becan and Porter.[19] The most that can be discerned is that he was in the import-export business, and that he had business connections with the Philadelphia Patent Floor-Cloth Manufactory firm at Bush Hill owned by Isaac Macaulay. The company had a warehouse at number 12 North Third Street in Philadelphia.[20]

Vandamme had an active social life. Living at the Mansion-House Hotel by the end of the year 1817, he was being invited to parties and balls. He attended a gala affair at the Masonic Hall in Philadelphia on 18 December and a grand ball to celebrate George Washington's birthday in February1818.[21] By 1818 Vandamme was able to afford a servant, and he traveled to Washington, D.C., where he spent several months during the summer.[22] While in the capital he met William Lee, who tried to introduce the general to land speculation deals. Lee sounds like a con man. He had offered Vandamme the opportunity to invest in land in Washington in 1817, and the general declined. Vandamme may very well have missed a good opportunity, as the city was expanding at a rapid rate. It would seem that he declined the opportunity again in 1818.[23]

In 1818 Vandamme was receiving mail and packages from Europe on a regular basis. The problem was that they were arriving in the United States by way of seaports from New York to Savanna, and his correspondence indicates the difficulties this was causing him. He was doing well enough financially by the end of the year that French refugees were seeking him out to ask for his help, both for business connections and for money.[24] He helped ex-officers who were not doing as well as he. Some had become cabinetmakers, albeit not terribly skilled; and Vandamme bought items from them, not because of the quality of their work, but rather to avoid giving them alms.[25] Despite the fact that his life was going well in America, Vandamme never intended to remain three thousand miles from his family or his beloved château La Frégate. His family ties were in France and Belgium, and it was there that he was determined to live out his last years. In Philadelphia he was making the best of his exile while awaiting news that he could return to Europe.

This happy day came in the spring of 1819. He sailed from New Orleans on *The Marcus* and landed at Le Havre on 1 June. Without a passport Vandamme was placed under police supervision until it could be determined just where he was going.[26] He had departed for America from the Dutch kingdom (Belgium), with official papers from neither the Dutch nor the French. When returning, he had not sought permission from either government, perhaps out of fear that it would be refused. Vandamme was permitted to pass through northern France to join his family in Ghent. His wife had been working for three years to secure permission from Paris to allow the general to return to Cassel.[27] In December 1819 Louis XVIII allowed those persons on the second list of the Ordinance of 24 July 1815 to return to France. Vandamme and his family were back in Cassel before the end of the year. The White Terror had reached its height during the summer and early fall of 1815. Four and a half years later tempers had subsided, and the Vandammes returned to a much subdued Cassel. They set about restoring La Frégate and the gardens to their previous conditions. Vandamme made every effort to win back the respect and affection of the inhabitants. He paid generous wages to those whom he employed; and in the winter months he distributed bread, firewood, and money to those in need. He was particularly helpful to veterans and the elderly. He enjoyed reminiscing and discussing political and military affairs with former officers who lived nearby, particularly generals Martin-Charles Gobrecht, a native of Cassel who commanded a cavalry brigade in Vandamme's First Corps at Kulm; Armand-Charles Guilleminot, who fought at Waterloo; and Louis-Marie Thévenet, who served briefly under Vandamme in 1815.[28]

On 1 April 1820, Vandamme, who had been removed from the army in 1815, was placed back on the rolls as being on leave of absence. Then, as the result of the Ordnance of 1 December 1824, he was granted full retirement pay beginning 1 January 1825. The general died at La Frégate on 1 July 1830. It is most unfortunate that he did not live a longer life. The Bourbon monarchy was overthrown in the last days of July 1830. King Charles X fled to England. Louis-Philippe became the "bourgeois" king of France, and the July Monarchy was very friendly with the old Bonapartists. Vandamme might very well have received the cherished marshal's baton and died a happy man. The absence of that title cast a dark cloud over the last twenty years of his life. General Dominique Vandamme was buried in the local cemetery at Cassel.

Following the death of Dominique, Sophie and their son Dionède returned to Ghent, her ancestral city. Dionède, who never married, died in July of 1836, and his mother passed away the following year on 9 February. They are both buried at Ghent.

Entering the aristocratic dominated army of King Louis XVI as a private at the age of 18, Vandamme rose to the highest rank of general of division during the years of the Revolution and into the ranks of the imperial nobility of the First Empire. His career is a classic example of the transformation of the French army from one dominated by privilege to one marked by ability.

His early years in the revolutionary army shed light on not only the military but also on the political ramifications of the life and career of a French officer during those troubled years. Denounced as a plunderer, a reactionary (read anti-Jacobin), a friend of a traitor (General Charles François Dumouriez), and twice removed from his command, Vandamme found himself all too frequently in Paris defending himself before the political leaders of France. These numerous bouts with the government of the "Terror" and the Directory provide an interesting insight into the perilous life of an officer whose career, if not his life, could be ended on frivolous or even false accusations. It also demonstrates how talent was rewarded despite adversities.

The Napoleonic years were quite different, if also troublesome. One served at the whims or pleasure of the Emperor. When out of favor, generals and marshals were given insignificant commands or simply lift without employment in the army. In the early years of the Empire Napoleon had an abundant supply of good generals who had gained experience and promotions in the wars of the Revolution. But as combat fatalities, age, and exhaustion took their toll, the number of good experienced commanders became thin, as evidenced in 1814 and the Waterloo Campaign in 1815.

Vandamme's career is a classic example of one who was in and out of favor during the Empire. A hero of the Battle of Austerlitz in 1805, he annoyed the Emperor in 1807 by his disrespectful treatment of Napoleon's youngest brother, Prince Jérôme. In favor once again by 1809 he fought at the Battle of Eckmühl to the satisfaction of Napoleon and was given command of an army corps in 1812. However, he again quarreled with Jérôme, and Napoleon sent him back to Paris in disgrace in the opening weeks of the Russian Campaign. In 1813 and again in 1815, Napoleon, in need of good field commanders, gave Vandamme command of a corps despite their previous difficult relationship. While Napoleon needed Vandamme in battle, he would not give him a marshal's baton.

Thus Vandamme has never received the attention bestowed upon the famous twenty-six who did receive that honor. Although Napoleon recognized and made good use of his military talents, his personal relations with the Emperor precluded his receiving the marshal's baton he so passionately desired. Even the name of the Polish Prince Josef Anton Poniatowski, in the French army but for a few years and a marshal for only a few days, is better known than that of Vandamme. Yet, Vandamme's name appears repeatedly in the accounts of the revolutionary wars from the campaigns in northern France and Belgium to the Rhine and the Danube; and as a prominent commander from Austerlitz to the Waterloo campaign.

Notes

PREFACE

1. See John G. Gallaher, "Political Considerations and Strategy: The Dresden Phase of the Leipzig Campaign," *Military Affairs* vol. XLVIV, no. 2 (April 1985).

CHAPTER 1. THE EARLY YEARS

1. Milot, "Portrait psychologique de Vandamme," 20.
2. Maurice van Damme wrote several pages of family history, now in carton 18 of the collection entitled "Fonds de Swarte-Revel, correspondance et papiers du Général Vandamme," at the Bibliothèque Municipale de Lille (hereafter cited as Vandamme Papers). This document is written in Flemish, and I am indebted to M. Max Deswarte of Blaringhem, France, for translating the Flemish into French for me. See also Gérard, "Dominique Vandamme."
3. Milot, "Portrait psychologique," 20.
4. On Vandamme's early years, see Gérard, "Dominique Vandamme," 7–8.
5. See "Etat des Services du Citoyen Dominique Joseph René Vandamme," Service Historique de l'Etat-Major de l'Armée, Archives de la Guerre, Château de Vincennes). I have in hand seven service records (*états des services*) for Dominique Vandamme. Some give more detail than others, but they all agree on the factual information and all are to be found in 303/GD 2e série.
6. Several letters quoted in Du Casse, *Vandamme et sa Correspondance*, 1:9–11.

7. Ibid., 1:9–10; Gérard, "Dominique Vandamme," 8.

8. Bertaud, *Army of the French Revolution*, 34.

9. Ibid., 40. On the transformation of the French army from the ancien régime, that is the king's army, to the revolutionary army of the republic, see Bertaud, *Army of the French Revolution*. On the rise of the Napoleonic marshals in the years of the Revolution, see Phipps, *Armies of the First French Republic*.

10. Napoleon would create the title marshal of the empire in 1804. However, the title of marshal was primarily a court title, not a military rank. Napoleon would remind his marshals (eventually twenty-six were named) that they were generals of division when serving with the army on campaign and marshals at court. Even so, Napoleon was careful not to place his marshals under the command of a mere general of division, as the marshals would have felt insulted.

11. See the document entitled "Au Nom de la Nation françoise," signed "Le Lieutenant Général, chef de l'Etat Major de l'Armée du Nord, J. H. Moreton," 24 August 1792, carton 1, Vandamme Papers. The first paragraph of this document reads: "Monsieur Vandamme, fusilier of the Twenty-fourth Infantry Regiment, is authorized to form at once a free company of one hundred men of which he will be the commander." Milot gives the date as 5 September 1794 ("La Compagnie franche," 787). Du Casse quotes the same document but calls it "Au nome de la Nation françoise," signed "J. M. Moreton" (*Vandamme et sa Correspondance*, 1:12–13n13).

12. Du Casse, *Vandamme et sa Correspondance*, 1:15.

13. There is general confusion surrounding the names of the various French armies between the English Channel and Switzerland in the first year of the war. Generals divided or united forces and assigned arbitrary names to suit their fancy. Thus Labourdonnaye's command is referred to sometimes as the Army of the North and sometimes as the left flank of the Army of the North. See Phipps's chapters on the Army of the North, in *Armies of the First French Republic*, vol. 1.

14. On the military operations in Belgium, see ibid., 1:151–57.

15. See Gérard, "Dominique Vandamme," 9.

16. On the political condition of the army during the years of the Terror (1793–94) and promotion in the officer corps, see Bertaud, *Army of the French Revolution*; Samuel F. Scott, *The Response of the Royal Army to the French Revolution: The Role and Development of the Line Army* (Oxford: Oxford University Press, 1978); and Phipps, *Armies of the First French Republic*, vol. 1.

17. On Vandamme's role in the Hondschoote campaign, see his own account in Du Casse, *Vandamme et sa Correspondance*, 1:45–48.

18. Phipps, *Armies of the First French Republic*, 1:232–34. Walmoden's force included four thousand cavalry, which were of little use to him in the battle because of the terrain.

19. Du Casse, *Vandamme et sa Correspondance*, 1:49. Early in the Revolution, French patriots began to date letters, documents, and reports "In the Year of Liberty" and in January 1790 the "Second Year of Liberty." Then, fol-

lowing the establishment of the Republic in September 1792, they dated documents "In the First Year of the Republic." On 1 January 1793 there was a question of whether they should use "The Second Year of the Republic" or wait until September. On 24 November 1793, the Convention settled the confusion by proclaiming a new calendar. It would begin with the creation of the Republic, on 22 September 1792, the most important date in history. Thus the year I (always in Roman numbers) ended on the Gregorian calendar 21 September 1793, and the year II began the next day. This calendar was used by the French until 1 January 1806 when Napoleon restored the Gregorian calendar. For a good brief (two pages) discussion of the revolutionary calendar, see Scott and Rothaus, *Historical Dictionary*, 1:145–46.

20. There is no documentary evidence to tell us Vandamme's feelings or his attitude with respect to the destruction of the two towns and the forest. If he believed that the inhabitants had cooperated with the enemy, or opposed the republican government in Paris, then he would have carried out his orders with enthusiasm. If he did not believe the antigovernment accusations, he may have carried out the burning with regret.

21. See Vandamme's orders, 13 September 1793, at Hondschoote, in Du Casse, *Vandamme et sa Correspondance*, 1:50–51.

22. See Vandamme's service records, Arch. Guerre, 303/GD 2e série.

23. Vandamme, in his correspondence at this time, frequently used "republicans" when referring to the French soldiers and the term "slaves" when referring to enemy soldiers. See Vandamme's correspondence for September–October 1793 in Du Casse, *Vandamme et sa Correspondance*, 1:45–75 (in particular, Vandamme to General Davaine, 22 October 1793, 1:66–67).

24. Vandamme to General Davaine, Dunkirk, 21 October 1793, ibid., 1:65.

25. Vandamme to Davaine, Vandamme to the Committee of Public Safety, both 22 October 1793, ibid., 1:67, 68.

26. Vandamme wrote to General Davaine or the members of the Committee of Public Safety every day during the siege of Nieuwpoort. On the first days of the siege, see Vandamme to Davaine, 23, 24 October 1793, ibid., 1:70–73.

27. Vandamme to Davaine, 25, 26 October, Vandamme to the Committee of Public Safety, 26 October 1793, ibid., 1:74–82.

28. Vandamme to Davaine, 27 October 1793, ibid., 1:82–84.

29. Davaine to Vandamme, 29 October 1793, ibid., 1:85–86.

30. Vandamme to Davaine, 29 October 1793, ibid., 1:86.

31. At the end of his letter to the Committee of Public Safety, 26 October 1793, Vandamme signed himself "Le général commandant l'armée républicaine devant Nieuport" (ibid., 1:82).

32. Ibid., 1:80–81.

33. Vandamme to the Committee of Public Safety, 2 November 1793, ibid., 1:88–92; Vandamme, "Journal des campagnes," 5.

34. For a detailed breakdown of his command, see Vandamme, "Journal des campagnes," 5–6; Vandamme to Moreau, 22 December 1793, carton 1, Vandamme Papers.

35. See Vandamme to the Committee of Public Safety, 18 November 1793, in Du Casse, *Vandamme et sa Correspondance*, 1:94–95.

36. Ernouf to Vandamme, 26 December 1793, ibid., 1:97–98.

CHAPTER 2. REVOLUTIONARY GENERAL

1. Phipps, *Armies of the First French Republic*, 1:270.

2. The Laws of 24 February are given in their entirety in the *Moniteur*, 26 February 1793. For a study of these laws in one particular département, see John G. Gallaher, "Recruitment in the District of Poitiers, 1793," *French Historical Studies* 3, no. 2 (1963).

3. On the French army in the early years of the war, see Bertaud, *Army of the French Revolution*.

4. See Vandamme to General Moreau, 26, 29 January, 21 February 1794, carton 1, Vandamme Papers.

5. See Vandamme to Moreau, 1 February 1794, ibid.

6. See the letter from "La Société Populaire et Montagnard de Cassel à citoyen Moreau, général de division, à Cassel," 27 February 1794, in Du Casse, *Vandamme et sa Correspondance*, 1:113–15.

7. Vandamme to Moreau, 21 February 1794, carton 1, Vandamme Papers.

8. Neither of these letters was dated or signed. They are quoted in their entirety in Du Casse, *Vandamme et sa Correspondance*, 1:118–19.

9. See Pichegru to Moreau, the Committee of Public Safety to General Vandamme, both 2 April 1794, ibid., 1:119–21.

10. Vandamme to Moreau, 4 January 1794, carton 1, Vandamme Papers.

11. Vandamme to Moreau, 12 April 1794, in Coutanceau and Leplus, *Opérations*, 49–50.

12. On the advancement and encirclement of Menen (sometimes also spelled Menin), see Moreau's instructions to Vandamme, 23 April 1794, carton 1, Vandamme Papers.

13. On the makeup of his command, see Vandamme, "Journal des campagnes," 11.

14. Phipps accuses Vandamme of his "usual carelessness" in allowing the Allied force to make its way north to safety (*Armies of the First French Republic*, 1:293). On the Allied breakout from Menen, see also Vandamme, "Journal des campagnes," 11–15.

15. See Vandamme to Moreau, 13 May 1794, carton 1, Vandamme Papers.

16. On French movements near Courtrai and Menen, see Moreau to Vandamme (two letters), General Souham to Vandamme, all 17 May 1794, ibid.

17. Vandamme, "Journal des campagnes."

18. See his three-page account of the fighting on 16–19 May in Vandamme to Moreau, 20 May 1794. He gives a lengthy account of the marching and fighting on 17–19 May in "Journal des campagnes." See also Moreau to Vandamme, 13, 16, 17, 18 May 1794. These are all in carton 1, Vandamme Papers.

19. Coutanceau and Leplus give the following figures for the Allied army: "100 officers, 4,000 men, 60 canons, 2 flags, 2 *étendards*, and 1,500 [French]

prisoners of war" (*Opérations*, 325–26). See also Jomini, *Guerres de la Révolution*, 5:98.

20. Vandamme, "Journal des campagnes."

21. Pichegru to Vandamme, General Souham to Vandamme, both 1 June 1794, carton 1, Vandamme Papers.

22. Vandamme to Moreau, 4 June 1794, in Du Casse, *Vandamme et sa Correspondance*, 1:151; Pichegru to Vandamme, Vandamme to Moreau, both 13 June 1794, carton 1, Vandamme Papers.

23. Moreau to Vandamme, 14 June 1794, ibid.

24. On the siege of Ypres, see Vandamme, "Journal des campagnes," 20–24; correspondence to and from Vandamme (ten letters in all), carton 1, Vandamme Papers; Phipps, *Armies of the First French Republic*, 1:312–13.

25. Moreau to Vandamme, 18 June 1794, in Vandamme, "Journal des campagnes," 23–24.

26. Vandamme to Moreau, 23 June 1794, carton 1, Vandamme Papers.

27. On the early operations at Nieuwpoort, see Vandamme, "Journal des campagnes," 32–33; Vandamme to Moreau, 5 July 1794, carton 1, Vandamme Papers.

28. Vandamme, "Journal des campagnes," 32–33; Vandamme to Moreau, 7 July 1794, in Du Casse, *Vandamme et sa Correspondance*, 1:170–71.

29. Vandamme, "Journal des campagnes," 34.

30. Ibid., 32–33; Phipps, *Armies of the First French Republic*, 1:314–20.

31. Vandamme, "Journal des campagnes," 33–34; Moreau to Representative Lacombe, 21 July 1794, carton 1, Vandamme Papers.

32. For the island of Cadsand and Fort Ecluse, see Vandamme, "Journal des campagnes," 35–36; correspondence dated 26 July–18 August 1794 (nine letters), carton 1, Vandamme Papers.

33. Davout found it necessary to rotate his garrisons so they did not spend more than one month at a time in the low country where the "fever" was rampant (Gallaher, *Iron Marshal*, 82–84). On the problems suffered by the Irish Legion on the island of Walcheren, see Gallaher, *Napoleon's Irish Legion*, 87–88.

34. Phipps, *Armies of the First French Republic*, 1:321.

35. Vandamme to Moreau, 9 August 1794, in Du Casse, *Vandamme et sa Correspondance*, 1:182.

36. Vandamme to Moreau, 4 August 1794, ibid., 1:180–82.

37. Vandamme to Moreau, 19 October 1794, ibid.; Laurent to Vandamme, 28 October 1794, carton 1, Vandamme Papers; Vandamme to Moreau, 30 October 1794, in Du Casse, *Vandamme et sa Correspondance*, 1:185.

38. On the siege of Nijmegen and the fighting at the battle of Buderich, see Vandamme's account, 11 November 1794, carton 1, Vandamme Papers.

39. On Vandamme's operations in the first week and a half of November, see his correspondence in Du Casse, *Vandamme et sa Correspondance*, 1:201–209. On the activity of the Second Division in late November and December, see Vandamme's correspondence to Moreau for those weeks, carton 1, Vandamme Papers.

40. Vandamme to Moreau, 20 December 1794, carton 1, Vandamme Papers.
41. For Ubrecht, see Vandamme to Moreau, 23 January 1795, carton 2, Vandamme Papers. On the brief French campaign in Holland, see Phipps, *Armies of the First French Republic*, 1:324–35.
42. Du Casse, *Vandamme et sa Correspondance*, 1:193; Moreau to Vandamme, 24 January 1795, ibid., 1:222; Vandamme to Moreau, 7 February 1795, carton 2, Vandamme Papers.
43. Major Charles (last name not legible) to the commander of the French troops, 3 February 1795, carton 2, Vandamme Papers; Commanding General of English Troops at Bremen to Vandamme, 4 April 1795, in Du Casse, *General Vandamme et sa Correspondance*, 1:243.
44. For example, Vandamme to Moreau, 23, 29 March, 8, 10 April 1795, carton 2, Vandamme Papers.
45. Vandamme to Moreau, 8 April 1795, in Du Casse, *General Vandamme et sa Correspondance*, 1:244.
46. Moreau to Vandamme, 27 April 1795, ibid., 1:248.

CHAPTER 3. WITH THE ARMY OF THE NORTH

1. Du Casse gives a good account of this affair in *Vandamme et sa Correspondance*, 1:248–55.
2. Pichegru to Vandamme, 13 June 1795, ibid., 1:248–51.
3. Moreau to Vandamme, 29 June 1795, ibid., 1:251–54.
4. Moreau to Vandamme, 30 June 1795, carton 2, Vandamme Papers.
5. Vandamme to Moreau, 1 July 1795, in Du Casse, *Vandamme et sa Correspondance*, 1:253.
6. Pichegru to Vandamme, 11 July, Moreau to Vandamme, 21, 22 August 1795, Vandamme to Isoré, no date (August 1795?), ibid., 1:254–57, 259–62.
7. Pichegru to Vandamme, 24 August 1795, ibid., 1:258.
8. "Ordre de la committée de sécurité publique," 29 September 1795, and "La Commission de l'Organisation et du Mouvement des Armées de Terre" to Vandamme, 5 October 1795, carton 2, Vandamme Papers.
9. Isoré does not make it clear which Merlin he wrote to. It could be either Philippe Antoine Merlin of Douai, who had been a member of the Committee of Public Safety after 9 Thermidor, and then Minister of Justice, or Antoine Christophe Merlin of Thionville, who was a member of the Convention and with the Army of the Rhine at the time. See Isoré to Vandamme, 28 September 1795, in Du Casse, *Vandamme et sa Correspondance*, 1:262.
10. Extract from the register of the Committee of Public Safety, 29 September 1795, signed by Cambacérès, Merlin, Dermont, Letourneur, and La Revellière—Lepeaux, carton 2, Vandamme Papers.
11. Pille to Vandamme (early October 1795), in Du Casse, *Vandamme et sa Correspondance*, 1:262–63.
12. See Minister of War (Jean-Baptiste Aubert-Dubayet) to Vandamme, 22 November 1795, carton 2, Vandamme Papers.

13. It may have been as early as June 1794 when Pichegru's name came up at the court of St. James as a possible friend of the Allied cause. Phipps, *Armies of the First French Republic*, 2:262, credits the Right Honorable William Wickham (*Correspondence from the Year 1794*, 1:85–86).

14. The Club de Clichy was a loose right-wing group of anti-republicans who took their name from the house on the rue de Clichy where they met. The club came into existence after 9 Thermidor (27 July 1794) and lasted only a few years. Its influence was at best minor during the Directory, and it virtually ceased to exist after 1797. See Challamel, *Les clubs contre-révolutionnaires*.

15. Phipps, *Armies of the First French Republic*, 2:262.

16. From the royalist point of view, the execution of Louis XVI had resulted in his son, though uncrowned and in prison, becoming Louis XVII. When the boy died at ten years of age in June 1795, his uncle the count of Provence was recognized as king of France with the title Louis XVIII.

17. On Pichegru's treason see Caudrillier, *La trahison de Pichegru*; Mitchell, *Underground War against Revolutionary France*.

18. See French agent Bacher from Switzerland, to the Directory, 13 February 1796, in Du Casse, *Vandamme et sa Correspondance*, 1:272.

19. See Phipps, *Armies of the First French Republic*, 2:268. Du Casse quotes the Directors to Pichegru, 25 March 1796, *Vandamme et sa Correspondance*, 1:285.

20. See Gouvion Saint-Cyr's *Mémoires sur les campagnes des armées du Rhin-et-Moselle de 1792 jusqu'à la paix de Campo-Formio*, 2:549–58.

21. See Du Casse, *Vandamme et sa Correspondance*, 1:282.

22. Vandamme to the Directors, April 1796, ibid., 1:287–89; Vandamme to Pichegru, 9 April 1796, carton 3, Vandamme Papers.

23. Directory to Rivaud, April 1796, in Du Casse, *Vandamme et sa Correspondance*, 1:289.

24. Carnot to Moreau, ibid., 1:297.

25. Vandamme to Woussen, 2 March 1796, ibid., 1:275.

26. Moreau to the Directory, 22 April 1796, ibid., 1:294–95.

27. The Army of the Sambre and Meuse already held a foothold on the right bank of the lower Rhine at Düsseldorf.

28. Phipps calls this plan "a monumental piece of folly, which was signed by Carnot and sent on the 29th March 1796 to Jourdan and Moreau" (*Armies of the First French Republic*, 2:277).

29. Desaix's corps had formed the center of Moreau's army and Saint-Cyr the left. On his switch to the center, Saint-Cyr wrote: "I always thought that Desaix, who for a long time preferred to fight in the valley of the Rhine, and who disliked very much fighting in the mountains, had demanded of Moreau that he form the left wing of the army; and Moreau, not wishing to offend him, consented to his demand." Saint-Cyr, *Mémoires*, 3:53. On the crossing of the Rhine, see ibid., 33–35; Jomini, *Guerres de la Révolution*, 8:203–213; Phipps, *Armies of the First French Republic*, 2:288–92.

30. On the Austrian plans, see Saint-Cyr, *Mémoires*, 3:33.

31. Du Casse discusses the problem of pillaging during this campaign, in *Vandamme et sa Correspondance*, 1:314–15.

32. Phipps, *Armies of the First French Republic*, 2:320.

33. On the battle of Neresheim, see ibid., 2:319–24; Saint-Cyr, *Mémoires*, 3:144–61; Phipps, *Armies of the First French Republic*, 2:319–24; Jomini, *Guerres de la Révolution*, 8:248–55.

34. Saint-Cyr, *Mémoires*, 3:126–33; Phipps, *Armies of the First French Republic*, 2:319–20.

35. On the Directory's Commissioners of the Government, see Doyle, *Oxford History of the French Revolution*, 227–64.

36. Haussmann to the Directors, 14 August 1796, in Du Casse, *Vandamme et sa Correspondance*, 1:322–23.

37. Ibid., 1:323.

38. Du Casse provides a very good discussion on this subject in ibid., 1:325–27.

39. Phipps, *Armies of the First French Republic*, 2:337–42.

40. Moreau to the Directory, 21, 27 October 1796, in Du Casse, *Vandamme et sa Correspondance*, 1:340, 342. Jomini gives a good account of the battle of Biberach in *Guerres de la Révolution*, 9:68–72.

41. Thompson, *Napoleon Bonaparte*, 74.

42. See Moreau to the Directory, 27 October 1796, in Du Casse, *Vandamme et sa Correspondance*, 1:342.

43. See Moreau's three long reports to the Directory, 15, 21, 27 October 1796, in which he describes in some detail his retreat from Bavaria back to the left bank of the Rhine (ibid., 1:333–43).

44. Minister of War to Moreau, n.d., Haussmann to the Directory, 18 October 1796, ibid., 1:346, 344–45.

45. See, for example, Vandamme to Moreau, 13 November, Vandamme to Desaix, 15 November 1796, ibid., 1:348–49.

46. Vandamme to Moreau, 16 November 1796, ibid., 1:350–51.

47. Vandamme to Moreau, 1 April 1797, ibid., 1:353.

48. Ibid., 1:355.

49. Vandamme, "Rapport sur le passage du Rhin," carton 3, Vandamme Papers.

50. On the crossing of the Rhine and the fighting on 20–21 April, see ibid. Vandamme wrote two reports on this brief campaign, Vandamme to Moreau, 21, 22 April 1797, ibid.

51. See Vandamme to Moreau, 23 April 1797, carton 3, Vandamme Papers.

52. Vandamme to Pinot, 27 April 1797, in Du Casse, *Vandamme et sa Correspondance*, 1:388.

53. See Thompson, *Napoleon Bonaparte*, 74.

54. Vandamme to Moreau, 4 May 1797, in Du Casse, *Vandamme et sa Correspondance*, 1:391.

55. Vandamme to Reynier, 6 May 1797, ibid., 1:391–94.

56. Abbot of Schwarzach to Vandamme, 30 May 1797, ibid., 1:396.

57. Abbot Bernard of Gengenbach to Vandamme, 30 May 1797, ibid., 1:396–97.

CHAPTER 4. CAMPAIGNS ON THE RHINE

1. In a letter to Pichegru dated 31 May 1797, for example, Vandamme wrote: "I will not speak for myself, my general, because I will probably quit the service." Du Casse, *Vandamme et sa Correspondance*, 1:400.
2. Du Casse, ibid., 1:405.
3. Phipps, *Armies of the First French Republic*, 5:7–25.
4. Du Casse attributes Vandamme's transfer from the Army of Mayence to the Army of England to General Bonaparte who had "great influence with the Directory," but he offers no evidence to back up this claim (*Vandamme et sa Correspondance*, 1:406).
5. Augereau to Vandamme, 11 April 1798, ibid., 1:414.
6. Vandamme's long report is entitled "Rapport du Combat du 18 Floréal, an VI, sur l'Attaque des Iles Marcouf," 7 June 1798, ibid., 1:419–23.
7. On this operation, see Vandamme's orders "Demont, Adjutant Général, Chef de l'Etat-Major, au Général de Brigade Vandamme," 28 June 1798, ibid., 1:423–25.
8. Farine, "Aide de Camp du Général Michaud, au Général Vandamme," 7 July 1798, ibid., 1:426–27. On the 1798 expeditions to Ireland, see Edouard Desbières, *Projets et tentatives de débarquement aux Iles Britanniques, 1793—1805*, vol. 5.
9. Minister of War (General Barthélemy-Louis Schérer) to Vandamme, 16 August 1798, carton 4, Vandamme Papers.
10. See Vandamme's correspondence from October 1798 to January 1799, carton 4, Vandamme Papers.
11. Letter of service, 5 February 1799, signed by the Minister of War, ibid.; Minister of War to Vandamme, 16 February 1799, ibid.
12. On the formation of the Second Coalition, see Rodger, *War of the Second Coalition*.
13. Jomini, *Guerres de la Révolution*, 11:94.
14. King Ferdinand of Naples had driven the French out of Rome in November 1798, and the Directory was preparing to send an army to punish the Neapolitans.
15. Jomini, *Guerres de la Révolution*, 11:94–95.
16. Ibid., 11:96. Jomini thought the Austrians did proportion their forces properly, putting too many men in the Army of the Tyrol and not enough in Germany.
17. Phipps, *Armies of the First French Republic*, 5:22. Jomini puts Jourdan's army at thirty-six thousand men in March. See "Etat de situation de l'Armée du Danube," *Guerres de la Révolution*, 11:96–97 (foldout).
18. Ernouf to Vandamme, 18 February 1799, carton 4, Vandamme Papers.
19. See Orders of the day, signed Jourdan, dated 28 February, 1 March 1799, ibid.

20. Jourdan to Vandamme, 4 March 1799, ibid.
21. See Jourdan to Vandamme, 18 March 1799, carton 4, Vandamme Papers; Jourdan to Saint-Cyr, 18 March 1799, in Saint-Cyr, *Mémoires*, 4:115.
22. Ernouf to Vandamme, 13 March 1799, carton 4, Vandamme Papers.
23. Jourdan to Vandamme, 18 March 1799, ibid.
24. Phipps, *Armies of the First French Republic*, 5:33, 50–51.
25. Compère to Vandamme, 19 March 1799, carton 4, Vandamme Papers.
26. Phipps, *Armies of the First French Republic*, 5:35. Jomini gives a breakdown of the Austrian army in *Guerres de la Révolution*, 11:99.
27. Jomini gives the date as 19 March (*Guerres de la Révolution*, 11:116–17).
28. Vandamme to Compère (no date given; about 20 March 1799?), in Du Casse, *Vandamme et sa Correspondance*, 1:444.
29. Jourdan to Vandamme, 19 March 1799, carton 4, Vandamme Papers.
30. Order of the day, signed Jourdan, 24 March 1799, ibid.
31. Jourdan to Vandamme, 24 March 1799, ibid.
32. On Vandamme's actions in the battle, see Saint-Cyr's report to Jourdan, 26 March 1799, in Du Casse, *Vandamme et sa Correspondance*, 1:448–49.
33. On the battle of Stockach (also called battle of Liptingen), see Saint-Cyr, *Mémoires*, 4:132–57; Phipps, *Armies of the First French Republic*, 5:43–50; Saint-Cyr's report to Jourdan, 26 March 1799, in Du Casse, *Vandamme et sa Correspondance*, 1:447–49.
34. Saint-Cyr to Vandamme, 26 March 1799, carton 4, Vandamme Papers.
35. See Saint-Cyr, *Mémoires*, 4:153–55; Phipps *Armies of the First French Republic*, 5:47–50.
36. On the retreat of the French army, see Saint-Cyr to Vandamme, 26 March, Order of the day, signed Jourdan, 30 March, Ernouf to Vandamme, 31 March 1799, carton 4, Vandamme Papers.
37. Ernouf to Vandamme, 3 April 1799, ibid.
38. Ernouf to Vandamme, 5, 10, 11 April 1799, ibid.
39. See Masséna to Vandamme, 18 April 1799, in Du Casse, *Vandamme et sa Correspondance*, 1:453–54.
40. "Instruction to generals of division," 20 April 1799, carton 4, Vandamme Papers.
41. Minister of War to Masséna, 7 May 1799, ibid.; Minister of War to Masséna, 12 May 1799, Dossier Vandamme, Arch. Guerre 303/7 Yd.
42. Le chef de l'Etat-Major Général to Coquengeiot, 18 June 1799, ibid.
43. Vandamme, "Mémoire justificatif."
44. Declaration du Comte de Zeppelin, 26 March 1799, in Du Casse, *Vandamme et sa Correspondance*, 1:458–59.
45. See "Traduction d'un rapport officiel, addressé à S. Alt. Monseigneur le Duc Régent [of Würtemberg], par son grand *Bailli* de Tübingen," 23 March 1799, Dossier Vandamme, Arch. Guerre, 303/7 Yd.
46. Ibid.

47. "Extract from the Letter of Citizen Roberjot to the ex-director Merlin," 17 April 1799, in Du Casse, *Vandamme et sa Correspondance,* 1:463–65.

48. Krauth, at Colmar, to Metzer, 23 April 1799, Dossier Vandamme, Arch. Guerre, 303/7 Yd. Vieux-Brisach had been besieged and shelled by the Austrians in the first year of the wars of the French Revolution. At that time, a large portion of the city was destroyed by fire.

49. "The Greffier of the Criminal Tribunal of the Upper Rhine to the Directors," Colmar, 22 April 1799, in Vandamme's "Mémoire justificatif."

50. The Administrators of the Department of the Upper Rhine to the Minister of War, 13 May 1799, ibid.

51. Extract from the Register of the Executive Directory, 12 July 1799, in Vandamme, "Mémoire justificatif."

52. There are two copies of Vandamme's defense, entitled "Mémoire Justificatif du Général de Division Vandamme," in carton 4, Vandamme Papers, Bibliothèque de Lille. One is a printed document published at Strasbourg by F. G. Levrault, 5 Thermidor, an VII (23 July 1799); the other is a handwritten manuscript. There is also a copy of the "Mémoire Justificatif" in the Dossier Vandamme, Arch. Guerre, 303/7 Yd. All references and page numbers will be made with respect to the document in the War Archives at Vincennes because it is easier for scholars to access than the document at Lille.

53. Vandamme, "Mémoire justificatif," 1–3.

54. Ibid., 4.

55. Ibid., 5.

56. Ibid., 6.

57. Ibid., 7. Vandamme was the "guest" of the prince of Hechingen for two nights, 19–20 March (ibid., 6).

58. Ibid., 9.

59. Ibid., 10.

60. Ibid., 11.

61. Ibid., 14. See also the letter from General Barbier to Coquengeiot, 12 May 1799, Dossier Vandamme, Arch. Guerre 303/7 Yd. Coquengeiot had written to Masséna about the interrogation of witnesses in Swabia, and Masséna's chief of staff replied that Swabia was occupied by Austrian troops; thus, he would not be able to interrogate anyone in Germany.

62. "Procès Verbal d'Information," signed Chef de Bataillon Coquengeniot, 27 May 1799, ibid., p. 9. This document is in the handwriting of Coquengeniot and begins with "Today, 8 Prairial an 7" (27 May 1799).

63. See Vandamme, "Mémoire justificatif," 15–16.

64. "Procès Verbal d'Information," signed Chef de Bataillon Coquengeiot, 27 May 1799, Dossier Vandamme, Arch. Guerre, 303/7 Yd, pp. 8–9.

65. Executive Order signed Sieyès, 19 August 1799, Dossier Vandamme, Arch. Guerre, 303/7 Yd.

66. On the political conditions in Paris during the spring and summer of 1799, see Lefebvre, *French Revolution,* 241–49.

67. The Letter of service, 18 August 1799, actually states that Vandamme was "to be employed as a General of Brigade" (carton 4, Vandamme Papers).

However, this was most likely a clerical error because there is no other reference to that rank in the Vandamme Papers for this time period. If it had been meant as a demotion, the general would surely have taken issue, and there would have been other references to him as a general of brigade.

68. Vandamme to Bernadotte (minister of war), 2 September 1799, ibid.

69. See Letter of service, 1 September 1799, ibid.

70. Vandamme to Bernadotte, 3 September 1799, in Du Casse, *Vandamme et sa Correspondance*, 1:423–25.

71. As Phipps put it: "The active French division was given to the hard-fighting, plundering Vandamme" (*Armies of the First French Republic*, 5:194).

72. See General Sir Ralph Abercrombie's report dated 28 August 1799, in Walsh, *Narrative of the Expedition*, 96–98; Moore, *Diary of Sir John Moore*, 1:343–45.

73. On the arrival of the duke of York with English reinforcements, see York's dispatch to the Prime Minister, 13 September 1799, in Walsh, *Narrative of the Expedition*, 110.

74. See Moore, *Diary of Sir John Moore*, 1:344–45; Brune's dispatches to the Minister of War, 30 August, 1 September, in Bourgoin, *Esquisse Historique*, 142–49 (Bourgoin was one of Brune's aides-de-camp).

75. Brune to the Minister of War, 10 September 1799 (official report), in Bourgoin, *Esquisse Historique*, 150–51 (150); Brune to the Minister of War, 10 September 1799 (official dispatch), in Du Casse, *Vandamme et sa Correspondance*, 2:14; Brune to Bernadotte, 10 September 1799 (personal letter), in Bourgoin, *Esquisse Historique*, 142–49 (148).

76. See General of Brigade Louis Fuzier to Vandamme, 14 September, Rostollant to Vandamme, 19 September 1799, carton 4, Vandamme Papers.

77. Bourgoin, *Esquisse Historique*, 155.

78. According to Phipps: "Napoleon remarked that Abercrombie might as well have been on the Thames as at Hoorn" (*Armies of the First French Republic*, 5:202).

79. On the battle of Bergen, as the French called it, see Adjutant General Charles-Ambroise Ardenne, Brune's chief of staff, to the Minister of War, 19 September 1799, in Du Casse, *Vandamme et sa Correspondance*, 2:20–23; Brune to Minister of War, 19 September 1799, in Bourgoin, *Esquisse Historique*, 152–54; York's description of the battle, dispatch to London, 20 September 1799, in Walsh, *Narrative of the Expedition*, 111–15; General Rostollant to Vandamme, 19 September 1799, carton 4, Vandamme Papers; Moore, *Diary of Sir John Moore*, 1:345–50. See also secondary accounts of the battle in Phipps, *Armies of the First French Republic*, 5:201–203, and Du Casse, *Vandamme et sa Correspondance*, 2:17–25.

80. Brune to the Batavian Directory, 19 September 1799, in Bourgoin, *Esquisse Historique*, 154; Brune to Vandamme, 20 September 1799, in Du Casse, *Vandamme et sa Correspondance*, 2:24.

81. See Brune to Vandamme, 22 September 1799, carton 4, Vandamme Papers.

82. See Du Casse, *Vandamme et sa Correspondance*, 2:24–25.

83. Moore, *Diary of Sir John Moore*, 1:350–51.

84. Brune to Vandamme, 26 September, Gouvion to Vandamme, 30 September 1799, carton 5, Vandamme Papers.

85. Brune to Vandamme, 1 October 1799, in Du Casse, *Vandamme et sa Correspondance*, 2:25–26.

86. On the Anglo-Russian drive south, see the duke of York's dispatch to London, 6 October 1799 (a detailed eight-page description of the battle), in Walsh, *Narrative of the Expedition*, 121–31. The following day, 7 October 1799, York sent another dispatch to London with further thoughts and casualties (ibid., 132–33). See also Brune to Minister of War, 4 October 1799, in Bourgoin, *Esquisse Historique*, 158–60; Du Casse, *Vandamme et sa Correspondance*, 2:27–35 (in particular, Rostollant to the Minister of War, 9 October 1799, at 2:32–34); Phipps, *Armies of the First French Republic*, 5:202–206.

87. Duke of York, dispatch to London, 9 October 1799, in Walsh, *Narrative of the Expedition*, 134.

88. Bourgoin, *Esquisse Historique*, 161.

89. On 20 October 1799, York again explained his reasoning for evacuating Holland and taking his army back to England (dispatch to London, in Walsh, *Narrative of the Expedition*, 138–39).

90. On the capture of the Dutch fleet, see Vice-Admiral Mitchel's dispatch, 30 August 1799, ibid., 104–106.

91. Brune's letter to the duke of York in response to the duke's request for negotiations, 16 October 1799, in Du Casse, *Vandamme et sa Correspondance*, 2:34–37.

92. On further negotiations, see Brune to Duke of York, 18 October 1799, ibid., 37–40.

93. The nine articles of the convention, signed by Major-General Know and Adjutant General Rostollant, are found in Walsh, *Narrative of the Expedition*, 139–40.

94. Bourgoin, *Esquisse Historique*, 162–63. For a further discussion of why Brune recommended that the government negotiate the withdrawal of the Anglo-Russian army, see Brune to the Minister of War, 16 October 1799, ibid., 163–66.

95. See ibid., 163–69. Bourgoin notes that these threats were contained in a letter concerning the suspension of hostility from Duke of York to Brune on 15 October 1799, but he does not quote the letter.

96. Chief Medical Officers to Brune, 19 October 1799, in Du Casse, *Vandamme et sa Correspondance*, 2:40–41.

97. Brune to Vandamme, 19 October 1799, ibid., 2:41–42.

CHAPTER 5. THE YEARS OF PEACE

1. On the Law of Hostages, see Lefebvre, *French Revolution*, 244–46; Patrick, "Law of Hostages," 563–64.

2. Lefebvre, *French Revolution*, 250–51.

3. On the conditions in France on the eve of the coup d'état of Brumaire, see Albert Vandal, *L'Avènement de Bonaparte*, vol. 1, *La Genèse du Consulat*

Brumaire; La Constitution de l'an VIII, 268–99; Lefebvre, *French Revolution from 1793 to 1799*, 241–51; Thompson, *Napoleon Bonaparte*, 146–55.

4. On the coup d'état of Brumaire and the establishment of the Consulate, see Vandal, *L'Avènement de Bonaparte*, vol. 1, *La Genèse du Consulat Brumaire; La Constitution de l'an VIII*, 300–402; Lefebvre, *French Revolution from 1793 to 1799*, 251–56; Thompson, *Napoleon Bonaparte*, 146–55.

5. On Moreau's role in the Brumaire coup d'état, see Dontenville, *Le Général Moreau*, 98–101.

6. Moreau to Vandamme, 8 January 1800, carton 5, Vandamme Papers.

7. Letter of service, signed Berthier, 26 January 1800, Berthier to Vandamme, 27 January 1800, Bonaparte to Berthier, 2 February 1800, ibid.

8. See "Situation et Emplacement des Troops de la 2e Division de l'Armée du Rhin," 2 April 1800, ibid.

9. See Moreau to Bonaparte, 2 April 1800, in Du Casse, *Vandamme et sa Correspondance*, 2:51–53. On their different plans, and how and why the First Consul eventually allowed Moreau to have his way, see "Plan de Campagne pour l'Armée du Rhin," 22 March 1800, Bonaparte to Moreau, 9 April 1800, *Correspondance de Napoléon*, nos. 4694, 4695, 6:201–203, 214–16; Thiers, *Histoire du consulat et de l'Empire*, 1:248–63.

10. On Austria's grand strategy, see Thiers, *Histoire du consulat et de l'Empire*, 1:231–34; Chandler, *Campaigns of Napoleon*, 270–71. The city of Toulon had opened itself to the English during the civil war of 1793, and Bonaparte played a major role in driving them out. To regain control of Toulon would provide the English Mediterranean fleet with an excellent naval base and with revenge for the defeat of 1793. It would also deprive the French of their finest naval facility in the Mediterranean.

11. For a good discussion of why Bonaparte gave in to Moreau against his better "military" judgment, see Thiers, *Histoire du consulat et de l'Empire*, 1:238–41, 246–49, 258–64. On Moreau's plan for the campaign in Germany, see General Dessolle to the Minister of War (Carnot), 10 April 1800, in Du Casse, *Vandamme et sa Correspondance*, 2:58–59.

12. On Bonaparte's plan for the 1800 campaign, see Chandler, *Campaigns of Napoleon*, 266–70; also Thiers, *Histoire du consulat et de l'Empire*, 1:248–49, 258–64.

13. Bonaparte hoped originally to cross the Alps further east by the Simplon and Gotthard passes, which would put him near Milan, astride the Po River at Stradella, which he believed the ideal point to block the Austrian retreat. See Bonaparte to Moreau, 9 April 1800, *Correspondance de Napoléon*, no. 4711, 6:214–16.

14. "Plan de Campagne pour l'Armée du Rhine," 22 March 1800, ibid., no. 4694, 6:201–203.

15. On the French crossing of the Rhine, see Thiers, *Histoire du consulat et de l'Empire*, 1:291–98.

16. On the battle of Stokach, see ibid., 1:303–304.

17. Ibid., 1:332–33.

18. Lecourbe to Vandamme, 22 May 1800, carton 5, Vandamme Papers.

19. See Du Casse, *Vandamme et sa Correspondance*, 2:78–79.

20. Vandamme to Molitor, 23 May 1800, carton 5, Vandamme Papers.

21. See Thompson, *Napoleon Bonaparte*, 179–82; Chandler, *Campaigns of Napoleon*, 298–304; Du Casse, *Vandamme et sa Correspondance*, 2:97–98.

22. See the letter of introduction written by Macdonald on behalf of Vandamme, 22 January 1801. Macdonald "Invited the generals and military commanders under my orders to provide General Vandamme all of the facilities for his voyage that he requests to understand civil and military Italy." In Du Casse, *Vandamme et sa Correspondance*, 2:98.

23. See, for example, Vandamme to the First Consul, 22 October 1801, ibid., 2:99.

24. The date 12 May 1803 is most frequently considered the resumption of the war between England and France, because that is the date the English ambassador, Whitworth, having been recalled, left Paris.

25. Lefebvre, *From 18 Brumaire to Tilsit*, 179, 170.

26. For Bonaparte's day-by-day itinerary on this tour of inspection of the north, see Garros, *Quel roman que ma vie!* 207–10.

27. Berthier to Vandamme, August 1803, in Du Casse, *Vandamme et sa Correspondance*, 2:101–102.

28. For example, General Alexander Dumas received one of a number of swords of honor from Bonaparte at the end of the Italian campaign of 1796–97, and a second sword in Egypt in 1798. See Gallaher, *Alexandre Dumas*, 88, 131.

29. Berthier to Vandamme, 30 August 1803, carton 5, Vandamme Papers; Gotteri, *Le Maréchal Soult*, 153–34.

30. See Gotteri, *Le Maréchal Soult*, 156, along with the voluminous orders of the day and the correspondence to and from Vandamme in cartons 6–10, Vandamme Papers (the material is organized in folders, by the months of the revolutionary calendar).

31. See, for example, the letter from General Gérard Christophe Duroc to Davout (no date), in Davout, *Correspondance*, 1:79n1.

32. Soult to Bonaparte, 12 April 1804, in Gotteri, *Le Maréchal Soult*, 162. See also Davout to Bonaparte, 30 April, 1804: "All of the generals, officers, noncommissioned officers, and soldiers of the camp of Bruges [the Third Corps of the army] have testified to me the greatest desire to express their affection and their desire [for an empire]. Tomorrow I will have the honor to send you the expression of the common wishes of the army and all of the declarations [of support] they have composed" (Davout, *Correspondance*, 1:78–79).

33. The generals named active marshals were, in the order that they first appeared, Berthier, Murat, Moncey, Jourdan, Masséna, Augereau, Bernadotte, Soult, Brune, Lannes, Mortier, Ney, Davout, and Bessières. The honorary marshals were Kellermann, Lefebvre, Périgonon, and Sérurier.

34. It has been alleged that Davout received his marshal's baton because he was married to Louise-Aimée Leclerc, sister of the late general Victor-Emmanuel Leclerc, the husband of Pauline Bonaparte. See Chandler, *Napoleon's Marshals*, xxxiv. It has also been pointed out that Davout was a

close friend of the late general Louis Charles Desaix de Veygoux, killed at the battle of Marengo (1800). Napoleon held Desaix in very high regard, and had he lived Desaix would certainly have been named marshal with the first group. Perhaps Davout received the baton of either Desaix or Leclerc. Napoleon's selection of Davout has often been cited as an example of his good judgment of men, because Davout went on to become one of the most celebrated field commanders and administrators of the Napoleonic army. See Gallaher, *The Iron Marshal*, 87–88.

35. The best study of the marshals of the empire, their relationship with Napoleon, why they were selected in 1804, and their relationships with each other, is Chardigny, *Les maréchaux de Napoléon*. Chandler also has a good overall introduction to the marshals in his *Napoleon's Marshals*, xxxiv–lxi. See also Jourquin, *Dictionnaire des maréchaux*.

36. Order of the day, signed Soult, 21 May 1804; Folder for the month of Prairial, year XII, both in carton 7, Vandamme Papers.

37. Order of the day, 21 May 1804, ibid.

38. For a good discussion of the creation of the Legion of Honor, see Durant and Durant, *Age of Napoleon*, 269–70.

39. "Legion of Honor," in Chandler, *Napoleonic Wars*, 246.

40. General Alexandre Dumas, father of the great nineteenth-century author, did not receive the Legion of Honor, although he had received two swords of honor from General Bonaparte. The First Consul was angry at Dumas for leaving the army in Egypt in 1799. See Gallaher, *Alexandre Dumas*.

41. Grand Chancellor of the Legion of Honor to Vandamme, 15 June 1804, carton 7, Vandamme Papers. There are several degrees within the Legion of Honor: chevalier, officer, and grand officer.

42. Napoleon placed the crown upon his own head. He did not wish to give the impression that it was the pope who made him emperor, nor to establish the precedent that his successors required the pope to crown the emperor of the French, a precedent established by Charlemagne in 800, when he was crowned by the pope as emperor of the Holy Roman Empire, that caused much trouble during the Middle Ages.

43. Vandamme to Prince Joseph, 6 March 1805, in Du Casse, *Vandamme et sa Correspondance*, 2:119.

44. Soult to Vandamme, 15 February, Chief of the General Staff to Vandamme, 24 February 1805, in ibid., 2:121–24.

CHAPTER 6. THE AUSTERLITZ CAMPAIGN

1. Most histories of the Napoleonic period deal with the formation of the Third Coalition. Among the best is Lefebvre, *From 18 Brumaire to Tilsit*, 198–213.

2. In a major reorganization of the numerous armies of the French Republic, Napoleon consolidated them all into one, which he named the Grande Armée on 29 August 1805. Various parts of the army would be in Italy, on the Rhine, in Hanover, or along the English Channel, but on paper

it was all one army. However, the term *Grand Army* is usually applied only to those army corps that were directly under the emperor's control operating in central and eastern Europe (including Russia in 1812) after the summer of 1805.

3. Chandler gives this figure in "The Formations of *La Grande Armée*, August 29, 1805," *Campaigns of Napoleon*, app. D, 1103. Discussing the size of the corps in preparation for the campaign of 1805, he writes: "The corps . . . varied in size according to their proposed roles, ranging from Soult's 41,000 to Augereau's 14,000 men" (386). Esposito and Elting, in *Military History* (47), put the strength of the Fourth Corps at 37,000 men as it crossed the Rhine at the end of September 1805. This figure could account for the loss of between 3,000 and 4,000 men in the march from Boulogne to the Rhine. On soldiers falling behind the march from Boulogne, see Soult to Vandamme, 8 September 1805, in Du Casse, *Vandamme et sa Correspondance*, 2:136–38.

4. Soult to Vandamme, 8 September 1805, in Du Casse, *Vandamme et sa Correspondance*, 2:136–38.

5. "Etat Militaire à Boulogne," no date (summer 1805?), carton 10, and "Situation et Rapport de la 2e Division," 19 September 1805, carton 12, Vandamme Papers.

6. Berthier to Vandamme, 1 August 1805, in Du Casse, *Vandamme et sa Correspondance*, 2:130–31.

7. Napoleon to Berthier, 25 August 1805, *Correspondance de Napoléon*, no. 9135, 11:140.

8. On the detailed instruction for the movement of the corps, see Napoleon to Berthier, 26 August 1805, ibid., 11:141–44.

9. "Situation et Rapport de la 2e Division," 19 September 1805, carton 12, Vandamme Papers.

10. "Order to the Army," 20 September 1805, *Correspondance de Napoléon*, no. 9245, 11:225–26.

11. General Saligny to Vandamme, 26 September 1805, carton 12, Vandamme Papers. Major Auguste-Julien Bigarré, with the Fourth Regiment of the Line in Vandamme's division, states that his regiment crossed the Rhine at Spire (*Mémoires*, 165). In some secondhand accounts, the Second Division crossed at Rhinhause.

12. Bigarré, *Mémoires*, 165.

13. On this march, see Vandamme to Commandant Cabau, 29 September, Vandamme to General Louis Meriage, his chief of staff, 30 September, "Ordre de Marche," signed Soult, 2 October 1805, and "Campagnes de l'An 14: Marche du 4e Corps de la Grande Armée," all in carton 12, Vandamme Papers. The document entitled "Campagnes de l'An 14" gives a day-by-day location of the Fourth Corps from the crossing of the Rhine on 27 September to the end of the campaign. It also has brief notes of interest after many of the days.

14. Soult to Vandamme, 3, 4 October 1805, and "Campagnes de l'An 14," carton 12, Vandamme Papers.

15. Soult to Vandamme, 6 October 1805, and "Campagnes de l'An 14," carton 12, Vandamme Papers; Napoleon's instructions to Soult, 27 September, 3 October 1805, *Correspondance de Napoléon*, nos. 9273, 9323, 11:251, 282.

16. Soult's instructions to Vandamme, 8 October 1805, and "Campagnes de l'An 14," carton 12, Vandamme Papers.

17. Vandamme to Soult, 9 October 1805, carton 11, ibid.

18. Soult to Vandamme, 11 October, two letters from Vandamme dated at Landsberg, 20 October 1805, and "Campagnes de l'An 14," carton 12, ibid.

19. Soult to Vandamme, 12 October 1805, ibid.

20. Soult to Vandamme, 14 October 1805, carton 11, ibid.

21. On the operations of the Fourth Corps south of the Danube, see 2e Bulletin de la Grande Armée, 9 October 1805, no. 9358, 11:302–303, 3e Bulletin de la Grande Armée, 10 October 1805, no. 9361, 11:305–307, 4e Bulletin de la Grande Armée, 11 October 1805, no. 9370, 11:313–14, Napoleon to Soult, two letters dated 12 October 1805, nos. 9373, 9374, 11:316–18, 5e Bulletin de la Grande Armée, 12 October 1805, no. 9380, 11:322–23, 6e Bulletin de la Grande Armée, 18 October 1805, no. 9392, 11:333–36, all in *Correspondance de Napoléon*; "Campagnes de l'An 14," carton 12, Vandamme Papers; Bigarré, *Mémoires*, 165–69; Du Casse, *Vandamme et sa Correspondance*, 2:138–45; Gotteri, *Le Maréchal Soult*, 179–81.

22. By the end of the sixteenth century the Julian calendar, in use in Europe since the days of Julius Caesar, had fallen ten days behind the sun. In 1582 Pope Gregory VIII had the calendar corrected, but at first only Catholic Europe adopted the new calendar. Gradually Protestant Europe switched from the Julian to the Gregorian calendar, but it was not until 1918 that the new Soviet Union gave up the old calendar. The result was that in 1805 the Russians were using a calendar that was eleven days behind the one used by the Austrians.

23. Napoleon to Soult, 12 October 1805, *Correspondance de Napoléon*, no. 9373, 11:316–17; Vandamme to "Officers of all grades," 12 October 1805, carton 12, Vandamme Papers.

24. Napoleon to Berthier, and 5e Bulletin de la Grande Armée, both 15 October 1805, in *Correspondance de Napoléon*, nos. 9383, 9384, 11:326, 327–29.

25. Huitième Bulletin de la Grande Armée, 20 October 1805, ibid., no. 9404, 11:342.

26. See "Campagnes de l'An 14," General Charles Saligny (Soult's chief of staff) to Vandamme, 24 October, Soult to Vandamme, 26 October 1805, all in carton 12, Vandamme Papers; Vandamme's Order of the day, 12 November 1805, in Du Casse, *Vandamme et sa Correspondance*, 2:147.

27. Soult to Vandamme, 20 November 1805, carton 12, Vandamme Papers.

28. See for example Soult's letters to Vandamme criticizing the conduct of the Second Division troops, 24 October, 20 November 1805, ibid. carton 12, Vandamme Papers.

29. Vandamme to Soult, 25 November 1805, "Registre du Correspondance."

30. Ségur, *Aide-de-Camp*, 213, 214.

31. On the extraordinary capture of the Tabor Bridge, see Manceron, *Austerlitz*, 130–31; Duffy, *Austerlitz*, 63–64.

32. Duffy, *Austerlitz*, 68. Duffy gives the source of this quote as "*Zapiski A. P. Ermolova*, Moscow: 1865–68, 1:29."
33. Manceron, *Austerlitz*, 153.
34. Gotteri, *Le Maréchal Soult*, 183.
35. On Alexander's visit to Berlin and the Treaty of Potsdam, see Manceron, *Austerlitz*, 114–15.
36. Chandler, *Campaigns of Napoleon*, 1:118. Esposito and Elting, *Military History*, 54, give the figure at 85,700.
37. See Chandler, *Campaigns of Napoleon*, 1:103, 118, for the French numbers. Chandler gives the French strength at 73,200 on the day of the battle; so do Esposito and Elting (*Military History*, 54).
38. On the position of the two divisions, see Soult to Vandamme, 1 December 1805, carton 12, Vandamme Papers.
39. Manceron, *Austerlitz*, 215. Manceron says he was quoting Bezin. Manceron gives a six-page account of this affair (ibid., 209–15). For eyewitness accounts, see Thiébault, *Mémoires*, 3:145–68; Ségur, *Aide-de-Camp*, 244–45.
40. Berthier to Davout, 8:00 P.M., 28 November 1805, in Davout, *Opérations du 3e Corps*, v—vi.
41. Ségur, *Aide-de-Camp*, 249.
42. Duffy, *Austerlitz*, 105–106.
43. Vandamme's report of the battle to Soult, 3 December 1805, "Registre du Correspondance."
44. For a detailed account of Saint-Hilaire's division in this battle, see Thiébault, who commanded one of Saint-Hilaire's brigades (*Mémoires*, 3:145–68).
45. Vandamme's report to Soult, 3 December 1805, "Registre du Correspondance."
46. After Buxhöwden drove Legrand out of the village of Telnitz, he held up his first column to wait for the second and third columns to reach their primary objectives on the Goldbach. This allowed Legrand time to regroup and for Davout's leading units to reach the battlefield (Duffy, *Austerlitz*, 104).
47. Bigarré wrote in his *Mémoires* (174) that Vincent was Vandamme's aide-de-camp, but he was not attached to Vandamme until 1806. See Six, *Dictionnaire biographique*, 2:559.
48. Bigarré gives this eyewitness account in his *Mémoires*, 175–76. See also Vandamme's report, 3 December 1805, "Registre du Correspondance."
49. Ségur, *Aide-de-Camp*, 252. It should be noted that Bigarré says (incorrectly) that it was the Twenty-fourth Regiment that fled from the battle (*Mémoires*, 176).
50. Bigarré, *Mémoires*, 180.
51. On this phase of the battle, see Vandamme's report, 3 December 1805, "Registre du Correspondance," and the two eyewitness accounts in Ségur, *Aide-de-Camp*, 249–54, and Thiébault, *Mémoires*, 3:156–64.
52. There has been debate concerning how many were lost in the legendary lake. Most eyewitnesses make the affair into a great disaster (Ségur, *Aide-de-Camp*, 246–47; Comeau, *Souvenir des Guerres d'Allemagne*, 230–31).

But the most reliable historians tend to play down the losses. For example, Chandler says: "Several thousand unfortunates [fell] into the freezing waters. The French bulletins later claimed that as many as 20,000 perished in this way, but this figure is undoubtedly a gross exaggeration; only 5,000 Allied troops were in the vicinity of the lakes at this time, and it is probable that 2,000 were drowned (some authorities put the figure as low as 200). However, it is certain that 38 guns and 130 corpses of horses were recovered from the waters of Lake Satschen after the battle" (*Campaigns of Napoleon*, 432). The 30e Bulletin de la Grande Armée gives the inflated figure of twenty thousand men. Coignet was an eyewitness to this event and wrote that most of the Allied troops who fled to the lake stayed close to the shore and that "even if a few platoons paddled in the water, it was not deep enough to drown them." See Coignet, *Les Cahiers du Capitaine Coignet (1799—1815)*, 231.

53. For the last phase of the battle, see Ségur, *Aide-de-Camp*, 255–56.

54. Thiébault, *Mémoires*, 3:158. Thiébault does not say he personally heard Vandamme say these words. Indeed, Thiébault was seriously wounded leading his brigade southwest from the Pratzen Plateau toward Sokolnitz, and Vandamme was marching south to Augezd, so it is unlikely they saw each other at all on the afternoon of the battle. Thiébault seems to be quoting an unidentified third party whose reliability we cannot verify. But it is the sort of statement Dominique Vandamme might well have made, given his character.

55. Vandamme's report, 3 December 1805, "Registre du Correspondance."

56. "To the Army," 3 December 1805, *Correspondance de Napoléon*, no. 9537, 11:443–44. There is also a printed copy of this document entitled "Soldats" in carton 11, Vandamme Papers.

57. In Du Casse, *Vandamme et sa Correspondance*, 2:157.

58. See Salipuy to Vandamme, 3 December 1805, carton 12, Vandamme Papers.

59. "Situation de 2e Division," 24 December 1805, and "Extrait de l'ordre du jour pour 4 nivôse, an XIV" (25 December 1805), both ibid.

60. Soult to Vandamme, 25 December 1805, ibid.

61. General Candras commanded Saint-Hilaire's First Division at Austerlitz.

62. Bigarré, *Mémoires*, 181–82. There is a second account of this affair in the order of the day, 25 December 1805, *Correspondance de Napoléon*, no. 9610, 11:499–500. The wording is a little different, but it relates the same story only in a more flamboyant prose.

63. "Etat Nominatif du Officiers, sous Officiers et soldats proposés pour être Membres de la Légion d'Honneur," 6 January 1806, carton 12, and "Situation," signed Vandamme, 7 January 1806, carton 11, Vandamme Papers; Soult to Berthier, 13 January 1806, in Gotteri, *Le Maréchal Soult*, 189. France gave up the revolutionary calendar on 31 December 1805 and went back to the Gregorian calendar on 1 January 1806.

64. Berthier to Vandamme, 20 February 1806, carton 11, Vandamme Papers.

65. Vandamme to Berthier, 18 June 1806, in Du Casse, *Vandamme et sa Correspondance*, 2:164.

66. Vandamme, Order of the day, 19 July 1806, carton 12, Vandamme Papers.

CHAPTER 7. SIEGE WARFARE IN SILESIA

1. On the Confederation of the Rhine, see Thiry, *Iéna*, 134–37.

2. On the role of Hanover in Franco-Prussian relations, see ibid., 138–39.

3. Thompson, *Napoleon Bonaparte*, 315.

4. Vandamme to Berthier, 27 September, Berthier to Vandamme, 30 September, 20 October 1806, carton 12, Vandamme Papers.

5. See Garros, *Ney: Le Brave des Braves*, 96–102.

6. On the siege of Magdeburg, see the "Rapport sur les événements militaires qui ont eu lieu sur Magdeburg, depuis le moment de son investissement jusqu'à la capitulation," 9 December 1806, carton 12, Vandamme Papers. The signature is not legible, but the author was "Le capitaine commandant du génie à la 3e Division" commanded by Vandamme.

7. Napoleon to Prince Jérôme, 3 November 1806, *Correspondance de Napoléon*, no. 11152, 13:461–62.

8. Berthier to Vandamme, 27 November 1806, carton 12, Vandamme Papers.

9. See Napoleon's orders to Jérôme, 3 November 1806, *Correspondance de Napoléon*, no. 11152, 13:461–62; Lamar, *Jérôme Bonaparte*, 30.

10. On the fortifications of Glogau and its garrison, see Du Casse, *Opérations du Neuvième Corps*, 1:57–60.

11. Jérôme, *Mémoires et Correspondance*, 2:64 (on the proposed attack on Glogau, see 2:63–64); Du Casse, *Opérations du Neuvième Corps*, 1:114–16.

12. Jérôme, *Mémoires et Correspondance*, 2:67.

13. Berthier to Vandamme, 27 November 1806, carton 12, Vandamme Papers.

14. Du Casse, *Opérations du Neuvième Corps*, 1:80.

15. See General Reinhardt's letter to Jérôme dated the second week of November 1806, in Jérôme, *Mémoires et Correspondance*, 2:60.

16. Vandamme to General Reinhardt, 1 December 1806, "Registre du Correspondance."

17. Vandamme to General Reinhardt, Vandamme to Berthier, Vandamme to Jérôme, 1 December 1806, ibid. (A copy of the five-page capitulation of Glogau dated 2 December 1806 is in carton 12, Vandamme Papers.)

18. Vandamme to Jérôme, 3 December 1806, "Registre du Correspondance."

19. "Order: by the Chief of Staff," 3 December 1806, carton 12, Vandamme Papers.

20. Trente-huitième Bulletin de la Grande Armée, 5 December 1806, *Correspondance de Napoléon*, no. 11393, 14:36–37.

21. Hédouville to Vandamme, 4 December 1806, carton 12, Vandamme Papers; Vandamme to Jérôme, 6 December 1806, "Registre du Correspondance."

22. Berthier to Vandamme, 5 December 1806, carton 12, Vandamme Papers.

23. Du Casse, *Opérations du Neuvième Corps*, 1:98–105. Du Casse gives the population of Breslau and surrounding suburbs at sixty-five or seventy thousand.

24. Order of the day, 7 December 1806, "Registre du Correspondance."

25. Prince Jérôme gave assistance to some of the population who lost their homes to the fire, but most of them took refuge behind the walls of Breslau. See the 41e Bulletin de la Grande Armée,14 December 1806, *Correspondance de Napoléon*, no. 11468, 14:87–89; Jérôme, *Mémoires et Correspondance*, 2:85–86.

26. Jérôme to Berthier, no date (about 15–16 December 1806), in *Mémoires et Correspondance*, 2:95; Vandamme to Jérôme, 16, 17 December 1806, "Registre du Correspondance."

27. Jérôme to Napoleon (requesting permission to join the army in Poland), no date, in Jérôme, *Mémoires et Correspondance*, 2:101.

28. Napoleon wrote Berthier on 17 December: "My cousin, you will send a Polish officer to the camp at Breslau, with orders to Prince Jérôme to leave the command of the siege to General Vandamme and to depart at once so as to arrive at Warsaw by 21 or 22 [December]." Napoleon to Berthier, *Correspondance de Napoléon*, 17 December 1806, no. 11495, 14:104.

29. Jérôme, *Mémoires et Correspondance*, 2:101.

30. Ibid., 2:103–104.

31. See General Minucci to "His Excellency Monsieur General of Division Vandamme, Commander of the Siege of Breslau," 27 December 1806, carton 12, Vandamme Papers.

32. Hédouville to Vandamme, 15 December 1806, ibid.

33. Vandamme to Hédouville, 22 December 1806, "Registre du Correspondance."

34. Du Casse read all the documents and found no explanation for the failure of the attack (*Opérations du Neuvième Corps*, 1:132). I have also searched the archives, in vain, for reasons it failed.

35. Montbrun to Vandamme, 23 December 1806, carton 12, Vandamme Papers; Vandamme to Hédouville, 24 December 1806, "Registre du Correspondance."

36. For a detailed description of the battle of Strehlen, see Montbrun's four-page report to Vandamme, dated Alt Grosburg, 24 December 1806, and General Minucci's three-page account of the battle, dated Grabischen, 27 December 1806, carton 12, Vandamme Papers.

37. On the battle of Strehlen, see Montbrun to Vandamme, 25 December, Minucci to Vandamme, 27 December 1806, carton 12, Vandamme Papers; Vandamme to Berthier, 26 December 1806, "Registre du Correspondance"; Du Casse, *Opérations du Neuvième Corps*, 1:134–36.

38. Vandamme to Montbrun, Vandamme to Thile, 25 December, Vandamme to Berthier, 26 December 1806, "Registre du Correspondance"; Thile

to Vandamme, 25 December 1806 (Thile wrote three letters to Vandamme that day), carton 12, Vandamme Papers.

39. Thile's second letter to Vandamme dated 25 December 1806, carton 12, Vandamme Papers.

40. Vandamme to Berthier, Vandamme to Montbrun, 27 December 1806, "Registre du Correspondance."

41. Hédouville to Vandamme, 24 December 1806, in Du Casse, *Opérations du Neuvième Corps*, 1:151–52.

42. Jérôme to Vandamme, 29 December 1806, in ibid., 1:152–53.

43. Montbrun to Vandamme, 29 December 1806, carton 12, Vandamme Papers.

44. On Prince Anholt-Pless's attempt to relieve Breslau, see Vandamme to Berthier, a five-page report dated 31 December 1806, "Registre du Correspondance"; Vandamme to General Deroy, 30 December 1806, carton 12, Vandamme Papers; Du Casse, *Opérations du Neuvième Corps*, 1:143–46. See also General Montbrun's account of scattering the Prussian army during retreat, Montbrun to Vandamme, 31 December 1806, carton 12, Vandamme Papers.

45. Order of the day, 1 January 1807, in "Correspondance Jérôme Napoléon," Archives Nationales, 400 AP 82.

46. See "Articles de Capitulation de Breslau," signed Vandamme, 3 January 1807, carton 13, Vandamme Papers.

47. Hédouville to Vandamme, 5 January 1807, ibid.

48. Jérôme to Vandamme, 1 January 1807, ibid.

49. Vandamme to Jérôme, 5 January 1807, "Registre du Correspondance."

50. Vandamme to Hédouville, 4 January 1807, ibid.

51. Vandamme to Jérôme, 5 January 1807, ibid. This is the second letter Vandamme wrote dated 5 January 1807. His report on the events following Jérôme's departure was the first.

52. Order of the day, signed Napoleon, Warsaw, 5 January, Order of the day, signed Hédouville, 11 January 1807, carton 13, Vandamme Papers.

53. Vandamme to Jérôme, 9, 10 January 1807, "Registre du Correspondance." Jérôme describes Schweidnitz in *Mémoires et Correspondance*, 2:235–37 (237). See also Du Casse, *Opérations du Neuvième Corps*, 1:189–92.

54. Vandamme to Jérôme, 10 January 1807, "Registre du Correspondance"; Jérôme to Vandamme, 12 January 1807, carton 13, Vandamme Papers; for numbers of men, "Situation of Württemberg Division," 12 January 1807, ibid.

55. Jérôme to Vandamme, 12 January 1807, carton 13, Vandamme Papers. See also Jérôme, *Mémoires et Correspondance*, 2:240.

56. On desertions from Schweidnitz, see Vandamme to Jérôme, 13 January 1807, carton 13, Vandamme Papers; Vandamme to Jérôme, 20, 23 January 1807, "Registre du Correspondance."

57. See Vandamme to Jérôme, 13 January 1807, carton 13, Vandamme Papers.

58. Vandamme to Jérôme, 19 January 1807, ibid.; Vandamme to Jérôme, 20 January 1807, "Registre du Correspondance"; Jérôme, *Mémoires et Correspondance*, 2:242.

59. Jérôme, *Mémoires et Correspondance*, 2:243; Du Casse, *Opérations du Neuvième Corps*, 1:201.

60. See Vandamme to Jérôme, 23 January 1807, "Registre du Correspondance"; Jérôme, *Mémoires et Correspondance,* 2:244; Du Casse, *Opérations du Neuvième Corps,* 1:202.

61. Jérôme to Vandamme, 28 January 1807, carton 13, Vandamme Papers; Jérôme, *Mémoires et Correspondance,* 2:250-53.

62. Jérôme, *Mémoires et Correspondance,* 2:254n1, 254.

63. Napoleon to Jérôme, 28 January 1807, *Correspondance de Napoléon,* no. 11716, 14:250-51.

64. See Jérôme, *Mémoires et Correspondance,* 2:256-59. Du Casse gives an inventory of the guns and munitions dispatched from Breslau to Schweidnitz on 30 January (*Opérations du Neuvième Corps,* 1:214-15).

65. A copy of the capitulation of Schweidnitz dated 7 February 1807 is found in carton 13, Vandamme Papers. There is also a copy of the capitulation on microfilm in the "Correspondance de Jérôme Napoléon," AP 82.

66. On the last days of the siege and the capitulation of Schweidnitz, see Jérôme, *Mémoires et Correspondance,* 2:262-63. On Vandamme's instructions for the ceremony of the surrender, see Hédouville to Vandamme, 15 February 1807, carton 13, Vandamme Papers.

67. Soixantième Bulletin de la Grande Armée, *Correspondance de Napoléon,* no. 11822, 14:308-309.

68. Du Casse, *Opérations du Neuvième Corps,* 1:230-34.

69. See Vandamme to Jérôme, 18 February 1807, Arch. Guerre, C2/396; Berthier to Jérôme, 17 February 1807, in Jérôme, *Mémoires et Correspondance,* 2:292.

70. "Journal du Siège de Neisse," 5 March 1807, signed "Fait au quartier Général à Breslau davant Neisse le 5e mars 1807, Le Capitaine Commandant du Génie. Amb. Pross.," carton 13, Vandamme Papers.

71. Vandamme to Jérôme, 23 February 1807, carton 13, Vandamme Papers; "Journal du Siège de Neisse," 5 March 1807, ibid.; Jérôme, *Mémoires et Correspondance,* 2:297-8.

72. "Journal du Siège de Neisse," 5 March 1807, carton 13, Vandamme Papers.

73. Jérôme to Berthier, 28 March 1807, in Jérôme, *Mémoires et Correspondance,* 2:310.

74. In Jérôme's memoirs, there is a lengthy discussion of the misunderstanding and the effect it had on operations in Silesia (ibid.).

75. Vandamme to Jérôme, 7 March 1807, carton 13, Vandamme Papers; Jérôme, *Mémoires et Correspondance,* 2:321-23.

76. Hédouville to Vandamme, 11, 19 March 1807, carton 13, Vandamme Papers.

77. "Situation," 10 March 1807, Arch. Guerre, C2/396. In his *Mémoires* Jérôme gives a detailed breakdown of the strength of his Ninth Corps toward the end of March as sixteen thousand men (2:311-13).

78. Hédouville to Vandamme, 20, 29 March 1807, carton 13, Vandamme Papers. See also Jérôme's discussion of the exchange of prisoners at this time, in *Mémoires et Correspondance,* 2:324.

79. Jérôme to Napoleon, 20 April 1807, "Correspondance de Prince Jérôme Napoléon," Archives Nationales, AP 82.

80. Jérôme to Napoléon, 2 May 1807, ibid., AP 83; Jérôme, *Mémoires et Correspondance*, 2:324.

81. On the rather uneventful siege of Neiss, see Vandamme's correspondence for March—May 1807, carton 13, Vandamme Papers; his correspondence and other letters in Arch. Guerre C2/396; Du Casse, *Opérations du Neuvième Corps*, 1:287–323.

82. On the capitulation of Neiss, see "Capitulation de la fortresse de Neisse," 1 June 1807, carton 13, Vandamme Papers; Vandamme to Jérôme, 2, 17 June 1807, Arch. Guerre, C2/396.

83. Jérôme to Napoleon, no date, in Du Casse, *Vandamme et sa Correspondance*, 2:241.

84. Marshal François-Joseph Lefebvre, duke of Danzig, is not the father of General of Brigade Charles Lefebvre-Desnouettes who served with Vandamme in Silesia. The marshal's son was named Marie-Xavier-Joseph; he was a captain in 1807 and later died with the rank of general of brigade at Wilna, during the retreat from Moscow on 15 December 1812.

85. Vandamme to Jérôme, 19 June 1807, carton 13, Vandamme Papers.

86. Jérôme to Vandamme, 27 April 1807. The prince added that one-third of Goerzten's troops were not armed at that time, but they were receiving additional arms every day.

87. Vandamme to General Camrer, 13 July 1807, Arch. Guerre, C2/396; Hédouville to Vandamme, 13 July 1807, carton 13, Vandamme Papers.

88. See the "Procès-verbal d'Inventaire des effets qui se sont trouvés ... dans le fouryon ... Général Vandamme," 11 May 1807, at the "Citadel, Strasbourg," Arch. Guerre, C2/396.

89. Both letters are quoted in Du Casse, *Vandamme et sa Correspondance*, 2:213–14. Vandamme refers to the general only by his last name, but I presume this person to be Louis-Melchoir Legrand. Vandamme to Minister of War, 28 April 1807, ibid., 2:213.

90. Du Casse provides a lengthy account of the Strasbourg Affair, in which he quotes the inventory of the eighteen boxes and chests sent to the minister of war, as well as other documents. He notes that the magistrates of Schweidnitz gave Vandamme four draft horses and a saddle horse, and that on 9 February the town of Landshut gave the general several bolts of Silesian cloth. The horses were used to pull the wagon back to France. This correspondence is not found in the Vandamme Papers at Lille or at Vincennes, but in general Du Casse has been found to be most accurate.

CHAPTER 8. THE AUSTRIAN CAMPAIGN, 1809

1. See correspondence for January–April 1809 in Davout, *Correspondance*, 3:2.

2. Figures for the strength of the Army of Germany vary only slightly from one author to another: Thiry, *Wagram*, 51–52; Esposito and Elting, *Military History*, 93–94; Chandler, *Campaigns of Napoleon*, 668–70.

3. Berthier to Vandamme, 13 March 1809, carton 14, Vandamme Papers.

4. Vandamme to Berthier, 31 March 1809, "Campagne de 1809: Correspondance." This booklet contains seventy-one pages of Vandamme's correspondence from 31 March to 3 December 1809.

5. Vandamme to Berthier, 1 April 1809, "Campagne 1809: Correspondance."

6. "Situation," and Vandamme to Berthier, both 5 April 1809, ibid.

7. Vandamme to Berthier, Berthier to Vandamme, 11 April 1809, ibid.

8. Napoleon had instructed Berthier to concentrate the army at Ratisbon, if hostilities began after 15 April, but to concentrate further west, behind the Ilm River in the vicinity of Ingolstadt, if the Austrians attacked before that date.

9. "Ordre au Capitaine Galbois," signed Napoleon, 18 April 1809, *Correspondance de Napoléon*, no. 15091, 18:486.

10. Napoleon to Masséna, 19 April 1809, ibid., 18:487.

11. "Ordre au Capitaine Galbois," signed Napoleon, 18 April 1809, ibid., no.15091, 18:486.

12. Berthier to Vandamme, 19, 20 April 1809, in "Campagne de 1809: Correspondance."

13. Napoleon to Vandamme, 20 April 1809, *Correspondance de Napoléon*, no. 15097, 18:490.

14. Napoleon to Davout, 21 April 1809, ibid., no. 15100, 18:491.

15. Berthier to Vandamme, 21 April 1809, in "Campagne de 1809: Correspondance"; 1e Bulletin de l'Armée de l'Allemagne, in *Correspondance de Napoléon*, no. 15112, 18:498–506.

16. Berthier to Vandamme, 22 April 1809, in "Campagne de 1809: Correspondance"; Napoleon to Davout, 5:00 A.M., 22 April 1809, *Correspondance de Napoléon*, no. 15104,. 18:493–94.

17. Napoleon to Lannes, 3:00 A.M., 22 April 1809, *Correspondance de Napoléon*, no. 15106, 18:495–96.

18. There is little information on his wound at Eckmühl. On 26 April the king of Würtemberg wrote him: "Monsieur General of Division, Count Vandamme, do not doubt the great interest inspired in me by hearing of the glorious days of the 22nd and 23rd, but also of the sorrow that I felt learning that you were wounded." In Du Casse, *Vandamme et sa Correspondance*, 2:275–76.

19. See Berthier to Vandamme, 23 April 1809, carton 14, Vandamme Papers.

20. Vandamme to General Neubronn, 24 April 1809, "Campagne de 1809: Correspondance." Du Casse provides a good discussion of this affair in *Vandamme et sa Correspondance*, 2:276–77.

21. Napoleon to Frederick, King of Würtemberg, 25 April 1809, *Correspondance de Napoléon*, no. 15104, 18:493–94.

22. Frederick to Vandamme, 5 May 1809, Du Casse, *Vandamme et sa Correspondance*, 2:275–76.

23. See Vandamme's correspondence, 24 April–1 May 1809, "Campagne de 1809: Correspondance"; Berthier to Vandamme, 25, 26, 27, 29 April 1809, carton 14, Vandamme Papers.

24. See Napoleon to Berthier, 1, 4 May 1809, *Correspondance de Napoléon*, nos. 15146, 15153, 15154, 18:526–27, 533.

25. Vandamme to Davout, 6 May 1809, "Campagne de 1809: Correspondance."

26. Vandamme to Napoleon, 6 May 1809, ibid.; Napoleon to Davout, 7 May 1809, *Correspondance de Napoléon*, no. 15168, 18:541; Davout to Napoleon for the second week of May, in Davout, *Correspondance*, 2:513–27.

27. Napoleon to Davout, 13 May 1809, *Correspondance de Napoléon*, no. 15199, 18:555–56.

28. Napoleon to Bernadotte, 15 May, Berthier to Vandamme, 16 May 1809, ibid., nos. 15213, 15218, 19:9–10, 13.

29. Vandamme to Bernadotte, 18 May 1809, "Campagne de 1809: Correspondance"; Bernadotte to Napoleon, 18 May 1809, in Du Casse, *Vandamme et sa Correspondance*, 2:297–301 (300). Vandamme puts the number at thirty thousand, whereas Bernadotte said twenty-five thousand Austrians.

30. Berthier to Vandamme, 19 May 1809, carton 14, Vandamme Papers.

31. Bernadotte to Napoleon, 21 May 1809, in Du Casse, *Vandamme et sa Correspondance*, 2:303–304.

32. Vandamme to Bernadotte, 21 May 1809, "Campagne de 1809: Correspondance"; "Situation," 17 May 1809, carton 14, Vandamme Papers.

33. Berthier to Vandamme, 24 May, 5 June 1809, carton 14, Vandamme Papers; 23e Bulletin de l'Armée de l'Allemagne, dated Vienna, 28 June 1809, in *Correspondance de Napoléon*, no. 15464, 19:189–91.

34. Vandamme to Berthier, 31 May, 1 June, Vandamme to his Chief of Staff, Colonel Kerner, 31 May 1809, all in "Campagne de 1809: Correspondance"; Berthier to Vandamme, Berthier to Bernadotte, both 31 May 1809, *Correspondance de Napoléon*, nos. 15284, 15285, 19:62–63.

35. Napoleon to Vandamme, 5 June 1809, *Correspondance de Napoléon*, no. 15302, 19:75; "Order," 9 June 1809, "Campagne de 1809: Correspondance."

36. Napoleon to Berthier, 16 July 1809, *Correspondance de Napoléon*, no. 15540, 19:255–56.

37. Berthier to Vandamme, 9 June, Vandamme to Berthier, also Vandamme to Colonel Kerner, 17 June 1809, carton 14, Vandamme Papers. There is no record that any other men were tried in connection with the death of the eleven Würtemberg soldiers.

38. Vandamme to Berthier, 9 June 1809, "Campagne de 1809: Correspondance."

39. Vandamme to Napoleon, 10 July, Vandamme to Eugène, 11 July 1809, ibid.

40. Napoleon to Eugène, 14 July 1809, *Correspondance de Napoléon*, no. 15526, 19:245; Vandamme to Berthier, 14 July 1809, "Campagne de 1809: Correspondance."

41. Vandamme to Berthier, 16 July 1809, and the Armistice, 16 July 1809, signed by Vandamme and General Zach, chief of staff for General in Chief Giulay, "Campagne de 1809: Correspondance."

42. Vandamme's correspondence to General Giulay and to Berthier, 16, 17 July 1809, ibid.

43. Orders to Colonel Kerner, 21 July 1809, ibid.

44. See Berthier to Vandamme, 23 July 1809, ibid.

45. Berthier to Vandamme, 2 August 1809, ibid. On the distribution of the Eighth Corps in the Neustadt region, see Vandamme to Kerner, 5 August 1809, ibid.

46. Berthier to Vandamme, 24 August 1809, in Du Casse, *Vandamme et sa Correspondance*, 2:316–17; Vandamme to Kerner, 29 August, Vandamme to Berthier, 6 September 1809, "Campagne de 1809: Correspondance."

47. Berthier to Vandamme, 14 September 1809, in Du Casse, *Vandamme et sa Correspondance*, 2:317–18.

48. Ibid., 2:319.

49. Wollowart to Vandamme, 19 October 1809, ibid., 2:322; Vandamme to Wollowart, 19 October, Vandamme to Berthier, 20 October 1809, "Campagne de 1809: Correspondance."

50. Wollowart to Vandamme, 21 October 1809, in Du Casse, *Vandamme et sa Correspondance*, 2:320–21.

51. Vandamme to Napoleon, 16 October 1809, in Du Casse, *Vandamme et sa Correspondance*, 2:320–21.

52. Vandamme to Wollowart, 15 October, Vandamme to his new chief of staff, Adjutant Commandant Revest, 20 October, Note dated 25 October 1809, "Campagne de 1809: Correspondance."

53. See "Ordre de l'Empereur," signed Napoleon and sent to Minister of War Clarke, 28 October 1809, ibid.

54. See the note at the end of the booklet, ibid.

55. "Rapport à l'Empereur," and "Note au Ministre" (of war), both 6 February 1810, carton 14, Vandamme Papers.

56. See Captain Fournier to Menneville, 12 February, Menneville to Fournier, 13 February, Menneville to the Minister of War (six pages), 28 February 1810, all in Dossier Vandamme, Arch. Guerre, 303/GD 2e série. Menneville details the whole affair in his 28 February letter.

57. Menneville to the Minister of War, 28 February 1810, ibid. Menneville's two-page report dated 10 March 1810 also presents the facts, along with the mayor's complaints and requests ("Rapport au Ministre," 10 March 1810, ibid.).

58. Menneville to the Minister of War, 28 February, Minister of Interior to Napoleon, 14 March, Vandamme to the Minister of War, 21 March 1810, ibid.

59. Born in Ireland in 1746, Harty served in the Irish Brigade before the Revolution and by 1793 had risen to the rank of general of brigade. His service was primarily that of an administrator in the French army. He never served in serious combat and became chief of staff of the camp at Boulogne in February 1808, a post he still held when Vandamme became commander in chief in 1810.

60. Because Menneville was not at the time the mayor of Boulogne, he did not live in the house.

61. Vandamme to Minister of War, 21 March 1810, Dossier Vandamme, Arch. Guerre, 303/GD 2e série.

62. There are two accounts of Sarrazin's defection quoted in Du Casse, *Vandamme et sa Correspondance*, 2:340–43. See also Vandamme to the Minister of War, dated Boulogne, 14 June 1810, and "Extrait d'une lettre écrite au général Harty, chef d'état-major du camp de Boulogne, par M. Renard, capitaine adjoint, commandant la 2e brigade de la 4e division, datée d'Etaples, le 10 juin 1810, à 10 heures du soir," ibid.; Dossier Vandamme, Arch. Guerre, 303/GD 2e série. Du Casse also provides a copy of Sarrazin's letter relieving the crew of the *Saint-Laurent* of any responsibility (*Vandamme et sa Correspondance*, 2:343).

63. Du Casse, *Vandamme et sa Correspondance*, 2:341.

64. See the details in Order of the day, 11 June, and Vandamme to the Minister of War, 14 June 1810, in Du Casse, *Vandamme et sa Correspondance*, 2:343–44, 341–42.

65. When Sarrazin returned to France after Napoleon's first abdication in 1814, he was not received warmly by the Bourbons. His death sentence was voided by the king, but he was put on inactive service. When Napoleon returned from Elba, Sarrazin was imprisoned at the Abbaye, then released and placed under police surveillance. In 1819 he was convicted of bigamy and given ten years of hard labor. In 1822 he was released, and he then settled in Brussels where he died on 11 November 1848. See Six, *Dictionnaire biographique*, 2:423–24.

66. See the *procès verbal* of the "Arrondissement d'Hazebrouck," 28–29 January 1811, carton 14, Vandamme Papers.

CHAPTER 9. CONFLICT WITH KING JÉRÔME

1. Du Casse, *Vandamme et sa Correspondance*, 2:345–46.

2. Berthier to Vandamme 12 February 1812, Dossier Vandamme, and the order signed by Minister of War, the duke of Feltre, 21 February 1812, both in Arch. Guerre, 303/GD 2e série.

3. There is a thirty-nine-page booklet containing Vandamme's correspondence from 9 March to 4 September 1812, "Vandamme Correspondance, 1812." See the note dated 9 March 1812, at the top of page 1.

4. Vandamme to Berthier, 9 March 1812, ibid.

5. Duke of Anhalt to Vandamme, 16 March 1812, in Du Casse, *Vandamme et sa Correspondance*, 2:348–49.

6. See the detailed marching orders issued by Vandamme in his correspondance dated between 25 March and 9 April: more specifically the orders dated 1, 9 April that give the position of each division each night. "Vandamme Correspondance, 1812."

7. See Vandamme's correspondence to Jérôme and two letters to the governor general of Glogau, all 9 April, "Vandamme Correspondance, 1812."

8. General Jean-Victor Tharreau, who commanded the Twenty-third Division, wrote Vandamme: "I am informing you that many inhabitants of the districts are leaving their homes and taking refuge in the forests taking with

them their livestock," thus the troops were unable to acquire food. Tharreau to Vandamme, 19 April 1812, carton 15, Vandamme Papers; Vandamme to the Major General of the Eighth Corps, 19 April 1812, "Vandamme Correspondance, 1812."

9. General Ochs to Vandamme, 22 April 1812, Dossier Vandamme, Archive Guerre, 303/GD 2e série.

10. Order of the day, 21 April 1812, "Vandamme Correspondance, 1812."

11. See "Situation sommaire du 8e Corps d'Armée," 25 June 1812, signed D. Vandamme, ibid. Chandler gives the figure at 15,885 men and 2,050 cavalry (*Campaigns of Napoleon*, 1112); Esposito and Elting put the total figure of the Eighth Corps at 16,700 men (*Military History*, 107).

12. Tharreau was killed in the battle at Borodino on 7 September 1812.

13. Vandamme to Jérôme, 23 April 1812, "Vandamme Correspondance, 1812."

14. Order of the day, 23 April 1812, ibid.

15. Jérôme to Vandamme, 29 April 1812, in Du Casse, *Vandamme et sa Correspondance*, 2:352–53; Vandamme to Jérôme, 29 April 1812, "Vandamme Correspondance, 1812."

16. See Vandamme to Jérôme, 29 April 1812, ibid.

17. Vandamme to Dupleix, 3 May 1812, in Du Casse, *Vandamme et sa Correspondance*, 2:356–57.

18. Fürstenstein to Vandamme, 12 May 1812, in Du Casse, *Vandamme et sa Correspondance*, 2:357–58. It was, of course, Napoleon who ordered that Vandamme command the Westphalian corps. From the beginning, Jérôme was not pleased with the arrangement.

19. Marchand to Vandamme, 12 May 1812, ibid., 2:356–57; Vandamme to Jérôme, 18 May, Vandamme to Marchand, 19 May 1812, "Vandamme Correspondance, 1812."

20. Marchand wrote a long letter to Vandamme, 24 May 1812, in great detail with respect to the demands for this affair. See Du Casse, *Vandamme et sa Correspondance*, 2:356–57, also 360–62.

21. Berthier to Vandamme, 1 June 1812, ibid., 2:356–57.

22. Vandamme to Berthier, 4 June 1812, "Vandamme Correspondance, 1812."

23. Vandamme to Dupleix, 26, 30 May, 1, 12 June 1812, ibid.

24. Some historians have put the number as high as six hundred thousand men engaged by the end of the campaign.

25. Clausewitz, *The campaign of 1812 in Russia*, 13.

26. Gallaher, *Iron Marshal*, 231–32.

27. See Lamar's excellent discussion of the matter in *Jérôme Bonaparte*, 85.

28. "Order for the Passage of the Niemen," 23 June, Napoleon to Berthier, 22 June 1812, *Correspondance de Napoléon*, nos. 18857, 18852, 23:531–35, 527.

29. See Napoleon's correspondence to Jérôme, 20, 21 June 1812, ibid., nos. 18831, 18850, 23:515, 525–26.

30. "Order for the Passage of the Niemen," 23 June, Napoleon to Jérôme, 20 June 1812, ibid., nos. 18857, 18831, 23:531–35, 515.
31. Vandamme to Jérôme, 21, 22 June 1812, "Vandamme Correspondance, 1812."
32. Vandamme to Jérôme, 3 July 1812, ibid.
33. Jérôme to Vandamme, 3 July 1812, ibid.
34. Jérôme to Catherine (no date), in Masson, *Napoléon et sa famille*, 7:309–10.
35. Vandamme to Napoleon, 3 July 1812, "Vandamme Correspondance, 1812."
36. Vandamme to Jérôme, 11 July 1812, ibid.
37. Napoleon to Jérôme, 4 July 1812, in Masson, *Napoléon et sa famille*, 7:311.
38. Napoleon to Berthier, 5 July 1812, *Correspondance de Napoléon*, no. 18905, 24:19–20.
39. Ibid., no. 18911, 24:24.
40. Du Casse, *Vandamme et sa Correspondance*, 2:372.
41. Masson quotes parts of Jérôme's letter in *Napoléon et sa famille*, 7:318–19 (19).
42. Vandamme to Berthier, 18, 27 July 1812, "Vandamme Correspondance, 1812."
43. Berthier to Vandamme, 6 August 1812, ibid. There is a copy of this letter in the Dossier Vandamme, Archive Guerre, 303/GD 2e série.
44. Napoleon to Berthier, 20 July 1812, *Correspondance de Napoléon*, no. 18984, 24:80–81.
45. See the notes at the end of "Vandamme Correspondance, 1812." See also Berthier to the Minister of War, 6 August 1812, Dossier Vandamme, Archive Guerre, 303/GD 2e série.

CHAPTER 10. DISASTER AT KULM, 1813

1. In his absence, General Claude-François Malet had unsuccessfully attempted to overthrow the government in Paris on the pretext that Napoleon was dead in Russia. On the Malet plot, see Serignan, *Un conspirateur militaire*.
2. On 14 October 1806, Marshal Bernadotte had failed to support Davout at Aurestädt, and he did not march to Jena. At the battle of Wagram on 6 July 1809, Bernadotte's corps broke and fled to the rear, whereupon Napoleon relieved the marshal of his command and sent him back to Paris in disgrace.
3. Sweden was also promised Hither (Swedish) Pomerania on the south coast of the Baltic Sea.
4. Vandamme to Minister of War, 15 February 1813, Arch. Guerre, 303/GD, 2e série.
5. Jomini lists them with the commander of each, in *Précis politique et militaire*, 238.
6. On Carra Saint-Cyr's evacuation of Hamburg, see Halzhausen, *Davout in Hamburg*, 40–41.

7. On Napoleon's reaction to Carra Saint-Cyr's evacuation of Hamburg, see Napoleon to Clarke (Minister of War), 26 March 1813, *Correspondance de Napoléon*, no. 9761, 25:122.

8. Napoleon to Eugène, 18 March, Napoleon to Clarke, 26 March 1813, ibid., nos. 9734, 9761, 25:103–105, 122.

9. See Napoleon to Eugène, 11 April, Napoleon to Ney, 6 April 1813, ibid., nos. 9843, 9818, 25:182–83, 166–67.

10. Thiébault, *Mémoires*, 5:51.

11. Vandamme's remarks from Ibid.

12. On Davout's movements in the first weeks of April, see Davout, *Correspondance*, 4:20–48.

13. Eugène to Vandamme, 1 April 1813, in Du Casse, *Vandamme et sa Correspondance*, 2:410.

14. Tettenborn to Vandamme, 12 April, Vandamme to Berthier, 19 April 1813, ibid., 2:410, 411–13.

15. See Vandamme's correspondence in the month of April 1813, ibid., 2:400–424.

16. Vandamme to Berthier, 4 April 1813, ibid., 2:392–94.

17. Vandamme to Berthier, 8 April 1813, ibid., 2:401–402.

18. Davout to Vandamme, 22 April 1813, in Davout, *Correspondance*, no. 1275, 4:47–48.

19. Vandamme to Berthier, 23 April 1813, in Du Casse, *Vandamme et sa Correspondance*, 2:416–17.

20. Blocqueville cites the entire letter in *Le Maréchal Davout*, 3:208–12; Du Casse quotes most of it in *Vandamme et sa Correspondance*, 2:430–33.

21. Davout responded to these astonishing orders: "Your Majesty will never make of me a duc d'Abbé! I would rather break in two my marshal's baton than to obey orders which you yourself would be the first to regret. War is already horrible enough without adding to it unnecessary cruelties." In Blocqueville, *Le Maréchal Davout*, 3:207. (The Abbaye was the prison in Paris where the massacre of September 1792 had taken place.)

22. On the fate of Hamburg after its capitulation, see Gallaher, *Iron Marshal*, 273–97; Halzhausen, *Davout in Hamburg*; and Joh. Christ Grohmann, *Hamburgs Gchicksale*.

23. See the account of this affair in Vandamme to Davout, 9 May 1813, in Du Casse, *Vandamme et sa Correspondance*, 2:434–35; Davout to Vandamme, 9 May 1813, in Davout, *Correspondance*, no. 1306, 4:88–89.

24. Davout to Vandamme, 10 May 1813, in Davout, *Correspondance*, no. 1308, 4:91–92.

25. See Vandamme's correspondance in Du Casse, *Vandamme et sa Correspondance*, 2:430–57 (in particular Vandamme to Davout, 12 May 1813, 2:444–45); Berthier to Davout, 7 May 1813, ibid., 2:433.

26. Davout to Berthier, 13 May 1813, in Davout, *Correspondance*, no. 1317, 4:103–104. A month earlier, when the marshal first learned that Vandamme would be serving under him, he wrote the general: "I have learned that you are part of my command with great satisfaction for the service of our sovereign, to whom men of your caliber are so necessary in the circumstance

that we find ourselves" (Davout to Vandamme, 8 April 1813, in Du Casse, *Vandamme et sa Correspondance*, 2:402–406).

27. Davout to Berthier, 13 May 1813, Davout, *Correspondance*, no. 1317, 4:103–104.

28. Berthier to Vandamme, 7 May 1813, in Du Casse, *Vandamme et sa Correspondance*, 2:433.

29. See Davout to Vandamme, 29, 30 May, Davout to Berthier, 30 May 1813, in Davout, *Correspondance*, nos. 1343, 1345, 1346, 4:130–35.

30. Davout to Vandamme, 30 May 1813, ibid., no. 1345, 4:132–33.

31. Davout to Berthier, 31 May 1813, ibid., no. 1350, 4:138–39. On Davout and the retaking of Hamburg in 1813, see Gallaher, *Iron Marshal*, 275–79.

32. Napoleon to Berthier, 24 May 1813, *Correspondance de Napoléon*, no. 20037, 25:312–13.

33. Davout to Berthier, 30 May 1813, in Davout, *Correspondance*, no. 1350, 4:138–39.

34. See Davout's instructions to Vandamme, 3 June 1813, ibid., no. 1353, 4:141.

35. Charles John to Vandamme, 18 June 1813, in Du Casse, *Vandamme et sa Correspondance*, 2:471–73.

36. Davout to Vandamme, 9 June 1813, ibid., 448–49.

37. Napoleon to Davout, *Correspondance de Napoléon*, 7 June 1813, no. 20104, 25:372–74.

38. On Napoleon's reasons for accepting the Armistice of Neumarckt, see J. P. Riley, *World War of 1813*, 110–26.

39. On the Prussian army in 1813, see Nafziger, *Dresden Campaign*, 14–27.

40. Riley provides a good discussion of the armistice in *World War of 1813*, 111–27.

41. See Caulaincourt's account of the Prague negotiations in his *Mémoires du Général de Caulaincourt*, 1:150–58. On Austria's "Justification" for renouncing its alliance with France and joining the Coalition, and for Napoleon's response, see "Observations sur la Déclaration de Guerre de l'Austriche," *Correspondance de Napoléon*, 14 August 1813, no. 20376, 26:49–59.

42. Napoleon to Berthier, 18 June, Napoleon to General Count Belliard, 2 July 1813, ibid., nos. 20145, 20217, 25:398–99, 452–53.

43. On Coalition strategy and the Trachenberg Plan, see Riley, *World War of 1813*, 116–21; Nafziger, *Dresden Campaign*, 11–12.

44. In a long letter to Marshal Davout dated 8 August 1813 (*Correspondance de Napoléon*, no. 20339, 26:13–21), Napoleon explained in great detail his plans for the renewal of hostilities.

45. Napoleon to Berthier, 11 August, Napoleon to Davout, 12 August 1813, ibid., nos. 20346, 20357, 26:23–24, 32–34.

46. Napoleon to Berthier, 17, 18, 20 August 1813, ibid., nos. 20396, 20397, 20415, 26:74–76, 98–99.

47. Napoleon to Vandamme, 23 August 1813, ibid., no. 20446, 26:119–20.

48. Vandamme to Berthier, 25 August 1813, in Du Casse, *Vandamme et sa Correspondance*, 2:490–91.

49. Napoleon to Gouvion Saint-Cyr, 25 August 1813, *Correspondance de Napoléon*, no. 20461, 26:129–30.

50. Napoleon to Vandamme, 25 August 1813, ibid., no. 20469, 26:136–39; Vandamme to Napoleon, 26 August 1813, Archives Nationales, AF IV 1661A Plaq. 4; Napoleon to Vandamme, 26 August 1813, *Correspondance de Napoléon*, no. 20474, 26:139–40.

51. On 26 August 1813, Napoleon wrote General François Nicolas Haxo: "I desire that General Vandamme move as quickly as possible to the plateau [of Pirna] . . . that he penetrate to Hellendorf" (*Correspondance de Napoléon*, no. 20474, 26:141–42).

52. On the details of the fighting on 26 August, see Haxo to Napoleon, 27 August 1813, Archives Nationales, AF IV 1661A Plaq. 4. General Haxo commanded the engineers of the Imperial Guard. Napoleon sent him to advise Vandamme because he was familiar with the terrain. See also Vandamme to Napoleon, 27 August 1813, ibid.

53. Vandamme to Napoleon, 27 August 1813, at 4:30 P.M., ibid.

54. See Commander of First Corps Artillery to Berthier, 27 August 1813, ibid.

55. At 7:00 P.M. Napoleon wrote that he thought "the enemy is not in retreat, that it regards the affair of yesterday as only a failed attack, and that it is doubtful if the enemy will retreat this night" (Napoleon to Berthier, 27 August 1813, *Correspondance de Napoléon*, no. 20479, 26:143–44).

56. Napoleon to Berthier, 28 August 1813, ibid., no. 20483, 26:147; Berthier to Mortier, 28 August 1813, Correspondence Berthier, Arch. Guerre, C17/179.

57. Berthier to Vandamme, 28 August 1813, Correspondence Berthier, Arch. Guerre, C17/179.

58. Berthier to Vandamme, 28 August 1813, ibid.

59. Vandamme to Berthier, 28 August 1813, in Du Casse, *Vandamme et sa Correspondance*, 2:499.

60. Vandamme to Berthier, 29 August 1813, Archives Nationales, AF IV 1661A Plaq. 4.

61. Napoleon to Murat, 29 August 1813, *Correspondance de Napoléon*, no. 20486, 26:148–49.

62. Haxo to Napoleon, 29 August 1813, Archives Nationales, AF IV 1661A Plaq. 4.

63. Vandamme to Berthier, 29 August 1813, ibid.

64. Napoleon to Berthier, 29 August 1813, *Correspondance de Napoléon*, no. 20485, 26:148–49.

65. Fain, *Manuscrit de mil huit cent treize*, 1:314.

66. On the fighting at Kulm, see Haxo to Napoleon, 6:00 P.M., Vandamme to Napoleon, 5:00 P.M., both 29 August 1813, Archives Nationales, AF IV 1661A Plaq. 4. For the movements of the Coalition, see Nafziger, *Dresden Campaign*, 215–21.

67. Both Chandler (*Campaigns of Napoleon*, 912) and Esposito and Elting (*Military History*, 137) give Vandamme's corps at 32,000 men, but Nafziger puts the French troop strength on the morning of 30 August at 39,000 men, 3,000 cavalry, and 83 guns, that is, 42,000 plus troops (*Dresden Campaign*, 222). Figures for the Coalition forces at Kulm are put at 54,000 by Chandler (912), 44,000 by Esposito and Elting (137), and at 41,000 men, 10,000 cavalry, and 136 guns by Nafziger (222), that is, over 51,000 troops. It is difficult to get exact figures as few historians give the same numbers. The archives do not provide a figure on the troop strength (a "Situation") for the days preceding the battle.

68. Vandamme to Napoleon, 30 August 1813, Archives Nationales, AF IV 1661A Plaq. 4.

69. Du Casse cites "notes in his [Vandamme's] handwriting, in which he records the events of 30 August 1813" (hereafter referred to as "Vandamme Notes on 30 August 1813"). See *Vandamme et sa Correspondance*, 2:517–19.

70. Philippon to Berthier, Archives Nationales, AF IV 1661A Plaq. 4.

71. On Kleist's retreat and arrival on the rear of Vandamme's First Corps, see Gorczkowsky, *Graf Kleist v. Nollendorf*, 15–17; Nafziger, *Dresden Campaign*, 228–31.

72. "Vandamme Notes on 30 August 1813," in Du Casse, *Vandamme et sa Correspondance*, 2:521.

73. Nafziger gives a good account of the French breakout to the rear (*Dresden Campaign*, 237–41).

74. Philippon to Berthier, 31 August 1813, Archives Nationales, AF IV 1661A Plaq. 4.

75. Napoleon to Berthier, 1 September 1813, *Correspondance de Napoléon*, no. 20497, 26:159.

76. Kolzakov was born in Toula in 1779. He entered the navy and rose to the rank of naval captain in 1809, at which time he became an aide to Grand Duke Constantine. He served in that capacity during the campaigns of 1812, 1813, and 1814. He eventually received the rank of admiral in 1843 and died at St. Petersburg in 1864.

77. I have only the six pages of Kolzakov's *Mémoires* that appear with an introduction and notes by Cazalas in "Comment Vandamme fut pris."

78. Ibid., 524, 527.

79. Ibid., 527.

80. Ibid., 528–29.

81. Fain was at French army headquarters as Napoleon's cabinet secretary at the time. He declared that "the Allies dragged him [Vandamme] in triumph to Prague." *Manuscrit de mil huit cent treize*, 319.

82. Ibid.

83. Ibid.

84. Napoleon to Murat, 1 September 1813, *Correspondance de Napoléon*, no. 20496, 26:159.

85. See two reports by the governor of Moscow, Fedor Vasiljevitch Rostopchin, to Alexander, in Cazalas, "Comment Vandamme fut pris," 34n1.

86. For a list of the French passengers see ibid.

87. On the "*Anne Dorothea* Affair," see Vandamme's eighteen-page report entitled "Mémoire en Réclamation pour Monsieur le Lieutenant Général Comte Vandamme, contre les Seiure Erick Nilson et compagnie négociante, armateure de la ville de Coppenhague. Et contre le Sieur John Peterson capitaine du navire *Anna Dorothea* dont les dit Erick Nilson sont armateur," carton 16, Vandamme Papers; Milot, "Le Retour de captivité."

CHAPTER 11. THE WATERLOO CAMPAIGN

1. Following the execution of Louis XVI in January 1793, the royalists recognized his son as "Louis XVII" even though the boy was never crowned and never reigned. When the youngster died in prison in 1795, the older of his father's two brothers, his uncle the count of Provence, became king of France with the title of Louis XVIII, albeit in exile until 1814. Thus, Louis XVIII dated his reign from the death of his nephew in 1795.

2. In December 1815 Vandamme had a twelve-page *Exposé* printed in which he explained and justified his behavior from the time he returned to France on 1 September through the fall of 1815 (Vandamme, *Exposé de la Conduite*, 4–5).

3. Ibid., 6. See also Vandamme to Minister of War, no date, Arch. Guerre, 303/7 Yd; and "Rapport fait au Ministre [de la Guerre]," signature not legible, dated January 1815, Arch. Guerre, 303/GD 2e série.

4. In Du Casse, *Vandamme et sa Correspondance*, 2:553. The same accusation is found in "Rapport fait au Ministre [de la Guerre]," signature not legible, dated January 1815, Arch. Guerre, 303/GD 2e série.

5. Vandamme to Minister of War, no date (September–October 1814?), Arch. Guerre, 303/7 Yd.

6. See d'Erlon to Vandamme, 5 September 1814, Arch. Guerre, 303/GD 2e série; Jourdan to Vandamme, Dejean to Vandamme, Macdonald to Vandamme, all 10 October 1814, Arch. Guerre, 303/7 Yd.

7. Jourdan to Vandamme, 10 October 1814, Arch. Guerre, 303/7 Yd.

8. If indeed Vandamme did take the andirons, it is most likely they never found their way back to Cassel in the middle of a campaign. The author has found no indication that they were in the château when the Russians arrived.

9. For a detailed account of this affair, see Hennerie, "Le pillage du château."

10. On his back pay, see Vandamme to "Monseigneur," 28 January 1815, Arch. Guerre 303/7 Yd. On his losses at Kulm, see "Motifs de la Liquidation," 5 November 1815, Arch. Guerre, 303/GD 2e série.

11. See Vandamme's justification for serving in the army during the Hundred Days, in his *Exposé de la Conduite*, 7.

12. Napoleon to Davout, 9 April 1815, *Correspondance de Napoléon*, no. 21782, 28:84.

13. Davout to Vandamme, 9 April 1815, in Davout, *Correspondance*, no. 1557, 4:414–15.

14. See Letter of service, 20 April 1815, carton 16, Vandamme Papers.
15. See Davout to Vandamme, 10 May 1815, in Davout, *Correspondance*, no. 1691, 4:522–23.
16. Davout to Vandamme, 12 May 1815, ibid., no. 1691, 4:522–23.
17. Napoleon to Vandamme, 2 June 1815, carton 16, Vandamme Papers.
18. The best account of the Coalition forces in Belgium on the eve of the campaign is found in Hofschröer, *1815 . . . Wellington.*
19. Soult to Vandamme, "Ordre de Mouvement" (signed "by order of the Emperor: Marshal of the Empire, Major General, duc de Dalmatie" [Soult]), 14 June 1815, Arch. Guerre, 303/7 Yd. This order is found also in *Correspondance de Napoléon*, 14 June 1815, no. 22053, 28:281–86.
20. See Marshal Soult, Order of the day, dated 14 June 1815, Arch. Guerre, 303/7 Yd; Houssaye, *1815: Waterloo*, 112.
21. Hofschröer, *1815 . . . Wellington*, 370.
22. There were two generals named von Pirch, and they are usually referred to as (1) and (2).
23. Houssaye, *1815: Waterloo*, 127.
24. Hofschröer gives a good account of the Prussian army on 15 June. See also Houssaye, *1815: Waterloo*, 120–28.
25. Hofschröer, *1815 . . . Wellington*, 236 (citing Muffling, *Aus meinem Leben*, 233 ff). Hofschröer quotes five other accounts of this meeting, by men who were present. All concur, in different wording, that Wellington agreed to support Blücher if attacked (233–39).
26. Kelly explains why Blücher fought at Ligny in five points (*Battle of Wavre*, 44).
27. Soult to Vandamme, 16 June 1815, "Campagne de 1815; 3ème Corps d'Armée. Lettres addressées au General Vandamme par le Major Général, etc., du 25 avril au 28 juillet 1815," Arch Guerre, C15/23.
28. See Becke, *Napoleon and Waterloo*, 100. Chandler accepts these numbers (*Campaigns of Napoleon*, 1038), while Esposito and Elting give the number as a total of 78,800 men (*Military History*, 159).
29. See Becke, *Napoleon and Waterloo*, 100. Once again Chandler accepts these numbers (*Campaigns of Napoleon*, 1038). Esposito and Elting give the number as 83,000 men (*Military History*, 159).
30. Historians today are still not sure who wrote the penciled order. For a good discussion of this affair, see Becke, *Napoleon and Waterloo*, 107–110.
31. Every historian who has written on the Waterloo Campaign has puzzled over the d'Erlon Affair and speculated as to the outcome of the campaign if d'Erlon had defied Ney's direct orders and arrived on the Prussian right flank as the Imperial Guard broke the enemy's center. Such are the fortunes of war. The best account of the d'Erlon Affair is still Houssey, *1815: Waterloo*, 204–11, 216–22.
32. See Grouchy, *Mémoires du Maréchal de Grouchy*, 4:45–46; Grouchy, *Observations*, 12.
33. Grouchy, *Observations*, 12.
34. On the retreat of the Prussian army, see Hofschröer, *1815 . . . Wellington*, 325–30.

35. In Kelly, *Battle of Wavre*, 90–91. See also Grouchy, *Observations*, 12.

36. Grouchy to Vandamme, 17 June 1815, Arch. Guerre, C15/23.

37. See Grouchy's explanation for his decisions in his *Observations*, 17.

38. Grouchy to Vandamme, midnight, 18 June 1815, "Campagne de 1815: 3ème Corps d'Armée," Arch. Guerre, C15/23.

39. Soult to Grouchy, 19 June 1815, ibid. Soult wrote two letters to Grouchy dated 19 June 1815.

40. In English in Becke, *Napoleon and Waterloo*, 266. It is also in French in Houssaye, *1815: Waterloo*, 474–75.

41. On the retreat of Grouchy's army, see Becke, *Napoleon and Waterloo*, 264–70; Kelly, *Battle of Wavre*, 133–42.

42. Grouchy himself was at Givet on 21 June. See Grouchy to Vandamme, 21 June 1815, "Campagne de 1815: 3ème Corps d'Armée," Arch. Guerre, C15/23.

43. See "Ordre de mouvement pour le 22 juin," signed Grouchy, 21 June 1815, "Ordre de mouvement pour le 23 juin," signed Grouchy, 22 June 1815, "Ordre de mouvement pour le 24 juin," dated 23 June 1815, ibid.

44. See Davout's correspondence beginning 22 June 1815, in Davout, *Correspondance*, 4:571.

45. Davout to Soult, 22 June 1815, ibid., no. 1762, 4:571–72.

46. Davout to Grouchy, 23 June 1815, ibid., no. 1763, 4:572–73.

47. See Executive Commission to Vandamme, 23 June 1815, carton 16, Vandamme Papers.

48. Grouchy to Vandamme, 24 June, Soult to Grouchy, 23 June 1815, "Campagne 1815: 3ème Corps d'Armée," Grouchy to Vandamme, 26 June 1815, all in Arch. Guerre, C15/23.

49. Grouchy to Vandamme, 27 June 1815, ibid. Grouchy actually wrote three letters to Vandamme on 27 June, all urging him to rush to the defense of Paris.

50. Grouchy to Vandamme, 29 June 1815, ibid.

51. Vandamme, *Exposé de la Conduite*, 7–8; "Itinéraire du 3e Corps depuis son entrée sur le Territoire ennemi jusqu'à son retour à Paris," no date, "Campagne 1815: 3ème Corps d'Armée," Arch. Guerre, C15/23.

52. Davout to Marshal Blücher and to Lord Wellington, dated Paris, 30 June 1815, in Davout, *Correspondance*, no. 1774, 4:581–82.

53. There is a detailed account of these affairs in Gallaher, *Iron Marshal*, 322–29.

54. See the four-page extract from the *Moniteur* dated 3 July 1815, "Bulletin du 2 juillet 1815," Arch. Guerre, X15/6.

55. See *Moniteur*, 2 July 1815.

56. The address was originally written as a patriotic declaration without political implications. Davout claimed he had signed a blank paper, and a revised address with the anti-Bourbon clause was written in above. See Davout, "Après Waterloo–Paris," *Revue de Paris*, 15 December 1897, 735.

57. "Le Gal Vandamme au président de la Chambre des Représentants, à Paris," presumed date 1 or 2 July 1815, Arch. Guerre, C15/6.

58. "The President of the Chamber to Lt. General, Count Vandamme," 3 July 1815, ibid. See also "Extrait du procès-verbal des séances de la Chambre des Représentants," 3 July 1815, ibid.

59. See the "Procès-verbaux" of the meeting, Archives Nationales, AF IV, 1936.

60. The armistice was signed at Saint Cloud by M. Bignon, the minister of foreign affairs, General Armand-Charles Guilleminot, Davout's chief of staff, and M. de Bondy, the prefect of the department of the Seine. The Baron Müffling signed on behalf of Blücher, and Colonel Hervey for Wellington. See Bertier de Sauvigny, *Bourbon Restoration*, 108.

61. Order of the day, 3 July 1815, Arch. Guerre, C15/6.

62. See Guilleminot (chief of staff of the Army of the Loire) to Vandamme, 4 July 1815, ibid.

63. Berthezène to Davout, 7 July 1815, ibid. On desertions from one of Vandamme's cavalry divisions, see General Louis Vallin to Vandamme, 7 July 1815, Arch. Guerre, C15/8.

64. Vandamme to Davout, 7 July 1815, and "Rapport du 7 juillet," signed Berthezène, ibid.

65. Vandamme received instructions from army headquarters at Orleans daily between 9 and 14 July. See Guilleminot to Vandamme, 9, 10, 11, 12, 13, 14 July 1815, ibid.

66. "Instructions and Powers given to Lieutenant Generals Count Valmy, Count Gérard, and Count Haxo to make known to the King and his Minister of War [Marshal Saint-Cyr] the submission of the French army that is retiring behind the Loire," no date, ibid.

67. Bertier de Sauvigny, *Bourbon Restoration*, 109–110.

68. Gérard, Kellermann, and Haxo to Davout, 10 July 1815, Archives Nationales, Fie, 1. 26.

69. Davout to Gérard, Kellermann, and Haxo, 13 July 1815, in Davout, *Correspondance*, no. 1788, 4:596–97.

70. See Milhaud to Gouvion Saint-Cyr, Naperville, 9 July 1815, Davout, "Après Waterloo," 157.

71. Davout to "the King," 14 July 1815, in Davout, *Correspondance*, no. 1791, 4:598–99; Davout to Vandamme, 13 July 1815, Arch. Guerre, C15/8; Vandamme, *Exposé de la Conduite*, 8–9.

72. Davout to Vandamme, 14, 15, 14 July, Vandamme to Davout, 26 July 1815, all in Arch. Guerre, C15/8.

73. For example, see the letter from Olivet (commander of the artillery of the Fourth Corps) to Vandamme, 16 July 1815, ibid.

74. On the Austrian advance and withdrawal, see Vandamme to Davout, 24 July, Davout to Vandamme, 25 July 1815, ibid.

75. Carnot's name was on the second list. He wrote to Fouché: "'Where do you want me to go, traitor?' 'Wherever you wish, idiot.' Replied the Duke of Otranto" (Bertier de Sauvigny, *Bourbon Restoration*, 117).

76. Davout to Vandamme, 28 July 1815, Arch. Guerre, C15/9.

77. Davout to Minister of War (Gouvion Saint-Cyr), 27 July 1815, in Davout, *Correspondance*, no. 1824, 4:629–32.

78. See Davout, "Après Waterloo," 168.
79. Gouvion Saint-Cyr to Macdonald, 30 July 1815, carton 16, Vandamme Papers.

CHAPTER 12. THE EXILE

1. On the White Terror, see Bertier de Sauvigny, *Bourbon Restoration*, 117–19.
2. See "Le Ministre Secrétaire d'Etat au Département de la Police Général," to Marshal Macdonald, signature not legible, Arch. Guerre, 303/GD 2e série.
3. Prefect of the Department of the Haute Vienne to Vandamme, 26 August 1815, carton 16, Vandamme Papers; Vandamme, *Exposé de la Conduite*, 9.
4. See the correspondence between the head of the police at Limoges and the Minister of War, 31 August–15 September 1815, Arch. Guerre, 303/GD 2e série.
5. See Baron de Talleyrand (Prefect of the Loiret) to "Monsieur le Comte," [Vandamme] 15 September 1815, ibid.
6. Fouché to Saint-Cyr, 11 October 1815, ibid.
7. See "Secrétaire d'Etat du Département de la Police Général" to the Minister of War, 25 January 1816, ibid.
8. See the letter from the Lieutenant Colonel, Chief of the Fourth Division (signature not legible) to Chief of the Bureau of Military Police, 2 February 1816, ibid.
9. To "Général Vandamme]," signed "Comte de Tryon, Colonel Comtle poste de Surveillance à Berny," 4 February 1815, ibid.
10. See Hennerie, "Le pillage du château," 276–77.
11. See Vandamme's own words in his *Exposé de la Conduite*, 10–11.
12. Hennerie, "Le pillage du château," 276–77.
13. See Decarer (secretary of state of the Department of Police) to the Minister of War, 26 December 1815, Arch. Guerre, 303/GD 2e série.
14. See Milot, "Une Lettre du général Vandamme à sa soeur," 278–79.
15. See "Motifs de la Liquidation," signed Montel, Arch. Guerre, 303/GD 2e série.
16. Du Casse, *Vandamme et sa Correspondance*, 2:579–80.
17. The Napoleon House, restaurant and bar at the corner of Saint Louis and Chartres streets in New Orleans, is still today a reminder of the Napoleonic influence.
18. There are about twenty letters related to these years, in the Vandamme Papers. However, it is difficult to determine from whom or to whom these letters were addressed. Frequently the signature is not legible. Even when the names can be read, I have, in most cases, no idea who the person was or how the individual fit into the life of Dominique Vandamme. In fact, Du Casse does not include any of the American correspondence. He gives less than two pages, of very general information, to the three years Vandamme was in the United States (*Vandamme et sa Correspondance* 2:580–81).

19. See Talcott to Vandamme, 11 November 1817, and the letters of introduction to Becan and Porter, no date, Philadelphia, carton 17, Vandamme Papers.

20. See the company flyer, ibid.

21. See the invitations, ibid.

22. See the letter to Vandamme, signature not legible, 16 April 1818, ibid.

23. Lee to Vandamme, 18 June, 16 April 1818, ibid.

24. See the correspondence in ibid. In particular, see the letter from the Countess Daphie from Ghent, 17 February 1819.

25. See Du Casse, *Vandamme et sa Correspondance*, 2:581. Du Casse, who had the advantage of knowing and talking with Vandamme's immediate descendents, wrote that the general, when he returned to France, brought some of that furniture back with him; and that in the 1870s it was in the family pavilion in Zélande (ibid.).

26. See the letter from the Commissaire Général de la Marine at Le Havre to the Minister of the Marine and Colonies, 1 June 1819, Arch. Guerre, 303/7 Yd.

27. See the correspondence to and from Madame Vandamme, Arch. Guerre 303/7 Yd.

28. The author is indebted to Du Casse for this information (*Vandamme et sa Correspondance*, 2:582–83).

BIBLIOGRAPHY

The principal primary documents relating to General Dominique Vandamme are the Vandamme Papers in the Municipal Library of Lille, eighteen cartons of documents cataloged under the title "Fonds De Swarte-Revel: Correspondance et papiers du général Vandamme." This is the largest single collection of documents, and by far the most important, relating to General Vandamme. The second major source of archival material is the Service Historique de l'Etat-Major de l'Armée (the war archives of the Ministry of War), housed at the Château de Vincennes on the east side of Paris. At Vincennes there are a number of cartons that deal with Vandamme, and the most significant is labeled "Dossiers Vandamme" (303/7 Yd). Other important cartons are found in the C2 series under the heading "Grande Armée: Correspondance du lieutenant-général Vandamme, du 23 mars au 22 août 1813" (C2/296); "Correspondance du général Vandamme, du 27 septembre 1805 au 30 janvier 1807" (C2/396–97); "1er corps de réserve au camp de Boulogne (Brune, Saint-Cyr, Vandamme)" (C2/487); "8e corps (Jérôme, Vandamme, Tharreau, Junot)" (C2/529); and the C15 series "Période des Cent Jours (1815): Copie des lettres addressées au général Vandamme, commandant le 3e corps par le Ministre de la Guerre, le major-général, etc., du 25 avril au 28 juillet, 1815" (C15 Grand format 23).

In addition, documents from, to, and about General Vandamme can be found in numerous other cartons at Vincennes. Primary sources can also be found at the National Archives in Paris and at the archives of the Department of the North at Lille. These are duly documented in the notes.

Arnold, James R. *Crisis on the Danube: Napoleon's Austrian Campaign of 1809*. New York: Paragon House, 1990.
———. *Napoleon Conquers Austria: The 1809 Campaign for Vienna*. Westport, Conn.: Praeger, 1995.
Beaujot, E. *Le Début de la Restauration et la Terreur blanche dans le Nord (1814–1818)*. Lille, 1933.
Becke, A. F. *Napoleon and Waterloo: The Emperor's Campaign with the Armée du Nord. 1815*. Reprint, London: Kegan Paul, Trench, Trubner, 1939.
Bertaud, Jean-Paul. *The Army of the French Revolution: From Citizen-Soldiers to Instrument of Power*. Translated by R. R. Palmer. Princeton, N.J.: Princeton University Press, 1988.
Bertier de Sauvigny, Guillaume de. *The Bourbon Restoration*. Translated by Lynn M. Case. Philadelphia: University of Pennsylvania Press, 1966.
Bigarré, Auguste-Julien. *Mémoires du Général Bigarré: Aide de Camp du Roi Joseph, 1775–1813*. Paris: Ernest Kolb, n.d.
Birtaut, J. *Le roi Jérôme*. Paris, 1946.
Blocqueville, Adélaïde-Louise de. *Le Maréchal Davout prince d'Eckmühl: correspondance inédite 1790–1815: Pologne, Russie, Hambourg*. Paris: Perrin, 1887.
———. *Le Maréchal Davout Prince d'Eckmühl raconté par les Siens et par Lui-Même*. 4 vols. Paris: Didier et Cie, 1879–80.
Bonaparte, Jérôme. *Mémoires et correspondance du roi Jérôme et de la reine Catherine*. 7 vols. Paris: Dentu, 1861–66.
Bottet, M. "Vandamme: Sabre de récompense nationale et brevet du comte d'Unsebourg." *Carnet de la Sabretache* (1903).
Bourgoin, L. *Esquisse Historique sur le Maréchal Brune*. 2 vols. Paris: Rousseau, 1840.
Bowden, Scott. *Napoleon and Austerlitz*. Chicago: Emperor's Press, 1997.
———. *Napoleon's Grande Armée of 1813*. Chicago: Emperor's Press, 1990.
Bruchet, M. "L'invasion et l'occupation du département du Nord par les Alliés." *Revue du Nord* (1920).
Burghersh, Lord. *The Operations of Allied Armies in 1813 and 1814: A Memoir of Lord Burghersh*. London: Worly, 1996.
Burturlin, D. Ainval, Christiane de. *Gouvion St.-Syr*. Paris: Copernic, 1981.
Caudrillier, Gustaaf. *La trahison de Pichegru*. Paris: F. Alcan, 1908.
Caulaincourt, Armand Augustin. *Mémoires du général de Caulaincourt, duc de Vicence: Grand Ecuyer de l'Empereur*. 3 vols. Paris: Plon, 1933.

Cazalas, E. "Comment Vandamme fut pris à la bataille de Culm." *Feuilles d'Histoire du 17e au 20e Siècle* 2.4 (July—December 1910): 523–29. Paris: R. Roger et F. Chernoviz.
Challamel, A. *Les clubs contre-révolutionnaires, cercles, comités, sociétés, salons, réunions, cafés, restaurants et librairies.* Paris: L. Cerf, 1895.
Chandler, David G. *The Campaigns of Napoleon.* New York: Macmillan, 1966.
———. *Dictionary of the Napoleonic Wars.* New York: Simon and Schuster, 1993.
———. *Napoleon's Marshals.* New York: Macmillan, 1987.
Chardigny, Louis. *Les maréchaux de Napoléon.* Paris: Flammarion, 1946.
Clausewitz, Karl von. *The campaign of 1812 in Russia.* London: John Murray, 1843.
Clément, G. *Campagne de 1813.* Paris: H. Charles-Lavauzelle, n.d.
Coignet. *Les Cahiers du Capitaine Coignet (1799—1815).* London: Peter Davies, 1928.
Comeau, Baron de. *Souvenir des Guerres d'Allemagne pendant la Révolution et l'Empire.* Paris: Plon, 1900.
Coutanceau, H., and H. Leplus. *La Campagne de 1794 à l'armée du Nord.* 2nd part, *Opérations.* Paris: R. Chapelot et Cie., 1908.
Croker, John Wilson. *The Correspondence and Diaries of J. W. Croker.* Edited by L. T. Jennings. 3 vols. London: Murray, 1884.
Davout, Louis N. "Après Waterloo—L'Armée de la Loire." *Revue de Paris* (January 1898): 151–72.
———. "Après Waterloo—Paris." *Revue de Paris* (December 1897): 705–43.
———. *Correspondance du Maréchal Davout Prince d'Eckmühl, ses commandements, son Ministère, 1801–1815.* Edited by Charles Mazade. 4 vols. Paris: Plon, 1885.
———. *Opérations du 3e Corps 1806–1807: Rapport du Marechal Davout, Duc d'Auerstaedt.* Paris: Calmann Lévy Frères, 1896.
Desbières, Edouard. *Projets et tentatives de débarquement aux Iles Britanniques, 1793–1805.* 5 vols. Paris: R. Chapelot, 1900–1902.
Dontenville, J. *Le Général Moreau, 1763–1813.* Paris: Ch. Delagrave, 1899.
Doyle, William. *The Oxford History of the French Revolution.* Oxford: Clarendon Press, 1989.
Du Casse, Albert. *Le Général Vandamme et sa Correspondance.* 2 vols. Paris: Didier et Cie., 1870.
———. *Mémoires pour servir l'histoire de la campagne de 1812, suivis des lettres de Napoléon au roi de Westphalie, pendant la Campagne de 1813.* Paris, 1852.
———. *Opérations du Neuvième Corps de la Grande Armée en Silésie sous le Commandement en Chief de S.A.I le Prince Jérôme Napoléon d'octobre 1806 à juillet 1807.* Paris, 1851.
———. *Les rois frères du Napoléon, documents inédits relatifs au Premier Empire.* Paris, 1883.
Duffy, Christopher. *Austerlitz: 1805.* London: Seeley Service, 1977.

Durant, Will, and Ariel Durant. *The Age of Napoleon: A History of European Civilization from 1789 to 1815*. New York: Simon and Schuster, 1975.
Duthilt, P. C. *Mémoires du capitaine Duthilt*. Lille, 1909.
Elting, John R. *Swords around a Throne: Napoleon's Grande Armée*. New York: Free Press, 1988.
Epstein, Robert M. *Napoleon's Last Victory and the Emergence of Modern War*. Lawrence: University of Kansas Press, 1994.
Esposito, Vincent J., and John Robert Elting. *A Military History and Atlas of the Napoleonic Wars*. New York: Praeger, 1964.
Fain, Agathon Jean François, Baron. *Manuscrit de mil huit treize, contenant le précis des événemens de cette année, pour servir l'histoire de l'empereur Napoléon*. 2 vols. Paris: Delaumay, 1824.
Fairon, E., and H. Heusse. *Lettres des grognards*. Paris: 1936.
Foucart, P., and J. Finot. *La Défense national dans le Nord de 1792 à 1802*. Lille, 1890.
Gachot, E. *Les campagnes de 1799: Jourdan en Allemagne et Brune en Hollande*. Paris: Perrin, 1906.
Gallaher, John G. *General Alexandre Dumas: Soldier of the French Revolution*. Carbondale: Southern Illinois University Press, 1997.
———. *The Iron Marshal: A Biography of Louis N. Davout*. Carbondale: Southern Illinois University Press, 1976.
———. *Napoleon's Irish Legion*. Carbondale: Southern Illinois University Press, 1993.
Garros, Louis. *Ney: Le Brave des braves*. Paris: Amiot-Dumont, 1955.
———. *Quel roman que ma vie!* Paris: Les Editions de l'Encyclopédie Française, 1947.
Gérard, Alain. "Dominique Vandamme, général de la Révolution et de l'Empire." In *Le Général Vandamme: Sa vie, ses campagnes, sa correspondance*, by the Association des Amis du Musée des Canonniers de Lille. Published in Lille by the Bibliothèque Municipale de Lille, 1980.
———. "Le général Vandamme, le département du Nord, et la fin du Premier Empire." *La Boute-Feu*. Lille, 1980.
———. "Vandamme et la Camp de Boulogne." *Souvenir Napoléonien* 44, no. 318 (July 1981): 3–10.
Gérard, Alain, and Jean Milot. "Vandamme et la Campagne de Silésie." *Souvenir Napoléonien* 44, no. 318 (July 1981): 11–18.
Goetz, Robert. *1805, Austerlitz: Napoleon and the Destruction of the Third Coalition*. London: Greenhill, 2005.
Gorczkowsky, V. *Graf Kleist v. Nollendorf, Königlich Preussischer General-Feld-Marschall*. Berlin, 1848.
Gotteri, Nicole. *Le Maréchal Soult*. Paris: Bernard Giovanangeli Edition, 2000.
Grohmann, Joh. Christ. *Hamburgs Gchidsale under Davoust und Meine Asmanderung*. Gotha: Beckerschen Buchhandlung, 1814.
Grouchy, Emmanuel de. *Mémoires du Maréchal de Grouchy*. 5 vols. Paris: Dentu, 1873–74.

———. *Observations sur . . . la campagne de 1815*. Philadelphia: J. F. Hurtel, 1818.
Halzhausen, Philip Paul. *Davout in Hamburg: Ein Beitrag zur Geschichte des Jahre 1813–1814*. Mülheim: Verlag von Max Röder, 1892.
Hamilton, William David. *Waterloo: New Perspectives, the Great Battle Reappraised*. New York: John Wiley and Son, 1993.
Hofschröer, Peter. *1815 The Waterloo Campaign: The German Victory— From Waterloo to the Fall of Napoleon*. London: Greenhill Books, 1999.
———. *1815 The Waterloo Campaign: Wellington, His German Allies and the Battles of Ligny and Quatre Bras*. London: Greenhill Books. 1998.
Houssaye, Henry. *1815: Waterloo*. Paris: Perrin et Cie, 1899.
———. *Iena et la Campagne de 1806*. Paris: Perrin, 1812.
"Inauguration à Cassel d'un monument commémorant la mémoire du général Vandamme." *Grand Hebdomadaire Illustré du Nord de la France*, 2 juillet 1922.
Jomini, Antoine-Henri, baron. *Histoire des Guerres de la Révolution*. 15 vols. Paris: Anselin et Pochard, 1820–24.
———. *Précis politique et militaire des campagnes de 1812 à 1814*. Genève: Slatkine-Megariotis Reprints, 1975.
Jourquin, Jacques. *Dictionnaire des maréchaux du Premier Empire*. Paris: Tallandier/Institut Napoléon, n.d.
———. *Dictionnaire des maréchaux du Premier Empire*. 5th edition. Paris: Christien/Jas, 2001.
Kelly, W. Hyde. *The Battle of Wavre and Grouchy's Retreat*. Felling: Worley, 1993.
Kolzakov, Paul Andréiévitch. "Comment Vandamme fut pris à la bataille de Culm." Edited by E. Cazalas, *Feuilles d'Histoire du 17e au 20e Siècle* 2.4 (July—December 1910): 523–29. Director, Arthur Chuquet. Paris: R. Roger et F. Chernoviz.
Lamar, Glenn J. *Jérôme Bonaparte: The War Years, 1800–1815*. Westport, Conn.: Greenwood Press, 2000.
Leconte, J. R. *Au musée royal de l'Armée. A propos des pistolets donnés par le Premier Consul au Général Vandamme (an XI)*.
Lefebvre, Georges. *The French Revolution from 1793 to 1799*. Translated by John H. Stewart and James Friguglietti. New York: Columbia University Press, 1964.
———. *Napoleon: From 18 Brumaire to Tilsit, 1799–1807*. Translated Henry F. Stockhold. New York: Columbia University Press, 1969.
———. *Napoleon: From Tilsit to Waterloo, 1807–1815*. Translated by J. E. Anderson. New York: Columbia University Press, 1970.
Lerecouvreux, M. "La manoeuvre de Kulm (août 1813)." *Revue Historique de l'Armée*. 1972.
Levi, C. *La défense nationale dans le Nord en 1793: La Bataille d'Hondschoote*. Dunkerque, 1907.
———. *Dominique Vandamme*. Cassel, 1914.
———. *Hondschoot et le siège de Dunkerque d'après les annales de Breynaert et d'autres documents nouveaux*. Dunkerque, 1922.

Lort de Serignan, Arthur de. *Un conspirateur militaire sur le premier empire: le général Malet.* Paris: Payot, 1925.
Lynn, John. *Bayonets of the Republic: Motivation and Tactics in the Army of the Revolutionary France.* Urbana: University of Illinois Press, 1984.
Manceron, Claude. *Austerlitz: The Story of a Battle.* Translated by George Unwin. New York: W. W. Norton, 1963.
Marbot, Jean-Baptiste, baron de. *Mémoires du général baron de Marbot.* 3 vols. Paris: E. Plon, Nourrit et Cie., 1892.
Markham, J. David. *Imperiala Glory: The Bulletins of Napoleon's Grande Armée, 1805–1814.* London: Greenhill Books, 2003.
Marmont, Auguste-Frédéric. *Mémoires du Maréchal Marmont, duc de Raguse, de 1792.* 9 vols. Paris: Perrotin, 1857.
Marshall-Cornwall, James. *Marshal Massena.* Oxford: Oxford University Press, 1965.
———. *Napoleon as Military Commander.* Princeton, N.J.: Van Nostrand, 1967.
Masson, Frédéric. *Napoléon et sa famille.* 11 vols. Paris: Albin Michel, 1900–1920.
Mathiez, Albert. *La Réaction thermidorienne.* Paris: Colin, 1929.
Maude, Frederic Natusch. *1813: The Leipzig Campaign.* London: Swan-Sonnenschein, 1908.
———. *The Jena Campaign, 1806.* London: Greenhill Books, 1998.
———. *The Ulm Campaign.* London: Swan-Sonnenschein, 1912.
Méneval, Baron C.-F. de. *Memoirs of Napoleon Bonaparte; The Court of the First Empire.* Vol. 1. New York: P. F. Collier and Son, 1910.
Milot, Jean. "La Compagnie franche de Vandamme." *Revue du Nord: Histoire et Archéologie* 71, nos. 282–83 (July—December 1989): 787.
———. "Une Lettre du général Vandamme à sa soeur." *Mélanges offerts à M. Robinet.* 1982, pp. 277–82. In author's possession.
———. "Portrait psychologique de Vandamme." *Souvenir Napoléonien* 44, no. 318 (July 1981): 19–29.
———. "Le Retour de captivité du général Vandamme." *Revue du Nord: Histoire et Archéologie* 66, no. 261/262 (April—September 1984): 587–98.
Mitchell, H. *The Underground War against Revolutionary France.* Oxford: Clarendon Press, 1965.
Moore, Sir John. *The Diary of Sir John Moore.* Edited by J. F. Maurice. 2 vols. London: Edward Arnold, 1904.
Nafziger, George. *Napoleon's Dresden Campaign; The Battles of August 1813.* Chicago: Emperor's Press, 1994.
Napoleon Ier. *La Correspondance de Napoléon 1er.* 32 vols. Paris: Imprimerie Impériale, 1858–70.
Pajol, Charles-Pierre, Comte. *Pajol Général en chef, par le général de division comte Pajol, son fils ainé.* 3 vols. Paris: Firmin-Didot, 1874.
Patrick, A. "Law of Hostages." In Scott and Rothaus, *Historical Dictionary,* 2:563–64.
Pelet, Jean-Jacques Germain. *Mémoires sur la guerre de 1809, en Allemagne, avec les opérations particulières des corps d'Italie, de Pologne, de Saxe,*

de Naples et de Walcheren; par le général Pelet, d'après son journal fort détaillé de la campagne d'Allemagne. 4 vols. Paris: Roret, 1824–26.

———. *Des Principales opérations de la campagne de 1813*. Paris: Spectateur Militaire, 1827.

Petre, Francis Loraine. *Napoleon's Campaign in Poland, 1806–1807: A Military History of Napoleon's First War with Russia, Verified from Unpublished Official Documents*. New York: Hippocrene, 1975.

———. *Napoleon's Conquest of Prussia—1806*. London and New York: J. Lane, 1907.

———. *Napoleon's Last Campaign in Germany, 1813*. New York: J. Lane, 1912.

Phipps, Ramsay Weston. *The Armies of the First French Republic and the Rise of the Marshals of Napoleon*. 5 vols. Westport, Conn.: Greenwood Press, 1980.

Quenson de la Hennerie, A. "Le pillage du château du général Vandamme à Cassel en 1814 et 1815." *Bulletin du Comité Flamand de France* (1922), 1er fascicule. Lille: L. Duytschaever, 1922.

Ratcliffe, Bertram. *Marshal de Grouchy and the Guns of Waterloo*. London: Frederick Muller, 1942.

Riley, J. P. *Napoleon and the World War of 1813: Lessons in Coalition Warfighting*. London: Frank Cass, 2000.

Rodger, Alexander Bankier. *The War of the Second Coalition, 1798–1801: A Strategic Commentary*. Oxford: Clarendon Press, 1964.

Saint-Cyr, Laurent de Gouvion. *Mémoires sur les campagnes des armées du Rhin-et-Moselle de 1792 jusqu'à la paix de Campo-Formio*. 4 vols. Paris: Anselin, 1829.

Saunders, Edith. *The Hundred Days: Napoleon's Final Wager for Victory*. New York: W. W. Norton, 1964.

Schom, Alan. *One Hundred Days: Napoleon's Road to Waterloo*. Oxford: Oxford University Press, 1992.

Scott, Samuel F., and Barry Rothaus. *Historical Dictionary of the French Revolution*. 2 vols. Westport, Conn.: Greenwood Press, 1985.

Ségur, Louis de. *An Aide-de-Camp of Napoleon, Memoirs of General Count de Ségur*. Translated by H. A. Patchett-Martin. London: Hutchinson, 1895.

———. *Histoire et Mémoires*. 2 vols. Paris: Firmin Didot, 1873.

Serignan, Arthur de Lot de. *Un conspirateur militaire sur le premier Empire: le Général Malet*. Paris, 1925.

Simon, G. *Die Kriegserignisse swischen Teplitz und Pirna im August und September des Jahres 1813. Die Schlacht bei Kulm am 29 und 30 August 1813 und Das Gefecht bei Arbesau am 17 September 1813*; Nach verläszlichen Quellen Bearbeitet 1911, Teplitz-Schönau Emil Seewald.

Six, Georges. *Dictionnaire biographique des généraux et amiraux français de la Révolution et de l'Empire (1792–1814)*. 2 vols. Paris: Georges Saffroy, 1934.

Swarte, Victor de. "Le général Vandamme." *Le Progrès du Nord*, no. 140, dimanche, 20 mai 1894.

Tack, D. *Mont Cassel historique, archéologique, pittoresque.* Dunkerque, 1923.
Tarlé, Eugene. *Napoleon's Invasion of Russia in 1812.* Oxford: Oxford University Press, 1942.
Teste, François-Antoine. "Souvenirs du général Teste." *Carnet de la Sabretache* (1912).
Thiébault, Paul-Charles. *Mémoires du Général Baron Thiébault.* 5 vols. Paris: Plon-Nourrit, 1895–97.
Thiers, Adolphe. *Histoire du Consulat et de l'Empire.* 21 vols. Paris: Paulin, 1845–69.
Thiry, Jean. *Iéna.* Paris: Berger-Levrault, 1964.
———. *Wagram.* Paris: Berger-Levrault, 1966.
Thompson, J. M. *Napoleon Bonaparte.* New York: Oxford University Press, 1952.
Uffindell, Andrew. *The Eagle's Last Triumph: Napoleon's Victory at Ligny, June 1815.* London: Greenhill Books, 1994.
Vandal, Albert. *L'Avènement de Bonaparte; La Genèse du Consulat Brumair; La Constitution de l'an VIII.* 3 vols. Paris: Plon, 1911.
Vandamme, Dominique. "Campagne d'Autriche 1809, Commandement du corps Würtemberg: Correspondance." Carton 14, Vandamme Papers. (Cited in notes as "Campagne de 1809: Correspondance.") This booklet contains seventy-one pages of Vandamme's correspondence from 31 March to 3 December 1809.
———. "Campagne de Russie, 1812, Correspondance." Carton 15, Vandamme Papers. (Cited in notes as "Vandamme Correspondance, 1812.")
———. *Exposé de la Conduite du Lieutenant-Général Comte Vandamme.* Paris: Imprimerie de Brasseur Ainé, 1815.
———. "Le journal des campagnes du général Vandamme pendant les IIe et IIIe années républicaines." Carton 1, Vandamme Papers.
———. *Mémoire justificatif du général de division Vandamme.* Strasbourg, an VII (1798–99). Dossier Vandamme, Arch. Guerre, 303/7 Yd.
———. *Récit abrégé des compagnes de II et III année républicaines.* Strasbourg, 1838.
———. "Registre du Correspondance du Général Vandamme du 27 septembre 1805 au 30 janvier 1807." Arch. Guerre, C2/396. (Cited in notes as "Registre du Correspondance.")
Walsh, E. *Narrative of the Expedition to Holland in the Autumn of the Year 1799.* London: Hamilton, Falcon, and Court, 1800.
Yermolov, Alexey. *The Czar's General: The Memoirs of a Russian General in the Napoleonic Wars.* Edited with notes by Alesander Mikaberidze. Welwyn Garden City, England: Ravenhall Books, 2005.

Index

Abbaye, in Paris, 15
Abbeville, 111
Abensberg, 201
Abens River, 59
Abercrombie, General Sir Ralph, 91, 93–96
Aboukir Bay, 75
Accusations, against Vandamme, 42, 67–70, 83–89, 180, 196, 286; by Haussmann, 58, 62–63; of Jacobin terrorism, 49–50; of Vieux-Brisach village extortion, 80. *See also* Jacobin Club, of Cassel
Active duty, 43–45, 102, 229
Aicha, 126
Aix-La-Chapelle, 121
Ajaccio, 160
Alexander, Emperor of Russia, 252; Napoleon's alliance with, 209–10
Alexander I, Tsar, 120–22, 155–56, 173, 181, 183, 219, 227–29, 241, 247, 251, 255; in Austerlitz Campaign, 133, 135, 138, 140, 143; Napoleon's peace talks with, 179
Alexandre, Charles-Alexis, 56
Alkmaar, 91, 93, 95
Allied Army(ies), 31, 33, 133, 163, 166, 170–71; Anglo-Dutch-German, 262; Anglo-Hanoverian, 12, 13; Anglo-Portuguese, 208; Anglo-Russian, 95–98; Anholt-Pless's Prussian, 168; in Belgium, 52; in Holland, 38–39; Russian-Austrian, 131; in Silesia, 164. *See also* Coalition Army; First Coalition; Second Coalition; Third Coalition
Alsace, 47, 87
Alten, 212
Altenberg, 245, 247, 249

Altenweerder, 236
Altheim, 191
Altona, 234, 236
Amberg, 53, 54, 59
Amiens, 111
Amsterdam, 39, 91
Ancenis, 45
Andelfingen, 80
Andréossy, General Victor-Antoine, 124
Angerville, 283
Anhalt, 211–12
Anholt-Pless, Prince, 165–67, 168, 172–73, 175
Anne Dorothea Affair, 255, 332n87
Antwerp, 9, 202
Appendorf, 60
Arbois, 47
Arcola, 144
Ardennes, 14
Armistice (1795): Austrians' denouncing of, 52; between French and Austrian armies, 45–46
Armistice of Neumarckt, 239–40, 329n41
Army(ies), 163, 166, 170–71; of Austerlitz, 256; of Austria, 76, 121–22, 128, 189, 193; of Batavia, 90–98; in Belgium, 52; of Bohemia, 241–44, 251, 254; of Coast of Brest, 44, 74; of Danube, 77–80, 99, 116; of England, 24, 38, 72–74, 113–15, 122; of France, 98, 99, 295; of Germany, 185–86; of Grisons, 109; of Italy, 51, 52, 65–66, 75, 76, 182, 194, 197; of Ligurie, 103–104; of Mayence, 72, 74–76; of Moselle, 18, 33, 65; of Naples, 75; of Napoleon, xi, 3, 107, 221, 234, 276, 287; of the North, 10, 26,

347

Army(ies) *(continued)*
28, 33, 38, 42–70, 298n13; of Observation, 75; of Paris, 280; of Portugal, 181, 207; of Prussia, 168, 179; of Reserve, 103–104, 106, 108, 109; of the Rhine, 102–103, 107; of the Rhine and Moselle, 45–46, 49–53, 56, 58–60, 62, 64, 69, 72; of Russia, 95, 132, 218–20, 228; of Sambre and Meuse, 33, 43, 52–53, 56, 59–60, 64–65, 72; of Silesia, 164, 243; of Switzerland, 72, 75, 80; of the West, 44–45, 218, 222. *See also* Allied Army(ies); Army Corps; Army Division(s); Coalition Army; First Army; French Army; French Republican Army; French Revolutionary Army; Grande Armée; Second Army; Third Army

Army Corps: Davout's First, 114, 222; Davout's Third, 113, 125–26, 136, 160, 189, 193–94; Eighth, 184, 186–87, 189, 191, 193, 197–99, 210, 213–18, 220–25; Fifth, 126, 160, 218; First, xii, 113–14, 125–26, 139, 142, 156, 222, 231, 234, 241–44, 249–50, 253–54, 264–65, 270; First Austrian, 186; First Prussian, 249, 265, 276; Fourteenth, 244; Fourth Austrian, 188; Fourth Cavalry, 218, 285; Fourth reserve cavalry, 224; Grande Armée Fourth, 124, 129, 313n3; Ninth, 171, 175, 193; Saxon, 193, 217; Second, 113, 126, 131–32, 184, 187–88, 264–65, 268–69, 277; Second Prussian, 266, 273, 276; Seventh, 122, 128, 184, 186, 217–18; Sixth, 113, 126, 157, 173, 189, 264, 267–68, 272; Tenth, 179, 218; Third, 113, 126, 136, 142, 160, 183–84, 186–89, 193–95, 262–67, 270–71, 273–79, 284; Third Prussian, 266, 268, 275, 277; Westphalian, 210–13, 216–18, 220, 222; Würtemberg, 202, 210, 244

Army division(s): Bavarian First, 161, 164; Bavarian Second, 164; Eleventh, 45, 283; Fifth, 230; First, 80, 91, 93, 242; Forty-second, 251; Fourteenth Infantry, 265; Fourteenth Military, 210; Second, 33, 37–39, 91, 94, 103, 118–19, 124–25, 143, 145, 157, 230, 242; Second Military, 262; Seventh, 50, 59, 60; Sixteenth, 112; Sixteenth Military, 210; Sixteenth Territorial, 109–10, 114; Tenth Territorial, 73; Thirty-second Military, 230–31, 233, 235; Twenty-fourth, 212–13, 249; Twenty-third, 213; Würtemberg division, 160–63, 168–73, 175–77, 179, 185–86, 190–91

Army of England, Vandamme's forays in, 73–74

Arnheim, taking of, 38–39
Artenay, 283
Aspern, 194
Assignat, 27
Aubert-Dubayet, Jean-Baptiste, 45
Aubrée, General of Brigade René-François, 94
Auenheim, on the Rhine, 74
Auerstädt, 183, 231
Auerstädt, battle of, 157–58

Augereau, Marshal Charles-Pierre, 73, 100, 122, 125, 128, 186–87
Augezd, 141
Augsburg, 54, 107, 126, 145–46
Aulic Council, 52, 61, 103–104, 127, 182; Austerlitz Campaign plan of, 121–22
Aumont, duke of, 257
Aussig, 246
Austerlitz, 123, 142–46, 152, 155–56, 182, 231, 256
Austerlitz, battle of, 129, 133–42, *134*, 296; armies' placements in, 135–36; final phase of, 141–42; retreating troops drown in, 141–42, 315n52; stalemate in, 139, 315n46; Vandamme's role in, 136–42. *See also* Austerlitz Campaign
Austerlitz Campaign, 4; of 1805 and 1809, *123*; Alexander I in, 133, 135, 138, 140, 143; Allied plan for, 127; armistice in, 132; Aulic Council plan for, 121–22; Austrian Army in, 121–22, 128; Davout's role in, 125–28, 135, 137; Grande Armée in, 122–23, 312n2; Kutusov's Army, deterioration in, 132; Mack's surrender in, 128; Napoleon's strategic command of, 122–42; Prussia in, 128–29, 133, 315n35; Russian troops in, 132; Soult's role in, 124–28, 130–33, 137–39, 141, 144–45; Vandamme's role in, 125–27, 129–30, 132–33, 313n11; Vienna occupied in, 131. *See also* Austerlitz, battle of
Austria, 7, 24, 40, 75, 108, 145–46, 155–57, 181–85, 207–10, 228; Army of, 121–22, 128, 189, 193; campaign of 1800, grand plan of, 103–104, 310n10; as defeated, 181, 202; honor of, 121; Maria Louise, princess of, 208, 240; Prussia's relationship with, 24, 26
Austrian Army: in Austerlitz Campaign, 121–22, 128; in Rhine Campaign (1799), 76
Austrian Campaign (1809): armistice in, 197; Austrian Army's defeat in, 189; Austrian plan for, 182; Davout's role in, 186–89; French Army in, 185; Napoleon's early strategy/tactics in, 187–88; Vienna march in, 191–96
Austrian Netherlands, 4, 5, 9, 19
Avignon, 289

Backer, Colonel, 175
Baden, 70, 72, 76
Baert, Barbara Françoise (mother), 4
Baert, Dominique (grandfather), 4
Bagration, General Peter, 135, 137–39, 218–20, 222–24, 226
Bailleul, 13, 26, 27
Bailli of Tübingen, 81, 82
Balinges, 79, 82
Balland, General Antoine, 29
Baltic Sea, 111
Bamberg, 52, 53
Bantry Bay, 65
Barclay de Tolly, General Michael, 218–20, 224, 227, 263

INDEX

Barenstein, 249
Barras, Paul-François, 71
Barthélemy, François, 71
Basel (Bâle), 76, 80, 83, 103, 105, 263
Basra, 243
Bassano, duke of, 253
Basse Wavre, 275
Bastille, 6, 285
Batavia, 90, 91
Batavian Directory, 92, 94, 98
Bautzen, 237, 242
Bavaria, 52, 59–60, 76, 107, 122, 127, 129, 146, 182, 184; army divisions of, 160–65; infantry of, 168
Beauharnais, Eugène, 184
Beaumont, 263
Becan, Mr., 293
Belgium, 4–5, 11–12, 16, 33, 52, 107, 111–12, 119, 183, 260–64, 283, 290, 294
Belgium Campaigns (1792–96), 25
Bellegard, General Heinrich, 184, 186
Bennigsen, General Levin August, 127, 173, 179
Bergen, 93, 94
Berg-op-zoom, 202
Berlin, 24, 40, 133, 156, 158, 160, 181, 226, 234, 237–38, 242
Bernadotte, Marshal Jean-Baptiste-Jules, 75, 90–92, 100, 126, 131, 139, 156, 193, 229, 237, 256. *See also* Charles John, Crown Prince of Sweden
Bernard, Abbot of Gengenbach, 70
Berthezène, General Pierre, 283, 288
Berthier, Marshal Alexander, 102–103, 112, 124, 184–86, 194–200, 217, 224–26, 232–33, 235–38, 245–46, 253; as chief of staff, 162, 163, 198; as Grande Armée commander, 145–46; Strasbourg Affair and, 180. *See also* Neufchâtel, prince of
Bertin, Philippe-Pierre, 180
Bertrand, General Henri-Gatien, 271
"Bertrand Orders," 271
Bessières, Marshal Jean-Baptiste, 126, 141
Bethuve, 38
Beurnonville, General Pierre, 64
Beverwyck, 95
Biberach, 60, 76, 106, 127–28
Bielitsa, 223–24, 226
Bierges, 275–76
Bigarré, Major Auguste-Julien, 139–40, 144, 315n47
Biron, Marshal de, 5, 6
Black Forest, 52, 60, 79, 105, 126
Blücher, Field Marshal Gebhard Leberecht von, 250, 256, 263, 279, 281, 284
Blücher, Prussian general, 241, 273
Boeschèpe, France, 26
Bohemia, 52, 53, 128, 183–84, 188–89, 192, 241, 243, 245–47, 251, 253
Bonaparte, Emperor Napoleon, xi, xii, 3, 144, 181, 207, 241; abdication of, 279, 280; coronation of, 117–18, 312n42; declared an outlaw, 261; defeat of, 267; divorce/remarriage of, 208; dynasty of, 214; empire of, 8, 257, 261; exile/return of, 260–62; Russian emperor's alliance with, 209–10
Bonaparte, General Napoleon, 76, 101–102, 110, 112, 116, 120–21, 155, 229; army of, xi, 3, 107, 221, 234, 276, 287; Army of England, commander, 72–73; Army of Italy, commander, 51–52, 65–66; Austerlitz Campaign, strategy/tactics of, 122–42; Austerlitz generals/troops, rewarded by, 143; Austrian Campaign (1809), early strategy/tactics of, 187–88; defeat of, 267; as First Consul for life, 111; French army retreat and, 276–80; Grande Armée, of, 218, 293; Jérôme's relationship with, 160–61, 174–75, 219–20, 224–25; Prussian invasion by, 158; Prussia's relationship with, 155–56; Vandamme rewarded by, 143–44; Vandamme's Legion of Honor from, 114, 117, 143, 145, 312n41, 316n63; Vandamme's relationship with, xi–xii, 3–4, 72–73, 102, 110, 112, 185, 192–93, 222–24, 229, 239, 253–54, 296; Waterloo Campaign preparations of, 262–63; Waterloo Campaign strategy of, 264. *See also* Bonaparte, Emperor Napoleon; First Consul Bonaparte
Bonaparte, Jérôme (brother of Napoleon), 160–65; Napoleon's relationship with, 160–61, 174–75, 219–20, 221–23, 224–26. *See also* Jérôme, King of Westphalia; Jérôme, Prince
Bonaparte, Joseph (brother): as Fourth Regiment colonel, 118–19; as prince of France, 118–19, 139, 140, 145, 183, 293; Spanish throne secured for, 181, 183; Vandamme's relationship with, 118
Bonaparte, Josephine (wife), 208
Bonaparte, Lucien (brother), 101
Bonapartists, 259, 295
Bonhomme, General, 94
Bonnaud, General Jacques-Philippe, 30
Bordeaux, 289
Borodino, 227, 231
Boryfeld, 232
Bouche-du Weser, 230, 232–33
Boudet, General Jean, 95, 97
Boulogne, 111–13, 117, 119, 125, 146, 185, 203–206, 210; Vandamme's arrival in, 203–204; Vandamme's humiliation in, 204, 324n60, 324nn57–58
Bourbon(s), 120, 257, 285; dynasty of, 24, 117; house colors of, 283, 286; monarchy of, 115, 295; regime of, 293; restoration of, 17, 257
Bourbon Restoration, 17
Bourdonnaye, 7
Bourges, 286–87
Bourmont, General Louis-Auguste, 265
Bousbeck, 30, 31; Vandamme's capture of, 31
Braunau, 186, 191
Breda, Holland, 10
Bremen, 38, 232–33, 237
Bremen troop training, by Vandamme, 232–33

Breskens, 35, 36
Breslau, 178, 180, 228; capitulation of, 171
Breslau, siege of, 163–69; failed French attack in, 165, 318n34; Thile's suburbs burning in, 163, 318n25; Vandamme's command of, 163–69, 318n28
Brieg, 165, 167, 171
Brie-Infanterie, 7
Brisach, 104–105
Britain, 207, 261
Britannique, Hôtel de, 203
British Isles invasion, 113, 119, 121
Bruchsal, 125
Brugant, General of Brigade, 18
Bruges, 26, 34, 113
Brumaire coup d'état, 71, 100–102
Bruneau, Albertine (stepsister), 5, 7
Bruneau, Eloi, 5
Brune, Marshal Guillaume-Marie, 90, 91–98, 100, 102, 109, 116, 203, 289
Brünn, 133–35, 137, 139
Brunswick, Charles William, duke of, 9
Brussels, 263, 265, 274, 277
Bry, 270
Bryeon, 267
Buderich, battle for, 37–38
Budweis, 193
Bülow, General Friedrich Wilhelm von, 241, 247, 265–67, 269, 271, 273, 276
Bush Hill, 293
Bussy, 267
Butschowitz, 143
Buxhöwden, General Friedrich Wilhelm, 127, 132, 135–38, 141–43

Cadsand, island of, 35
Caestre, 29
Caffarelli, General Louis-Marie, 137
Calais, 111
Calvados, 73
Calw, 62
Cambrai, 285, 287
Campaign of 1800, 103–109; Austrian grand plan for, 103–104, 310n10; First Consul Bonaparte's plan for, 104, 310n13
Campaign of 1805, Eastern European war and, 119
Campo Formio, Treaty of, 72, 75, 108
Camrer, General, 179
Candras, General Jacques-Lazare, 124–25, 145
Capetian, 117
Capet, Louis, 10. *See also* Louis XVI, King
Carlsruhe, 62
Carnot, Lazare, 15, 17, 22, 28, 49, 51, 52, 59, 60, 71; Austrian battle plan of, 51–52, 303n28; as "Organizer of Victory," 51
Carolingian empire, 121
Carra Saint-Cyr, General Claude Carra, 230, 232–33
Cassel, France, 4, 5, 43, 44, 64, 98, 109–10, 145–46, 180, 259–60, 290–92, 294–95; Jacobin Club of, 26–27, 42–43, 300n1, 300n6; Vandamme's Free Company at, 11–12

Castricum, 95
Casualties, in Menin-Courtrai battle, 31–32, 300n19, 301n20
Catherine, Princess of Würtemberg, 160
Catholic Church, 118; Revolution's impact on, 7
Catholics, of France, 45
Caulaincourt, General Armand, 240
Central Europe (1809): Napoleon's assessment of, 183; Napoleon's forces in, 184; rumors of war in, 185
Chamber of Elders, 101
Chamber of Five Hundred, 71, 83, 88, 101
Chamber of Representatives, 279–82
Chambord, 47
Chanlaire, M. de, 203
Charlemagne's relics, 121
Charleroi, 33, 264–66
Charles, archduke of Austria, 52–55, 59–62, 65, 76, 77, 122, 128, 129, 131, 182–84, 186–89, 192, 194–95, 197
Charles John, crown prince of Sweden, 229, 237, 239, 241, 256. *See also* Bernadotte, Marshal Jean-Baptiste-Jules
Charles, Major, 39
Charles X, King, 295
Chartres, canon of (Sieyès), 100
Chasseurs du Mont-de-Cassel, 9, 29
Chatham, Lord, 96
Chaumont, 277
Cherbourg, 73, 210
Cher River, 286
Cindy, 265
Clairfayt, General, 29–32, 45, 47
Clarke, General Henry-Jacques, 202, 205
Clausewitz, Carl von, 219
Cleves, 38
Club de Clichy, 47, 303n14
Coalition Army, 241, 243; retreat of, 245, 330n55; role of in Kulm disaster, 246–51, 254; Vandamme's defeat and, 254. *See also* Allied Army(ies); First Coalition; Second Coalition; Third Coalition
Coalition forces, in Belgium, 263
Coburg, prince of, 10, 17, 29, 33
Collège des Récollets, 5
Colmar, 81, 83
Commissioners of War, 28
Commission of Organization, 43
Committee of Public Safety, 17, 19, 20, 41, 43, 44, 56; dominant members of, 22; Vandamme's relationship with, 28, 41, 300n9
Compère, General Claude-Antoine, 37, 41, 77, 82, 85
Concordat, 110
Condé, prince of, 47, 48
Confederation of the Rhine, 156
Constance, Lake of, 77, 104, 106
Constantine, Grand Duke, 135, 140, 251–52
Constitutional monarchy, 7, 9
Constitution Club, 26
Continental System, 209
Copenhagen, 235, 237, 255

INDEX

Coquengeiot, Chef de Bataillon, 80, 88
Corbineau, General, 248
Cossacks, of Russia, 236, 251, 259–60
Coster, Thérèse de (grandmother), 4
Courtrai, battle for, 29–31, 32, 300n14
Coutard, Colonel, 188
Couthon, Georges-Auguste, 22
Crossen, 160–61
Custine de Sarreck, General Adam-Philippe, 12
Cuxhaven, 232

Daendels, General Hermann-Wilhelm, 36, 92, 93
Danes, 229, 234–37
Danton, Georges-Jacques, 23
Danube, campaigns of, 57
Danube River, 52–54, 59, 105–107, 126–27, 129–32, 156, 182, 184–89, 191–97
Danzig, siege of, 179
Davaine, General Jean-Baptiste, 16–20
David, Jacques-Louis, 118
Davout, General Louis N., 116; brigade of, 66; malaria, in troops of, 36
Davout, Marshal Louis N., 139, 157, 183–84, 186–89, 191–92, 219, 223–24, 230–31, 233–39, 262, 279, 280–81, 283–87; army divisions of, 143, 187; Austerlitz Campaign and, 125–28, 135, 137; authority of, 230; First Corps of, 114, 222; headquarters of, 282; reputation of, 191, 236; Third Corps of, 113, 125–26, 136, 160, 187, 189, 193–94; Vandamme praised by, 236–39, 328n26
Declaration of the Rights of Man and Citizen, 6
Dejean, General Pierre-François, 259
Delaborde, Henri-François, 80
Delmas, General Antoine-Guillaume, 62
Denmark, 209, 238; neutrality of, 229, 234
Dennewitz, 254, 256, 265
d'Erlon, General J. B., 259, 264, 269, 333n31
Deroy, General Bernhard, 161–67, 175–76
Desaix, General Louis-Charles, 53, 55, 59, 62–67
Desenfans, General Nicolas-Joseph, 30
Desept, 88
Dessau, 211, 242
Dessolle, General Jean-Joseph, 104
Deswarte: Alcide, 292; Charles (brother-in-law), 292; Marie-Thérèse, 292; Pauline, 292; Uranie, 292; Valentine (sister), 290–92
Deux-Ponts, 46
Deventer, 39
Diepenbroeck, General, 35
Dieppe, 73
Diersheim, 65, 66
Diersheim River, Vandamme's crossing at, 65, 66, 67, 304n50
Digner, Leopold, 196
Dijon, 103
Dillingen, 55, 186
Dinant, 278–79

Dionède (son), 295
Directory, government of, 44, 46–51, 56, 58, 60, 64, 74–76, 78–80, 89, 90, 95, 97–98, 296; corruption of, 115–16; overthrow of, 99–101, 309n3
Dixmude, 17
Dohna, 245, 247, 249
Domon, General Jean-Simon, 268
Donauwörth, 62, 126, 186, 201
Don Quixote, 78
D'Oubril, Monsieur, 155
Dover, 110
Dresden, 160, 230, 234, 237, 242–45, 247–48, 254
Drouet, General Jean-Baptiste, 141, 264
Duben, 242
Du Casse, Albert, xii
Ducos, Roger, 101
Dufour, General François-Marie, 230, 239
Dufour, General Georges-Joseph, 64
Duhesme, General of Division Philibert-Guillaume, 50, 52, 53, 55, 56, 58, 59, 65, 66
Dumonceau, General Jean-Baptiste, 91–94, 230, 239, 249
Dumouriez, General Charles-François, 9–11, 295
Dundas, General, 95
Dunkirk, France, 4, 15, 16, 19, 20, 111, 255, 262; siege of, 12–13
Dupleix, Jérôme's supply chief, 215–16, 217, 220
Durnstein, battle of, 128
Düsseldorf, 52, 61
Duveyrier, Adjutant Commander, 166, 168–69
Dyle River, 273, 275–77

Eckmühl, 188–89, 191, 201, 231; Battle of, 296
Eckmühl, prince of, 151, 219, 224–26, 233, 237. See also Davout, General Louis N.
Ecluse, capture of, 36
Education, of Vandamme, 4–5, 297n4
Egypt, 74–76, 100, 102, 112, 114, 120, 185
Eilenburg, 242
Elba: Napoleon exiled to, 257; Napoleon returns from, 260–61
Elbe, lower region of, 230, 232, 237
Elbe River, 156, 158, 211–12, 228, 230, 232–37, 240, 243–45, 247
Elbhause, 212
Ellwangen, 125
Elysée, 279
Emperor Napoleon. See Bonaparte, Emperor Napoleon
Empire, of Napoleon, 296
Engen, 105–106
England, 18, 38, 234, 295; Anglo-Russian army and, 95; army of, 24, 38, 72–74, 113–15, 122; Austrian support from, 75, 108, 121; Bonaparte's conflict with, 111; Coalition armies support by, 24, 26, 75; French hostilities and, 114; French insurgents and, 45, 73; invasion of, 73; pope and, 118; Prussians and, 133; sea

England *(continued)*
  domination by, 110–11; at war with France, 109–11, 183, 209
English Channel, 73
Enns River, 145, 194
Erfurt, 183
Ergoldsbach, 188–89
Ernouf, General Jean-Augustin, 20, 76, 79–80
Erzgebirge Mountains, 243, 245
Escaut River, 32
Essenbach, 188, 189
Essen, General, 95, 96
Essling, 194
Esslingen, 77
Estates General, 6
Etampes, 283
Etaples, 206
Eugène (Beauharnais), Prince, viceroy of Italy, 184, 197, 219, 228, 230–31, 244
Europe, 109, 127, 183, 209; aristocrats of, 120; control of, 155–56, 181; Napoleon's desire for peace in, 157, 209; ports of, 181; reshaping map of, 240. *See also* Central Europe (1809)
European ports, Napoleon's control of, 181
Executive Directory, 62, 71, 72, 81, 84, 88, 89
Exelmans, General Rémy-Joseph, 264, 266, 271, 273–75, 277, 281
Eylau, 173, 211, 231; battle at, 175

Fain, Baron Agathon Jean, 253
Family, of Vandamme, 4–5, 297nn2–3; Albertine (stepsister), 5, 7; Baert, Barbara Françoise (mother), 4; Baert, Dominique (grandfather), 4; Coster, Thérèse de (maternal grandmother), 4; Deswarte, Alcide, 292; Deswarte, Charles, 292; Deswarte, Marie-Thérèse, 292; Deswarte, Pauline, 292; Deswarte, Uranie, 292; Dionède (son), 295; family life and, xi–xii, 4–6, 7; Joseph-François (uncle), 4; Louis François Corneille (brother), 4, 292; Maurice Joseph Bruno (father), 4–5; origins of, 4; Pyn, Jeanne Marie (paternal grandparent), 4; René (paternal grandparent), 4; Termyn, Catherine (stepmother), 5, 7, 221; t'Kint, Sophie (wife), 108, 290, 292, 295; Valentine Barbara Isabelle (sister), 290–92
Farine, Captain Pierre-Joseph, 74
Feldbach, 198
Ferdinand, Archduke, 122, 127
Ferey, General Claude-François, 124, 139
Férino, General Pierre-Marie, 53, 55, 56, 62, 76–78
Ferrand, General Jacques, 20, 26
Finland, 209, 229
First Army, 218, 220, 223
First Coalition, 24, 26, 40, 75, 155
First Consul Bonaparte, 101–104, 107–12, 114–15, 156, 160, 310n4; Campaign of 1800, plan of, 104, 310n13; emperor aspirations of, 114–15, 311n32; as French emperor, 115–16; Moreau versus, 103, 104, 106–107, 310n4, 310n11; northern inspection tour of, 111–12; Vandamme rewarded by, 112, 114, 311n28
First Empire, 295
First Gentleman of the Chamber, 257
Flanders, 5, 36, 146
Fleurus, 33, 264–66, 270, 273, 282
Flushing, 36
Fontainebleau, 257
Food, shortage of, 40, 61, 126–27, 129–31, 212–13, 215–16, 218, 286
Fort Ecluse, siege of, 35–36
Fouché, Joseph, 100, 279, 282–84, 287
Fournier, Captain, 203
Fourth Auxiliary Battalion of the Colonies. *See* Martinique colonial regiment
Fourth Regiment, 118, 144–45; eagle flag, loss of, 140–41; of Light Infantry, 139; Napoleon replaces eagle flag of, 144–45, 316n62
Fox, Charles James, 156
Fraint, General Louis, 136–37
France: civil war in, 45; continent dominated by, 110; in 1812, 208; financial crisis in, 157; Imperial Guard of, 141; Prussian peace treaty with, 41; Prussia's relationship with, 155–56; Vandamme returns to, 257
France, Hôtel de, 203
Francis I, emperor of Austria, 108, 131, 133, 135, 143, 182, 202, 228
Frankenstein, 176
Frankfort, 52, 53, 60, 160
Frederick I, king of Würtemberg, 185
Frederick, Peter, duke of Oldenburg, 210
Frederick the Great, 164, 175, 190
Frederick William III, king of Prussia, 133, 156–57, 183, 229, 247
Freiburg, 56, 105
French Allied Army, 171
French Army: Austrian Campaign (1809) and, 185; Belgian occupation by, 36; condition of, 23–24, 46–47, 50–51, 75–76, 300n1, 300n3; conduct of, 80–84; deterioration of, 8, 51, 54, 60–61, 303n25; drafting soldiers for, 23–24, 99–100, 208, 300n2; Emperor Napoleon's return and, 262; French émigrés versus, 29, 34–35, 73; generals' fate in, 14, 19–20, 41, 124, 125; Holland campaign of, 38–39, 98; of Italy, 99; "king's army" versus "bourgeois" army of, 8; local population and, 26–27, 50, 300n7; looting/pillaging by, 42, 46, 51, 54, 58–59, 60–61, 82, 89, 280, 304n31; Louis XVIII, rejection by, 281–83, 334n56; Louis XVIII's purge of, 285–88, 335n75; malaria and, 36, 301n33; monarchy's restoration and, 284–85, 335n66; Napoleon's defeat and, 276–80; Napoleon's reorganization of, 113–14, 229–30, 241; officer corps of, 8, 11, 298n16, 298nn8–9; Paris evacuation by, 282–83; reorganization of, 33, 64, 72, 75; Revolution's impact on, 4, 6–8, 11, 298n16, 298nn8–9; Rhine Campaign and,

75, 79–81; transformation of, 295; volunteers in, 9, 23; Waterloo Campaign, placements of, 264–68. *See also* Grande Armée; Laws of 24 February
French duplicity, over Hanover, 156
French émigrés, 47; captured, fate of, 17, 34–35, 39, 301n31, 301nn28–29; French Army versus, 29, 34–35, 73; Vandamme's capture of, 17, 34–35, 39, 301n31, 301nn28–29. *See also* Law of Hostages
French monarchy, Vandamme's relationship with, 257–59
French monarchy, restoration, 257; Coalition forces support for, 284; French army support for, 284–85, 335n66; French officers submit to, 285–86
French Republic, 8, 24
French Republican Army, 12, 23, 34, 60
French Revolution, xii, 3, 4. *See also* Revolution
French Revolutionary Army, xi, 8, 295
Freudenstadt, 53
Friederichstadt, 176
Friedland, battle of, 176, 179, 209, 211
Frimont, General, 263
Frise, 39
Fructidor coup d'état, 71, 99; Vandamme affected by, 71–72, 89
Furnes, 16–20, 29, 42
Furnes, capture of, 17
Fürstenberg, prince of, 85
Fürstenstein, count of, 215

Gabel, 242
Galles, Chef de Bataillon Morard de, 291
Gambsheim, 53
Garrau, Pierre Anselme, 56
Gazan, General Honoré Theodore, 128
Geismar, Colonel Baron, 259–60
Gembloux, 273–75
"General of Division," "Marshal of Empire" versus, 298n10
Generals, republican, 114
Gengenbach, 66, 70
George III, King, 156
Gérard, General Maurice-Etienne, Count, 112, 264, 267–69, 271–78, 284
Germany, 52, 58, 59, 82, 85–87, 89, 102–105, 108–109, 120–22, 125, 157, 182–87, 210, 228; Army of, 185–86
Ghent, 4, 26, 108, 292, 294–95
Gilly, 266
Girard, General Jean-Baptiste, baron, 267–68
Girondin faction, of Jacobins, 22–23
Girzikowitz, 137
Giulay, General, 197
Glatz, 171, 175–77, 179
Gleisdorff, 198
Glogau, 168, 171, 212; capture of, 176–77; surrender of, 163; Vandamme's siege of, 161–63
Goerzten, count of, 175, 179, 321n86
Goettweig, abby of, 195
Goldbach, 137–39, 141–42

Goldbach Brook, 135–36
Gottweg, 195
Gougelot, General Jean-Florimond, 17–18
Goullu, General François, 105
Gouvion, General of Brigade Louis-Jean, 94, 95
Government, revolutionary, 11, 12, 24
Grand Bailli of Tübingen, 81, 85, 86
Grande Armée, 112, 124–25, 143, 146, 158, 160–64, 166, 169, 179, 181–82; Austerlitz Campaign, readiness of for, 122–23, 312n2; looting/pillaging by, 129–31; of Napoleon, 218, 293; Sixtieth Bulletin of, 174; Thirty-eighth Bulletin of, 163. *See also* Army Corps; Army Division(s); French Army
Grande Armée officers, immigration of to United States, 293–94, 336n17, 337n25
Grand Leez, 277
Gratz, 197
Gregorian calendar, 127, 314n22
Grenoble, 261
Grodno, 218, 220, 222–24
Groningen, 39
Gross Beeren, 247, 254, 256
Grouchy, Marshall Emmanuel, 264, 293; Vandamme's relationship with, 3; Waterloo Campaign, command of, 266–80
Gudin, General Charles-Etienne, 137, 143, 187–89
Guicchivitz, 168
Guilleminot, Armand-Charles, 295
Gulf of Juan, 260
Guntzbourg, Vandamme's attack on, 54
Gunzburg, 126

Haarburg, 235
Haarlem, 95
Haeuw, Clement, 291
Haffner, Colonel, 234, 236
The Hague, Holland, 92
Hamburg: government of, 238; Napoleon's punishment of, 235, 238, 328n21; siege of, 230–39, 241
Hammerstein, General, 213
Hanover, 113, 125, 133, 156; French duplicity over, 156
Hanseatic Legion, 235, 237–38
Hapsburgs, 120–21
Hardewick, 39
Harty, General Olivier, 204
Haussmann, Commissioner Nicolas: army generals denounced by, 62–63; report on Heidenheim battle, 56–59
Haute Vienne, 289
Haxo, General Nicolas, Count, 249, 284
Haxo, Lieutenant Colonel, commander of Schweidnitz, 172
Hazebrouck, 26, 27, 207
Hébertists, 23
Hébert, Jacques-René, 23
Hechingen, prince of, 85, 86
Hédouville, General Joseph, 161; Vandamme's relationship with, 164–68, 170–71, 177, 216

Heer, baron of, 86
Heidenheim, 59, 186; Vandamme's defeat at, 55–56
Helder, 39, 91, 97
Hellendorf, 246; Vandamme's capture of, 243–44, 330nn51–52
Helvétie, 72, 75
Herberstein, 198
Hermann, General, 91, 93, 96
Hessians, 38
Hezongen, 37
Hiller, General Johann von, 184, 187, 189
Hoche, General Louis-Lazare, 16–18, 44, 45, 64–68, 73
Hoffenberg, 53, 66–68
Hohenlinden, 109
Hohentwiel, fort of, 105
Hohenzollern, Prince Friedrich Franz, 174, 184, 187–88
Hollabrünn, 132
Holland, 5, 11, 33, 52, 102, 107, 112, 116, 183; conquest of, 38–39
Holland Campaigns (1799), 25, 90–98, 309nn93–95; Vandamme's role in, 90–98
Hollenburg, 195
Hollendorf, 244, 246
Holstien, 237
Holy Roman Emperor, 121
Hondschoote, 18; battle of, 12–16; Vandamme's role at, 12–14, 298n17; victory at, 15
Hoorn, 93, 94
Horb, 82
Houchard, General of Division Jean-Nicolas, 12–15
Hoyerswerda, 242
Hube, 167
Hugel, General of Brigade, 190, 199, 200
Hulot, General Etienne, 268
Humbert, General Jean-Joseph, 206
Hundred Days, 287
Huningue, 61, 62, 64
Hussardes, of Austria, 54, 58

Iberian Peninsula: Napoleon's focus on, 181–83, 208; Napoleon's setbacks on, 207
Iller River, 106–107, 126–27
Imperial Guard: of France, 141; of Russia, 135, 138, 139, 141, 144, 264, 268
Ingolstadt, 126, 186–87
Inn River, 129, 184, 186, 191
Ionian Islands, 120
Ireland. 65, 74, 206
Irish Legion, 36
Iron Marshal, 191, 238. See also Davout, Marshal Louis N.
Isar River, 59, 129, 186–87
Isoré, Representative of the People, 44
Italian campaign, 112
Italy: end of war in, 109; kingdom of, 121

Jacobin Club, of Cassel, 26–27, 42–43, 300n1, 300n6; Vandamme's denouncement by, 26–27, 42–43, 49–50, 300n6, 302n1
Jacobin Representatives, 43

Jacobin(s), 11, 41, 42, 44–47, 89, 99–101, 115, 287, 291; Club, of Cassel, 26–27, 42–43, 300n1, 300n6; Girondin faction of, 22–23; rise/fall of, 22–23; impact on Vandamme's military career, 26–27, 42–43, 49–50, 300n6, 302n1; Vandamme's dissatisfaction with, 28, 42. See also Reign of Terror
Jardon, General of Brigade Henri-Antoine, 77, 103
Jargeur, 283–84
Jellacic, General Franz, 128
Jemappes, battle of, 9–10
Jena, 183, 187; battle of, 157–58
Jena-Auerstädt, 155, 256
Jérôme, king of Westphalia, 3, 149, 208, 211, 215, 218; Vandamme's relationship with, 211, 214–17, 221–23, 225–26
Jérôme, Prince, xii, 3, 149, 160–67, 172–78, 211, 213–26, 229, 296; Glogau siege and, 161–63; Vandamme's relationship with, 3, 163–71, 174–75, 177, 178. See also Bonaparte, Jérôme; Jérôme, King of Westphalia
"Jesuit Bark," for malaria, 36
Joachim, king of Naples, 228, 253. See also Murat, Marshal Joachim
John, Archduke, 109, 122, 128, 129, 131, 182, 193
Jomini, General Antoine-Henri, 75
Joseph, King, 207. See also Bonaparte, Joseph (brother)
Joubert, Marshal Barthélemy-Catherine, 56, 100, 255, 258
Jourdan, Marshal Jean-Baptiste, 13, 15, 17, 20, 23, 26, 33, 38, 52–55, 59, 64, 74–81, 87, 259; resignation of, 80; Vandamme's relationship with, 77–78
Jourdan's *levée en masse*, 99
Julian calendar, 127, 314n22
Junot, General Andoche, 181

Kalisch, 162, 212–13
Kamensky, General of Division Alexander, 138
Karwitz, 248
Kastrikum, 95
Katzbach, 254, 256
Kaunitz, prince of, 133
Kebl, 53
Kechler, Major, 195
Kehl, 61–64, 74, 79, 105
Kellermann, General François-Etienne, 9, 264, 284
Kerner, Colonel, 190, 197
Kilchberg, 81
Killem, 13
Kindberg, 197
Kinzig River, 53, 66, 76, 79, 105
Kivov, 255
Kléber, General Jean-Baptiste, 52
Kleinburg, 168
Klein-Schottgau, 168
Kleist, General Frederick Heinrich, 247, 249–51, 254, 268
Klettendorf, 168

INDEX

Klosterneuburg, abby of, 195
Klundert, Holland, 10, 12
Knights Hospitaler of Saint John of Jerusalem (Knights of Malta), 75, 120
Kobelnitz, 135, 137, 139
Koenigstein, 242
Koenigstein Plateau, 243
Kollowart, General John Charles, 135, 138, 141, 184, 186, 188
Kolzakov, Paul Andréiévitch, 251, 331n76; *Mémoires* of, 251–52
Kosel, 171; siege of, 175–76
Kovno, 218, 220
Krauth, Léopold, 81, 83, 88
Kray, General Paul, 103, 106–109
Krems, 192–93, 195, 202
Kristern, 168
Krumbach, 79
Kulm, xii, 227, 229, 231, 233, 235, 237, 239, 241, 243
Kulm, disaster at, 245–51; Coalition forces' role in, 254; Napoleon places blame for, 253–54; Vandamme as prisoner after, 252–53, 260, 331n81
Kutusov, General Mikhail, 127–29, 129, 131–33, 138, 227–28

Laber River, 187
La Bourdonnaye, 7
Labourdonnaye, General Anne-François, 7, 10, 298n13
Lacombe, Representative, 35
Lacour, General, 41
La Frégate, 153, 260, 290, 294–95
Lahn, 53
La Hougue, 73
Laix, 79
Lake of Constance, 77, 104, 106
Landau, 53
Landsberg, 126, 129
Landshut, 146, 187–88, 191
Langeron, General A., 138
Lannes, Marshal Jean, 125–29, 132, 135, 137, 139, 160, 187–89, 194
Laon, 263, 277, 279
Laroche-Dubouscat, General Antoine, 53, 55, 62
Latour, General (Austrian), 53, 54, 59–61, 65
Latour-Maubourg, General Marie-Victor, 218
Laurent, General François-Guillaume, 33–37
Laval, General, 103
Law of Hostages, 100, 309n1
Laws of 24 February, 24, 300n2
Lech River, 77, 126, 186
Lecourbe, General Claude-Jacques, 103–107
Lee, William, 293
Lefebvre, Marshal François-Joseph, 74, 76, 78, 166, 175–76, 179, 184, 186–89, 321n84
Lefol, General, 268
Légion de La Châtre, 29
Legion of Honor, 312n40; Vandamme nominates officers/men for, 145, 316n63; Vandamme's receipt of, 114, 117, 143, 145, 312n41, 316n63

Legislative Assembly, 7, 8
Legrand, General Claude-Juste, 80, 124, 126, 136–38, 141–42; Strasbourg Affair and, 180, 321n89
Le Havre, 73, 294
Lehe, 38
Leipzig, 234, 254–56
Lenz, 192
Leoben, 66, 109
Leval, General of Division Jean-François, 76, 106, 146, 157
Leyden, Holland, 10
Lichtenau, 62
Lichtenstein, 188
Liechtenstein, Prince Johann, 138
Liège, 263, 265–66, 273–74
Ligny, 265–70, 272–74, 279, 282
Ligny Campaign, *258*
Ligny Stream, 268
Lille, France, xii, 4, 7, 11, 12, 29–33, 108, 110–12, 207, 263, 292
Limale, 275
Limoges, 289–90
Lindach, 189
Lintz, 131
Linz, 191–94, 202
Lippe, 230
Lipsk, 220
Liptingen, 78
Lisbon, 181, 207
Lissa, 163–64
Lobau, General Georges, 194–95, 264, 268, 272
Lodi, 52
Loiben, 128
Loire River, 125, 279, 283–84, 286–87, 290
London, 24, 96, 97
Lonjumeau, 283
Loo, 39
Lorge, General Jean-Thomas, 105, 107
Lorient, 6
Lorraine-Vaudemont, prince of, 105–106
Louis XIV, King, 39
Louis XVI, King, 3, 6, 24, 287, 295; fate of, 10, 22–23
Louis XVIII, King, 47, 254; French Army, purging by, 285–88, 335n75; French Army's rejection of, 281–83, 334n56; restoration of, 257, 260–61, 281, 283–87, 289, 293–94, 332n1
Louis, Archduke, 184, 187
Louise, Queen, 156
Louis-Philippe, king of France, 295
Louvre, 118
Lubeck, 235
Lutzen, battle of, 235
Lyon, 23, 261
Lys River, 30–32, 110

Macaulay, Isaac, 293
Macdonald, Etienne-Jacques: as general, 39, 75, 108–109, 201, 211; as marshal, 197–98, 254, 256, 259, 287–88
Mack, General Karl Freiherr, 30, 122, 126–29
Macon, General Pierre, 131

Magdeburg, 158, 163, 168, 230–31, 234, 241; Vandamme's seige of, 158, 160
Mainburg, 59
Malaria: French Army and, 36, 301n33; "Jesuit Bark" for, 36
Malas, General, 104
Malbrancq, General, 31
Malet, General Claude-François, 327n1
Malher, General Jean-Pierre, 157
Malines, 43
Malmaison, 279
Malta, 75
Manche, 73
Mannheim, 45
Mansion-House Hotel, 293
Mantua, 65, 122
Marchand, General Jean-Gabriel, 214, 216
Marcus, The (ship), 294
Marengo, battle of, 108
Maret, Hughes-Bernard, duke of, 253
Margaron, General Pierre, 124
Maria Louise, princess of Austria, 208, 240
Marie, Colonel, 140
Marmont, Marshal Auguste-Frédéric, 113, 125–27, 126, 131, 201
Marseilles, 289
Marshal de Biron, military school, 5–6
"Marshal of the Empire," 116, 311nn33–35; "General of Division" versus, 298n10
Marshal of France, 278
Martinique, 6
Martinique colonial regiment, 5
Masonic Hall in Philadelphia, 293
Masséna, 80, 95, 99, 100, 103–104, 131, 187, 189, 207
Masséna, General, 75
Masséna, Marshal, 122, 184, 207
Matis, Colonel, 268
Mautern, 199
Maxen, 247, 249
Mayence, 45, 157; Army of, 72, 74–76
Meaux, 280
Mecklenburg, 238
Meerdick, 12
Melas, General Michael Friedrich, 103–104
Mellery, 273, 277
Memmingen, 126–27, 127, 129
Ménard, General Jean-François, 80
Menin, 15, 16, 32, 34
Menin-Courtrai battle: casualty figures for, 31–32, 300n19, 301n20; Vandamme's role in, 29–31, 34, 300n14
Menitz Lake, 141
Menneville, M. Mayor of Boulogne, 203–205, 207
Merlin, Representative, 44
Merveldt, General Max, 129
Metternich, Prince Clemens Lothar, 240
Metzer, 88
Meuse River, 37
Mézières, 262, 279
Michaud, General Pierre-Antoine, 29, 32, 74
Milan, 52, 121–22, 181
Milet de Mureau, General Louis-Marie, 80

Milhaud, General Edouard-Jean, 285
Military campaigns, of Vandamme: Army of England, forays in, 73–74; Austerlitz battle, 136–42; Austerlitz Campaign, 125–27, 129–30, 132–33, 313n11; Bousbeck capture in, 31; Bremen troop training in, 232–33; Breslau siege in, 163–69; Diersheim river crossing in, 65, 66, 67, 304n50; French émigrés captured during, 17, 34–35, 39, 301n31, 301nn28–29; Furnes capture in, 17; Glogau siege in, 161–63; Guntzbourg surprise attack in, 54; Heidenheim defeat in, 55–56; Hellendorf capture in, 243–44, 330nn51–52; Holland Campaigns (1799), 90–98; Hondschoote battle, 12–14, 298n17; Legion of Honor nominations in, 145, 316n63; Magdeburg siege, 158, 160; Menin and Courtrai battle in, 29–31, 34, 300n14; Moesskirch capture in, 106; Neiss siege, 175–80, 320n77; Nieuwpoort siege, 17–19, 34–35, 301n27; Poland invasion (1812), 212–15; prisoners of war captured in, 39, 126–27, 193, 302n43, 323n29; Rhine Campaign (1799), 76–77; Silesian Campaign, 185–86; Stokach battle, 105–106; Töeplitz, march on, 245–49, 252–53; Waterloo Campaign, 264–68. *See also* Accusations, against Vandamme; Military career, of Vandamme; Relationship(s), of Vandamme
Military career, of Vandamme, xii, 3–6, 27, 41, 63, 296; army discharge, 6, 225–26; denouncements in, 80–89, 307n52; deterioration of, 210–26; dissatisfaction in, 3, 201–202, 288; end of, 27, 288; First Consul rewards, 112, 114, 311n28; Free Company formation, 8–9, 298n11; French émigrés' impact on, 17, 34–35, 39, 301nn28–29; Fructidor coup d'état, impact on, 71–72, 89; government's support in, 50–51; Hondschoote command, 14–15, 299n20; Italy familiarization trip, 109, 311n22; Jacobin Club denouncement, 26–27, 42–43, 49–50, 300n6, 302n1; Kulm disaster, 245–51, 331n67; Legion of Honor award, 114, 117, 143, 312n41; in Martinique, 6; medical leave in, 62, 63–64, 72, 98, 145–46, 202; military school and, 5–6, 297n4; Mont-de-Cassel and, 12; Pichegru relationship, impact on, 48–50; rapid rise in, 15–16, 299n22; reinstatement in, 44, 229, 302nn9–11; relieved of command, 19–20, 221–23, 225–26; resignation attempt, 233; Revolution's impact on, 6–7, 12, 15–16, 89, 298n16, 299n22; Strasbourg Affair and, 180, 321n90; talent display in, 8, 298n10; threat to abandon career, 69, 71, 305n1; "Vandamme Affair," 80–84, 89, 307nn66–67; Vandamme as war trophy prisoner, 252–53, 260; Vendée exile assignment, 45; Westphalian troop command in, 210–21; Würtemberg division command in, 160–63, 168–73, 175–77, 179, 185–86, 190–91.

See also Accusations, against Vandamme; Military campaigns, of Vandamme; Personality/character, of Vandamme; Relationship(s), of Vandamme
Military headquarters, of Vandamme: Andelfingen, 80; Bautzen, 242; Boulogne, 203–206; Bremen, 232–33; Cherbourg, 73; Courtrai, 30; Dessau, 211; Hondschoote, 14; Lille, 108; Lissa, 163; Magdeburg, 241; Saint-Omer, 112; Steenvoorde, 26; Strasbourg, 74; Vierzon, 286; Wurben, 172; Zillebeke, 32
Military rank, of Vandamme: captain, 8–9, 12; corporal, 6; general, xi, xii, 4; general of brigade, 3–4, 15–16, 43–45, 65, 69, 74; general of division, 4, 37, 40, 43, 74, 76, 84, 103, 112, 124, 166; lieutenant colonel, 12; lieutenant general, 257; marshal's baton and, 201–202; military governor, 110, 114; private, 3, 7; sergeant, 6
Military school, 5–6, 297n4
Miloradovitch, General Mikhail Andreivitch, 138, 141
Minucci, General, 164–65, 167–68, 168, 172
Mir, 225
Mitchell, Vice-Admiral Andrew, 91
Moelk, abby of, 195
Moesskirch, capture of, 106
Moldavia, 209
Molitor, General Gabriel-Jean, 103, 105–106, 108
Montbrun, General, 165–68, 172, 176, 188
Mont-de-Cassel, Chasseurs du, 9, 29
Montreuil, 113
Montrouge, 281
Mont St. Jean, 276
Moore, General Sir John, 91, 94, 96
Morand, General Charles-Antoine, 187–88, 232–33
Morard, Chef de Bataillon, 291–92
Moravia, 132–33
Moreau, General of Division Jean-Victor, 28–41, 46, 48–55, 59–69, 100, 102–109; First Consul Bonaparte versus, 103, 104, 106–107, 310n4, 310n11; Vandamme's relationship with, 26, 42–44, 63–64, 67–69, 102–103
Mortier, Marshal Adolphe-Edouard, 113, 245, 249–50, 254
Moscow, 152, 227, 253–55
Moulin, Jacobin Jean-François, 99
Müffling, Major General Friedrich Carl von, 267, 333n25
Muhldorf, 191
Munich, 54, 59, 107–108, 126, 129–30, 186
Münster, 126
Munsterberg, 176
Murat, Marshal Joachim, 126–29, 132, 135, 137, 139, 228, 245–47, 262. *See also* Joachim, King of Naples
Murg River, 53, 57

Nammerhof, 82
Namur, 263, 265, 272, 277–78, 282

Nansouty, 187
Naples, 75, 140, 228, 262
Napoleonic era, xi, xii, 124, 296
Napoleonic France, 257
Napoleon's return from exile, 260–61
National Assembly, 6–8
National Convention, 20, 22
National Guard of Cassel, 94
Necker River, 125
Neerwinden, 10
Neiss, 171
Neiss River, 176
Neiss, seige of, 175–78; capitulation/surrender in, 178; Jérôme credits Vandamme with, 178–79; Vandamme's role in, 175–80, 320n77
Nelson, Lord Horatio, 209
Neresheim, battle of, 54–57
Nesstadt, 198
Netherlands, kingdom of the, 263, 290
Neubronn, General, 190, 191
Neuburg, 126
Neufchâtel, prince of, 213. *See also* Berthier, Marshal Alexander
Neulemback, Drechsler de, 196
Neustadt, 187, 197–98
New Breisach, 79
New Orleans, 293–94
Ney, Marshal Michel, 113, 125–28, 157–58, 160, 162, 173, 245, 247, 254, 256, 265–66, 268–69, 271–72, 274, 333n31
Niemen River, 114, 179, 209, 218, 220
Nienburg, 233
Nieuport, 259
Nieuwpoort, 65; capture of, 35; Vandamme's siege of, 17–19, 34–35, 301n27
Nijmegen, siege and fall of, 37–38, 301n38
Nile, 75
Ninth Corps of the Grande Armée. *See* French Allied Army
Nollendorf, 250
Nordlingen, 54, 125–26
Normandy, 73, 112
North Sea, 93, 112
Norway, 229, 234
Notre Dame Cathedral, 117–18
Nürnberg, 53, 54

Oberkirch, 53, 57
Ochsenhausen, 126–27
Ochsenwerder, 236
Ochs, General Adam von, 212–13, 215
Oder River, 160–61, 163–66, 171, 212, 242
Oder Valley, 160, 176
Offenburg, 68, 76, 79
Ohlan, 165
Oise River, 280
Oldenburg, 210, 232
Old Guard, 276
Olivet, 290
Olmütz, 135, 139
Organizer of Victory, 51
Orleans, 283, 286
Oschen-Werder, Island, 237

Ostend, 16–18, 26, 34
Ostermann-Tolstoy, General Ivan, 244, 246–48, 254
Ostrach River, 78
Otrante, 287
Ottmarshein, 80
Ottoman, 75, 209
Oudinot, Marshal Nicholas-Charles, 184, 202, 242, 247, 256
Outreau, 113, 118
Over-Yssel, 39

Pajol, General Charles-Pierre, 264, 268, 271–72, 275–77
Palace of Peers, 263
Palatinate, 53
Paradies, 105
Paris, France, 11, 19, 20, 99–101, 183–85, 257–61, 279–87; French Army's evacuation from, 282–83; government in, 12, 40; military orders from, 14–16; political intrigue in, 71–73; rumor mill of, 64–65; Vandamme ordered out of, 258, 332n2
Parliament of Paris, 6
Parsdorf, 108
Pas-de-Calais, 110
Patton, General George, 3
Paul I, Tsar, 75, 120
Pavlovna, Princess Anne, 210
Peace of Amiens, 110
Pérignon, General Jean Charles, 44
Personality/character, of Vandamme, xi, 3–5, 15, 26, 49–50, 87, 205, 297n4; compassion in, 70; courting influential friends, 20–21; criticism of authority in, 19, 28, 211, 300n10; currying favor, 20, 299n34; excessive self-confidence in, 16, 29–30, 299n23; Jérôme's assessment of, 178; local populations and, 26–27, 50, 70, 300n7; political values of, 115, 295–96; self-destructive behavior in, 19. *See also* Family, of Vandamme; Military career, of Vandamme; Relationship(s), of Vandamme
Petersburg, 155, 229, 254
Peterson, Johan, 255
Peterswalde, 243–45, 250, 253
Petite-Garenne, 206
Petit Montrouge, 283
Pfaffenhofen, 187
Pforzheim, 53
Philadelphia Patent Floor-Cloth Manufactory, 293
Philippeville, 263, 279
Philippon, General, 249, 251
Pichegru, General Jean-Charles, 32, 33, 37–40, 42–49; resignation of, 48, 303n19; treason of, 46–48, 71–72, 303n13, 303nn14–17; Vandamme's relationship with, 42–43, 48–49, 71–72
Pilica River, 214
Pille, General Louis-Antoine, 44, 302n11
Pinot, Colonel Charles-Antoine, 67
Pirch, 265, 268, 276–77
Piré, General Hippolyte-Marie, 281

Pirna, 243–45, 247, 249, 251
Pitt, William, 96, 156
Pius VII, Pope, 117–18; Concordat with, 110
Plains of Pratzen, 136
Pleiswitz, 239
Poischwitz, 239
Poitevit, Colonel, 124
Poitiers, 286
Poland, 24, 40, 157, 167, 175–76, 179, 184–85, 209–10, 212–13, 219–20, 227–28, 261; Grande Armée attacked in, 173; Vandamme's invasion of, 212–15
Poniatowski, Prince Joseph Anthony, 218, 224, 225, 243, 296
Pont-à-Marcq, 30
Poperinghe, 13, 26; destruction of ordered, 14, 298n19
Po River, 65, 99, 103
Porter, Mr., 293
Portugal, 73, 75, 181; French defeat in, 207–208
Posen, 226
Potsdam, 133, 156
Po Valley, 104, 122
Prague, 240, 242, 244, 247, 252
Pratzeberg, 138
Pratzen Heights, 135–39, 137, 139, 141–42
Pratzen Plateau, 143, 145
Pressburg, 137, 143, 145, 155, 193–94
Priesten, 248
Prina, 251
Pripet Marshes, 218–19
Prisoners of war, 33, 93, 128, 301n25, 308n77; exchange of, 177, 320n78; Vandamme's capture/treatment of, 39, 126–27, 193, 302n43, 323n29
Promised Land, Italy as, 61
Prossnitz, 132
Provan, 13
Provence, count of, 24
Prussia, 7; Austerlitz Campaign and, 128–29, 133, 315n35; Austria's relationship with, 24, 26, 40; France's relationship with, 155–56; French peace treaty with, 41, 86, 118, 121, 155–58, 179, 183, 209–10, 261; Louise, queen of, 156–57; Napoleon's drive into, 158; Napoleon's relationship with, 155–56
Prussian garrison, at Beslau, 175
Prussians, 26, 40, 156–58, 163–68, 170–72, 174–78, 228–31, 240, 250, 262–78, 271, 280–81
Puntowitz, 137
Pyn, Jeanne Marie (paternal grandparent), 4
Pyrenees, 12, 181, 183, 207–209, 240

Quatre Bras, 263–66, 269, 271–72, 274
Quellain, Léon Nicolas, 83, 87, 88

Radziwilow, 129
Raigern, abbey of, 134, 136–37
Rampon, Senator, 204
Rastatt, 53, 57, 72, 81, 82
Ratisbon, 186–89, 201

Raygord, 220
Regensberg, 53
Regiment: Eighty-second, 268; Fourth, 118–19, 139, 140–41, 144–45, 316n62; Martinique colonial, 5; Twenty-eighth, 124; Twenty-fourth of Light Infantry, 7, 124, 140; Twenty-fourth of the Line, 7
Reign of Terror, 22, 28, 41, 42–43, 47, 115–16, 296
Reille, General Honoré-Charles, 264, 280–81
Reims, 262, 280
Reims, Cathedral of, 117
Reinhardt, governor of Glogau, 162
Relationship(s), of Vandamme, 296; with Bonaparte, Napoleon, xi–xii, 3–4, 72–73, 102, 110, 112, 185, 192–93, 222–24, 229, 239, 253–54, 296; with Bonaparte, Prince Joseph, 118; with Carra Saint-Cyr, 232–33; with Coalition armies, 259–60; with Committee of Public Safety, 28, 41, 300n9; with Davout, 191–92, 230–31, 233–34, 236–39, 328n26; with English agents, 27–28, 300n8; with family, 5; with Fredrick I, 185–86, 190–91; with Grouchy, 3; with Hédouville, 164–68; with Isoré, 44; with Jérôme, king of Westphalia, 211, 214–17, 221–23, 225–26; with Jérôme, Prince, 3, 163–71, 174–75, 177, 178; with Jourdan, 77–78; with local populations, 26–27, 50, 300n7; with Marchand, 216; with Maurice Joseph Bruno (father), 5; with Menneville, mayor of Boulogne, 203–206; with Moreau, 26, 42–44, 63–64, 67–69, 102–103; with officers/troops, 145–46; with Pichegru, 42–43, 48–49, 71–72; with restored French monarchy, 257–59; with Soult, 3, 130; with Valentine (sister), 292; with Wollowart, 199–201; Würtemberg officers, 189–90, 199–201; Würtemberg troops, 196, 199
Religious education, 5
Renchen, 67, 68
Reningelts, 13
Rennegels, 26
Representatives: of the Convention, 14; of the People, 11–14, 28, 35, 56
Republic, 8, 14, 20, 23, 27, 28, 35, 39, 42, 46–49, 81, 84, 85, 102, 114–16
Republican ideals, 114
Republicans, 16, 22, 26, 43, 49, 99, 102, 115
Rethel, 279
Reuss-Schleiz, Prince, 246
Reutlingen, 82
Revest, Adjutant Commandant, 213, 236, 248
Revolution, 12, 15, 21, 22, 24, 27, 28, 47, 100, 110, 115, 257, 295–96; impact on French Army, 4, 6–8, 11, 298n16; Vandamme's support for, 7
Revolutionaries, 8
Revolutionary ideals, 27
Revolutionary years, xi, 117
Rexpoede, 13
Reynier, General Jean-Louis, 55, 68, 218, 225

Rhine, 9, 37–38, 64–68, 79–81, 89–91, 102–105, 107–109, 125–26, 262–63
Rhine Campaign (1799), 75–81; Vandamme's role in, 76–77
Rhine campaigns, 57
Rhine/Danube Campaign (1796), 52–54, 59–62, 64–67
Rhine, Upper, 80–83, 87, 88
Rhône River, 289
Richardot, M. de, 239
Riga, 255
Riss River, 106
Rivaud, Commissioner, 49
Rivet, General Jean-Baptiste, 45
Roberjot, French plenipotentiary, 82, 86
Robespierre, Maximillien-François, 22, 47
Rochefort, 279
Rocroy, 263, 279
Romanovs, 120
Rome, 111, 118, 279
Roquencourt, 281
Rosenberg, General, 125, 188
Rosenbert, Prince Franz, 184
Rostollant, Adjutant General Claude, 93
Rottenburg, 82
Rotterdam, Holland, 92
Rottweil, 79
Rousbruge, France, 14, 298n19
Rousbruge-Poperinghe region, France, 14; destruction of villages ordered for, 298n19
Rousseau, Jean-Jacques, 8
Royalists, 35, 45, 46, 89, 100, 257, 259, 261–62, 285, 287, 289
Rozan, 218
Rubicon, 11
Rumburg, 242
Russia, 24, 75, 76, 114, 118, 121, 133, 155–57, 179, 207–11, 229, 234, 239–41, 261; Imperial Guard of, 135, 138, 139, 141, 144, 264, 268
Russian Campaign, 211–25, 296
Russians, retreat of, 239

Saal River, 187, 211
Saarbruck, 49, 50
Saar River, 46
Sackingen, 105
Saint Bernard Pass, 104, 106
Saint-Cyr, Marshal Laurent Gouvion, 45, 46, 48, 53–55, 59, 60, 62–64, 66, 67, 78, 79, 104–107, 204, 242–45, 247, 254, 285, 288
Sainte-Suzanne, General Filles-Joseph, 74, 105–107
Saint-Hilaire, General Louis-Vincent, 126, 135–38, 141–43, 194, 315n44
Saint Just, Louis-Antoine, 22
Saint-Laurent of Camiers, 206
Saint-Louis, cordon rouge of, 47
Saint-Morcouf, 73
Saint-Omer, 112–13
Saint Petersburg, 140
Saint-Poelten, 192
Saint-Six, destruction of ordered, 14, 298n19
Salicete, Cristofora-Antonio, 56

Saligny, General of Division Charles, 124–25, 125
Salome, M., 260
Salzweld, 231
Sambre River, 265, 277–78
San Domingue, 206
Santon Hill, 135
Saratitz, 141
Sardinia, 103
Sarrazin, General of Division Jean, defection of, 206–207, 325n65
Sarrebruck, 46, 57
Satschan Lake, 134–35, 141
Saulty, 12
Sauvenière, 274
Saxe Weimar, duke regent of, 260
Saxony, 158, 209, 212, 242, 244
Schaff, 105
Schaffhausen, 80, 104–105
Scharnhorst, Gerhard Johann, 240
Scheldt River, 36, 203
Schérer, General Barthélemy-Louis, 75
Schiner, General of Brigade Joseph-François, 125, 139, 142
Schnadow, Colonel, 190
Schönbrunn Palace, 132, 144, 156, 202
Schoorl, 93
Schorel, 93
Schwarzach, abbot of, 70
Schwarzenberg, Prince, 218, 220, 241, 244–45, 246, 247–49, 256, 263
Schweidnitz, 171, 178; siege of, 169, 171–74; capitulation in, 174; Jérôme credited with, 171–74; Russian surprise attack in, 173; Vandamme commanding during, 171–74, 173
Schwirchtal, Abbey of, 85
Seckendorf, General Reinhart, 161, 167
Second Army, 109, 218, 219–20, 222
Second Coalition, 75, 84, 99, 108–10
Sedan, 125
Ségur, Philippe-Paul, Napoleon's aide-de-camp, 140, 142
Seine River, 281
Semring Pass, 197
Siegenburg, 187
Sierock, 218
Sieyès, Emmanuel-Joseph, 89, 90, 100–101
Sigmaringen, 79
Silberberg, 171, 179
Silesia, 4, 161, 165, 171, 173–74, 176–80, 210–12, 215–16, 237, 241–43
Silesian Campaign, xii, *159*, 159–66, 234; Vandamme's Würtemberg division in, 185–86
Smolensk, 227
Society of the Friends of the Constitution, 7
Soissons, 280
Sokolnitz, 136, 138, 141
Sokolnitz Castle, 134
Sombreffe, 264–67, 270–71
Sorsum, Baron, 224
Souham, General Joseph, 16, 29, 30, 37, 78, 79

Soult, Marshal Nicolas-Jean de Dieu, 76, 78, 112, 114–17, 203, 266–67, 271, 276, 279, 280; in Austerlitz Campaign, 124–28, 130–33, 137–39, 141, 144–45; Vandamme's relationship with, 3, 130
South German Confederation, 182
Spain, 24, 111, 118, 121, 187, 202, 228; King Joseph's throne in, 181–83, 207, 208
Spire, 125
St. Amand, 267–70
Stanitz, 132–33
St. Anthony, Chapel of, 141
Staré Vinohrady, 138–39
St. Denis, 277, 290
Steenvoorde, 13, 26
Stein, 105
Steinitz, 132
Stendal, 231
Stettin, 160
Steyer, 193–94
Steyr, 145
St. Germain, 281
St. James, Court of, 229
Stockach, battle of, 78–79
Stockholm, 49
Stokach, Vandamme's battle at, 105–106
Stolpen, 242
St. Petersburg, 155, 229
St. Polten, 194–95
Straden, 248
Straits of Gibraltar, 181
Strasbourg, 52, 53, 57, 62–65, 74, 76, 79, 84, 85, 88, 105, 125–26, 180, 185–86
Strasbourg Affair, 180, 321n90
Strehlen, 165, 167; battle of, 318nn36–37
St. Sulpice, 187
Stuttgart, 55, 77, 81, 82, 185
Styrie, government of, 198
Suchet, General Louis-Gabriel, 124
Suvorov-Rymmikski, General Aleksandra V., 76, 96
Suzanne, General (Senator), 203–205
Swabia, 81, 82, 87
Sweden, 49, 229, 237, 239, 241, 256
Swedes, 229, 237, 239
Swiss battalion, 263
Swiss Campaign, 96
Switzerland, 72, 75, 76, 80, 83, 102–103, 106, 109, 116, 121

Talcott, Mr., 293
Talleyrand, Prince Charles-Maurice, 100–101, 157, 202, 261, 287
Taponnier, General Alexandre-Camille, 53
Te Deum, 121
Telnitz, 134–37, 139, 141
Temploux, 258, 277
Termyn, Catherine (stepmother), 5, 221
Teschen, 246
Teste, General François-Antoine, 278
Tettenborn, General, 232, 237
Teugen, 187
Texel, 98

INDEX

Tharreau, General Jean-Victor, 213, 221, 224–25
Thermidorian Directory, 47
Thermidorian Reaction, 41, 51, 56
Thermidorians, 41, 44, 99
Thermopylë, 247
Thévenet, Louis-Marie, 295
Thiébault, General of Brigade Paul-Charles, 142, 230–31
Thielemann, General Johann Adolf von, 265, 268, 270, 273, 275–78
Thile, General, 164–66, 168, 171
Third Army, 218
Third Coalition, 120–21, 312n1
Tilly, 273
Tilsit, 181, 183, 209–10, 218; peace talks at, 179
t'Kint, Sophie (wife), 108, 290, 292, 295
Töeplitz, 245–49, 252–53; Vandamme's march on, 245–49, 252–53
Torgou, 242
Tormassov, General A. P., 219
Torres Vedras Line, 207
Toulon, 23, 104
Toulouse, 73, 289
Tourinnes, 277
Tournai, 32
Tourneur, Vandamme's aide-de-camp, 82, 85
Trachenberg Plan, 241, 245
Trafalgar, 209
Treaty: of Amiens, 110–11, 208, 311n24; of Campo Formio, 72, 75, 108; of Luneville, 109; of Potsdam, 133, 156; of Pressburg, 143, 145; of Schönbrunn, 156, 202; of Tilsit, 210
Triberg, 79
Tribunal, revolutionary, 15, 16
Tübingen, 77; Grand Bailli of, 81, 85, 86
Tuileries, 8, 160
Twedee (Twedel), Lord, 27
Tyrol, 52, 76, 103, 122, 127–28

Ubrecht, 39
Ulm, 78, 79, 104–107, 123, 126–30, 133, 155
United Irishmen, 74
United States, 118, 279, 292–94
Unsebourg, count of (Vandamme), xi, 2, 3, 185, 257
Urach, 82
Uranie, 6, 292

Vallin, General Louis, 278
Valmy, battle of, 9–10
Valmy, Count de (Kellermann), 284
Valois, 117
Van Damme, 4; Louis François Corneille (brother), 4, 7, 292; Maurice Joseph Bruno (father), 4, 5; René (paternal grandparent), 4; Valentine Barbara Isabelle (sister), 4, 7, 292. *See also* Vandamme
"Vandamme Affair," 80–84, 89, 307nn66–67
Vandamme, Commandant at Hondschoote: maintaining order/discipline as, 14–15, 299n20; orders destruction of French villages, 14
Vandamme-Davout conflict, Napoleon and, 192–93
Vandamme, Dominique-Joseph-René, xi, xii, 3, 5, 6, 12; as Citizen Dominique, 43–44; civilian life of, 289–90; death/burial of, 295; France exile of, 290; France, return of, 294; Ghent exile of, 292; immigration to United States, 293–94, 336n18. *See also* Family, of Vandamme; Military campaigns, of Vandamme; Military career, of Vandamme; Personality/character, of Vandamme; Relationship(s), of Vandamme
Vandamme family estate: Coalition forces invade, 259–60; public invades, 290–92
Varé, General of Brigade Louis-Prix, 138
Varennes, France, 8
Var River, 104
Vendée, 23, 45, 64, 65, 89, 110
Vento, 37
Verdun, 125
Versailles, 281
Vervins, 263
Viatka, 255
Vienna, 24, 52, 65, 76, 107–108, 123, 129, 131–32, 135–37, 144–45, 182–84, 191–97, 260–61
Vienna, Convention of, 156
Viervoet, fort of, 18
Vierzon, 286, 290
Vieux-Brisach, 80, 81, 83, 84, 87, 88, 105
Villeneuve, Admiral Pierre-Charles, 120–21
Villers-Cotterêts, 280
Villette, 281
Villingen, 76
Vilna, 222–24
Vincennes, xii, 259
Vincent, Captain Henri-Catherine, 139, 191
Vistula River, 160, 162, 213–15
Vohburg, 187

Waal River, 37, 38
Wachendorf, 82
Waghausel, 125
Wagram, 4, 123, 201, 209, 211, 231; battle of, 195, 197
Wagram Campaign (1805, 1809), 123
Walcheren, 34, 36
Waldenburg, 176
Wallachia, 209
Walmoden, General, 13, 38, 125–26
War Archives, 259
War of 1812: European readiness for, 209; French readiness for, 208–209; Napoleon's army affected by, 227–28; Napoleon's readiness for, 210; Russian army affected by, 228; Vandamme's readiness for, 210–11
Warsaw, 164, 174, 214–16, 218, 221–22, 224
Wars, revolutionary, 87, 111, 122, 206, 221, 259, 296
Wartensleben, General, 52–54, 59

Warthe, 172
Washington, D.C., 293
Waterloo, 118, 263, 273, 279–80; battle of, 275–77; Napoleon's defeat at, 276
Waterloo Campaign, *258*, 295–96; armistice signed in, 283, 335n60; Coalition forces' readiness for, 263–64; early skirmishes in, 268–74; French Army placements for, 264–68; Napoleon's preparations for, 262–63; Napoleon's strategy for, 264; Vandamme's role in, 264–68
Watoue château, destruction of, 14, 298n19
Wattignies, 17
Wavre, 273–77, 282
Wegener, General, 234, 237
Weimar, 233
Weiss (innkeeper), 88
Weistritz, 171–72
Welhain, 275
Wellesley, General Arthur, 207
Wellington, duke of, 207
Werneck, Austrian general, 37
Wervik, 29, 30
Wesel, 226, 230
Weser River, 159, 230–33
West Indies, 44
Westoutre, 12
Westphalia, king of, 3, 149, 210–11, 215, 217, 219–20, 222, 224–26, 229, 231
West River, 232
West Scheldt River, 34
White Terror, 289–90, 294
Wilhemsburg, 235–36
Wilhousbourg, 196

Willenstadt, 12
Winzgerode, General Baron, 132
Wittgenstein, General Ludwig Adolf von, 228
Wittgenstein, Prince, 234
Wollowart, Count, 199
Wollowart, General, 190, 193, 199–201
Woussen, Representative, 50
Wrede, General Karl Philipp von, 163–64, 188
Wurben, 172
Würmser, General, 52
Würtemberg, 52, 80; Catherine, princess of, 160; duke of, 81, 85; Frederick I, king of, 185; prince of, 82, 246
Würtemberg chasseurs, 196
Würtemberg division: in Silesian campaign, 185–86; of Vandamme, 160–63, 168–73, 175–77, 179, 190–91
Würtemberg officers/troops, behavior of, 189–90, 196, 198–201

York, duke of, 12–15, 38, 91–98
Ypres, 13, 16, 26, 27, 30; siege of, 32–33, 301n24

Zabingen, 125
Zeiten, General Hans Joachim, 265
Zeppelin, Count, 81, 85, 86
Zieten, General Hans Joachim von, 265–66, 268, 270, 276
Zillebeke, 32
Zittau, 242–43
Znaim, 132, 197
Zuider Sea, 93
Zurich, 80, 95, 96